GILBERT ACHCAR, who grew up in Beirut,
and African Studies, University of London.
of Barbarisms: The Making of the New Wo
published in thirteen languages, *The 33-Day War: Israel's War on Hezbollah in Lebanon and Its Aftermath* (with Michel Warschawski, Saqi Books, 2007), and *Perilous Power: The Middle East and U.S. Foreign Policy*, a book of dialogues with Noam Chomsky.

'A work of breath-taking empathy, examining one of the most painful and emotion-laden topics in the modern world with dispassion, sensitivity and high erudition ... [A] magisterial study' Rashid Khalidi, Edward Said Professor of Modern Arab Studies, Columbia University

'Essential reading for anyone who seeks a balanced understanding of the place of Jews and the Holocaust in Arab thinking today. Whether or not one agrees with Gilbert Achcar on every issue, he provides a welcome and well-informed counterpoint to caricaturists and hate-mongers and fear-promoters of every persuasion.' Michael R. Marrus, Chancellor Rose and Ray Wolfe Professor Emeritus of Holocaust Studies, University of Toronto

'An erudite, perceptive, and highly original study that shines much-needed light on a field which has tended to be dominated by partisanship and propaganda' Avi Shlaim, Professor of International Relations, St Antony's College, University of Oxford

'A sensitive and insightful exploration of an important dimension of the Middle East conflict ... Achcar's book, which combines meticulous scholarship and an engaging style, is a significant contribution to the mutual understanding that is in such short supply.' Peter Novick, Professor Emeritus of Modern History, University of Chicago

'A penetrating analysis of the multiplicity of attitudes and responses in the Arabic-speaking world toward Nazism, anti-Semitism, and the Holocaust' Francis R. Nicosia, Raul Hilberg Distinguished Professor of Holocaust Studies, University of Vermont

'A courageous undertaking ... [Achcar] succeeds in treating the subject of the relationship of Palestine and the Nazi Holocaust with original thinking, profound scholarship, and meticulous analysis.' Naseer Aruri, member of the Palestine National Council; Chancellor Professor (Emeritus) of Political Science, University of Massachusetts, Dartmouth

To Richard
with hope!
Gilbert Achcar

THE ARABS AND THE HOLOCAUST

Gilbert Achcar

The Arabs and the Holocaust

The Arab–Israeli War of Narratives

Translated from the French
by G. M. Goshgarian

SAQI

First English edition published in hardback in 2010 by Saqi Books

This paperback edition published in 2011

ISBN: 978-0-86356-458-1

Copyright © Gilbert Achcar, 2010 and 2011

Translation copyright © G. M. Goshgarian, 2010 and 2011

Originally published in France by Actes Sud as *Les Arabes et la Shoah*

Indexer: ed.emery@thefreeuniversity.net

A full CIP record for this book is available from the British Library.
A full CIP record for this book is available from the Library of Congress.

Printed and bound by CPI Mackays, Chatham ME5 8TD

SAQI

26 Westbourne Grove, London W2 5RH, UK

www.saqibooks.com

And why beholdest thou the mote that is in thy brother's eye, but considerest not the beam that is in thine own eye?

MATTHEW 7:3

Contents

Preface

This book had its inception early in 2006, when my friend Enzo Traverso asked me to contribute a chapter on the reception of the Holocaust in the Middle East to the monumental work on the history of the Shoah that he and three other scholars were co-editing for the Italian publishing house UTET in Turin.[1] The editors were looking for someone who could write about the reception of the Holocaust in the Middle East. I accepted the invitation, but only after much hesitation: the short six months I was given to complete my essay – an author who had been approached before me had bowed out late in the day – made the task, given its scope and complexity, a perilous one.

I took it on nonetheless, motivated by what might be called a sense of duty. The work being put together would, I knew, be a good one, and I did not want to see the issue I had been asked to discuss – a delicate question if ever there was one – treated incompetently or left aside. Out of a concern for intellectual rigour, I limited the field of my research to countries that lay directly in my area of competence, countries whose language I knew – those of the Arab world from which I come. After my editors had approved this restriction, I began intensively researching and writing, and I eventually turned out the long chapter that closes the second and final volume of that work.[2] Enzo was the first to suggest, insistently, that I work this chapter up into a book. At the time, I was not particularly inclined to plunge back into intensive research on the same topic.

But I continued to give it thought, since the questions raised were being posed ever more sharply in the Middle East. For example, late in 2006 a Tehran conference called 'Review of the Holocaust: Global Vision' promoted Holocaust denial, with the Iranian president, Mahmoud Ahmadinejad, contributing his own deliberately provocative statements. Urged on both by readers of the original chapter – including the publishers of the French, British and American editions of the present book – and by my own desire to discuss the problem in a form more widely accessible than the voluminous compendium published solely in Italian, I undertook the project of transforming the chapter into a book.

It was obvious that it was going to take enormous effort to depict the reception of the Holocaust in the Arab world, where the diversity of countries and conditions is multiplied many times over by the diversity of political tendencies and sensibilities, even as the inhabitants' views of the Jewish tragedy are rendered infinitely more complex by their relationship to the Palestinian drama, the Nakba. The Introduction to the book is accordingly devoted to this very complex relationship between the Holocaust and the Nakba.

To make my task somewhat more manageable, I have focused on the countries most directly affected by the creation of the state of Israel, those of the Arab East. Maghreb countries – those of the Arab West, in North Africa – are treated only incidentally. This restriction notwithstanding, the slim volume initially envisioned has mushroomed into a thick book. The discussion of the Holocaust period – the 1930s and 1940s – takes up more than half of it. I have construed the Shoah (the 'catastrophe') broadly in the following pages, not restricting it to the post-January 1942 phase of systematic liquidation that the Nazis called the 'Final Solution' but including the entire period of Jewish persecution – both in Germany and, later, in the lands conquered by the Nazis – that began with Hitler's assumption of power in 1933.

I have privileged these years over the following decades for several reasons. First, they are the main object of the historical controversy fought out in the battle of the narratives. (Wherever good secondary sources were not available, I have explored primary sources.) Second, it was between the end of the First World War and that of the Second that the main ideological currents of the Arab countries took shape; their diverse relations to the Holocaust provide an excellent index of their own nature. As a result, this book provides an ideological mapping of the Arab world – and, as I see it, as much of its interest lies therein as in the title subject. Finally, a detailed discussion of the attitudes toward the Holocaust that have taken shape in the six decades since the state of Israel came into being is impossible here, for the simple reason that it would fill several volumes.

I certainly have not titled my book *The Arabs and the Holocaust* because I share the grotesque view that the Nazis had no closer collaborators in their persecution of the Jews than the Arabs. I do not even suggest that 'the Arabs' participated in the crime, actively or passively, as many population groups across Europe did.[3] Yet as a result of the Zionist enterprise and Jewish immigration to Palestine, the Arabs were deeply affected by the Holocaust, and my main ambition has been to render the complexity of their relation to it. To be sure, one finds many odious attitudes toward the Holocaust in the Arab world; but one also finds absurdly distorted interpretations of the Arab reception of the Holocaust in Israel and the West. My aim is to open up avenues of reflection that make it possible to go beyond the legion of caricatures, founded on mutual incomprehension and sustained by blind hatred, that plague discussion of the subject.

Finally, though it would be impossible to provide an exhaustive account of Arab reactions to the Holocaust, I do believe that a more narrowly focused investigation of Palestinian perceptions of the Shoah is both possible and necessary. I would hope that a Palestinian scholar will soon produce, on this subject, the equivalent of what Tom Segev and Peter Novick have produced, respectively, on the Israelis' and the Americans' relationship to the Holocaust,[4] with the same admirable concern for objectivity and the same critical distance from nationality and ethnicity that they demonstrate. And, in the interests of mutual comprehension, I would also hope that an Israeli scholar will soon produce an in-depth study of the history of the Israeli receptions of the Nakba, the drama of the Palestinian people.

LONDON, AUGUST 2009

A note on the transliteration of Arabic

I have transliterated Arabic names and terms using a simplified version of the rules for romanization applied in the specialized literature, with the aim of making them more accessible to lay readers yet still recognizable to those who know the language. To the same end, names of well-known individuals are transliterated in accordance with common practice. Finally, in the case of Arab authors who have published in a European language, their own transliterations of their names have generally been respected. However, the romanization of Arabic names by the various authors is respected in the citations, as is the rule.

Words Laden With Pain

Anyone who sets out to write about the genocide of the Jews by the National Socialist state confronts a delicate terminological problem. What name should be given a calamity that, from the standpoint of a humanist ethics, will remain forever 'unnameable'?

Shoah, Holocaust, Jewish Genocide

All the words used to name the genocide of the Jews are heavily connoted; none is neutral. Even formulas apparently inspired by Émile Durkheim's scientific imperative to avoid 'prenotions' in approaching 'social facts', such as Raul Hilberg's title *The Destruction of the European Jews*,[1] are plainly the result of a difficult choice: subjecting the object under study to a distanced, clinical gaze. Hilberg clearly declares, in the preface to the first edition of his book, 'We shall not dwell on Jewish suffering ... '[2] This is an entirely respectable and even ineluctable choice when, as in the case of his monumental work, keeping a scientific distance does not indicate a lack of empathy but, rather, reflects a desire to control it so as to remain as objective as possible. The aim in such cases is to ensure the credibility of the facts on which subsequent empathy may be solidly based without incurring the suspicion that empathy has tailored the facts to its needs. This attitude, of course, is utterly different from the pseudo-scientific detachment of the deniers' approach, which is hard put to hide the antipathy that is its basic motivation.

The most satisfactory objective designation seems to me 'Jewish genocide', an expression that makes use of the generic term 'genocide' while particularizing it by invoking the identity of the victims, as do the terms 'Armenian genocide', 'Roma genocide' and 'Rwandan genocide'. These terms by no means contradict either the contention that every genocide is a singular occurrence or the undeniable fact that the Jewish genocide surpasses all other twentieth-century genocides in scope – an objective observation that can and should be acknowledged without entering into the 'competition of the victims' that Jean-Michel Chaumont has admirably studied in his book of that name.[3]

Naturally, the designations sanctioned by public discourse and the media are not motivated by this same quest for rigour. Two terms have become established as designations of the Jewish genocide in its singularity: 'Shoah' and 'Holocaust'. The first is a Hebrew word generally translated as 'catastrophe': employed with the definite article in the singular (*Ha-Shoah*), it is the natural expression in the language of the Jewish religion for the terrible tragedy that befell the European Jews (along with other, non-European Jews, who are all too often forgotten). It is not, to be sure, a 'scientific' term, but a way to accentuate the singularity of the Jewish genocide.

Esther Benbassa, however, criticizes the use of the term Shoah, arguing that, with its biblical origins, it designates a punishment inflicted by God. She also emphasizes that the expression used in Yiddish, the language of the majority of victims and survivors of the Jewish genocide, was different.[4] Despite its secularization, she asserts, the term Shoah contains all the ingredients of a 'secular theology' of the Jewish tragedy. Her objection is well-founded, but she herself, paradoxically, uses the term Holocaust, to which the same criticisms apply a fortiori.

'Holocaust', indeed, has the same function in present-day usage. It is derived from a Greek word, *holokaustos*, that means 'entirely consumed by fire'. More precisely, it comes from the Greek translation of the Hebrew Bible (Leviticus 1:3) and has entered the Western languages by way of Church Latin. The word refers to the ancient Israelites' practice of burning sacrificed animals as an expiatory offering. The Hebrew text has no equivalent for the Greek word, utilizing only the term *olah*, which means 'ascension' or 'elevation' (the word *aliyah* has the same root) to designate 'immolation' – probably because what is burned rises towards heaven in the form of smoke. The burnt offering, or *olah*, is a variant of *qorban*, which means 'sacrificial offering'. In the Bible, the word *olah* is used only to describe animals that were to be entirely consumed by fire, which is why it was translated as 'holocaust'. Other offerings, such as 'meal-offerings' of flour or cakes, were only partially burned; the rest had to be given to 'Aaron and his sons', that is, the priests.

In view of its original meaning, the use of the word 'holocaust' to designate the Jewish genocide is eminently contestable and a subject of fierce controversy. The criticism focuses above all on the fact that its etymological meaning makes its utilization as a name for the Jewish genocide – and in particular for the funereal sequence of gas chamber/crematorium – macabre if not indeed reprehensible. Moreover, the very idea that the victims of the Jewish genocide might be considered 'expiatory offerings' is quite simply appalling.

The website of the United States Holocaust Memorial Museum in Washington, DC, offers an account of the historical development that has led to this incongruous use of the term:

> In secular writings, *holocaust* most commonly came to mean 'a complete or wholesale destruction,' a connotation particularly dominant from the late nineteenth century through the nuclear arms race of the mid-twentieth century. During this time, the word was applied to a variety of disastrous events ranging from pogroms against Jews in Russia, to the persecution and murder of Armenians by Turks during World War I, to the attack by Japan on Chinese cities, to large-scale fires where hundreds were killed.
>
> Early references to the Nazi murder of the Jews of Europe continued this usage. As early as 1941, writers occasionally employed the term *holocaust* with regard to the Nazi crimes against the Jews, but in these early cases, they did not ascribe exclusivity to the term. Instead of '*the holocaust*,' writers referred to '*a* holocaust,' one of many through the centuries ...
>
> By the late 1940s, however, a shift was underway. *Holocaust* (with either a lowercase or capital H) became a more specific term due to its use in Israeli translations of the word *sho'ah*. This Hebrew word had been used throughout Jewish history to refer to assaults upon Jews, but by the 1940s it was frequently being applied to the Nazis' murder of the Jews of Europe. (Yiddish-speaking Jews used the term *churbn,* a Yiddish translation of *sho'ah*.) The equation of *holocaust* with *sho'ah* was seen most prominently in the official English translation of the Israeli Declaration of Independence in 1948, in the translated publications of Yad Vashem throughout the 1950s, and in the journalistic coverage of the Adolf Eichmann trial in Israel in 1961.[5]

It was, however, Elie Wiesel who definitively established the use of the term by insistently designating 'The Holocaust' a unique event. And he did so in full awareness of the implications, as Zev Garber and Bruce Zuckerman have shown in a remarkable critical discussion of the use of this term as a proper name for the Jewish genocide:

> While it is certainly true that the vast majority of people (Jew and Gentile) continue to use 'The Holocaust' without understanding its religious/sacrificial connotations, it strains credulity to argue that those Jewish thinkers and writers who first adopted this term and even more

importantly, allowed it to flourish, totally ignored information that could easily be found simply by opening a dictionary. ... there is little doubt that the one man who has done the most to establish 'The Holocaust' in the modern consciousness was well aware of what he was doing and well aware of what the term 'holocaust' meant in all its nuances. ... And the motivation for Wiesel's use of 'The Holocaust' has unmistakable religious/ sacrificial overtones, as his own writings reveal.[6]

We believe that he well understood all of the factors that could come into play ... he chose this term nonetheless to preserve the specialness of the tragedy as a Jewish tragedy.[7]

Arno Mayer, for his part, contests the term 'holocaust' on the grounds that this 'religiously freighted' word takes its place in an 'overly sectarian' cult of the memory that has spawned, in his estimation, 'a collective prescriptive 'memory' unconducive to critical and contextual thinking about the Jewish calamity'.[8] For the Durkheimian reason evoked earlier, Mayer's argument is legitimate insofar as it aims to challenge the use of the term in scholarly studies of the Jewish genocide. However, usage has ultimately conferred on 'Holocaust', as on other terms, a meaning that transcends its origins: it now names the Jewish genocide in particular, as Michael Marrus has stressed.[9] Furthermore, Mayer himself has forged a term, 'Judeocide', which, unlike Hilberg's, puts the Jewish genocide as a whole in a category of its own, much more, indeed, than the word 'holocaust', which continues to be used as a generic term to designate a considerable number of other tragedies – a circumstance that Elie Wiesel deeply deplores.

Thus, if the aim is to name the Jewish genocide in its singularity while also communicating the emotional force with which its memory is fraught, the term 'Shoah' is certainly far more appropriate. Indeed, the website of Yad Vashem, the Jerusalem-based Israeli institution created to memorialize the Holocaust (its official English name is The Holocaust Martyrs' and Heroes' Remembrance Authority), today advocates the use of Shoah.[10] Yet 'Holocaust' has come into general use in most Western languages, including English and German, whereas Shoah has gained wide currency in French and, albeit to a lesser extent, Italian. The latter term is, however, gaining ground in Europe as well as in the United States. This book thus uses both terms, depending on the context as well as the languages in which it is published.[*]

---

[*]   The U.S. Holocaust Memorial Museum's website points out that the term that the museum itself has chosen to use won out over its competitors in the USA in a way typical of that society of the spectacle par excellence: it came into common use thanks to the 1978 television series *Holocaust*, directed by Marvin Chomsky

Zionism, Colonialism, Uprootedness

Zionism, considered as the political movement to create a *Judenstaat* ('state of the Jews') in the title of the famous book by its principal founder, Theodor Herzl, was first and foremost a reaction to anti-Semitism that envisioned an ethnic-nationalistic segregation and regrouping of Jews on a territory of their own. It often found itself in virulent opposition to competing options that promoted the individual and collective rights of Jews, where they already resided, whether via autonomy or social integration.

The beginnings of the Zionist colonization of Palestine considerably antedate Hitler's assumption of power, as do the first hostile Arab reactions. The Arab inhabitants of Palestine perceived the Zionist undertaking there as one more avatar of European colonialism, particularly since it mostly unfolded under the post-First World War British colonial mandate. In his famous 1917 letter addressed to the Zionist movement, British Foreign Secretary Lord Arthur Balfour declared His Majesty's government favourable to 'the establishment in Palestine of a national home for the Jewish people'.

From the inception of European-Jewish colonization in Palestine in the latter half of the nineteenth century – a movement accelerated above all by pogroms in Russia – to the outbreak of the First World War, Arab peasants squared off with Jewish settlers in repeated and sometimes bloody confrontations. These were not xenophobic or even anti-Jewish reactions on the part of the Palestinian villagers, at least initially, but rather altogether predictable reactions by farmers who had been expelled from their lands. The clearest proof is that when the settlers allowed the peasants to remain on the land and gave them the opportunity to continue working it, they acquiesced in the new arrangements. When, in contrast, the new owners sought to expel them or to induce the Ottoman authorities to do so, as they increasingly did after the turn of the century, the farmers rebelled.[11]

The hostility of the native population, both Muslim and Christian, would increase over the years in direct proportion to the expansion of this colonization and to the growing awareness that the Zionist movement was seeking to create a state in Palestine. Thus, well before the First World War, opposition to Zionism was a key component in the formation of a Palestinian

---

from a screenplay written by Gerald Green. In France, the term Shoah, now widely employed, was made popular by another audiovisual work, the solemn sobriety of which sharply distinguished it from the common run of fictional treatments of the Jewish genocide: *Shoah*, a documentary directed by Claude Lanzmann that was first broadcast in 1985.

identity and of an Arab nationalistic consciousness. Witness the articles published from the late nineteenth century on – with greater frequency after mid-1908, thanks to the political liberalization in the Ottoman Empire at that time – in newspapers in not only Palestine but Cairo, Beirut and Damascus as well.[12]

The number of Jews living in Palestine doubled between the dawn of the twentieth century and the First World War. It increased by a factor of ten under the British mandate, rising from 61,000 in 1920 (out of a total population of 603,000) to more than 610,000 (of a total population of nearly 1,900,000) on the eve of the proclamation of the state of Israel.[13] In the early 1920s, Jews were migrating to Palestine at an average annual rate of 8,000; this migration then intensified, cresting at 34,000 in 1925.[14] Inevitably, the first major anti-Jewish Arab riots broke out shortly after the de facto establishment of the British mandate. Beginning in Jerusalem in 1920 and Jaffa in 1921, the initial violence culminated in the riots of 1929.[15]

The fact remains, however, that the Nazis' seizure of power in 1933 and its aftermath were much more than a mere stimulant to Jewish immigration to Palestine. They were the decisive factor lending credence to the views of the Zionists and leading ultimately to the realization of their project – as the immigration statistics make clear. After the 1925 peak (a result, in particular, of both the Depression and of anti-Jewish measures in Poland coinciding with new restrictions on immigration to the United States) the number of immigrants sank to fewer than 20,000 for the entire five-year period 1927–31 – that is, an annual average of fewer than 4,000. In 1931, Jews made up one-sixth of the population of Palestine: according to the British census, the country counted 175,000 Jews and 880,000 Arabs that year.[16] Immigration levels rose to higher than 12,500 in 1932, then shot up to more than 37,000 in 1933, 45,000 in 1934, and 66,000 in 1935. The influx was then slowed by the 1936–9 Palestinian uprising, after which the British colonial administration imposed restrictions on Jewish immigration.[17]

Over the forty-year period 1882–1931, a total of nearly 187,000 immigrants arrived in Palestine. Between 1932 and 1938, a period of only seven years, more than 197,000 people poured into the country, followed by 138,300 more in the ten years between 1939 and 1948. In sum, a total of nearly 313,000 immigrants settled in the area between Hitler's assumption of power in 1933 and the end of the British mandate in 1948, according to official Israeli statistics.[18] One hundred and fifteen thousand of them came illegally.[19] In the three years between the end of the war in Europe in May 1945 and the proclamation of the state of Israel in May 1948, 80,000 Holocaust survivors came to Palestine illegally, according, once again, to official Israeli figures.[20]

In 1932, the Jewish population of Palestine – almost 181,000 – constituted 18.3 per cent of the total population. By 1946, it represented more than 35 per cent,[21] reaching 37 per cent at the moment the state of Israel was proclaimed two years later. Of the 716,700 Jews living in the new state six months after it declared its independence, 463,000, that is, nearly two-thirds, had been born abroad, according to the 11 November 1948 census.[22]

Thus the 'state of the Jews' plainly owes its creation to the Holocaust, for more than one reason. The Nazis' anti-Semitic policies were initiated with the expulsion, under increasing duress, of German Jews.[23] Until 1939, the Nazis preferred that these Jewish émigrés leave Germany for Palestine:

> Jewish emigration to Palestine ... is a lesser evil for Germany. 'I know from my own experience,' wrote an official of the *Auswärtiges Amt* [the German Foreign Office], 'how unusually unpleasant the influx of Jewish intellectuals is for us.' He pointed out that the emigration of Jews to the United States, Turkey and Iran influenced intellectual life in the direction of strengthening anti-German feeling, and that Jewish immigrants in Latin America caused the Germans much economic, propagandistic and political harm ... But in Palestine, argued that official, the Jews are among themselves and cannot harm the Third Reich.[24]

> Within Germany, Hitler actively intervened in the debate over Palestine in 1937 and early in 1938. He insisted on the stepped-up promotion of Jewish emigration and deportation by all possible means, regardless of destination. According to Hitler, Palestine was to continue as a prime destination for German Jewish refugees, and became an even more significant factor in Nazi emigration policies in 1938 and 1939 as the Gestapo and the Sicherheitsdienst collaborated with underground Zionist organizations in the 'illegal' immigration of Jewish refugees past the British blockade into Palestine.[25]

Nearly 53,000 Jews from Germany alone left for Palestine between 1933 and 1939, taking only legal emigration into account. German Jews represented one-quarter of all legal Jewish immigrants in 1933; by 1939, the proportion had risen to 52 per cent.[26] Their emigration was facilitated by a 25 August 1933 agreement between German Zionists and representatives of the Jewish Agency, on the one hand, and the Nazi government on the other. Known as the *Haavara* ('transfer' in Hebrew), it authorized German Jews emigrating to Palestine, and these Jews alone, to transfer part of their assets there in the form of goods exported from Germany.[27] The agreement was the more controversial in that it subverted the economic boycott of Nazi Germany which many believed capable of precipitating the downfall of the Hitler regime, which at that time was still being put in place. On the other hand, the *Haavara* agreement shored up the then almost bankrupt Jewish Agency for Palestine,[28] the institution responsible for organizing Jewish immigration and overseeing the *Yishuv*.[*]

In spite of all the Zionist movement's efforts, a majority of the German and Austrian Jews who left continental Europe by September 1939 went to the Americas – 95,000 of them to the United States and 75,000 to Latin America, over against the 60,000 who emigrated to Palestine.[29] Yet the fact remains that, in 1948, 170,000 Jews from Poland constituted the largest segment of the *Yishuv*.[30] When all is said and done, it is obvious that National Socialism, by substantially boosting Jewish emigration to Palestine, allowed the movement to attain the critical mass that enabled it to triumph politically and militarily in 1948. 'The rise of the Nazis thus proved advantageous for the Zionist movement,' Tom Segev has accurately pointed out.[31]

History was thus confirming Herzl's vision – in a way that he could not have imagined in his worst nightmares. 'The present scheme', Herzl had declared in the preface to his 1896 manifesto in book form, 'includes the employment of an existent propelling force ... And what is our propelling force? The misery of the Jews.'[32] This vision underlies the same 'philosophy of the beneficial disaster' that Shabtai Teveth, the biographer of the president of the Jewish Agency's executive committee and the most important of the founding fathers of the state of Israel, David Ben-Gurion, attributes to the man whom he knows better than anyone else does. Teveth cites Ben-Gurion: 'The harsher the affliction, the greater the strength of Zionism.'[33] [†]

This philosophy explains, in Teveth's view, Ben-Gurion's relative indifference to the Holocaust, for which he has been much criticized: 'Two facts can be definitely stated: Ben Gurion did not put the rescue effort above Zionist politics, and he did not regard it as a principal task demanding his personal leadership ... '[35]

The head of the Jewish Agency gave stark expression to the implacable

---

[*]   *Yishuv*, a Hebrew word meaning 'settlement' or 'population', is the name given to the community of Jews living in Palestine.

[†]   Michel Abitbol speaks in similar terms of the attitude of the 'Zionist mainstream establishment' of the Jewish communities of North Africa, 'which, faithful to the Herzlean dialectic, welcomed the rise in consciousness triggered by anti-Semitic agitation' in 1936.[34]

logic of Zionist priorities when he declared, in December 1938, not long after the Nazi pogrom known as *Kristallnacht*: 'If I knew that it was possible to save all the children in Germany by transporting them to England, but only half of them by transporting them to Palestine, I would choose the second – because we face not only the reckoning of these children, but the historical reckoning of the Jewish people.'[36] He added: 'Like every Jew, I am interested in saving every Jew wherever possible, but nothing takes precedence over saving the Hebrew nation in its land.'[37]*

In the opposing camp, the most eminent members of the Brit Shalom and, later, Ihud circles, both of which rejected Zionist statism in favour of a binational state in Palestine – Hugo Bergmann, Martin Buber, Judah Magnes, and Henrietta Szold – waged, unsurprisingly, a desperate struggle to persuade the Yishuv to put rescuing Europe's Jews ahead of all else. Late in 1942, when news of the 'Final Solution' began to reach the Yishuv, members of these circles played a pivotal role in founding an association called Al-domi (biblical Hebrew meaning 'do not remain silent') that worked actively, albeit in vain, to attain this end. The very existence of this association appears to have been blotted from memory.[39]

The American Council for Judaism (ACJ) followed an equally consistent line. An anti-Zionist organization founded by Reform rabbis and lay-people in the 1940s,[40] the ACJ favoured a single democratic, secular Palestinian state in which Jews and Arabs would enjoy equal rights. The UN Special Commission on Palestine took note in 1947 of the ACJ's position that 'proposals to establish a Jewish State ... are a threat to the peace and security of Palestine and its surrounding area, are harmful to the Jews in Palestine and throughout the world, and are also undemocratic'.[41]

The ACJ, which boasted more than 14,000 members at its apogee, fought energetically to open America's doors to the displaced. This was the logical corollary of its opposition to the Zionist project in Palestine in a context of solidarity with European Jews. Its attitude was not unlike that of the British writer Israel Zangwill who broke with the Zionist movement when it

---

* The attitude of the British Jewish organizations was even worse than Ben-Gurion's. Raul Hilberg describes the reaction of the latter to the influx of Jewish refugees that followed *Kristallnacht* in Nov. 1938: 'At this point, the Home Secretary, Sir Samuel Hoare, declared at a cabinet meeting that the Jewish organizations did not want an inundation of Jews, lest anti-Semitism increase. They also did not wish publicity about the number of refugees admitted, lest the Jewish leadership become the target of criticism that there were either too few or too many. From this moment, Britain's Jewish organizations no longer played a major, let alone leading, role in the rescue of the European Jews.'[38]

opted for Palestine as the only territorial objective of the future 'state of the Jews' – this despite the fact that Zangwill is said to have been the author of the notorious phrase that has it that Palestine was 'a land without a people for a people without a land' (an attribution that is imprecise and has been contested).[42] Zangwill – who knew well that, unless the Arabs were driven from Palestine, creating a Jewish state in this country implied domination of an Arab majority by a Jewish minority[43] – militated in favour of 'territorialism', the project of regrouping Jews on a territory better suited to the purpose than Palestine, wherever it might be – preferably in the United States. 'America,' he wrote,

> has ample room for all the six millions of the Pale [i.e. the Pale of Set-
> tlement, home to most of Russia's Jews]; any one of her fifty states could
> absorb them. And next to being in a country of their own, there could be
> no better fate for them than to be together in a land of civil and religious
> liberty, of whose Constitution Christianity forms no part and where
> their collective votes would practically guarantee them against future
> persecution.[44]*

Conversely, the Palestinian project determined the American Zionists' position on the question of immigration to the United States by Holocaust survivors. The extraordinary Congress that brought American Zionists together with leaders of the world movement in New York's Biltmore hotel in May 1942 demanded only that the doors of Palestine be opened to Jewish refugees – not those of every country at war with the Axis, beginning with the United States.[46] As Aaron Berman has shown, this stance was not mod-ified – quite the contrary, in fact – when it was learned that the Nazis were carrying out a systematic genocide:

> American Zionist leaders decided that their primary task had to be
> the building of support for the immediate establishment of a Jewish
> state in Palestine. Their decision did not reflect a callousness about or
> disinterest in the terrible fate of the European Jews. Rather, American
> Zionists believed that there was nothing unique about Hitler's plan for
> genocide ... Believing that Jewish homelessness was the basic cause of all
> anti-Semitism, American Zionists resolved to put a final end to Jewish
> statelessness ...

---

*   A fundamentally identical attitude, as well as the conviction that it was urgently
    necessary to find a refuge for Jews fleeing Nazism, motivated Isaac Steinberg, former
    People's Commissar for Justice in the first government headed by Lenin after the
    1917 'October Revolution' and another activist in the 'territorialist' cause.[45]

Sadly, the American Zionists' calculation was faulty. ... once the Nazis embarked on their program of genocide, the American Zionist decision to make the establishment of a Jewish state their primary goal handicapped any attempt to build a powerful lobby to force the American government to undertake the rescue of European Jewry.[47]

David Wyman, who can hardly be accused of hostility to American Zionists, has drawn up a balance sheet of their actions in this field: 'An unavoidable conclusion', he writes, 'is that during the Holocaust the leadership of American Zionism concentrated its major force on the drive for a future Jewish state in Palestine. It consigned rescue to a distinctly secondary position.'[48] However, he adds, 'substantially more was possible than they recognized'.[49]

Of all the arguments invoked to justify the Zionists' undeniable lack of enthusiasm for the demand that the United States, Great Britain and the other allied countries open their gates before continental Europe's Jewish refugees, even the most reasonable constitute mitigating circumstances at best. The political motivation for this lack of enthusiasm is equally undeniable, as is indicated by a comment of Ben-Gurion's that Segev cites: 'In the wake of the *Kristallnacht* pogroms,' Segev reports, 'Ben-Gurion commented that "the human conscience" might bring various countries to open their doors to Jewish refugees from Germany. He saw this as a threat and warned: "Zionism is in danger!"'[50]

Francis Nicosia sums up the consequences of the Zionists' attitude towards Nazism:

> If, as the Zionists had always claimed, the assimilationists had been living an illusion, the Zionists had undoubtedly lived one of their own. It was rooted in the fallacy that if anti-Semitism was natural and understandable, as Herzl and others had insisted, there was room for its accommodation to the principles and goals of Zionism. Herzl and others believed that anti-Semites would accept Zionism, even if they disliked or hated Jews, and that they might indeed do everything necessary to support Zionist efforts until Jews and non-Jews reached their common goal of removing Jews from Germany. What they had not understood, and what post-World War I German Zionists apparently would not understand until after 1933, was that whatever appeal Zionism had for most anti-Semites, even for the Nazis after World War I, it was of a purely pragmatic nature, and therefore problematic. Indeed, an understanding of National Socialism and precisely how Zionists should respond to it seemed to elude the entire Zionist movement, including the Yishuv, until well into the Second World War.[51]

The fact remains that responsibility for the failure to grant haven to European Jewish refugees ultimately lies with the governments of the allied countries that were in a position to do so. Although Berman's judgement can seem excessively severe, he is not wrong that 'while Germany was primarily responsible for the Holocaust, the democratic governments of the United States and the United Kingdom must be considered at least accomplices in genocide'.[52] Nothing is more revealing in this regard than the international conference held in Evian, France, from 6 to 15 July 1938. Initiated by Franklin D. Roosevelt, its mission was to reflect on the fate of the Jewish refugees from Germany and Austria, whose numbers had increased considerably as a result of the *Anschluss* and the intensification of the Nazis' anti-Semitic program. Thirty-two countries sent delegations.

> As the conference proceeded, delegate after delegate excused his country from accepting additional refugees. The United States delegate, Myron C. Taylor, stated that his country's contribution was to make the German and Austrian immigration quota, which up to the time had remained unfilled, fully available. The British delegate declared that their overseas territories were largely unsuitable for European settlement, except for parts of East Africa, which might offer possibilities for limited numbers. Britain itself, being fully populated and suffering unemployment, also was unavailable for immigration; and he excluded Palestine from the Evian discussion entirely. The French delegate stated that France had reached 'the extreme point of saturation as regards admission of refugees.' The other European countries echoed this sentiment, with minor variations. Australia could not encourage refugee immigration because, 'as we have no real racial problem, we are not desirous of importing one.' The delegates from New Zealand, Canada, and the Latin American nations cited the Depression as the reason they could not accept refugees. Only the tiny Dominican Republic volunteered to contribute large, but unspecified areas for agricultural colonization.[53]

It was due to this set of historical circumstance that the Jewish tragedy, which peaked in the Shoah, also culminated in the Palestinian tragedy, the Nakba. In a pivotal essay, Edward Said underscored the 'link to be made between what happened to Jews in World War II and the catastrophe of the Palestinian people',[54] going so far as to add that 'the Jewish tragedy led directly to the Palestinian catastrophe by, let us call it, "necessity" (rather than pure will).'[55] Of course, the Holocaust was incomparably crueller and bloodier than the Nakba. This consideration, however, in no way diminishes the tragedy of the

Palestinians, particularly since they did not, as a people, bear any blame for the destruction of European Jewry.

In an attempt to show conversely that 'the Jewish tragedy did not create the Palestinian catastrophe', Joseph Massad criticizes Said's contention. The Zionist project, he argues, antedated National Socialism and the Holocaust; furthermore, 'only one-third of holocaust survivors ended up in Palestine, mainly because they could not go to the United States.'[56] His argument, however, is aimed at the wrong target. When Said speaks of 'the Jewish tragedy' he obviously means the Holocaust in the broad sense of the tragedy spawned by the Nazis' accession to power and its aftermath, not in the narrow sense of the 1942–5 'Final Solution'.

Moreover, the direct relationship between the Palestinian drama and the Jewish tragedy was inscribed in the fact that Zionism was first and foremost a reaction to anti-Semitism. Certainly, if one takes the Holocaust in the narrow sense of the 'Final Solution' initiated in 1942, it becomes harder to maintain that the state of Israel owes its existence to the Holocaust. And it is indeed primarily pro-Zionist authors who have combated such a thesis.[57] Yehuda Bauer, who, like Massad, reformulates the idea in narrow terms ('Israel was created by the Holocaust'), advances the opposite thesis:

> On the contrary, if the German Reich had held out one more year, it is doubtful whether there would have been any survivors at all ... The Holocaust prevented a Jewish State from coming into existence with, as new-minted citizens, the millions of Jews who were murdered. Indeed, because of the Holocaust, the attempt to establish a state almost failed. There were almost not enough Jews left to fight for a state. The ones who survived the Holocaust were central to that effort, and had there been more, the effort would have been easier and the outcome more certain. My answer, therefore, is unequivocal: The view that Israel was created by the Holocaust is erroneous. The opposite is true.[58]

Bauer's contention is the more surprising in that a few lines earlier he declares: 'If the United States had opened its gates to Jewish immigration ... it is highly probable, in my view, that a much larger proportion of Jewish D.P.s would have gone to the United States than did.'[59] The notion that the 'millions of Jews who were murdered' might have constituted 'new-minted citizens' of the state of Israel, many of whom would have fought for its creation, is of a piece with the one that led Mordecai Shenhabi – the man credited with the idea of founding Yad Vashem – to propose in 1950 that Israeli citizenship be posthumously conferred upon all Holocaust victims.

Discussing the debates that this proposal touched off, Segev describes it as 'utterly spurious': 'There is no way of knowing which, or how many, of the Holocaust's victims considered themselves "potential citizens" of Israel. Many of them died precisely because they had preferred not to move to Palestine when that option was opened to them. And most of the world's Jews, Holocaust survivors among them, chose not to come to Israel even after the state was founded.'[60]

It remains true, however, that Holocaust survivors in the strict sense made up about one-third of the Zionist forces who fought in the 1948 war.[61] Nevertheless, the motive common to the authors just cited, over and above the fundamental differences dividing them, is their legitimate rejection of the idea that the creation of Israel was an answer to the Jewish genocide. Bauer passionately disputes it: 'I do not think I have to deal with this because the very line of thought is so repugnant. I think most Jews would have preferred saving the lives of the Jews who died in the Holocaust to establishing the state.'[62]

Said's thesis is no different. His recognition of the 'necessity' informing the historical process that culminated in the creation of the state of Israel by no means implies approval or legitimization of its creation or of the ways in which it was achieved: 'I do not accept the notion that by taking our land Zionism redeemed the history of the Jews, and I cannot ever be made to acquiesce in the need to dispossess the whole Palestinian people.'[63] Historical 'necessity' implies no political or moral justification for such acquiescence. Nor does it imply any imperative reason to endorse Zionism. As Isaac Deutscher explained in 1954:

> From a burning or sinking ship people jump no matter where – on to a lifeboat, a raft, or a float. The jumping is for them an 'historic necessity'; and the raft is in a sense the basis of their whole existence. But does it follow that the jumping should be made into a programme, or that one should take a raft-State as the basis of a political orientation?[64]

The rising tide of refugees to Palestine was not Nazism's only contribution to the creation of the state of Israel. In 1947 there also existed a mass of concentration-camp and other Jewish survivors of Hitler's genocidal enterprise who had been reduced to a state of extreme poverty and profound distress. Supporting the creation of the state of Israel was the way that North America, Europe and the Soviet Union solved, on the cheap, the embarrassing problem represented by this multitude of unfortunates whom neither the Americans nor the Europeans nor the USSR wished to take in.

While the Soviet authorities encouraged illegal Jewish immigration to Palestine from the Central and Eastern European countries under their control,[65] Washington asked London to allow Jews to immigrate legally into the country, which was still under British mandate. 'On June 6, 1946, President Truman urged the British government to relieve the suffering of the Jews confined to displaced persons camps in Europe by immediately accepting 100,000 Jewish immigrants [in Palestine]. Britain's Foreign Minister, Ernest Bevin, replied sarcastically that the United States wanted displaced Jews to immigrate to Palestine "because they did not want too many of them in New York."'[66] Long before Bevin, Mussolini had responded in much the same vein to Truman's predecessor, who asked him, in 1939, to grant the Jews refuge in Italian colonies: 'President Roosevelt asked Benito Mussolini to allow Jews to move to Ethiopia, which was under Italian rule; Il Duce wondered why the refugees could not be settled in the United States.'[67]

Once the war had ended and the horror of the camps had been fully revealed, the desire to get rid of the devastated Jews by sending them elsewhere persisted. The foundation of the state of Israel directly served that end: 200,000 Holocaust survivors settled there in the year following its creation.[68] According to the official statistics, more than 76,500 immigrants arrived there from Europe between 15 May 1948 and the end of the year, followed by another 122,000 in 1949.[69] In addition to the sordid fact that certain states sought to resolve the problem of the Holocaust survivors at the Palestinians' cost – as some states nowadays seek to rid themselves of their radioactive waste by exporting it to poor countries – the Zionist movement naturally tried to exploit the shock waves that followed the liberation of the camps in 1945. A former foreign minister of Israel, Shlomo Ben-Ami, has explained this stratagem:

> The target of Zionist diplomacy was no longer Britain but the United States and international opinion. There was little hope of averting an open clash with the mandatory power now entangled in the conflicting pledges and promises to Arabs and Jews. And as has happened frequently in the history of Zionism, the cause was enhanced by the Jewish catastrophe. It was the full truth and the awesome impact of the Holocaust of European Jewry, as it was exposed worldwide after the war, that served now as the platform upon which Zionist diplomacy could mobilise governments and international opinion in order to attain its major political objective, a Jewish state in Palestine. Once again, Jewish catastrophe was the propellant of the Zionist idea and a boost to its prospects.[70]

Finally, the National Socialist enterprise steeled the Yishuv for war in both the physical sense, since Palestinian Jews took part in the British war effort, and also the psychological sense, since it imbued Zionist militants with great determination, born of the feeling (the illusion, in the view of critics and sceptics) that they were fighting to establish the definitive response to the Holocaust. From the moment it was proclaimed, the state of Israel laid full claim to its legitimization based on the Holocaust and the anti-Nazi struggle. The terms of the 'declaration of independence' read out by David Ben-Gurion on 14 May 1948 are well known:

> The catastrophe which recently befell the Jewish people – the massacre of millions of Jews in Europe – was another clear demonstration of the urgency of solving the problem of its homelessness by re-establishing in Eretz-Israel the Jewish State, which would open the gates of the homeland wide to every Jew and confer upon the Jewish people the status of a fully privileged member of the community of nations.
>
> Survivors of the Nazi holocaust in Europe, as well as Jews from other parts of the world, continued to migrate to Eretz-Israel, undaunted by difficulties, restrictions and dangers, and never ceased to assert their right to a life of dignity, freedom and honest toil in their national homeland.
>
> In the Second World War, the Jewish community of this country contributed its full share to the struggle of the freedom- and peace-loving nations against the forces of Nazi wickedness and, by the blood of its soldiers and its war effort, gained the right to be reckoned among the peoples who founded the United Nations.[71]

The subsequent war between the new state and the Palestinians and surrounding Arab countries ended with the defeat of the Arab camp and the emergence of the Palestinian refugee problem.[72] The two narratives of these events, Israeli and Palestinian-Arab, inevitably turned, from the outset, on two very different sequences. The Israeli narrative featured *extermination* – the Shoah – and rehabilitation by the state. The Palestinian and Arab narrative revolved around the usurpation carried out by the state and the attendant *expulsion* – the Nakba.[73]

Nakba

Few people know, and even fewer point out, that the Arabic word *nakba*, which has been circulating in the Western languages for a few years now, is one possible equivalent of Shoah in Arabic. The other is *kāritha*, a word that is today employed as the Arabic translation of Shoah as distinct from Holocaust, translated *mahraqa*. *Nakba* means 'grievous catastrophe'. The term has been in use in the Arab countries since 1948 to describe the foundation of the state of Israel and its consequences: the first Arab–Israeli war, the defeat of the Arab armies, the massive exodus of the Palestinians from the territories that came under the control of the new state, and that state's refusal to allow Palestinians back to their homes and lands after the cessation of hostilities.[74]

Among the most powerful illustrations of the tragic nature of the conflict in the Middle East is that a state created as a refuge for persecuted Jews who had been reduced to the condition of refugees or 'displaced persons' in turn created the problem of the Palestinian refugees. The Law of Return, by which anyone recognized as a Jew has the right to settle in Israel and acquire Israeli citizenship, became a cornerstone of the legitimization of the new state, which simultaneously denied Palestinian refugees the right to return that they have not ceased to demand ever since.

The symmetries between the various terms – Shoah/Nakba, displaced person/refugee, law of return/right of return, UNRRA/UNRWA[*] (the list could be extended) – should give us pause, even if the two situations are not perfectly symmetrical. They offer a particularly striking illustration of the complexity of the issue and a partial explanation of why it arouses so much passion that some have even accused the Palestinians of imitating Israel. The accusation calls to mind the Palestinian poet Mahmoud Darwish's remark to the Israeli poet Helit Yeshurun, during a 1996 interview, that Israelis 'are jealous of anyone whom the world recognizes as a victim. That's an Israeli monopoly.'[75]

Thus two Israeli academics, Ruth Linn and Ilan Gur-Ze'ev of the University of Haifa, have accused the Arabs of plagiarizing as it were the term *shoah*, without having bothered to find out which Arabic word is used to designate the Palestinian tragedy. They seem not even to have heard of the term *nakba*. 'Following the Israeli use of the Hebrew word *shoah* "Holocaust" to refer to the annihilation of the Jews by the Nazis, the Arabs employ the Arabic word *karita* [sic] "Holocaust" [sic] to convey the magnitude of their disaster following the establishment of the Jewish state,'[76] they claim, going so far as to suggest that the Arabs borrowed the idea of the 'right to return' from Holocaust narratives.[77]

---

[*] The United Nations Relief and Rehabilitation Administration (UNRRA), created in 1943, concerned itself with 'displaced persons' in Europe until 1947; the United Nations Relief and Works Agency (UNRWA), created in 1949, continues to concern itself with Palestinian refugees.

Similarly, Meir Litvak and Esther Webman, Israeli academics affiliated with Tel Aviv University's Moshe Dayan Center, contended not long ago that the Israeli 'terminology and discourse of the Holocaust had a profound effect on the Palestinian discourse on the *Nakba* from its early emergence'.[78] In support, they cite a source that hardly qualifies as authorized: the Arabic translator of a book by a French Holocaust denier. 'Other aspects of Holocaust terminology', they continue, 'have been cast into the Palestinian discourse on the *Nakba*. "Destruction and redemption" (*shoah u-geula*), "Holocaust and rebirth" (*shoah u-tehiya*) turn into "*Nakba* and resistance" (*Nakba wa-muqawama*), "perseverance and resistance" (*israr wa-nidal*)'.[79] In fact, these formulas do not correspond in the slightest; moreover, the pairs of Arabic words cited are not even formulas in general use in 'the Palestinian discourse'.

In a recent book, Litvak and Webman extend this argument, although they now acknowledge that the use of the term *nakba* – a very common Arabic word – predated the Nakba itself in warnings against the impending catastrophe in Palestine. They accordingly date the plagiarism of which the Palestinians are accused to an earlier period: 'Indeed, the terminology and discourse of the Holocaust highly affected the Arab discourse on the Nakba from the mid-1940s, when immigration to Palestine emerged as the solution for the displaced Jews in Europe.'[80]

In point of fact, the Arab 'terminology and discourse' of the Nakba developed from 1948 on in complete independence from 'the terminology and discourse of the Holocaust', which had not yet come into general circulation, as the studies on the reception of the Holocaust in both the West and Israel attest. The word *nakba* began to establish itself in the Arab world from 1948 on as a means of underscoring the gravity of a defeat (*hazima*) that some sought to minimize as a mere *naksa* (a setback) – a move the Nasserites would repeat in 1967 with no better success.

The Syrian academic Constantine Zurayk (Qustantīn Zurayq), a liberal Arab nationalist, is generally credited with having put the term *nakba* into broad circulation as a designation for 'The Catastrophe' (*al-nakba*) in a pamphlet that had a profound effect on public opinion: *The Meaning of the Catastrophe* (or disaster), published in 1948 and reissued in a second edition the year after. In the introduction, the author declares: 'The Arab defeat [*hazima*] in Palestine is not a mere setback [*naksa*] or a simple, transitory misfortune, but a catastrophe [*nakba*] in every sense of the word, a calamitous ordeal among the most difficult that the Arabs have undergone in the course of a long history full of ordeals and calamities.'[81]

The extraordinary complexity of the problem before us, like the passion it arouses, is more than just the result of two experiences of persecution. History, after all, abounds in instances of the emigration or forced exile of persecuted people who become persecutors in their turn. Oppressed religious sects and people deported for ethnic or political reasons are among the examples that spring to mind. What makes the Israeli–Palestinian problem exceptional is, above all, that no other population actively involved in a colonial–settler project was fleeing a form of persecution as long-standing and brutal as European anti-Semitism, or was made up of survivors of such a stupefying crime against humanity.

It was with this circumstance in mind that Mahmoud Darwish exclaimed, in his exchange above with Helit Yeshurun, 'Do you know why we Palestinians are famous? It's because *you* are our enemy. Interest in the Palestinian question flows from interest in the Jewish question. Yes. People are interested in you, not me ... ! The international interest in the Palestinian question merely reflects the interest people take in the Jewish question.'[82] This was, of course, an exaggeration blurted out in the heat of the moment: the Palestinian tragedy would certainly have resounded if the Westerners who settled in Palestine had been, say, members of a Protestant sect rather than Jews. How, then, are we to explain the importance accorded to the Palestinian tragedy apart from the Jewishness of Israel?

It cannot fairly be said that the 'uprooting' of the Palestinians – to borrow the expression used by Pierre Bourdieu and Abdelmalek Sayad to describe the rural populations 'regrouped' by the French army in camps in colonial Algeria[83] – has been exceptionally extensive or cruel. Compare it with the Algerian case, in which some two million 'regrouped persons' came under the direct control of the French colonial army: measured against its standards of brutality, the Israeli army pales. None of the massacres of Palestinians carried out by Israeli forces compares in scope to the one perpetrated by the French army in May 1945 in the Algerian cities of Setif and Guelma, to cite only that case: several thousand Algerians – *tens* of thousands, by Algerian estimates – were massacred there in the space of a few weeks. And what the black population of sub-Saharan Africa had to endure during the long 'civilizing' period in the history of the colonial empires, from slavery to veritable genocides (which all too often go unmentioned even today), was far more terrible than even the Algerian horror.

As colonial abominations go, the fate of the Palestinians is far from being the worst. The only people who can be excused for thinking differently are those who are directly subject to this fate and lack the necessary basis for comparison. The Palestinians cannot, however, advisedly and legitimately apply to their own case the superlatives appropriate to the Jewish genocide. 'Who would want morally to equate mass extermination with mass dispossession?' Said exclaims in the essay cited above. 'It would be foolish even to try.'[84] Similarly, Benny Morris is correct to point out that Deir Yassin – the Palestinian village where 120 people were massacred by the Revisionist Zionist Irgun in 1948 – 'was no Srebrenica' (the Bosnian city in which eight thousand people were slaughtered by the forces of the Serbian Republic of Bosnia in 1995).[85]

How, then, are we to explain the immense place that the oppression of the Palestinians at the hands of the Israelis holds among the passionately debated issues of our day? There are several reasons for this. One is that Israel is the only European colonial settler state in which the political rights of the native population have yet to be restored (apart from places like North America and Australia, where colonization all but wiped out the native population). With the disappearance of the South African apartheid system in 1994, the Palestinian question became the last major burning issue of European colonialism. Israel is currently the only state in the world that combines three modes of colonial oppression: members of the indigenous minority who remained after 1948 (the 'Israeli Arabs') have the status of second-class citizens; since 1967, the inhabitants of the West Bank and Gaza have had the status of a population under either foreign occupation or direct control by the former occupiers; and the great majority of Palestinians have the status of people uprooted from their land and barred from returning. Most of this last group live in refugee camps on the periphery of the colonial state or in the territories it controls; others have joined the vast Palestinian diaspora; still others are living uprooted within the 1949 borders as 'internally displaced persons'.

The persistence of these colonialist modes of oppression makes Israel, in some sense, an anachronism. A colonial state born at the very moment in which the process of decolonization was first gaining strength, it both proved the rule and constituted an exception. Hence the profound ambiguity of a 'war of independence' that grew into a war of colonial conquest, by way of a declaration of independence perceived as a declaration of annexation by a majority of the people of the country – Mandatory Palestine – on whose soil it was solemnly read out on 14 May 1948.

Even on the territory attributed in November 1947 to the 'Jewish state' by a United Nations General Assembly in which the future 'Third World' was barely represented[86] – a territory that would be substantially enlarged *manu militari* in the course of the first Arab–Israeli war – close to half the resident population received Israel's declaration of independence as an outrage. At the time, a yawning gulf separated those who regarded the creation of Israel as an act of liberation of the first importance – the redemption of European Jewry's centuries-old history of oppression – and those who perceived it as the establishment of a colonial entity at the cost of the indigenous population. As the American journalist I. F. Stone wrote in 1967: 'The fact that the Jewish community in Palestine afterwards fought the British is no more evidence of its not being a colonial implantation than similar wars of British colonists against the mother country, from the American Revolution to Rhodesia.'[87]

Nevertheless, the notion of Israel as the product of an anti-colonial war of independence long held sway in the West. It was decisively modified by the June 1967 war, when the myth of Israel as a David facing the Goliath of the surrounding Arab countries gave way to an image of Israel as the state of 'an elite people, self-assured and domineering', as General Charles de Gaulle put it. The phrase was widely criticized because it was not free of anti-Semitic overtones: the French president was targeting what, in his view, the Jews 'had always been'.[88]

Recognition that Israel is a colonial power was long in coming in the West – longer on the left than the right – and, of course, in Israel itself. The considerable distance covered runs from the period when Jean-Paul Sartre's review Les Temps modernes published a thick issue on the Israeli–Arab conflict on the eve of the 1967 war,[89] in which the title of Maxime Rodinson's remarkable contribution characterizing Israel as a 'colonial-settler state' could still be qualified by a question mark,[90] to the unabashed 1999 admission by the most famous of the 'new Israeli historians', Benny Morris, that 'Zionism was a colonizing and expansionist ideology and movement.'[91] Uri Ram has summed up Israeli 'post-Zionist' discourse on the question:

> Israel is a settler-colonial society on a par with other white European societies such as Australia or South Africa. Whether or not the expulsion of Palestinians in 1948 was premeditated (the transfer issue), or an unintentional consequence of the war, Israel is largely responsible for the refugee problem. The conquest of land and labor was an avowed principle of labor Zionism, and its logical derivative is dislocation of, and discrimination against, Palestinians.[92]

Against this backdrop, the Palestinian struggle appears for what it is: the last major anti-colonial struggle. The indigenous population of 'Rhodesia' obtained the same political rights as the population of colonial origin in 1980; the country then experienced a second independence and genuine decolonization under the name Zimbabwe. South Africa's indigenous population, in its turn, had gained the same rights as the population of colonial origin by 1994.[93] Yet the indigenous population of Palestine is still waging a bitter struggle for recognition of its right to sovereignty over as little as one-fifth of its ancestral lands – the portion that Israel did not immediately conquer in 1948, but occupied nineteen years later.

The persistence of Israeli colonial oppression, flying in the face of the prevailing tendency of world history, has been made worse by a rising curve of violence. Israel has fought seven major wars in its six decades, in 1948, 1956, 1967, 1973, 1982, 2006 and 2008–9, the latter two the most brutal of all. Each one profoundly alarmed the world because of the strategic location of the conflict. (Contrast the 5.4 million war-related deaths in the Congo in the ten years since 1998 – 45,000 a month or 1,500 a day in 2008, on the estimate of an American NGO.[94] Black skins are of small worth in comparison with black gold.)

The international implications of the conflicts in the Middle East do not, however, alter the fact that Israeli oppression of the Palestinians is now at its highest level ever. In recent years, it has soared from one peak to the next, beginning with Ariel Sharon's assumption of the leadership of the Israeli government in 2001, followed by the 2002 reoccupation of the West Bank for the purpose of crushing the Second Intifada, continuing to the 2006 blockade of Gaza and the repeated assaults on it since. Zionist colonial power clings to its 1967 conquered territory in the face of resistance of an intensity and tenacity that would surely have beaten back other forms of colonialism, at considerable cost to Israeli society.

The result is hardly surprising: Israel's image has, inevitably, deteriorated. According to a BBC poll conducted in thirty-four countries and published on 2 April 2008 – several months before the cruel assault on Gaza unleashed at the end of the year, which has surely had a powerfully negative influence on perceptions of the country – Israel was, after Iran, the state with the poorest image: 54 and 52 per cent cited the influence of Iran and Israel, respectively, as negative.[95] Another poll, in 2003, indicated that 59 per cent of Europeans considered Israel a threat to peace, whereas only 53 per cent thought Iran was.[96] The more the image of the 'Jewish state' suffers – above all in the West, where its image counts for a great deal – the more it turns to the Holocaust to shore up its legitimization.

The reason is that the West (vestiges of Judeophobia and anti-Semitism aside, which today persist only among a minority) continues to regard the Shoah from the standpoint, and sense of responsibility, of the *culprits*, whereas the Arab world and most of the Third World regard the state that claims to represent the victims of the Shoah from the standpoint of the *victims* of both the Nakba and Israel's subsequent acts. This fact weighs very heavily on the reception of the Holocaust in the Arab East, which got ever more complicated from the time of the Shoah itself to the time of the Nakba up to our own day.

PART I

THE TIME OF THE SHOAH

Arab Reactions to Nazism
and Anti-Semitism
1933–1947

Prelude

It ought to be a truism that 'the Arabs' do not exist – at least not as a homogeneous political or ideological subject. Yet such use of a general category known as 'the Arabs' is common in both journalism and the specialist literature. 'The Arabs' are supposed to think and act or react in unison. Of course, like 'the Jews' or 'the Muslims', 'the Arabs' as a politically and intellectually uniform group exist only in fantasy, engendered by the distorting prism of either ordinary racism or polemical fanaticism.

Like any large, diverse group, the Arab population is criss-crossed by different ideological currents, shaped by varied forms of education and political experience in different countries, a circumstance no well-informed work on political thought in the Arab world fails to point out. Only a perception distorted by 'Orientalism', in the pejorative sense of the term made famous by Edward Said – i.e. the cultural essentialization of the peoples of the East that reduces them to a stereotyped immutable being or 'mind'[1] – can obscure the very deep divisions in the Arab world.

The diversity of the Arabs' historical relations to Nazism and Zionism is no less pronounced. There have even been a few Arab allies of the Zionist movement: recall the Palestinian 'collaboration'[2] and the unacknowledged 'collusion' of leaders who had ties to the British, such as King Abdullah of Jordan,[3] or allies motivated by the idea of making common cause with the Zionists as 'enemies of their enemies,' notably some Christian Maronites in Lebanon.[4]

In the Arab anti-colonial independence movement, whose opposition to the Zionist project in Palestine reflected what was by far the dominant Arab attitude in the 1930s and 1940s, we may distinguish four basic ideological currents:

1) the liberal Westernizers
2) the Marxists

3)   the nationalists
4)   the reactionary and/or fundamentalist Pan-Islamists.

Note that none of these currents has a monopoly on the central value inspiring it. Thus there is widespread adhesion to Islam among liberal Westernizers and nationalists. Nationalism, moderate or radical, animates Westernist liberal advocates of independence and, in a specifically religious form, Pan-Islamists as well. Similarly, it can be argued that both Marxists and most nationalists are Westernizers who even, at times, embrace the same liberal values.

Moreover, each current comprises several distinct variants, and there are a number of intermediate and combined categories. Regarding nationalism in particular, we may distinguish a right wing that often works in close alliance with Islamic fundamentalism, a left wing influenced by Marxism and a liberal version.[5] On certain questions, the positions of these sub-groups can differ sharply.

Nevertheless, a qualitative difference sets each of the four major categories apart: the nature of its guiding principle, its determinant system of political values. They choose their political positions with reference, first and foremost, to a distinctive political and ideological system of thought – liberalism, Marxism, nationalism or Islam conceived as a source of political inspiration adapted to contemporary conditions.

CHAPTER I

The Liberal Westernizers

As used here, 'Westernism' has nothing to do with the concept of 'Occidentalism' forged in symmetrical opposition to Said's 'Orientalism' as a caricature for a certain Islamic perception of the West.[1] Nor is it my intention to stand the concept of Orientalism on its head in order to paint the Westernizers as unconditional admirers of the 'West' and its governments. The term is, rather, patterned after nineteenth-century Russian 'Westernism'.

The Russian Westernizers, in opposition to the Slavophiles, urged adoption of the Enlightenment values that dominated Western Europe together with the industrial civilization that, in their view, functioned properly only when accompanied by those values.[2] Russian Westernism did not imply uncritical admiration of Western Europe but, rather, a set of values that might equally be described as 'modernist' and could perfectly well accommodate a political critique of the West.[3] Thus, alongside liberal Westernism, there existed a Marxian Westernism and even a Europeanist Russian nationalism. The situation is no different in the Arab world.

Following Nadav Safran, I use the word 'liberalism' here not in its nineteenth-century sense, designating a limitation of the role of the state, individualism and 'the sanctity of property,' but rather to mean 'a general commitment to the ideal of remolding society on the basis of an essentially secular conception of the state and rational-humanitarian values'.[4]

Steeped in a democratic, humanist culture, the Westernizing liberals among the advocates of independence in the Arab world opposed National Socialism from the outset – a stand that by no means mitigated their anti-colonialist hostility to Zionism. As those best qualified to criticize the premises of Zionism while defending the values of Western anti-fascist culture, the Westernizing liberals were a deep embarrassment to the Zionist movement. They did not, however, hold the greatest appeal for the Arab masses, given the contradiction between those very values and the colonialist behaviour of the Western powers posing as their champions – a problem still acutely relevant in the Arab world today.

The twofold denunciation of Nazism and Zionism made it possible to contest the use of Nazi abominations as a way of legitimizing the Zionist enterprise. The liberals' main argument was based on plain common sense: why should the Palestinians have to pay for the Nazis' crimes? This objection stands as a constant in the long history of the Arab polemic against Zionism; the various ideological currents of the Arab world have all taken it up.

My own father, Joseph Achcar, a pro-independence but also Francophile Lebanese, provided an early statement of this argument. It appeared in the dissertation he submitted in 1934 to the University of Lyons for a doctorate in law, in which he deplored Hitler's assumption of power the previous year:

> It goes without saying that we condemn, as the world's conscience has done since then, the atavistic, savage conception that ... professes to purify the German nation by eliminating elements foreign to it ...
>
> A government that springs from this reactionary, antiquated attitude readily ostracized the heterogeneous minorities among the people. The result was to drive away 'the undesirables,' the Jews, who had to appeal to the hospitality of other countries. It was accorded to them only on precisely defined conditions, [given] the difficulty of finding them employment in the current period of economic crisis.
>
> The Zionist leaders accordingly returned to the assault on the obstacles to creating a Jewish state in Palestine ...
>
> It is not possible to redress one injustice, if an injustice has been committed, by another, more serious and more costly injustice. That the Jewish people inhabited Palestine more than twenty centuries ago is beyond doubt. That it should aspire, after so long an interval, to take the country back and lay down the law there is sheer utopia.[5]

This point of view was anything but exceptional. Indeed, there is every reason to wonder why liberal Westernist anti-colonialism, the vehicle of the Enlightenment in the Arab world, has attracted so much less attention than the most reactionary Arab currents, even those that were infinitely less influential.

Israel Gershoni, a specialist in Egyptian intellectual history at the University of Tel Aviv, has taken up the task of 'deconstructing the hegemonic narrative' that maintains, contrary to all the documentary evidence, that a majority of Egyptians supported Nazism in the 1930s.[6] His research established that 'the overwhelming majority of Egyptian voices – in the political arena, in intellectual circles, among the professional, educated, urban middle classes and even in the literate popular culture – rejected fascism and Nazism both as an ideology and a practice, and as "an enemy of the enemy.'"[7]

> The Egyptian public's attitude toward fascism and Nazism was expressed principally through three types of representation. The first, *imperialistic representation*, viewed fascism and Nazism as imperialist forces; the second, *totalitarian representation*, perceived the Third Reich and the fascist regime in Italy as extreme forms of modern totalitarianism. And the third, *racist representation*, scathingly denounced the ideology of Nazism and its racist theories and practices.[8]

Gershoni paid special attention to the Islamic variant of liberal Westernism in Egypt. In a study on Egyptian liberalism's attitude towards Nazism from 1933 to the outbreak of the Second World War, he focuses on the weekly review *Al-Risāla*, the first issue of which appeared in 1933.[9]

Boasting a circulation that rose, late in the decade, to 40,000 copies, a third of which were sold in Arab capitals beyond Egypt's borders, *Al-Risāla* provided a forum for some of the most prestigious Egyptian and non-Egyptian Arab intellectuals of the period: its contributors included Ali 'Abdul-Rāziq, Ahmad Amīn, 'Abbās Mahmūd al-'Aqqād, Muhammad Husayn Haykal, Tāha Hussein, Tawfiq al-Hakīm,[10] Mahmūd Taymūr and Sāti' al-Husri.[11] Together with a clear Arabist and Islamic orientation (*Al-Risāla* means 'the message' – an allusion to that of the Prophet Muhammad) along reformist lines,

> it regularly devoted space to a methodical, highly critical review of internal developments in Nazi Germany and in fascist Italy, as well as of the policies of Hitler and Mussolini in the international arena. It was not a solitary voice in doing so. Consistent support of liberal democracy and liberal values, attended by the rejection of fascist and Nazi totalitarianism, can also be found, for example, in the monthly *Al-Hilal*, in the daily *Al-Ahram*, and in the illustrated weekly *Ruz al-Yusuf* [*Rose al-Yūsuf*] throughout the entire decade.[12]

Gershoni shows that the critiques appearing in the review were comparable to the best analyses and refutations of Nazism published in Europe. The review denounced not only the racial exclusion organized by National Socialism, but also the 'racist madness' of its scientific pretensions and their translation into medical practice. Avoiding the trap into which ultranationalists and religious conservatives fell, it struggled against all forms of the illusion that Nazi Germany was pro-Arab because it was anti-Jewish: *Al-Risāla* denounced

Nazism 'as a "white imperialist attack" on the Semitic peoples, first and foremost against the Arabs and Muslims',[13] while assailing the specific form of anti-Judaism peculiar to Nazi anti-Semitism. Yet all this went hand in hand with fierce denunciation of the Zionist enterprise in Palestine.[14]

Gershoni insists that *Al-Risāla* was in no sense marginal or exceptional: 'It was actually the pro-fascist and pro-Nazi intellectual voices that were peripheral.'[15] He offered further proof a few years later in a study of another liberal Westernist publication, the Egyptian monthly *Al-Hilāl* (The Crescent), which played a key role in shaping culture in the Middle East.[16]

Like *Al-Risāla*, *Al-Hilāl* methodically denounced the totalitarian, imperialistic and racist nature of Nazism and Italian fascism. Gershoni dwells in particular on two essays that appeared in July and August 1933, one about the great mass slaughters of history, the other about anti-Semitism; *Al-Hilāl* warned that the Jews might fall victim to a massacre on a scale with the one that had decimated the Armenians, which it cited as the most terrible in modern history.[17]

Gershoni thus corroborates what his colleague at the University of Tel Aviv, Ami Ayalon (not to be confused with the Ami Ayalon who has moved from the head of Shin Beth, the Israeli internal security service, to the highest levels of the Labor Party), noted in an earlier essay on Egyptian intellectuals in the 1930s:

> The voices of democracy's champions were louder than those of its critics who were fascinated by the Führer and the Duce. They grew still louder toward the end of the decade. Egyptian thinkers and writers may have undergone a crisis of orientation during that period regarding issues of communal and individual identity in the extreme complexities of modernity. Most of them, so it seems, nevertheless remained dedicated to the democratic idea, with its implied liberties and rights, and were prepared to defend it at all times against the perils of totalitarianism.[18]

Today this stance is generally effaced by anti-Arab propaganda that depicts 'the Arabs' as Nazis deep down, dovetailing with its complement in the Arab world, which does its utmost to convey the same impression because it corresponds to its own vision of things. Yet the Zionists themselves were capable of making the distinction in the 1930s. Philip Khoury, relying on documents discovered in the Central Zionist Archives (CZA) in Jerusalem, describes a 1936 meeting in Syria between Eliahu Epstein, the representative of the Jewish Agency for Palestine, and Fakhri al-Bārūdi, one of the main leaders of the National Bloc, the leading Syrian organization of pro-independence liberal Westernizers, and a later meeting with other Bloc leaders, including Shukri al-Quwwatli, a radical nationalist, who would in time twice serve as president of independent Syria.[19] Epstein was exploring the possibility of an agreement with the advocates of Syrian independence; Bārūdi laid out preconditions, underscoring his party's moderating role:

> Thousands of people wanted to go from Syria to Palestine to help their brethren but we prevented them from doing so ... We also defended Syrian Jews from attacks by the press and the street mob ... The slogans which are raised now and around which the struggle takes place are, 'an end to immigration.' And the Arab leaders cannot stop the clashes unless some gain is made in regard to stopping immigration.[20]

Bārūdi was not talking through his hat. The Syrian independence advocates had indeed defended the Jews of Syria and had taken active measures on their behalf. Witness an English-language Palestinian daily's February 1935 report on the reaction of the main Syrian pro-independence daily, *Alif Bā'*, to the bloody anti-Jewish riots in Constantine* the preceding August:

> Condemnation of the Moslems of Algiers [Algeria] for provoking anti-Jewish riots and of the German government in driving Jews from Germany without reason, is contained in a leading article published in 'Alif Ba,' the Moslem daily of Damascus, in its issue of February 12. 'The Jewish religion is one of the most honored in the world, and it is the duty of members of all other religions to treat it with esteem,' says the article. 'It is true that we are fighting Zionism, but we are not fighting the Jews as such. Judaism is not necessarily Zionism.' Arabs should strongly oppose anti-Semitism, the paper urges, and refuse to help those who advocate it as the North African Moslems are doing. That is a sin which can never be atoned.[22]

Quwwatli explained that an agreement depended on whether the Zionists intended to 'make of Palestine a Jewish National Home or to make a Jewish National Home in Palestine. If the former, then we are categorically opposed

---

*   According to Norman Stillman, the riots 'took place in Constantine, Algeria, from August 3 to 5, 1934, after a drunken Jewish army tailor insulted some Muslims in the courtyard of a mosque and urinated on them. During the rioting that ensued, twenty-three Jews, including men, women, and children, were killed and thirty-eight injured according to the official statistics ... Throughout much of the pogrom, the French police and security forces stood by and did little or nothing to stop the rioters.'[21]

46   THE ARABS AND THE HOLOCAUST

to it and there is no way to come to an understanding. But if it means the latter then we are ready ... to find a solution to the mutual advantage of both parties.'[23]

This attitude was widespread among liberal Arab nationalists. The Egyptian 'Abdul-Rahmān 'Azzām, who was to become the first secretary of the League of Arab States at its creation in 1945, said in a November 1935 speech delivered in Palestine itself, in the city of Nablus, on the eighteenth anniversary of the Balfour Declaration:

> What is the Balfour Declaration worth? It is a commitment on the part of those who do not own to give what is not theirs. It aims to fool the Jews into clinging to hopes whose objective is collision with the East and capitulation to the West. The result can only be a state of eternal hostility with the Arab peoples and the nations of Islam ... The Balfour Declaration is detrimental for the Jews as well as the Arabs ...
>
> The West will not deal justly with the Jews for as long as it continues to be the West that we know and that the Jews know. Do the Zionists wish to inherit Palestine and, along with it, the unending hostility of the East? I think that the Jews will avoid that. Who knows? Perhaps we will one day be able to celebrate the burial of the Balfour Declaration together with them, after all of us have come to see that this Declaration is a harbinger of evil for Arabs and Jews alike.[24]

Consider also the first gathering of Arab feminists, held in Cairo from 15 to 18 October 1938 in solidarity with Palestine. It was convened three months after the July 1938 International Conference in Evian mentioned in the Introduction, which the pioneer of Egyptian and Arab feminism, Huda Shaarawi (Sha'rāwi), attacked in her opening address: 'Not a single representative of one of the participating states, not even the representative of Great Britain or the United States, has dared declare that his government was prepared to provide a haven to these rejected, shelterless people, while Palestine, to which they have no familial or national ties, has taken in four hundred thousand of them down to the present day.'[25] The Palestinian Arab nationalist Akram Zu'aytir, who provides a report on her speech, adds: 'She called on Jewish compatriots to show solidarity with us in order to bring the Zionists to renounce their mad dreams.'[26]

How did the Arab liberal Westernizers in Palestine itself position themselves? A good example is George Antonius who, after a stint as an official in the British colonial administration in Palestine, became one of the political and intellectual leaders of the Arab nationalist movement in general and the liberal current in particular. A member of the Palestinian and Arab delegations, he was the main Palestinian Arab spokesperson at the important London Conference of 1939. The year before, in *The Arab Awakening* – a book that Said rightly calls '*the* classic and foundational book on Arab nationalism'[27] – Antonius wrote, remarkably:

> There seems to be no valid reason why Palestine should not be constituted into an independent Arab state in which as many Jews as the country can hold without prejudice to its political and economic freedom would live in peace, security and dignity, and enjoy full rights of citizenship ...
>
> The relief of Jewish distress caused by European persecution must be sought elsewhere than in Palestine, for the country is too small to hold a larger increase of population, and it has already borne more than its fair share ...
>
> The treatment meted out to Jews in Germany and other European countries is a disgrace to its authors and to modern civilisation; but posterity will not exonerate any country that fails to bear its proper share of the sacrifices needed to alleviate Jewish suffering and distress. To place the brunt of the burden upon Arab Palestine is a miserable evasion of the duty that lies upon the whole of the civilised world. It is also morally outrageous. No code of morals can justify the persecution of one people in an attempt to relieve the persecution of another. The cure of the eviction of the Jews from Germany is not to be sought in the eviction of the Arabs from their homeland; and the relief of Jewish distress may not be accomplished at the cost of inflicting a corresponding distress upon an innocent and peaceful population.[28]

Antonius was by no means an isolated voice, as René Wildangel (now an adviser to the Green fraction in the German Bundestag) has shown in a book that, like Gershoni's, seeks to deconstruct the dominant narrative.[29] Wildangel's thorough examination of the 1930s and 1940s Palestinian Arab press, in all its diversity, marshals a wealth of quotations from articles, as well as reproductions of cartoons, that provide solid support for his conclusion that

> Voices critical of National Socialism were not at all rare in Palestinian Arab newspapers of the 1930s. ... Whatever the motivation for such criticism – whether it was moral and humanistic (denouncing the brutality of the German dictatorship), political and ideological (taking issue with the idea of fascism), religious (critical of the Nazis' policy toward the churches) or, rather, pragmatically inspired by the situation in Palestine (pointing, for example, to the consequences of Jewish immigration) – the range

of such diverse motivations is impressive, and gives the lie to one-sided judgments of the position taken by the Arab Palestinians.[30]

With the exacerbation of tensions, especially from 1936 on, the radical wing of the national movement led by the Mufti of Jerusalem, Hajj Amin al-Husseini, came to represent the Arab majority view in Palestine. However, the pro-independence current opposed to the Mufti remained very influential, and had major media at its disposal, including a broad array of publications, notably the daily *Filastīn* and the weekly *Al-Akhbār*, which frequently aired virulent anti-Nazi criticisms.

Filastīn (*Palestine*, transliterated '*Falastin*', the most common colloquial pronunciation, immediately under the paper's Arabic name) was one of the oldest and most important. Rashid Khalidi characterizes it as 'Palestine's main Arabic-language daily' during the period 'and probably the country's fiercest and most consistent critic of the Zionist enterprise':[31]

> As time went on, moreover, *Filastin* came to be relied upon throughout the Arab world for news of Zionist policy initiatives and the progress of Zionist colonization in Palestine, thereby playing an important role in establishing Zionism as an issue that concerned all Arabs. Even before World War I, the paper's editorials and articles on Zionism were picked up and reproduced by other newspapers, not only in Palestine but in Beirut, Cairo, Damascus, and other centers throughout the Arabic-speaking world.[32]

'Abd-ul-Rahmān 'Abdul-Ghani, in his 1995 examination of the Palestinian press between 1933 and 1939, deplores, somewhat unfairly, the general poverty of its treatment of Nazism. The more systematic investigation of the same publications that René Wildangel carried out twelve years later led him to underscore the richness of the information they transmitted. 'Abdul-Ghani's quotations from *Filastīn* are, nevertheless, instructive, showing that from 1933 on it depicted Nazism as reactionary and dictatorial while voicing the conviction that democracy would eventually triumph.[33]

The newspaper's opposition to Nazism also flowed from an acute awareness, which can only be termed premonitory, that Hitler's accession to power would reinforce the Zionist enterprise. Hence the ironic April 1933 editorial Wildangel describes, which declares 'that the Zionist association in Palestine had decided to include, in a gallery of personalities who had made significant contributions to the construction of the country, such as "Herzl, Nordau, Balfour, Lloyd George and others," "a portrait of Hitler as well."'[34]

In an article that appeared on 17 June 1934 under the title 'Nazi Palestine!!!' *Filastīn* reacted vigorously to Zionist accusations of Arab pro-Nazism:

> Palestine needs neither fascism nor Nazism in order to arouse the feelings of her sons against Zionism and its designs in the Arab world. This repulsion already exists; it had already taken root in people's minds several years ago, well before Nazism. ... What authorizes the Jews to announce sorrowfully to the Arabs that a Nazi movement has sprung up among them? Is it the Arabs who have driven the Jews from their land, or is it rather the Jews who are driving Arabs from their homes and persecuting them to the point of depriving them of human beings' most basic right, the right to life?[35]

According to Orayb Aref Najjar, who has studied the editorials published in *Filastīn* during the Second World War,

> The newspaper supported the pro-Allied argument in two ways. First, it made distinctions between the universal and local, creating a hierarchy of values that explained why the paper sided with the Allies. Second, by drawing upon traditional Arab-Islamic values (and by mining the historical record for examples), the editors suggested that Islamic values precluded fighting with Nazi Germany and urged 'tolerance in trying times' to deal with continued colonial rule Palestinians found cruel and unacceptable.[36]

Even as *Filastīn* vigorously attacked the Axis powers, and, especially, Nazism, it mobilized the classic argument on the issue of Jewish immigration. Why should the blameless Palestinians be made to pay for the appalling European persecution of the Jews? Why did the United States, Britain and Britain's overseas allies not open their doors to Jewish immigration? The daily pursued a campaign for Palestinian rights, calling for the liberation of Palestinian political prisoners and the return of exiled Palestinian leaders – most of whom were numbered among its political adversaries.

All things considered, the attitude of the Palestinian liberals was one of the most remarkable and commendable forms of opposition to Nazism in the world. Not only did they refuse to side with 'the enemy of their enemy', or, more precisely, 'the enemy of their two enemies' (as did a large segment of the nationalist elites under the lead of the Mufti of Jerusalem) or even to take refuge in a prudent semi-neutrality (as did a number of Arab governments that were officially allied with London or controlled by it); they went so far as to support the oppressor of their own nation in its war against the sworn enemy of those who were trying to conquer their land. They did so, Najjar emphasizes, in the name of an ethical hierarchy that put liberal values, both secular and religious, above every other considerations in the hope (or, perhaps, wish) that those values would lead the nations fighting for them to render the Palestinians justice. In this regard, Najjar cites a *Filastīn* editorial of 9 September 1939 – that is, a mere week after the outbreak of the Second World War (and four days after the United States had proclaimed its neutrality): 'War has placed us in a new situation with regard to our relations with Britain. We are connected to it today in a matter that is more universal than our private cause. We are not calling on Arabs to sacrifice their cause, but we are asserting that the present conflict between the democratic forces and dictatorial forces has dictated that we take sides with one or the other.'[37]*

All this is very remote from the currently prevailing image of a Palestinian people that supposedly responded to Mufti Amin al-Husseini's exhortations by chanting hallelujah in unison. The shroud of silence cast over the real positions of a major segment of the Palestinian elite is explained by political motives that have not varied since the 1939 London negotiations when Zionist leaders admitted they preferred dealing with the underlings of the much maligned Amin al-Husseini. 'It will be much easier for us to counter their claims,' Ben-Gurion explained. 'We can say that they stand for terrorism and represent only a small part of the Arab population. A broad delegation including "moderates" will display the Arab public's general resistance to the Jews.'[39] Propaganda literature has always projected the Mufti's stance onto all the Arabs of Palestine, with a view to portraying them as ardent partisans of the Axis powers. The Zionist intelligence services' internal communications were more circumspect:

> The Arab position on the war was the subject of much speculation. The Jewish Agency's sources stressed the Arab inclination to support the Nazis for mostly obvious political reasons but also, at times, out of ideological identification. The Zionist intelligence services reported a few German secret agents working among Palestine's Arabs but assumed that no single organization could really be considered a fifth column. By one estimate [dated 7 December 1941], some 60 percent of the country's Arabs supported the Nazis.[40]

---

*   On 18 Feb. 1942, the weekly *Al-Akhbār* described Hitler as 'humanity's greatest enemy' ('*adū al-insāniyya al-akbar*).[38] The underlying premiss of this characterization is a ranking of enemies according to a general humanist criterion at odds with the narrowly nationalist vision of the 'enemy of our enemy'. We shall have occasion to return to it.

It is in fact remarkable that *no more than* 60 per cent of Palestinian Arabs supported the Nazis at that point, when Germany was at the height of its military success. Only later would reversals on the Soviet front and the United States' entry into the war put a new face on matters. (No more than 60 per cent, let us add, according to a source predisposed, for a host of reasons, to overestimate the number of pro-Nazi Palestinians.)

The official position put forward by the founders of the League of Arab States on the Palestinian question in 1944 has also been relegated to the shadows. It was due to the dominant role played by the liberal Westernizing current – thanks to the leading position of Cairo's Wafdist government – in the League's foundation. Indeed, Egypt's Wafd was the party that best represented liberal Westernism within the Arab independence movement throughout the first half of the century; it enjoyed the support of its co-thinkers in the governments of both Beirut and Damascus.

At the 7 October 1944 meeting, in Alexandria, delegations led by the heads of the Egyptian, Iraqi, Jordanian and Lebanese governments adopted a protocol that was the prelude to the creation of the League of Arab States. The special resolution on Palestine contained in the Alexandria Protocol declares that the Committee

> is second to none in regretting the woes which have been inflicted upon the Jews of Europe by European dictatorial states. But the question of these Jews should not be confused with Zionism, for there can be no greater injustice and aggression than solving the problem of the Jews of Europe by another injustice, i.e., by inflicting injustice on the Arabs of Palestine of various religions and denominations.[41]

The April 1946 report of the Anglo-American Committee of Inquiry contains exactly the same discourse:

> Arab spokesmen profess the greatest sympathy for the persecuted Jews of Europe, but they point out that they have not been responsible for this persecution and that it is not just that they should be compelled to atone for the sins of the Western peoples by accepting into their country hundreds of thousands of victims of European anti-Semitism. Some Arabs even declare that they might be willing to do their share in providing for refugees on a quota basis if the United States, the British Commonwealth and other Western countries would do the same.[42]*

---

* In this connection, it is worth pointing out that the Arab countries took in very many Armenian survivors of the 1915 genocide. In 1925, there were 150,000 Armenians in

The official position of the Arab states explicitly ruled out the expulsion of Jews who had already settled in Palestine. Witness a speech delivered by the first Secretary General of the League of Arab States, the Wafdist Egyptian 'Abdul-Raḥmān 'Azzām, six months after the end of World War II, at a moment when Arabs had reason to think that they would enjoy military superiority in an armed conflict with Zionists. The continuity with his previously cited speech of 1935 is striking.

> You will no doubt remember that the Arab league has in the last six months collided with the Jews. It was a violent collision with a weak and dispersed people who, of all peoples, most need our sympathy, for they are our persecuted cousins. ... The Zionists are a curse on the Jews themselves and, indeed, on us Arabs. We still extend to the Jews the hand of friendship, and we do not want to share in the crime of persecuting them. ... I say, confident in God and guided by the witness of current events, that in this matter we will win a victory which will not disperse the Jews as the Europeans dispersed them, for this is not in our nature nor in the nature of our fathers before us. They will realize ... that we are their brothers, with whom they can live as our Christian brothers have done, and that they can reach in the common homeland of the Arabs the highest functions and positions.[44]

The proposals for a resolution of the Palestine conflict put forward by the Arab states in 1946–7 were entirely in keeping with this approach. They were laid out in the report presented by the United Nations Special Committee on Palestine (UNSCOP) to the General Assembly in September 1947 as a preliminary to the debate and vote on the partition plan recommended in the same report:

(a) That Palestine should be a unitary State, with a democratic constitution and an elected legislative assembly,
(b) That the constitution should provide, inter alia, guarantees for (i) the sanctity of the Holy Places and, subject to suitable safeguards, freedom of religious practice in accordance with the status quo; (ii) full civil rights for all Palestine citizens, the naturalization requirement being ten years' continuous residence in the country; (iii) protection of religious and cultural rights of the Jewish community, such safeguards

Syria and Lebanon, according to an Armenian estimate; a full 90,000 of them lived in Aleppo and its environs.[43]

to be altered only with the consent of the majority of the Jewish members in the legislative assembly,

(c) That the constitution should provide also for (i) adequate representation in the legislative assembly of all important communities, provided that the Jews would in no case exceed one-third of the total number of members [that is, the proportion of Jews in the Palestinian population in 1947]; (ii) the strict prohibition of Jewish immigration and the continuation of the existing restrictions on land transfer, any change in these matters requiring the consent of a majority of the Arab members of the legislative assembly; (iii) the establishment of a Supreme Court which would be empowered to determine whether any legislation was inconsistent with the constitution.[45]

As the Arab states thus came out in favour of integrating the Jews living in Palestine in what would have effectively been a binational state, they also made a proposal about the Jewish refugees then in Europe. That same year, 1947, the UN ambassadors of the Arab countries then members of the international organization – Egypt, Iraq, Lebanon, the Saudi Arabian Kingdom, Syria and Yemen – joined those from Afghanistan, Colombia and Pakistan on a subcommittee that opposed the partition of Palestine and submitted a draft resolution to the General Assembly on the problem of resettling 'Jewish refugees and displaced persons' from Europe.

The gist of the resolution, put to the General Assembly for a vote, was that the task of finding a home for the refugees should be equitably shared. The subcommittee pointed out that 287,000 Jewish immigrants had been admitted to Palestine between 1933 and 1946, compared with 188,000 to the United States, 65,000 to the United Kingdom and some 110,000 to a number of other countries including Canada, Australia, South Africa and certain countries of Latin America. In other words, Palestine had 'absorbed a disproportionately large number of Jewish immigrants and [could] not take any more without serious injury to the economy of the country and the rights and position of the indigenous population'. As for the problem of the refugees still waiting in camps, the subcommittee offered the following recommendations:

(i) That countries of origin should be requested to take back the Jewish refugees and displaced persons belonging to them, and to render them all possible assistance to resettle in life;

(ii) That those Jewish refugees and displaced persons who cannot be

repatriated should be absorbed in the territories of Members of the
United Nations in proportion to their area, economic resources, per
capita income, population and other relevant factors;

(iii) That a Special Committee of the General Assembly should be set up
to recommend for acceptance of the Members of the United Nations
a scheme of quotas of Jewish refugees and displaced persons to be
resettled in their respective territories, and that the Special Committee
should, as far as possible, work in consultation with the International
Refugee Organization or its Preparatory Commission.[46]

Submitted to the General Assembly on 24 November 1947, the draft
resolution received sixteen votes in favour – including those of the nine
subcommittee members – and sixteen opposed, with twenty-six abstentions.
It was, consequently, not adopted. A remark that Walid Khalidi made twenty-
four years later reflects the bitterness that well-informed individuals in the
Arab world must have felt at the time: 'Jewish immigration to Palestine, even
if it means flooding the Arabs out – by all means; but a modest contribution
by each Western country to reflect the ostensibly humanitarian concern for
Jewish refugees – nothing doing. Such are the ways of Charity.'[47]*

The most common Arab attitude to the Holocaust would continue to be
grounded in the conviction that people entirely innocent of the crime had
been forced to pay for it, and that the governments that professed to be the
most deeply shaken by it were hypocrites seeking, above all, to shirk their
duties, neglecting the obligations dictated both by their own responsibility for
the Jewish genocide – or their failure to save the Jews – and by humanitarian
considerations. A sense of profound injustice and Western hypocrisy has
continued to rankle Arab public opinion to the present day.

---

*   On 'charity', let us cite the following report by the International Refugee Organization: 'Despite the fact that the General Assembly of the United Nations established
a budget of $155,860,500 for the first year of operation of the IRO, as of September
1947, contributions were at the rate of only $90,000,000 a year, and actual payments
represented only one-fourth of the annual contributions of the twelve governments.
With these funds the Preparatory Commission ... maintained 640,000 people
in European and Middle Eastern camps, and was providing legal assistance and
administrative aid to 900,000 others not in camps ... During July 1947, it became
necessary ... to establish a "freeze order" which closed the care and maintenance
facilities of the Preparatory Commission to new applicants with the exception of
so-called "hardship cases." This decision was made in an effort to use the Commission's
limited resources as efficiently as possible for the benefit of persons already in its
care.'[48]

CHAPTER 2

The Marxists

For ideological reasons, Marxists in the Arab world, including many indigenous and immigrant Jews, were consistently hostile to Nazism. The only exception came during the interlude of the Stalin–Hitler pact (1939–41), which Communist leaders tried hard to justify to their rank and file as a defensive tactical manœuvre on Moscow's part.[1] It was the Marxists who were mainly responsible for branding Zionism a racist movement, as well as for the specious equation 'Zionism = Nazism' – whose first logical implication (as is all too often forgotten) is equal aversion for both. Marxist Arabs tended to dismiss Nazism and Zionism as equally reactionary ideologies and movements – two sides of the same coin.

The Nazi seizure of power in Germany occurred at a time when the world Communist movement was squarely on the ultra-left course dictated by Moscow, opposing fascism and 'social fascism' – that is, Social Democracy – with the same vehemence. Communists also applied this line to Zionism, whose dominant faction was in the social democratic fold. Hence *Rundschau*, the German-language review of the Executive Committee of the Communist International, could say of 'the inhibitions' exhibited at the summer 1933 Zionist Congress in Prague, just before the signing of the Haavara agreement: 'True, Hitler is the enemy of the Jews, but Hitler is a national German racist and the Zionists are national Jewish racists. At bottom they speak the same language. And in fact it seems as though there might be some kind of understanding between Hitler and the Zionists.'[2]

It was in this context that Palestine's Communists underscored the 'remarkable similarity' between Nazism and Zionism and forged the label 'Zionist-fascist' on the model of 'social-fascist'. They accused the Zionists of banding together with the Nazis to combat the Soviet Union and the Arab national movement. As Walter Laqueur has shown, 'Party propaganda did not fail to point out [in 1933] the "remarkable similarity" between Nazism and

Zionism ("Only two parties exist today in Germany – the Nazi Party and the Zionists") and, as evidence, it referred to the fact that the Zionist newspaper published in Germany did not attack the Nazi regime in its columns.'[3]

This type of accusation was of course much less shocking and defamatory then than it has become in the wake of the Holocaust. It is undeniable that the Zionists initially had dealings with the Nazis, as we have already seen. The extracts that Israel Shahak cites from *Wir Juden*, a 1934 book by Joachim Prinz, a German Zionist rabbi and future president of the World Jewish Congress, are as appalling as they are instructive. Prinz makes no bones about his admiration for Nazism and its goal of racial 'purification'; he contends that Zionists who recognize a Jewish nation and race have no choice but to honour this Nazi principle of 'purity'.[4]

In addition to the German Zionists' attempt to draw closer to the Nazis,[5] the Revisionist wing of the world Zionist movement – the Maximalist faction, in particular – had clear affinities with Italian fascism.[6] The phrase 'Zionist-fascist' was not, however, reserved for this wing alone (a use of the term that, at the time, seemed legitimate even to socialist Zionists[*]) but was applied to the whole of the movement and most frequently to its socialist leaders. The tag exemplifies the same ultra-left extremism that pinned the label 'fascist' on Social Democracy.

When in 1935 the international Communist movement prioritized the struggle against fascism in the strict sense, the extreme severity of this language was attenuated. However, the 1936–9 Arab revolt inflamed the situation in Palestine again. Thereafter, the August 1939 Stalin–Hitler pact forced the Communist movement as a whole to justify its stance of 'neutrality' towards both camps in the world war that broke out the same year. The Arab Communists had to put their anti-Nazi activities on standby, in some cases very abruptly, after a good, very promising start.

Take, for example, the Syrian and Lebanese Communists who had founded a League for the Struggle against Fascism (*'Usbat mukāfahat al-fāshistiyya*) in June 1937 and had convened an anti-fascist conference in Beirut, two years later, on 6 and 7 May 1939, with great pomp and circumstance. Several members of parliament attended, as did prominent members of literary

---

[*]   In the early 1930s, Ben-Gurion did not hesitate to compare Vladimir Jabotinsky's Revisionism to fascism and Nazism.[7] The meetings between Ben-Gurion and Jabotinsky and their 1934 pact (which was aborted due to the opposition of the Zionist left) nevertheless afforded the two men an opportunity to affirm their 'like-mindedness'.[8] It was Ben-Gurion's Rafi which, in 1967, forced through the participation of Menahem Begin's Gahal in the Israeli government of national unity.[9]

and press circles. The conference received letters of support from various celebrities, including well-known figures of the independence movement, such as the Syrian Shukri al-Quwwatli.

This 'Conference of Struggle against Fascism' adopted a conciliatory attitude toward both Britain and France, the colonial power in Syria and Lebanon, in line with Moscow's projected alliance with the 'democratic front' against the 'fascist front' – to borrow the terms used by Syrian Communist leader Khālid Bikdāsh in his speech at the conference.[10] But the Communist initiators of these anti-Fascist and anti-Nazi actions were caught off guard by the signature of the Ribbentrop–Molotov Pact. They resumed their anti-fascist activities only after the Wehrmacht's *June 1941 invasion* of the Soviet Union shattered the Pact. This explains why there is a 'hole' of almost two years in the account of these activities provided by Arab Communist historians.[11]

The case of Najāti Sidqi is telling in this regard. A prominent Palestinian Communist leader and former delegate to the congress of the Red International of Labor Unions in 1931, Sidqi had been charged with the publication, in Paris, of a Communist bulletin in Arabic from 1933 to 1936 and of another in Spain that was aimed at Moroccans involved in the Civil War (in which he himself participated actively). In 1936, Najāti Sidqi crossed Germany on his way from Paris to Moscow: this journey hardened his anti-Nazi convictions. When the German–Soviet Pact was signed, he did not hesitate to criticise publicly what he rightly perceived as a grave error on Moscow's part. In Beirut, where he had settled in 1938, Sidqi published a series of articles on the incompatibility of Nazism and Islam in a new Lebanese magazine of which he was one of the editors. These articles were collected and published the same year in a book that was also published in London in English translation. Sidqi's attitude led to his expulsion from the Communist Party by 'comrades' so subservient to Moscow that they did not hesitate to risk repression and imprisonment as the price of their defence of Stalin's pact with yesterday's sworn enemy.[12]

Just as it renewed and intensified the Communists' anti-fascist activity, the Wehrmacht's invasion of the Soviet Union precipitated yet another zigzag in the attitude of Palestine's Communists toward the Zionists. Fascism became again the *main* foe; Zionism was explicitly demoted to secondary rank. In this connection, Ridwān al-Hilū, the Arab secretary of the Palestinian Communist Party in the period just before it split, gave an interesting speech at a March 1943 meeting in Jaffa celebrating the twenty-fifth anniversary of the creation of the (Soviet) Red Army.[13] After explaining that 'the Zionist movement is the fruit of the terror and massacres perpetrated against the Jews', but also the product of the Jewish capitalists' desire to prevent Jewish workers from rallying to the revolutionary movement, he rattled off a list of statistics indicating that Jewish immigration to Palestine came from countries in which anti-Semitism had wrought havoc, such as Poland or pre-Revolutionary Russia. Emigration from countries such as England or the United States was virtually non-existent, and because the Russian Revolution had overthrown anti-Semitic Czarism, the stream of Jewish immigrants from Russia had dried up after 1925. Conversely, emigration from Germany, Austria and Czechoslovakia to Palestine had been negligible until Nazism drove the Jews to emigrate en masse. 'Anti-Jewish terror in the fascist countries is in reality a criminal act perpetrated by fascism that undermines the Arab cause and helps Zionism.' Zionism, Hilū continued,

> knows this very well; it knows that the liquidation of racism and chauvin-
> ism in Europe would entail its own liquidation and that of its projects
> and ambitions. That is why it welcomes anti-Jewish terror and thwarts
> all plans that might channel emigration toward a country other than
> Palestine. This happened, for example, at the 1939 [*sic*] Evian Confer-
> ence, when, at a meeting of the representatives of the Jews of England,
> America, and Poland, the Jewish Agency opposed all plans that might
> divert Jewish emigration from Palestine. It was happier to see the Jews
> remain in Germany, where they are subject to torture, terror, and privation,
> than to transport them to any country other than Palestine. This clearly
> shows that Zionism's concern is not to save Jews from the terror that is
> overwhelming them; its sole concern is to profit from that terror ...

Hilū concluded that 'Zionism is not the main enemy in this period, which is why the struggle must exclusively target Nazism and fascism', whose defeat would inevitably bring on Zionism's as well.

During this period, the only visible association of Arab Marxists independent of Moscow was an Egyptian Trotskyist group active between 1938 and 1948 under a series of different names. Jacques Berque offers an elegant description of this group in his magnificent book on Egypt:

> Anwar Kamil, president of the 'Bread and Liberty' group, the poet Georges
> Hinain [Henein], the painter Ramsis Yunan, the logician Mahmud al-
> 'Alim, the bookseller Lutf Allah Sulaiman [Lotfallah Soliman], and many
> others put forward conflicting views which were almost all Marxist, but
> each in its own way. Mutual accusations abounded, but the quest was
> ardently pursued. Many of the analyses then proposed were to bear fruit
> in the future. The intelligentsia which grew up at the paradoxical meet-
> ing-point between the University, proletarian activism, and upper-class

aestheticism did not always adjust its theories adequately or realistically to the facts. But it *was* that very maladjustment. Whence its significance, so much greater than its real weight or even than its formulations.[14]

Even the very orthodox pro-Soviet Communist Rif ʿat al-Saʿīd, today president of the National Progressive Unionist Party (al-Tagammuʿ), acknowledged, many years later, that this 'experiment' was distinguished from other Marxist groups in that it was 'purely Egyptian'[15] – an allusion to the domination of the country's various pro-Soviet groups by leaders of foreign extraction, most of them Jewish. The Egyptian Trotskyist group energetically contributed to the Marxist anti-Zionist propaganda effort, playing a game of one-upmanship against the Moscow partisans who had been forced to engage in ideological acrobatics. Thus, unlike them, it could consistently insist on the symmetrical denunciation of Zionism and Nazism.

In 1944, Anwar Kāmil published a pamphlet that is certainly one of the most unusual documents we have on the Zionist question.[16] This eclectic pamphlet is very heavily indebted to two sources, one Stalinist, the other Trotskyist – so heavily, indeed, that more than 90 per cent of it may be said to have been plagiarized, even though Kāmil acknowledges them both. The first is a book by the orthodox British Communist I. Rennap (the anagrammatic penname of Israel Panner),[17] which counterposed the integrationist tradition of the Jewish Enlightenment (the Haskala) to Zionism and reflected Moscow's new, post-1941 anti-Nazi priorities. The second is an 'Open Letter to the Labour Party Congress', written by a Trotskyist 'Group of Palestine Socialists', which calls on members of the Labour Party to reject a resolution supporting Zionist objectives.[18]

After a short introduction, the first four pages of Kāmil's pamphlet – apart from the conclusion, they are the only pages that are not lifted from the two sources just mentioned – are given over to a combined denunciation of anti-Semitism and Zionism that is quite similar to the conventional critique put forward by the Egyptian intelligentsia.[19] It then goes on to dismiss Nazism and Zionism as twin dangers:

> The Jews are biologically inferior to Aryans! The Jews are biologically inferior to the other peoples! This is the cry of the most extremist of the schools that fan hatred of Jews, and the most violent by virtue of its recourse to campaigns of extermination of the Jews: the Hitler-Streicher

school.[*] However, there also exists, on the other side of the fence, a school that is no less extremist and fanatical than the first: the Zionist school, whose leaders seek to confer an aura of sanctity on the Jewish people with the help of methods that are often less audacious and frank than those of the Hitler-Streicher school. Thus the Jews are biologically superior to other peoples! The Jews are 'God's chosen people'! The Jews are the people with the greatest right to live![20]

The reference to the biblical notion of the 'chosen people', in this context of a simultaneous rejection of both anti-Semitism and Jewish claims to supremacy, seems to have been influenced by the Islamic critique of Judaism. At any rate, the pamphlet pleased Hassan al-Banna, the founder and leader of the Egyptian Muslim Brotherhood, then at the height of its influence. Banna invited its author to his office in Cairo to congratulate him.[21][†] The pamphlet's dedication is, moreover, an unusual one, coming from a Marxist: 'To the free mujahidin [used, here, in the sense of fighters] who have shed their blood in Palestine in defence of the Arab cause' – a combination of Islamic (the term 'mujahidin' means those who practise jihad) and Arab nationalist connotations that also attests the impact of the nationalist current, tinged with Islam, that was extremely active in the Egyptian opposition in the same period.

The conclusion nevertheless hews to the canons of Marxist internationalism. After explaining that anti-Semitic persecution aims to punish the Jews for their contribution to 'the army of horizontal liberation' – in other words, the army of the world revolution[23] (several expressions used in the text are calculated to get around the censorship) – the pamphlet concludes by exhorting poor Jews to abandon Zionism and stay far from Palestine so as to avoid the great catastrophe (*nakba*) that may otherwise befall them.[24][‡]

---

*   Julius Streicher was one of National Socialism's main propagandists and the publisher of the infamous anti-Semitic weekly *Der Stürmer*.

†   This twofold critique may also be an echo of the French Jewish anarchist Bernard Lazare's 1894 book, in which we are told: 'Antisemites and philosemites join hands to defend the same doctrines, they part company only when it comes to award the supremacy. If the antisemite reproaches the Jew for being a part of a strange and base race, the Jew vaunts of belonging to an elect and superior race.'[22] Nothing, however, proves that Kāmil had read Lazare's book.

‡   According to 'Abdul-Qādir Yāsīn, Anwar Kāmil published, in the wake of the Nov. 1947 Soviet vote in favour of the partition of Palestine at the UN, a pamphlet entitled *Ufyūn al-Sha'b* (The Opium of the People) that sharply criticized the Soviet Union and culminated in a denunciation of the 'Kremlin bureaucracy' for its support of partition.[25] Rif'at al-Sa'īd, in his book on the Egyptian left between 1940 and 1950, brands this book a 'crime', in classic Stalinist fashion. He accuses Kāmil of having

Whatever the fluctuations in communist attitudes toward Zionism, militant opposition to Jewish immigration to Palestine was common to all Arab Marxists, as well as the rest of the movement until at least the early 1940s. So were the condemnations of anti-Semitism, the depiction of Jewish 'workers' as potential recruits to the movement, and the critique of Zionist socialism as reactionary and colonialist – a position in fact that dates from the beginnings of the Communist International in 1919–20. When the break between the majority of Poale Zion and the movement was consummated in 1922, the denunciation of Zionism by the Executive Committee of the International became still sharper. It set what would continue to be the movement's line for the next two decades:

> The theme of Palestine, the attempt to divert the Jewish working masses from the class struggle by propaganda in favour of large-scale Jewish settlement in Palestine, is not only nationalist and petty-bourgeois but counter-revolutionary in its effect, if the broad working masses are moved by this idea and so diverted from an effective struggle against their Jewish and non-Jewish capitalist exploiters.[27]

The anti-Zionist opposition to Jewish immigration to Palestine, adopted by the Communist movement in the Arab East from its 1919–20 beginnings, did not change with the Nazis' assumption of power in Germany and the steady increase in anti-Semitic persecution. The impact of these events was counterbalanced by a rise in the level of violence in Palestine, confirming the Communists' conviction that the Zionist project was drawing Jews into a trap. They insistently repeated that the only way to save European Jews, in view, above all, of their numbers, was to defeat Nazism itself.

Walter Laqueur has rightly called the position of Palestine's Communists on immigration 'the *central issue*'.[28] Writing in 1955 with the benefit of hindsight, he mocked them for underestimating the fate in store for the European Jews.[29] The Communists, however, were not opposed to Jewish emigration in general, but to their immigration to Palestine and, at war's end, in 1945, the majority Arab faction of Palestinian Communists, the National Liberation League, believed that history had proved them right:

> The majority of the Jews in Palestine were seen to have arrived in the country 'to escape the Nazi terror,' and the victory of the Allies in the

---

published it 'in very close collaboration with the secret services', without producing a scrap of proof.[26] At the same time, he is careful not to say anything about the connection between the pamphlet and the Soviet stance on Palestine.

war, which supposedly had 'put an end to racial discrimination and the oppression of peoples,' was regarded as having signalled 'the end of Zionism.' It was held to be inconceivable that Zionism could flourish in a democratic society, and already in 1945 it was being claimed that 'immigration has now stopped' and that 'many Jews are now returning to their countries of origin.'[30]

This was, of course, wishful thinking, as would become clear after the 4 July 1946 Kielce pogrom in Poland gave a fillip to the 'propelling force' of Zionism:

> For a moment, it seemed as if the situation of Polish Jewry had been stabilized.
> However, in the summer of 1946, there was a terrible pogrom, shocking in its cruelty, in the city of Kielce. It took place in broad daylight, under the gaze of the local police (and some say with their participation). Jews who had managed to survive the German occupation now found their death in the city of Kielce and its environs, at the hands of Polish murderers. More than 70 Jews were killed; the government was too weak to prevent the catastrophe. The axe blows in the heads of the Kielce victims reverberated throughout Poland; Jews who had hoped to return and to rebuild their lives in that country experienced a rude awakening. After Kielce, there was no longer any hope for Polish Jewry except in flight. The great 'Escape Movement' (*bericha*) began to take on mass proportions.[31]

The biggest flaw in the pro-Soviet Communists' immigration argument lay, however, in the absence of an international Communist campaign to open the gates of all the countries in which Jews fleeing Nazism could have found refuge, and to which the 'displaced persons' of the post-war period wished to go. The overwhelming majority of both groups wanted to emigrate to the United States, which, tragically, as we saw in the Introduction, granted access to only a small minority.[32]

Not even the American Communists mobilized behind the demand that Jews be granted refuge there. The 1944 Open Letter from the 'Group of Palestine Socialists' to the Labour Party, cited above, curtly criticizes the US Communists, quoting their Yiddish organ, *Morgen Freiheit*, which endorsed Zionist positions on the creation of 'a national home' in Palestine to save the persecuted Jews – 'instead of demanding "Open the doors of America for the refugees."'[33] As an American Trotskyist later wrote: 'The [US Communist Party's] Kremlin mentors had failed to lift even a finger to make the vast territories of the USSR available as a place of refuge for capitalism's victims in Europe. So the very existence of the demand on Washington that it "Open the Doors!" was an embarrassment – particularly after the signing of the Stalin–Hitler pact in August 1939.'[34][*] He goes on to describe the drive launched by his comrades, unhampered by Soviet constraints, to abolish immigration quotas and open America's doors to all asylum-seekers, Jews in particular. The American Fund for Political Prisoners and Refugees was set up by American Trotskyists in June 1938; on its National Committee were John Dewey, Suzanne La Follette, Sidney Hook and Meyer Schapiro.[36]

These positions show, once again, that opposition to a 'Jewish state' in Palestine by no means implied either anti-Semitism or indifference to the fate of European Jewry. Quite the contrary: Arab Marxists constantly battled manifestations of anti-Jewish hatred.[37] In spring 1941, as Iraq's Communists were adopting a favourable stance toward Rashid 'Āli al-Gaylāni's anti-British government, they wrote to Gaylāni to express their abhorrence at the rise in anti-Jewish exactions, which would soon peak with the bloody riots of 1 and 2 June 1941.[38] Even in Palestine, notwithstanding the high tensions reigning there and the fact that most of the Jews were colonial settlers, the Arab Communists of the National Liberation League pleaded against confounding anti-Zionism with anti-Judaism or anti-Semitism, firmly rejecting calls to expel Jewish immigrants. Musa Budeiri provides a description of one of their press organs:

> Al Ghad's articles maintained a careful distinction between Zionists and the Jewish inhabitants in Palestine. While the former were seen to present a threat to the Arab people, the interests of the Jewish inhabitants did not conflict with those of the Arabs. They were seen to be natural allies in the struggle to establish 'a just economic order' which itself would result in the destruction of Zionism. Rejecting those 'bourgeois nationalists' who called for the expulsion of the Jews from Palestine, Al Ghad pointed to the past history of Arab tolerance. It called on the Arab national movement to show the Jews that the Arabs did not bear them any racial enmity, by striving for a democratic regime which would provide the framework for 'peace and co-operation between the two peoples.' To this end, Al Ghad put forward its own proposals for a democratic Palestine state guaranteeing the Jewish inhabitants 'complete cultural and administrative autonomy.'[39]

---

[*] This circumstance did not prevent Palestine's Jewish Communists from embracing the myth according to which the Soviet Union, the saviour of the Jews fleeing Nazism, had magnanimously granted them asylum.[35]

What is more, the Marxist organizations in the Arab world, Palestine aside, counted many Jews in their ranks – sometimes in leading positions, as in Egypt. The Jewish Marxists were often more militantly anti-Zionist than their Gentile comrades.[40] In 1947, Jewish members of the Democratic Movement for National Liberation, the main Egyptian Communist organization, founded a Jewish League for the Struggle against Zionism – which was promptly dissolved by the government.[41] The League's June 1947 manifesto declared:

> We denounce the Zionists for taking an interest in deported Jews only to the extent that it serves their own narrow egotistical interests, for they refuse to consider any solution to the problems of these unfortunates other than emigration to Palestine. Thus they prolong the deportees' suffering for the purpose of exploiting it to Zionist political ends ...
>
> We believe that the Jewish refugees in the camps in Germany and Austria must be given the possibility to return without delay to the countries from which Fascism deported them ... As for those refugees who, for psychological reasons, wish to start a new life far from the sad memories of the past, we believe that it is the duty of all countries, especially the biggest, to take them in and help them settle in their new homes.[42]

The Jewish members of the Iraqi Communist Party, grouped in a League against Zionism, had a premonition of Moscow's impending turn several months before the fateful 1947 UN vote.[43] They accordingly wrote to Stalin in May 1946 to demand that he support the Palestinian cause at the UN: 'The right of its Arab people to independence is unambiguous, and their question is unrelated to the plight of the Jewish displaced persons.'[44] For their part, Palestine's Arab Communists, a majority of whom had formally parted company with the majority of Jewish Communists, pinned the blame on the Mufti and his partisans:

> With partition clearly on the agenda, the NLL [National Liberation League] turned its fury against the leadership of the Arab national movement. It accused it of having paved the way for partition with its 'negative' and 'racialist' policy toward Palestine's Jewish inhabitants. The traditional leaders' rejection of the 'democratic solution,' and their refusal to recognise the civil rights of Jewish immigrants who had arrived in Palestine after 1918, were declared to have given credence to Zionist claims that partition was necessary as a means of 'protecting the Jewish minority from the aggression of the Arabs,' and to lie at the root of the Arabs' failure to gain international support for their 'just cause.' The attitude of the NLL

towards the leadership of the national movement was transformed from one of preferred collaboration to outright hostility.[45]

Thus one can imagine the disarray into which Arab Communists were thrown when, in November 1947, the 'beloved leader and teacher' – Stalin – instructed the Soviet delegation in the UN General Assembly to vote for the plan to partition Palestine.[46] The Egyptian Communists, led by Henri Curiel, tried to extricate themselves from the embarrassing situation by playing a game of one-upmanship that turned on denouncing British imperialism, identified as the main enemy in both Egypt and Palestine.[47] Palestine's Arab Communists had to carry out a wrenching revision of their positions.[48] The way the members of the National Liberation League living in the Palestinian territories annexed by the Jordanian monarchy summed up this ordeal, on the eve of their 1951 transformation into the Jordanian Communist Party, is not without a certain piquancy:

> The position of the glorious Soviet Union in defence of the independence of Palestine and the freedom of its two peoples, Arab and Jewish, as well as their right to self-determination, was tantamount to a warning for the National Liberation League. The League found itself facing a choice between two paths, and two paths alone. It could continue to defend its old political line, which would have meant collaborating with the colonialists and their spies and lackeys; it would further have meant taking up arms in order to join in racist massacre and oppose the independence of Palestine and the freedom of its two peoples, while defending colonialism. Alternatively, it could liquidate its old political line and adopt a new one, a Marxist-Leninist line, opposing colonialism and its bloody plots against Palestine.
>
> ... the League came to abandon its former, opportunistic and chauvinist political line, and to opt for the Marxist-Leninist path, that of struggle against colonialism, for the independence of Palestine, and for the freedom of the two peoples, Arab and Jewish, as well as their right to self-determination.
>
> Since that time, our party has been subject to oppression by the colonialists and their underlings, the treacherous leaders of Palestine, and the commanders of the armies of the Arab governments.[49]

For its part, the Iraqi Party, shocked by the Soviet vote in favour of partition, temporarily broke ranks with the rest of the Arab Communist movement. In an act of insubordination altogether exceptional among Stalinist parties, it refused to line up behind Moscow's position for more than six months,[50] returning to the fold only under severe pressure, exerted, to a large extent, by the French Communist Party.[51] In the meantime, an internal party directive of December 1947 had lambasted Moscow's stance and listed six reasons for the Iraqi Party's continued rejection of the partition plan:

a)   Zionism is a movement that is racist, religious, reactionary, and false to the Jewish masses ...

b)   Jewish immigration ... does not solve the problems of displaced Jews in Europe but is an organized invasion directed by the Jewish Agency ...

c)   The partition of Palestine is an old imperialist project ... which rests on the presupposed impossibility of an understanding between Jews and Arabs ...

d)   The form of government for Palestine can rightfully be determined only by the Palestinian people, by the people who live actually in Palestine, and not by the United Nations ...

e)   Partition is bound to lead to the subordination of the Arab majority to the Zionist minority in the proposed Jewish state.

f)   Partition and the creation of the Jewish state will increase racial and religious enmities and will affect seriously the prospects of peace in the Middle East.[52]

Like Communists everywhere, those in the Arab countries had, after Stalingrad, basked in the glorious image of the triumphant Soviet Union. However, Moscow's 1947 change of heart on the Palestinian question – it took the form of both political and (with the delivery of Czechoslovakian arms) military support for the creation of an Israeli state and that state's first war against the Arab armies[53] – put a sharp brake on their expansion and left them isolated in Arab public opinion for some time to come. They would not surmount this handicap until the USSR concluded a new alliance with Arab nationalism in the 1950s. They never managed to rid themselves of it for good.

CHAPTER 3

The Nationalists

The members of the Axis were perceived in different ways in the Arab world: the further away each power was, the greater the sympathy for it. Thus imperial Japan enjoyed the broadest support (among those who were aware of its existence); ultranationalists often invoked it as a model of modernization without cultural Westernization. Conversely, fascist Italy was perceived as a colonial power even more odious than France and Britain, owing mainly to the Italians' tyrannical occupation of Libya – an aversion that became especially intense with the execution, in 1931, of the Libyan 'Lion of the Desert', Omar al-Mukhtar.*

Nazi Germany was perceived, first and foremost, as England's foe, and as such it inevitably attracted support – of widely varying intensity and extent – especially from those struggling against British domination in Palestine, Egypt and Iraq. This sympathy was the greater, especially in Palestine, in that anti-Semitism made the Nazis, in the view of the most primitive, an ally in the struggle against the Zionists. By the same token, it diminished in lands under French domination – in Syria and Lebanon in the Arab East, as well as in North Africa – when the Vichy government, allied with the Axis powers, replaced Paris as the seat of colonial authority.

Without entering into the interminable debates about what constitutes fascism, I shall here hazard a generic definition of fascism proper as a combination of four elements: paramilitary organization, ultranationalism, economic corporatism and a totalitarian 'revolutionary' political project. Fascism in this sense was only marginally an object of (even approximate) imitation in the Arab world.

---

* At the Islamic Conference held in Jerusalem in December 1931, the Egyptian Wafdist 'Abdul-Rahmān 'Azzām harshly condemned the Italian atrocities in Libya, going 'so far as to argue that the Italian threat to the Islamic faith in Libya was stronger than the Jewish-Zionist threat to Palestine'.¹ When the Italian consul lodged a protest with the British Mandatory Authority, 'Azzām was expelled.

In a (lamentably) influential 1985 study of Nazism's impact on the region during the 1930s, Stefan Wild identifies 'five parties and movements in the Arab world which to a greater or lesser degree had taken over certain elements of National Socialism or Fascism':[2] the Arab Baath in Syria, the 'Syrian' Social Nationalist Party (SSNP), the Lebanese Phalangist Party (Kataeb), the Young Egypt movement (Misr al-Fatāt) and the Iraqi youth movement Futuwwa. While this is a short list, it is nevertheless highly questionable, not least because of the looseness of the criteria on which it is based: 'certain elements' and 'to a greater or lesser degree'.

What is more, Wild arbitrarily ignores the organization that hewed perhaps most closely to the fascist model: Zionist Revisionism, some of whose most prominent members would scale the summits of the Israeli state. Yaacov Shavit emphasizes that Revisionism bore 'more than a passing resemblance' to fascism in its conception of the nation as well as

> the cult of the undisputed leader, the uniforms (brown shirts and leather bandoliers), the disciplinary hierarchical organization of *Betar*, the propaganda style and populist appeal, and the conviction among its opponents that Revisionism was ready – and willing – to achieve its objectives through organized violence and political terror.[3]

Let us nevertheless examine Wild's five cases. Of the five, only the Baath, the SSNP and the Lebanese Phalange were still in existence in the latter half of the twentieth century. The Baath has played a major role in contemporary Arab history, holding power in Syria and Iraq from the latter half of the 1960s on; as everyone knows, its rule in Iraq came to an end with the 2003 American invasion. The SSNP's real political role was confined to Lebanon after the fleeting period in the late 1940s when the party had an impact on the course of Syrian history. The activity of the Lebanese Phalange, for its part, has always been confined to Lebanon, in line with the party's mission.

The Baath Party

In his 1985 study, Wild devotes just one page to the Baath. This page, however, contains so many errors, distortions and deliberate omissions that it has become an obligatory source for polemics hostile to Arab nationalism. Yet Wild's essay has been called a 'scrupulously objective study' by Bernard Lewis[4] – who has himself become less and less scrupulous over the years, to the point that his work on the Middle East is now a standard reference for American neo-conservatives.[*]

On this single page, Wild claims that Michel Aflaq ('Aflaq) – one of the two founders and the chief ideologue of the Party of the Arab Renaissance (*al-Ba'th al-'Arabi*) – came into contact with Nazi ideas as a student at the Paris Sorbonne between 1928 and 1932; that he was fascinated by Hitler's programme; that he bought the abridged French translation of Alfred Rosenberg's *The Myth of the Twentieth Century*, the second most important Nazi book after *Mein Kampf*; and that in Damascus in 1939–40 he created, with Zaki al-Arsūzi, the embryo of the future Baath Party. He then offers two quotations from Elie Kedourie's English translation of excerpts from a book that Sami al-Jundi based on his personal experience of the Baath. Wild calls Jundi a 'founder member of the Baath party', although neither Kedourie nor Jundi ever advances that claim. Jundi's book reconstructs the political and intellectual atmosphere of Damascus in the period 1939–40.

Here are the two quotations:

> Whoever has lived during this period in Damascus will appreciate the inclination of the Arab people to Nazism, for Nazism was the power which could serve as its champion, and he who is defeated will by nature love the victor.
>
> We were racialists, admiring Nazism, reading its books and the source of its thought, particularly Nietzsche's *Thus Spoke Zarathustra*, Fichte's *Addresses to the German Nation* and H. S. Chamberlain's *Foundations of the Nineteenth Century*, which revolves around race.[†] We were the first to think of translating *Mein Kampf*.[5][‡]

Let us closely examine Wild's allegations. On the origins of the Baath, I shall cite the testimony of both Jundi himself and a founding member of the party, Jalāl al-Sayyid.[6] I shall also make use of several reliable and respected historical works: Patrick Seale's classic 1965 *The Struggle for Syria*;[7] 'The Rise

---

[*]   In 2007, Lewis was given the American Enterprise Institute's Irving Kristol Award, the American neo-conservative community's most prestigious honour.

[†]   This last phrase represents an erroneous translation on Kedourie's part. Instead of 'which revolves around the race' it should read: 'and [Richard Walther] Darré's *The Race*'. The book by the SS leader and, subsequently, Nazi minister Darré, *Neuadel aus Blut und Boden,* Munich, 1930, was translated into French under the title *La Race: Nouvelle Noblesse du sang et du sol,* Paris, 1939.

[‡]   Wild notes that the latter claim is incorrect, inasmuch as there existed Arabic translations of *Mein Kampf* well before 1939. Indeed, a good part of Wild's essay examines such translations.

of the Syrian Ba'th', a 1972 essay by Nabil Kaylani;[8] John Devlin's 1976 *The Baath Party*, which provides an accurate account of the party's origins;[9] and, finally, Hanna Batatu's 1978 magnum opus, *The Old Social Classes and the Revolutionary Movements of Iraq*.[10]

Nothing indicates that Michel Aflaq had the least affinity for Nazism in his student days in France, unless one assumes that his purchase of a Nazi bestseller proves that he was fascinated by Nazi doctrine. When Jundi reports in a note that, at a time when he was looking for the Rosenberg book, he learned that Aflaq owned a French translation of it, he presents the matter as a 'strange coincidence'.[11] Kedourie seizes on the mere fact that Aflaq possessed the book to affirm that Aflaq took his inspiration from Nazi authors.[12] (Incidentally, Kedourie ought to have known that Rosenberg's book contains statements that are, from an Arab nationalist point of view, so abhorrent that even the pro-German, pro-Italian Emir Shakib Arslan publicly criticized it; see below.)

In fact, Aflaq and his close friend Salāh-ud-Dīn (generally shortened to Salāh) al-Bītār, the future co-founders of the Baath Party, were far more fascinated by *Marxism* during their stay in France, impressed as they were by the Communists' support for the cause of Syrian independence. This is attested both by their own accounts and by historians of the Baath movement like Batatu and Seale.[13]

In addition, Syrian Communist historian 'Abdallah Hannā reports that Aflaq was on the four-member editorial committee of the Communist-controlled weekly *Al-Talī'a* (Avant-garde), which published such articles as 'The Nazi Brutes Murder their Adversaries' (December 1935) and 'Everyday Racism under Hitler' (March 1936).[14] A December 1935 article of Aflaq's, 'Between Revolution and War', from which Hannā cites extracts, sings the praises of the 'communist revolutionary', whom Aflaq contrasts with the 'fascist warrior'.[15]

The Popular Front's victory in the French elections held in spring of the same year, 1936, indirectly led Aflaq to break with the Communists: he was offended by the volte-face of the Syrian Communists, who endorsed the Franco-Syrian treaty and began collaborating with the colonial authorities as soon as their French comrades joined the coalition of left parties that made up the new government in France.[16] Aflaq nevertheless renewed his ties with the Communists in 1941, after war broke out between the Soviet Union and Nazi Germany, contributing to the review *Al-Tarīq*, the organ of the League to Combat Fascism and Nazism ('Isbat mukāfahat al- fāshistiyya wa al-nāziyya) founded by Syrian-Lebanese Communists.[17] Sami al-Jundi and Jalāl al-Sayyid both came to know him thanks to these articles.[18]

Pace Wild, in 1939–40 Aflaq formed the core of the future Baath Party not with Zaki al-Arsūzi but rather with his friend Salāh al-Bītār. Arsūzi, for his part, had quite independently created a parallel group that was probably the first to use the name 'Baath'. Jundi, who confirms this historical fact, describes Arsūzi as paranoid, suspecting 'colonialist plots' against his group – which never had more than two dozen members.[19]

Jundi calls Arsūzi 'the Master', as did most of the members of Arsūzi's group, who had been high-school students of his. Arsūzi was a partisan of racial theories directly influenced by Nazi ideology. From Jundi's account, it appears that Arsūzi was especially taken with the writings of Houston Stewart Chamberlain, Nazism's immediate spiritual ancestor. Arsūzi, however, turned Chamberlain's racism upside down, forging a doctrine of his own that made Semites superior to Aryans and assigned Arabs a pivotal role among the Semites. (He went so far as to attribute Arab origins to the Jews.[*])

Wild's two quotations from Jundi occur in the opposite order in the original, with the second cut in a way that seriously deforms its meaning. Here is what actually appears in Kedourie's translation:

> Whoever has lived during this period in Damascus will appreciate the inclination of the Arab people to Nazism, for Nazism was the power which could serve as its champion, and he who is defeated will by nature love the victor. But our belief was rather different....
>
> We were idealists, basing social relationships on love. The Master used to speak about Christ ...[22]

There is no excuse for Wild's omission of the passage beginning with the word 'But'. The fact remains, however, that Arsūzi was influenced by Nazism's racial theses[23] – which is one reason why his ideas failed to attract much interest. His Arab nationalist party's proclamation in its statement of principles that 'the Arabs comprise a single nation' and have 'a single leader' (*zaʿīm*)[24] was directly patterned after the Nazis' *ein Volk, ein Reich, ein Führer*. Jundi himself characterizes Arsūzi as a 'racist who believed in authenticity and nobility, a man of an aristocratic temperament and turn of mind'.[25]

Jalāl al-Sayyid, who founded the Baath party with Aflaq and Bītār, has

---

[*] In this connection, Hazem Saghieh cites, in his remarkable book on the nationalists of the Arab East,[20] a 1938 essay in which Arsūzi declares: 'As for the Jews, my opinion is that Arabs and Jews should come to an understanding in this world and cooperate in order to re-establish the Arabs' glory and realize the Semitic genius, which is the Judeo-Arab genius.'[21] The condition was that the Jews abandon their plan to create a state in Palestine.

explained what led them to exclude Arsūzi from the new party: 'his education had made him too categorical. He made no place for socialist values in his political philosophy and had greater affinities for Nazi or even ancient Roman thought, categorizing people as slaves or masters, nobles or plebeians.'[26]

In 1944, the members of Arsūzi's group went their separate ways; most of them joined Aflaq and Bītār's group a year later.[27] Arsūzi never did, not least because he detested Aflaq.[28] Sami al-Jundi, the last of Arsūzi's disciples to betray the Master, did not join until 1946,[29] although he made one final attempt to convince Arsūzi to join with him. The former members of Arsūzi's group constituted a de facto faction within the Baath, since they continued to bear their mentor's influence.[30]

The radical faction of the Baath (the Syrian 'Regional Command') of the 1960s, which took power in Damascus on 23 February 1966, is responsible for falsifying Arsūzi's role. Its leaders wanted to downplay Aflaq who had supported the other faction (the Pan-Arab 'National Command'), the Iraqi branch of which took the reins of government in Baghdad on 17 July 1968.[*] Sami al-Jundi, a member of the Damascus faction, served as the Syrian ambassador to France but was eventually ordered to return to Syria, where he was briefly imprisoned after the Six-Day War on the charge of cultivating contacts with the enemy. He published his book on the Baath in 1969 in the wake of this bitter experience.

Another vehicle for spreading similarly distorted allegations to the West under the influence of Syrian sources is Eric Rouleau's 1969 essay published in the Paris *Le Monde Diplomatique* and then in English translation in the London *New Left Review*.[31] Rouleau downplays Aflaq's left-wing past and indicates that Aflaq, like Arsūzi, had had 'sympathies for Nazism' at the beginning of the war.[32] He goes on to imply that Arsūzi had been hostile and Aflaq sympathetic to Nazism. His information came from Arsūzi himself, whom he interviewed in a Damascus café. Thus, we are told, Aflaq supported Rashid ʿAli al-Gaylāni's nationalist Iraqi government in 1944, while Arsūzi rejected it.[33]

In fact, the two men's attitudes toward the Iraq episode had nothing at all to do with their attitudes toward Nazism. Jundi points out, actually, that Arsūzi had opposed the putsch in Iraq because he 'thought that it was a mistake to take action against the Allies before the Germans arrived in the Taurus Mountains; the error lay in the timing'.[34] Quoting an unnamed professor from the University of Damascus, Rouleau then repeats the accusation that

---

[*] It has been suggested that a religious motivation was also at work here: Arsūzi was of Alawite origins, as were most of the leaders of the Syrian faction.

Aflaq had been fascinated by Nazism in 1937, once again citing Rosenberg's book[35] – all the more irresponsible in that he had an opportunity to interview Aflaq and could easily have verified the matter with him.[36]

Batatu has accurately described Aflaq's eclectic ideology as 'a mixture of an essentially humanitarian nationalism and aspects of the individualism of the Enlightenment, the democratism of the Jacobins, the youth idealization of Mazzini, the class standpoint of Marx, the elitism of Lenin, and over and above that, a strong dose of Christian spirituality, and a nationalistically interpreted Islam'.[37] (He might also have pointed to the powerful influence of Emmanuel Mounier.)

What is more, in a 1941 essay, Aflaq explicitly warned against the 'nationalism that comes to us from Europe.' No reader could have doubted whose nationalism he had in mind.[38] In a 1950 essay* on the differences between the Baath's socialism, on the one hand, and Communism, and National Socialism on the other, Aflaq rejects 'Germany's and Italy's national socialism' at the theoretical level because it 'is based on the ideal of racial supremacy and discrimination between nations, that is, the supremacy of one race over another and its right to dominate the world, and also on discrimination between individuals belonging to the same nation, which inevitably leads to individual or class dictatorship'. He is also, he writes, opposed to fascism on practical grounds, since fascism 'is bent on expansion and colonialism and cannot be realized unless this expansion is realized, which makes it an auxiliary to colonialism'.[39]

In a recent book based on a doctoral dissertation of which Stefan Wild was a co-supervisor, Götz Nordbruch, commenting on a 1944 pamphlet in which Aflaq and Bītār sought to refute communist theory, sees in it a striking parallel to the Nazis' anti-Communist agitation.[40] This is a strange interpretation of a pamphlet that basically accuses Moscow of having abandoned Marx's internationalism and replaced it with Soviet nationalism in practice, while criticising the Syrian Communists for putting loyalty to Moscow above Arab interests; the two observations are hardly open to doubt and were, indeed, shared by most contemporary critiques of Stalinism, liberal or left-wing. The two authors of the pamphlet are, moreover, intent on establishing their distance from knee-jerk anti-Communism;[41] they conclude by advocating friendship between the Arabs and a Soviet Union praised for its support of peoples' liberation struggles.[42] In reality, Aflaq's intellectual inspirations inclined his

---

* This is the date given in a collection in which the essay cited here has been reprinted. The content of the essay, however, leaves one with the impression that it was written in the period in which fascism still held sway over Berlin and Rome.

brand of nationalism to be, on the whole, in the 1930s and 1940s, less emphatic and militaristic than that found in the 'red book' on Arab nationalism of a thinker of liberal inspiration such as Constantine Zurayk, an admirer of Giuseppe Garibaldi.[43]

What remains of Wild's allegations? Not one has withstood examination. Yet it is this one-page distillation of slanderous counter-truths (along with other passages in Wild's essay) that Bernard Lewis cites in *Semites and Anti-Semites*, the 1986 book in which he develops his thesis about the 'new anti-Semitism'.[44] In the process, he contributes to the 'demonization of Pan-Arab nationalism' denounced by Ralph Coury,[45] who puts the main blame for it on Kedourie. Lewis has given considerable play to Wild's allegations in his 'scrupulously objective study'; they have consequently been utilized by many others who purport to find a close affinity between anti-Zionism, Arab or Muslim, and Nazi anti-Semitism.[46]

As a secular nationalist Arab party, the Baath of the early years was also demonized by those nostalgic for the 'Arab-Islamism' of the inter-war period. Basheer Nafi, for example, depicts the Baath Party as the final product of a movement toward ethnic cleansing inaugurated, he claims, by the 1933 massacre of Assyrians in Iraq. This tendency, he says, 'reached its climax in the Ba'th Party's covenant whereby founders of the party envisaged the expulsion of non-Arab minorities if they proved disloyal to the Arab nation'.[47] In reality, the accusation is based on the very special interpretation of an article of the party's constitution (*dustūr*) that Jalāl al-Sayyid makes before going on to explain that the Iraqi Baath did not apply this article to the Kurds.[48]

The passage that Nafi takes to task (he feels no need to cite it, although his book is full to bursting with quotations and footnotes) is Article 11 of the April 1947 Baath constitution. It consists of a single sentence: 'Anyone who advocates creating an anti-Arab racist bloc or joins one, as well as anyone who has immigrated to the Arab fatherland with colonialist aims, shall be expelled.'[49] *Pace* Nafi, this is by no means a programme for ethnic or racial cleansing in the strict sense. Rather, it alludes first and foremost to the Palestinian question (as it stood in 1947) and advocates expelling supporters of Zionism from the Arab world, while driving colonialist settlers from Palestine and other colonialist populations from the Arab countries in which they had settled (Algeria and Libya in particular). This position, very different from that of the liberal Westernizers and Marxists, was common to the secular ultranationalists and 'Arab-Islamists'. The positions of the Mufti of Jerusalem (of whom Nafi is far less critical) were much more severe.

The fact remains that this article represented a concession to the ultranationalists. The wording of it was probably the result of a compromise, included as it was in a set of statutes reflecting the heterogeneity of the tendencies that made up the party in its early stages, from the far right through the liberals and on to the Marxian far left, as Sayyid has explained.[50] Sayyid, for his part, merely repeats an idea that had already found expression in an official Baath text introducing the 1947 statutes, included in a collection of party documents published in 1963. Distorting its meaning, Nafi calls it proof of 'Nazi influences' on the nascent Baath.[51] The document in question was most probably written by Aflaq himself:

> The nationalist vision was, perhaps, over-emphasized in the constitution. Yet the First Congress took action to considerably diminish the nationalist emphasis that marked the party's genesis in the first years. This emphasis was not entirely unrelated to the influence of the intellectual and psychological climate fostered in the Arab countries by Nazism, in which a traditional nationalist vision based on pride in the past and ancestral glories was combined with fragments of then popular ideas about racism and the biological vision of society. All this came on top of patriotic demands for independence, aimed at foreign colonialism. The thought of the party was, from the outset, situated at a level that was higher and more sophisticated than these views and beliefs, which were far from scientific; in the early stages, the minds of the young must have been influenced to some extent by this simplistic explanation proposed by Nazism as an easy solution to the problems of the Arab countries. It set out from the idea that foreigners and intruders in the Arab world ranked, along with colonialism, among the main factors promoting decadence, sabotage, and conspiracy.
>
> This is why great care was taken to make the constitution a line of demarkation that would entirely eliminate the influence of these stupid ideas.[52]

The text refers to the third principle in the preamble to the party's 1947 constitution, the second point of which – inspired by the principles of the preamble to the UN Charter, adopted two years earlier – declares that: 'Humanity comprises a whole with shared interests and common values and culture. The Arabs are sustained by world culture and help sustain it in their turn; they stretch out a fraternal hand to the other nations and work together with them to establish equitable rules capable of ensuring that all peoples will benefit from peace and prosperity, refinement of customs and intellect.'[53]

The foregoing is by no means intended to excuse the Baath's later degeneration, which, as we will see, was aggravated in the 1960s. Indeed, it is precisely the Baath's decline into dictatorship that makes claims such as

Wild's credible in the eyes of non-specialists. Those who have knowingly spread them, such as Lewis, who can hardly be accused of ignorance of the subject (wilful ignorance aside), have done so in the context of a campaign to retrospectively denigrate Arab nationalism and its anti-Zionism. The political motivation is patent.

Moreover, as Wildangel points out, arguments based on such isolated elements as the two quotations from Sami al-Jundi – to say nothing of the fact that one has been truncated, a circumstance of which Wildangel himself seems unaware – are made by certain academics with no regard for the scholarly precaution that is one of the elementary intellectual standards of their profession.[54]

The reality of the matter is that no one has found the least trace of anti-Semitism in Aflaq's writings; had such evidence ever been found, the discovery would quite certainly have been broadcast far and wide. The only article on Palestine in the principal collection of Aflaq's writings dates from 1946 – it was published in his party's organ, *Al-Ba'th*, on 6 August of that year – when the hatred bred by the Palestinian conflict was near its height. Yet this text is imbued with the deep admiration of a fledgling nationalist for a nationalism about to succeed:

> While we must insist on our characterization of Zionism as injustice and aggression and denounce that aggression before the whole world, we must not lose sight of the solid conviction that informs it, inspiring the Jewish people with courage and a spirit of sacrifice, and its leaders with firmness and self-denial, thus endowing the movement in its entirety with strength, zeal, and discipline.[55]

The party's official declarations and the unsigned articles on Palestine published in *Al-Ba'th* from 1945 on are in the same spirit.[56] Relatively rare, given the importance of the issue – the Baath has been criticized for paying too little attention to the Palestinian question – they are distinguished by the much greater space they devote to denouncing all the Arab regimes without exception than to denouncing Zionism or the Western powers, and by the caustic tone in which they do so. In the spirit of Aflaq's tribute, the detestable attitude of the Arab regimes is contrasted with the Zionists' efficiency and determination. Only one article, about the danger represented by the creation of a Jewish state in the heart of the Arab world, contains a sentence of an anti-Semitic nature. Written by Salāh-ud-Dīn al-Bītār and published on 21 December 1947, when tension was at its height after the UN vote on partition, it affirms that the

Jews are 'known to bore away at every society from within'. Then follow some commonplace clichés about Jewish economic power.[57]

The Syrian Social Nationalist Party

Antun Saadeh (Antūn Saʿāda), the Greek Orthodox Lebanese who founded the Syrian Social Nationalist Party (SSNP) in 1932, was a Germanophile well acquainted with Nazism thanks to his knowledge of German, which he taught at the American University of Beirut (AUB), and an early admirer of Hitler. The SSNP – 'Syrian' refers to the 'Greater Syria' of the 'fertile crescent', encompassing the Sinai, Palestine, Jordan, Lebanon, Syria and Iraq, to which Saadeh would later add, oddly enough, the island of Cyprus – is a Levantine clone of the Nazi party in almost every respect: political ideology, including hostility to the Enlightenment and a geographic-racial-nationalist theory with scientific pretensions; organizational structure; and leadership cult. Even the party's flag is patterned after that of the Nazis, with the red and black in opposite places and a helix with four blades in place of a swastika.

Patrick Seale writes that Saadeh's

> pseudo-science cannot have made many converts; few members of his party read his long and abstruse book.[58] But he relied less on argument than on organization. What was attractive was the accent on youth, the rigid discipline, the Fascist conception of the role of the leader, as well as the simple thesis that 'natural Syria' was a great nation which had played, and would play once more, a great role in history. Saʿada was perhaps the first Arab to produce a wholly indigenous version of the youth formations which flourished in Italy and Germany in the 1930s.[59]

In November 1935, in a secret political report informing Berlin that Saadeh's party had been discovered and punished for planning a putsch, the German consul in Beirut depicted this 'Syrian People's Party' – '*Syrische Volkspartei*', a translation reflecting an erroneous but persistent French translation of *qawmi* as 'people's' or 'popular' rather than 'nationalist' – as a party 'that has obviously been deeply influenced by national-socialist or fascist ideas and models in its worldview, organization, and external forms'.[60]

In an informative chapter on Saadeh,[61] Hazem Saghieh, himself a former SSNP member, describes the Christian sectarian fanaticism that underlies Saadeh's thought, which rejects Arabs (especially African Arabs), Islam and even the East in favour of the supposed superiority of the 'Syrians', with their Mediterranean civilization. Moreover, hatred of the Jews, for Saadeh, is not a Muslim monopoly. Indeed, it is even a fundamentally Christian specialty, since the Jews were the enemies of Christ before they were the enemies of Muhammad, and 'oppressed him and crucified him and combated his disciples.' Islam and Judaism ... have compatible codes and differ from Syrian Christianity, the religion of reason.[62]

The SSNP had, nonetheless, made a poor impression on the sharp-eyed German consul, who reported:

> The leadership, however stupid this may seem, is supposed to have contemplated staging a rebellion against the French mandatory government should the occasion offer, and to have conducted training sessions and tried to sap police morale to that end ...
>   This spring, the movement tried to sound me out on the question as to whether Germany might provide its young partisans with military training and also make arms deliveries to it. I made it so clear that I did not wish to be approached with such requests that the question was never again broached.[63]

The great frustration that this must have caused Saadeh, whose ego was immense, explains why he later denied that his party was fascist or national-socialist (it was not 'democratic' or communistic, either, he added, but simply 'Syrian nationalist'[64]). The party again found itself in a hot spot after two abortive putsch attempts, in 1949 and 1961. The first resulted in the summary execution of Saadeh.

The SSNP still exists in Lebanon and Syria, although it has become much less virulent; it even acquired a leftist patina in the late 1960s, in defensive reaction against the sweeping far-left wave of the period. Basically, it has now become an appendage of the Syrian regime, like other Lebanese organizations, and also a 'partner' of the Baath Party in Syria's 'Progressive Patriotic Front' – a form of 'multi-party government' reminiscent of those prevailing under certain Stalinist regimes in Eastern Europe.

The Lebanese Phalange

Although the Lebanese Phalange (Kataeb) was founded in 1936 by Pierre Gemayel, a Lebanese Maronite pharmacist who came home from the Berlin Olympic Games deeply impressed by the Nazi regime, it was more closely patterned after the Spanish Francoist model, to which its name refers, than after German Nazism or Italian fascism. Its closest affinities are with the 'clerical fascism' inaugurated by the pro-fascist wing of the Italian People's Party (the precursor of the Christian Democrats), a variant of fascism associated with Francoism (with its 'national Catholicism'), Salazar's regime in Portugal, Dollfuss-Schuschnigg's dictatorship in Austria, the Pétain regime in France and other such historical movements.[65]

The Lebanese Phalange was ultra-conservative on the social level and typically fascist in its structure. It has always posed as the protector of Lebanese Christians in general and Maronites in particular, as well as of the Lebanese entity carved out by the French colonial authorities in 1920 – in contradistinction to any form of nationalism seeking to incorporate that entity into a larger territorial unit, be it Pan-Arab or 'Syrian'. The Phalange played a significant role in the 1958 religious sectarian clashes, the first of their kind in independent post-war Lebanon. It was a fierce enemy of Saadeh's SSNP in the period of the French colonial mandate.

Although predisposed to anti-Semitism by both its fascist and Maronite Catholic sources of inspiration, the Phalange cannot fairly be accused of it. The party is concerned, above all, to ensure the survival of Lebanon in the face of any effort to absorb it into its Muslim Arab surroundings; all its political manœuvres have been dictated by this one overriding aim. Thus, even as it endorsed anti-Zionism in 1945 so as not to alienate its Muslim allies in the struggle for independence (including the Najjadeh movement, the counterpart to the Kataeb), and also because it feared the competition a Jewish state might offer the Lebanese state,[66] it presented itself as the protector of Lebanese Jews with the exacerbation of tensions accompanying the march toward the creation of the state of Israel and the 1948 war.[67] The Phalange has, moreover, traditionally maintained good relations with Lebanon's non-Muslim minorities, both for electoral reasons and because of convergent interests in the preservation of the Lebanese state.

An attempt to establish cooperative relations between the Lebanese Phalange and the Jewish Agency foundered in 1946 because Palestine's Zionist leaders already had close dealings with the party's Maronite rivals.[68] With the radicalization of Arab nationalism fuelled by the 1948 war, however, the Phalange forged an alliance with the young Israeli state, although it provided rather thin support in the early stages. As Benny Morris has pointed out,

> the foundation of the Israeli-Phalange relationship, the Jewish State's most lasting with any minority in the Arab world, was laid in secret contacts during 1948–51 ... The dealings always seemed to be one-sided ... Zionists and Israelis aided the Phalange propaganda effort in the U.S.; Israel was

asked to materially and politically assist a Phalange revolution in Beirut; and Israeli financial assistance was sought, and obtained, for the Phalange election campaign of 1951.[69]*

This alliance ultimately emerged as one of the key factors in the long Lebanese war, especially in its pre-1982 phase. It was promoted by the Phalange's far-right wing, led by Bashir Gemayel, who, under the banner of the 'Lebanese Forces', kept his distance from the more traditionally conservative wing of the party led by his older brother Amin.[70]

Young Egypt and Egyptian Nationalism

The political trajectory of the movement known as Young Egypt (Misr al-Fatāt) has consisted of a series of zigzags. They are explained by the versatility of its founder and leader, Ahmad Hussein (Husayn).[71] Founded in 1933, and plainly inspired by the rising tide of European fascism, Young Egypt aped its modes of organization and its paramilitary activities, creating 'greenshirts' on the pattern of the German brownshirts and Italian blackshirts.[72] Its ideology evolved towards ultranationalism tinged with Islamic elements, leading it to envisage merging with the Muslim Brotherhood in 1939, before it decided instead to compete with it under the provisional name of the Islamic Patriotic Party.[73] Young Egypt quickly took back its old name, only to become the Socialist Party of Egypt in 1949. It continued to operate under that label until the Egyptian military outlawed all political parties in January 1953.[74]

As with the SSNP – and with even better reason, given Young Egypt's frequent changes of tack – neither the German nor the Italian authorities took the movement seriously, their scepticism heightened by their extreme prudence in everything touching on the territories under British colonial domination. As Wolfgang Schwanitz explains,

> From his election in 1933 until World War II, Adolf Hitler pursued a secondary peace policy toward the Middle East. He was much more interested in a division of labor with London: he accepted the British Empire while believing that Eastern Europe ought to be a completely German domain for *lebensraum* ... Hitler's racial views, known to the

---

*   Morris's essay was written in 1984, i.e. after Israel's 1982 invasion of Lebanon and the massacres of the Palestinians of Sabra and Shatila carried out under Israeli supervision in Sept. 1982 by partisans of Bashir Gemayel, who had been assassinated shortly before. The essay was produced in a context of opposition, widespread in Israel at the time, to the alliance between the Phalange and the Israelis.

public since 1920, must have influenced his lack of interest in creating German colonies or territories in the lands of 'colored people.'[75]

Young Egypt was initially very critical of Mussolini's Italy, to which Ahmad Hussein had paid a disillusioning visit in 1934;[76] this did not prevent the organization, however, from supporting Italy one year later in its war against Ethiopia.[77] The movement's attitude towards Rome continued to zigzag thereafter, alternating between collaboration and criticism.[78] The same held for Germany as well:[79] whereas in the mid-1930s, Young Egypt emphasized its own 'spiritual dimension' against the 'materialism' of European fascism,[80] Ahmad Hussein tried to build a relationship with the Third Reich as early as 1934, openly declaring his admiration for Hitler.[81] In 1938, however, Hussein visited Germany and, for the second time, Italy, and came back marvelling over the Third Reich. He had got a closer look than many admirers from afar – past counting in the 1930s, among the Arabs no less than in the rest of the world – who were fascinated by the German recovery in the midst of the worldwide economic crisis.[82]

Nevertheless, given Hussein's frequent political changes of direction, it is obvious that his infatuations with foreign models were basically impressionistic, springing from the same attraction to the strongmen of the moment that led him to praise the Soviet Union after the war.[83] These zigzags have been well described by James Jankowski and 'Ali Shalabi, as well as P. J. Vatikiotis,[84] and Rif'at al-Sa'id.[85] Sa'id, citing Hussein's contradictory statements, has an easy time making him look like a fool in the book he devoted to him. (In his introductory chapter, he points out that Hussein went from supporting to opposing the monarchy and from denouncing Hitler and Mussolini as partisans of violence in September 1938 to identifying two months later the many points that fascism had in common with Islam.[86])

With the exacerbation of tensions in Palestine during the latter half of the 1930s, it was not long before Young Egypt – especially given its 1938 pro-fascist turn – lapsed into anti-Semitism. It was an anti-Semitism not only of words, but also of deeds. Whereas Ahmad Hussein had criticized Nazi anti-Semitism in 1938 as regressive, blaming it for the negative impact it had had on Palestine,[87] his movement organized, in 1939, an energetic anti-Jewish campaign,[88] calling for a 'Boycott of Jewish Commerce'[89] and compiling lists of Jewish-owned businesses in various Egyptian cities. Unlike the 1930s anti-Zionist boycott launched in other Arab countries, such as Syria,[90] which was restricted to the products of the Palestinian Yishuv, or one of 'Zionist' products – defined as 'Jewish goods produced in Palestine' – that the League of Arab States called for in 1945,[91] this boycott was undeniably anti-Semitic. On 2 November 1945, on the twenty-eighth anniversary of the Balfour Declaration, Young Egypt and the Muslim Brothers organized attacks on Jewish stores or institutions – the first of their kind, according to Rif'at al-Sa'īd.[92] Young Egypt also organized a new anti-Jewish campaign during the 1948 war.[93]

Lotfallah Soliman provides a good picture of this current in his panorama of the Egyptian political scene at the beginning of the Second World War. He begins by pointing to 'two very small minorities at the two extremes of the political spectrum, of which it would be hard to say which was the more insignificant'.[94] We have already discussed the first of these currents, the Marxists. 'The other tiny minority,' Soliman writes,

> which was more or less modernist, but fundamentally authoritarian, discovered echoes of its own fantasies and, above all, its primitive anti-communism in fascism and, especially, National Socialism. Yet, allergic as it was to elaborate conceptualizations, it took from the German and Italian models only their outer manifestations, their brown or black shirts, parades, exaltation of strength, and, first and foremost, their outrageous xenophobia. This fascistically inclined minority was anti-Semitic; it justified its anti-Semitism by pointing to the Zionist colonization of Palestine, the heavy proportion of Jews in the local communist movements, and also with arguments based on contemporary Egyptian history.[95]

Of course, it can hardly be doubted, in view of the prevailing political circumstances, that the influence exercised by the Marxists was outweighed by the ideological influence of a nationalist, fascistically inclined minority on a younger Egyptian generation whose patriotism was exacerbated by the joint effect of British colonial oppression and the progress of the Zionist enterprise in Palestine. This is even easier to understand when we recall that the Marxists were handicapped by the dominant perception of them as both ethnic and cultural outsiders. Nevertheless, contrary to a propaganda legend cultivated to political ends by the enemies of the Nasserite movement, none of the 'Free Officers' who overturned the Egyptian monarchy on 23 July 1952 was a 'Nazi'. It is true that several of these officers had been involved with Young Egypt in the 1930s; Gamal Abdel-Nasser himself had been a member of the movement for close to two years, in 1935–7, before he concluded that it was inane and quit.[96] But that happened before Ahmad Hussein's visit to Germany, the pro-Nazi turn and Young Egypt's first anti-Semitic campaign.

P. J. Vatikiotis nevertheless makes a great deal of Nasser's brief membership in the organization, repeatedly returning to it in his 1978 book *Nasser and his Generation*. He goes so far as to affirm categorically that 'From Young Egypt Nasser and his colleagues had learned as early as 1938 that working closely with the army, a *coup* could "wipe out the "old gang", suppress the Constitution and run a régime modeled on that of the totalitarian states.'[97] Leaving aside the fact that Nasser had resigned from the movement in 1937, let us ask a more basic question about Vatikiotis's methodology. Did one have to belong to Young Egypt to know that a *coup* could sweep away the existing ruling class and establish a dictatorial regime? Or did Young Egypt itself simply take its inspiration from what was well known to everyone in a region fascinated by the Turk Mustafa Kemal[*] and, long before him, by Napoleon Bonaparte? To ask the question is to answer it. It would, moreover, be easy to multiply questions of this kind. For example, did Ahmad Hussein hold the patent on aspirations to nationalize the Suez Canal, justifying Vatikiotis's claim that he was at the origins of this ambition of the Free Officers?[98]

That Hussein and the Young Egypt movement, which was narrowly focused on his person, so often changed political orientation is in itself enough to show that he was less a producer of ideology than a political weathervane. Study of his movement illustrates the diversity inherent in the ideological force field of anti-colonial nationalism in the period. But one must beware of taking the weathervane for an electric fan.

Observers of the period have of course been subject to precisely that temptation. Vatikiotis defends himself rather ineptly against the charge that he has succumbed to it, leaving the reader with the clear impression that he has:

> Without suggesting that Nasser and his fellow-officers who acceded to power in 1952 acquired all their political ideas and lifted all their policies from Young Egypt, their view of power and their approach to it, their attitude and policies toward the British, Europe or the West, the Arab Middle East and the world, as well as their perception of the Egyptian national problem and their remedy for it all appear, upon careful examination, too close to those of Young Egypt for the connection to be lightly dismissed as conjecture, or over-reading.[99]

---

[*] It would be interesting and, no doubt, edifying, to compare the contrasting treatments of Gamal Abdel-Nasser and Mustafa Kemal in the extensive Western scholarly literature that demonizes the former while defending the latter, notwithstanding the many points the two men had in common. Does what counts as truth within the limits of the North Atlantic Treaty Organization count as error beyond them?

A few pages on, however, Vatikiotis gives his argument a twist that makes it more tenable: 'It is not so much that several of the younger officers commissioned after 1936 were members or sympathisers of the Society as it was the convergence of the attitudes, beliefs and personalities of a whole generation of young subalterns who had undergone similar social and economic vicissitudes and psychological shocks in adolescence and secondary school, particularly in the years from 1933 to 1936.'[100]

Even this statement is dubious, however, since it internalizes the 'convergence of attitudes' as if it were a basic personality type when it resulted, more prosaically, from the encounter between a colonial situation and international or regional ideological tendencies. These tendencies were, moreover, sharply contradictory, running the gamut from Marxism to fascism, from secular nationalism to fundamentalist Pan-Islamism. The situation spawned diversity rather than homogeneity, as we have seen; and the Free Officers – whose individual affiliations ran from the Muslim Brotherhood to Communism – offer an excellent illustration of the political and ideological heterogeneity of anti-colonialism. As Vatikiotis himself had written several years earlier, with greater objectivity: 'There were perhaps as many shades of political belief as there were members of the Free Officers Executive ... Any contention therefore that the Society embraced a group of officers with a common ideological or political persuasion is erroneous.'[101]

Anwar al-Sadat, generally considered the most 'pro-Nazi' of the Free Officers (Vatikiotis, whose contention that Sadat joined Young Egypt is based on a police report,[102] does not hesitate to add that his membership in the organization 'helped radicalise' him[103]), does not mention Hussein's movement or, for that matter, its founder in the highly romanticized personal narrative that he wrote in 1954, shortly after the 'Revolution'.[104]* Yet he certainly was not seeking to hide anything – he dwells at length on his contacts with two German agents in the summer of 1942, established as Rommel's Afrikakorps was marching on El-Alamein (the two agents were promptly apprehended by British counterintelligence, followed by Sadat himself), and happily acknowledges his admiration for the Muslim Brotherhood and its founder, Hassan al-Banna.

---

* Similarly, in the very narcissistic autobiography that Sadat published after his 1977 visit to Jerusalem, he makes no mention of his membership in Young Egypt. He does, however, declare that he 'had joined every single political party in Egypt, either out of curiosity or in the hope that it might provide a way out'.[105] The occasion for this remark is an allusion to his brief membership in the league founded by the very pro-British Amin Osman, whose career ended with his 1946 murder; Sadat himself was complicit in the crime.

Sadat's account, written in Arabic, was heavily abridged and freely reconstructed/adapted by its English translator, contrary to what the publisher suggests in the preface to the 'translation'. While the book is 'biased', he explains, the 'British public' should have the opportunity to inform itself about the situation, however unpalatable it may find the book's contents. He then offers two contradictory statements: 'This book emerges, therefore, exactly as it was received. No attempt has been made to edit it, except for length.'[106]

This is significant, because it is almost always the English 'translation' and translations from the English into other languages that are quoted. The pro-German passage cited by Bernard Lewis[107] and others after him does not exist in the original; its style clearly indicates that it has been written by the 'translator'. Still, Sadat never made any secret of his sympathy for the Germans in the Second World War. More serious is the way Lewis adduces this passage as proof that the Free Officers 'were at least in sympathy with the same cause' as the Mufti of Jerusalem – after labelling that cause anti-Semitic and bringing up the June 1941 anti-Jewish riots in Baghdad in the same passage.[108]

Yet there is nothing at all in Sadat's account or, for that matter, the English adaptation of it, including the passage cited by Lewis,[109] indicating the slightest sympathy for Nazi doctrine in general or anti-Semitism in particular. There does breathe on every page a burning if hardly surprising hatred for the British colonial power, which is what impelled the publisher to offer his excuses and which was toned down in the abridged version.

Thus the German sympathies of Egyptian or Arab public opinion in the early years of the war must not be confused with the adhesion of a very small minority to fascism or Nazism – no more than British or Jewish hopes for a Soviet victory after 1941 can be taken, in and by themselves, for Stalinism. As Lotfallah Soliman recalls,

> Those who, in Cairo, demonstrated to cries of 'Go, Rommel!' saw in the German field marshal nothing more than 'the enemy of their enemy.' They were guided by political agendas unburdened by ideology, nationalist political agendas for which the omnipresent foe was Great Britain, which had been occupying their country for almost sixty years, not Germany, which had never had a colonial history in either Egypt or any other Arab or Muslim country. Nazi Germany represented 'absolute evil' only for the tiny cosmopolitan, internationalist minority to which we belonged.[110]

Sadat himself castigates the demonstrators who marched to cries of 'Go, Rommel!' Their demonstration took place on 4 February 1942, touching off the British putsch of the same day that forced the king to name a new government. The change profited the Wafdist partisans of an alliance with London against the Axis powers. Sadat marshals several arguments in defence of the thesis that the demonstrations had been organized for the express purpose of justifying the British use of force.[111]

A majority of nationalist Egyptians, including Sadat and his comrades among the officers, were partisans of the position that 'Ali Māhir, the prime minister at the beginning of the war, put forward in hopes of 'sparing Egypt the horrors of war'.[112] It was, moreover, Māhir to whom the Free Officers appealed to form the first Council of Ministers after their 23 July 1952 *coup d'état.*

The young Egyptian soldiers viewed the Second World War as nothing more than a repetition of the first, for which their ancestors had been conscripted by their colonial oppressors and used as cannon fodder in a fight in which they had no stake. In his account, Sadat voices this feeling in terms far stronger than the bowdlerized English adaptation suggests:

> Egypt's destiny was in, not its own hands, but those of the English. We regarded the future from this standpoint, and thus did not fail to look to the past – to the First World War, in which marching columns of our captive fathers were led toward battlefields where they dug trenches in order to die in them, transported manure in order to be buried under piles of it, and licked their own sweat so that the English could sip their wine![113]

The High-School Student Movement Futuwwa in Iraq

In Wild's accurate presentation, 'The futuwwah-movement in Iraq was a youth-organization, not a political party. The Futuwwah was an official youth movement which comprised all students of the higher [upper] classes of high schools. They received a paramilitary training.'[114] Wild classifies this movement among his five organizations of Nazi-fascist inspiration, in an essay he titles 'National Socialism in the Arab Near East' – which goes to show how easily loose criteria can become a source of untenable categorizations.[115]

Wild points to the participation of a delegation of the Futuwwa (the word means both 'youth' and 'valour') in a 10 September 1938 Hitler Youth parade in Nuremberg, at the annual Nazi party rally. But it was one delegation among many from around the world that had been invited to the Nazis' main annual ceremony, and it had, incidentally, been sent by the very pro-British Iraqi government (five days before British Prime Minister Neville Chamberlain paid his first visit to Hitler). Wild also points to the Nazi leanings, which he calls anti-Semitic, of Sāmi Shawkat, director-general of the Iraqi Ministry of Education, whom the pro-British Iraqi Prime Minister Nūri al-Saʿīd had personally charged with reorganizing the Futuwwa along the lines of the German model.

For their part, Britain's representatives in Iraq opined, in 1939, that the movement 'should be physically and socially beneficial because it provides for discipline on the square (the British teachers all say that lack of discipline is one of the worst difficulties in the classes)'.[116] It was by no means in Iraq alone that non-Nazi organizations formed paramilitary youth groups in the 1930s. Other examples include the liberal Egyptian Wafd party, with its 'blueshirts', and its Syrian counterpart, the National Bloc, with its (grey-blue) 'ironshirts': both were eager to retain the allegiance of young members who, they feared, might be lured away by the radical nationalists. Here is how one of those nationalists, the Syrian Akram al-Hūrāni,[*] later mocked his country's 'ironshirts':

> Thus the leadership of the patriotic guard, thanks to both its mentality and training, was very far from welding this popular army full of ardor and enthusiasm into a true combat unit, to say nothing of the contradiction between the patriotic guard's so-called liberal-democratic principles and the fascistic appearance of its organizations ... It did, however, take a great interest in the organization's external appearances, its uniforms and insignia, for instance, which were in the fashionable Nazi and fascist style that appealed to people in those days.[117]

Of course, the uniformed youth organizations that came into vogue in the first half of the twentieth century were hardly an Arab monopoly. The British Lieutenant-General Robert Baden-Powell had founded the Boy Scouts in 1907.

Peter Wien suggests that the Futuwwa was more on the order of a state-run scouting movement than a Nazi youth organization in the conclusion to his book *Iraqi Arab Nationalism*.[118] His argument is, however, unconvincing, given that members of the Futuwwa received military training under Colonel Salāh-ud-Dīn al-Sabbāgh, who played a central role in the 1941 events.[119] Moreover, both the historical context and their political education

---

[*]   In 1952, Akram al-Hūrāni's Arab Socialist Party merged with Aflaq's and Bitar's Party of the Arab Renaissance (Baath) to form the Party of the Socialist Arab Renaissance, generally known as the Baath Party.

predisposed the young people of the Futuwwa to behave more like a fascistic youth group than ordinary boy scouts.

That is in fact how they did behave during the 1 and 2 June 1941 Baghdad pogrom known as the *Farhūd* (a term that evokes anarchy and pillage in dialectal Iraqi Arabic), according to sources that Wien himself cites.[120] Wien attributes the behaviour of these young people to the Futuwwa's failure to control them, but hardly convincingly. Reeva Simon has provided a more cogent description of the Futuwwa's nationalist zeal during the clashes with British troops in May 1941 and the chaos of the *Farhūd*.[121]

Iraqi Arab Nationalists and Nazism

There existed in 1930s Iraq an ultranationalist current that, like so many others across the globe, particularly in countries colonized by Britain, reflected the enchantment with fascism that marked this period. Its main representatives belonged to the Al-Muthanna Club, founded in 1935. Sāmi Shawkat was one of its most eminent members, while the four colonels who constituted the backbone of the Rashid 'Āli al-Gaylāni government during the nationalist episode of April–May 1941 sympathized with it.[122] The Al-Muthanna Club had an authoritarian, populist orientation; the degree to which its members subscribed to Nazi ideology varied. Police reports and documents of the Al-Muthanna Club published in Baghdad in 1998[123] show that Al-Muthanna was above all ultranationalist, anti-Communist and Pan-Arab, and cultivated an anti-Jewish or anti-Semitic tone that was implicit rather than explicit. Some Iraqi and Palestinian members were Nazi sympathizers who had contact with the Germans.[124] A police report of April 1942, written shortly before the club was dissolved by Nūri al-Saʿīd's government, attributes the club's pro-Nazi turn to the influence of the Mufti of Jerusalem, Amin al-Husseini, who had arrived in Baghdad in October 1939.[125]

A pamphlet on Nazism that the club published the same year Husseini arrived sharply criticizes Hitler's Germany and its ideology, without, however, taking issue with German anti-Semitism.[126] It denounces Nazi Germany as an expansionist power that violates both international treaties and the right of peoples to freely determine their future; is animated by an anti-Arab theory of racial supremacy; and terrorises its own people. The pamphlet concludes by calling on Arabs to 'maintain an attitude of reserve and suspicion toward the current war and to direct their efforts toward defense of their true interests', and also 'to resist Communist, Zionist, Nazi, fascist and other colonialist movements detrimental to [their] identity and progress.'[127]

Gaylāni was guilty of collaborating with Nazi Germany after the British army overthrew his government. Condemned to death in his own country and put on the British authorities' wanted list, he ultimately joined Husseini in Berlin, where he cooperated with the Third Reich on matters of Arab foreign policy, although he played second fiddle to the Mufti.[128] Gaylāni was much less deeply involved than the Mufti in anti-Semitic activities, confining himself basically to anti-British nationalism – Iraqi rather than Pan-Arab nationalism, as Lukasz Hirszowicz shows in *The Third Reich and the Arab East*, still the standard work on relations between Nazi Germany and the Arab world.

Gaylāni's collaboration with Berlin nevertheless lent credence, after the fact, to London's depiction of the 1941 nationalist putsch as pro-Nazi and German-manipulated. The British were seeking to counter the putschists' popularity in Arab public opinion, which was much more enamoured of them than of the Axis as such and was frankly hostile to Italy. In George Lenczowski's accurate description, Arab public opinion 'presented a combination of pro-German and neutral attitudes. There was, moreover, a widespread belief that the war was a conflict of the big powers and as such of no direct concern to the Arabs. This explains why there was relatively little anti-Ally unrest in the Middle East during the war.'[129]

This suspicion towards the great powers turns up in the memoirs that Colonel Salāh-ud-Dīn al-Sabbāgh, a pivotal figure in the 'Golden Square' behind the 1941 putsch, wrote in the interlude between his flight to Turkey and his subsequent extradition to Iraq, where the British authorities had him executed in 1945. Sabbāgh relates telling a German officer in 1939, before the outbreak of the war:

> Suppose that Germany were to emerge from the war victorious over Great Britain: what guarantee would the Arab countries have their situation would be better than it is today? ... Neither a German nor a British victory, should war break out, is in any sense in the Arabs' interests. We want neither the victory nor the defeat of the one side or the other; rather, we wish to see them emerge from the war with matching forces, so that the balance between them is maintained.[130]*

Sabbāgh describes the nationalists' two different positions after the war broke out: the relatively moderate one taken by General Tāha al-Hāshimi before

---

*   Let us note in passing that a situation similar to the one that nationalist Arabs sought did indeed prevail at the end of the Second World War, with the difference that the two powers holding each other in check were the USA and the USSR.

he became president of the Council of Ministers in February 1941 and the pro-Axis position of the Mufti of Jerusalem. They agreed on three points: to keep the British happy within the limits of the Anglo-Iraqi treaty; to build up the Iraqi army; and to keep out of the war while waiting to see how it would develop.[131]

Their two main points of divergence had to do with the stance to adopt towards the Axis and the best place to wage the national battle. Hāshimi, who wanted to stay on Britain's good side, advocated breaking off relations with the Axis and fomenting a revolt in Syria against the colonial authorities of Vichy France. The Mufti advocated launching a revolt against the British in Palestine, who were likely, he thought, to bow to the Arabs' demands under the circumstances. Like Sabbāgh, who adopted a position midway between the two, both Hāshimi and Husseini thought that if the Soviet Union entered the war on the side of the Axis and proceeded to invade Iran, the Arabs should enter the war in their turn in order to liberate their lands.

The subsequent collaboration between Gaylāni and Berlin heavily distorts perceptions of the 1941 Iraqi nationalist episode. Gaylāni himself, even more than Sabbāgh, was an Iraqi nationalist intent on keeping his country out of the war. His attitude was thus identical to that of Egyptian nationalists such as 'Ali Māhir. As Majid Khadduri has explained, it was London's colonial arrogance that radicalized Gaylāni, impelled the Iraqi nationalists to make contact with the Axis and precipitated the anti-British *coup d'état* of 1 April 1941.[132]

Nevertheless, even after the *coup*, Gaylāni's government continued proclaiming its intention to respect Iraq's international commitments, including, it explicitly said, the Anglo-Iraqi treaty that the nationalists had so strongly condemned.[133] When the British forces that had been dispatched to Iraq after the *coup* arrived in Basra, Gaylāni even hastened to give them permission to land, 'as evidence of the friendly attitude of his Government towards Britain'.[134] It quickly became clear, however, that London intended to overthrow the new Iraqi government *manu militari*. Faced with the inevitability of a confrontation, Gaylāni and his military allies, whose resources were far inferior to those of the British, naturally sought assistance from London's enemies – the Axis, but also the Soviet Union, which Hitler did not attack until three weeks after the end of the Gaylāni episode.[135]

Sabbāgh maintains that he abandoned neutrality only at 'five o'clock in the morning of Friday, 2 May 1941, the day the English betrayed us, taking us by surprise and bombing our units and camps from the air. Our soldiers were torn to bits, although we had peaceful positions and were endeavouring to respect the treaty while defending our rights.'[136] The account clearly indicates that he was not, in the proper sense of the word, a partisan of Hitler's Germany.

Even Yūsuf al-Sab'āwi, generally considered the most pro-Nazi of the leaders of the 1941 putsch (largely because he translated *Mein Kampf* in 1934 for a Jesuit anti-Jewish Arabic-language daily[137]) cultivated ties with the Communists from 1936 on.[138] After the government that the putsch had brought to power was overthrown by British forces, Sab'āwi, who had taken refuge in Iran, made contact with the Soviet ambassador and asked for Moscow's help in organizing a rebellion, explaining that the 1941 episode was 'a patriotic movement directed against the imperialists' and had 'no connection with Nazism'.[139]

The events of April–May 1941 were perceived neither in Iraq nor in the rest of the Arab world as a pro-Nazi *coup d'état*. Witness the reaction of the Iraqi Communists, who were fiercely anti-Nazi and stood above all suspicion of anti-Semitism. On 7 May, they sent a letter to Gaylāni proudly recalling the support they had given his government very early in the day and congratulating him on his popularity.* At the same time, they called on him to rely exclusively on the forces of the people and drew his attention to the need to oppose the provocative anti-Jewish acts that the party 'abhor[red]' and also to avoid making pro-Axis propaganda. 'You, no doubt, agree with us, your Excellency,' they added, in urging him to seek an alliance with the USSR alone, 'that the powers in question are no less imperialist than Britain.'[141]

In spring 1941, the Axis was at the height of its military success. Until the tide began to turn in spring 1942, very many pro-independence activists in the Arab countries, Westernizers included, sought the support of the winners of the moment. The Syrian Shukri al-Quwwatli is an example.[142] Even the eminently pro-British Iraqi Nūri al-Saʿīd briefly attempted to establish contact with the fascist powers. Majid Khadduri has shown how London's 1939 rejection of the solution to the Palestinian problem that Nūri al-Saʿīd urged it to adopt on the basis of the British White Paper of the same year pushed the nationalist Iraqis into hostility towards Britain, leading even its most faithful Iraqi ally to make overtures to the Axis.[143]

With the reversal of the situation, the dominant forces among the Arabs changed tack, as Hirszowicz relates:

> By 1943 Arab politicians who had been sympathetic to the Axis broke with the watchful waiting policy and began to throw in their lot with

---

* In 1941, the Communist Party leadership charged those critical of its stance with 'Trotskyism,' before disowning the consequences of its own line two years later.[140]

Allies. Early that year Iraq declared war against the Axis, and Egypt followed two years later. In Palestine the moderate Arab politicians began to organise their forces, although the British authorities did not fully support them, against the Huseini clan.[144]

Syrian Arab Nationalists and Nazism

While the 1941 Iraqi episode sharply exacerbated Arab nationalists' hostility to England, they continued to distrust the Axis powers. The collaboration of Gaylāni and, especially, the Mufti of Jerusalem with Rome and Berlin hardly commanded universal assent even among their closest allies. The Syrians, in particular, had had occasion to observe that the colonial authorities of Vichy France had been no more inclined than their predecessors to promise them independence during their few months of control over Syria and Lebanon, before the British swept them aside and replaced them with representatives of Free France after overthrowing Gaylāni's Iraqi government. Under pressure from their British allies, the Gaullists went so far as to promise the Lebanese and Syrians independence, which neither the Vichy regime nor even Rome or Berlin had ever done.

Fawzi al-Qāwuqji was Arab nationalism's leading military figure in the inter-war period. An Ottoman Army officer during the First World War who had fought in the campaign against the British, he later served as a commander in all the Arab national battles of the period: the 1925–7 Syrian revolt, the 1936–9 Palestinian revolt, the 1941 Gaylāni episode in Iraq and, finally, the 1948 war for Palestine, in which he led the Arab Liberation Army (Jaysh al-Inqādh).

After being wounded in combat in 1941 in Syria, the comatose al-Qāwuqji was transported to Berlin, where he was nursed back to health. In his memoirs, he tells how, during his stay in hospital, he came under heavy pressure from German civilian and military officials to declare his allegiance to the Führer. He even had an altercation with an SS officer who proffered threats when Qāwuqji insisted that Germany first formally acknowledge the Arabs' right to independence. The next day, his son died of poisoning. Qāwuqji, convinced that the Nazis had murdered the young man, refused to take part in the funeral they organized.[145]

His stay in Berlin ended in 1945. He found the Mufti's intrigues and his rivalry with Gaylāni no less bewildering than the German and Italian leaders' foot-dragging over Arab and Syrian national demands. In particular, he opposed Axis plans to create Arab units and incorporate them into their own armed forces, rather than supporting the formation of an independent army.

Nabīh al-'Azmeh, one of the main Arab nationalist political leaders in Syria and the region as a whole, belonged to a minority who had cultivated contacts with the Axis and been obliged to leave when the representatives of Free France, allied with the British, assumed control after the 1941 events in Iraq. He refused, however, to go to Berlin (preferring Turkey), despite the fact that his brother 'Ādil had found refuge with Gaylānī and Husseini there. "I do not wish to go to Europe," he wrote his brother on 3 July 1941, "and stretch out my hand to anyone before I know the fate that they hold in store for my nation and the designs Italy has on our country ... Between us, the situation is unclear, [so that] the commitments we make in the dark represent a threat to [our] interests simply by virtue of our presence in their country.'[146]

On 20 April 1942, 'Azmeh wrote a letter to the Mufti, then in exile in Rome, in which he criticized him for, among other things, taking up residence in Europe and attributed his mistrust of the Axis powers to his fear of 'the replacement of one foreign power by another and one yoke by another, even if the terms employed change. To my mind,' he went on, 'the fact that the colonized are enemies of England and France and that Germany is powerful and victorious is not reason enough for nations subject to the yoke of [Germany's] enemies to adopt a favourable attitude towards Germany or take its side.'[147]*

Four months later – in August 1942, according to the editor of 'Azmeh's posthumous papers – he broke with Germany in a letter to the German foreign minister that is an acerbic denunciation of Germany's imperial policy toward the Arab Middle East.[149] In September, 'Azmeh sent a letter to the Iraqi authorities, occasioned by the visit of President Roosevelt's personal envoy to Baghdad, explaining his vision of the political positions that the Arabs should adopt in the world conflict:

Today, we are confronted with two foreign fronts and two corresponding

---

*   Accompanying the draft of this letter, found in Nabīh al-'Azmeh's archives, is a sheet bearing the following notes: 'Germany's objectives: Iraqi oil – the railroad from northern Irak to Basra – Syrian oil – the oil of the Hejaz, Kuwait, and Bahrain – Palestine and the Sinai, Suez and the Gulf of Aqaba, Aden, and Bab-el-Mandeb. Italy: Syria, Lebanon, and Palestine – Egypt – Yemen and its islands, especially Khorasān [probably an error for Kamarān] – 'Asīr and part of the Hejaz coastline – protection of the Eastern Christians and the minorities – Cyprus – Tunisia, Algeria, Morocco – Tripolitania.'[148]

Arab fronts: the Germans, the English; Rashid 'Āli together with Hajj Amin, and Nūri al-Saʿīd together with those who share his views. The foreigners all have designs, objectives, and desires involving our countries, and the patriots all have their arguments. A third Arab front clings to the principles of true independence and total, full-fledged unity of the kind that would bring all Arabs together. This front has no contact with a [foreign] front; it is watching and waiting, with an eye to eventually putting the nation on the path dictated by its interests, or to joining whichever of the two Arab fronts carries the day. This third front is stronger than the two other Arab fronts in terms of popularity and influence.[150]

'Azmeh pointed out that the Germans had so far made the Arabs more promises than the English had, and urged the Iraqis to step up the pressure on London with Washington's help. 'You will see,' he assured them, 'that the day the results of the efforts of the two Arab fronts are proclaimed and confirmed, the nation will be on the side of those who have succeeded in procuring the most advantages for it, just as it will be hostile to the front that has failed. Finally, if its aspirations are not fulfilled by whatever one or the other of the two fronts has achieved, it will take sides with the third, even ranging itself against the other two.'[151]

Arab Nationalism and Anti-Semitism

We have already mentioned the anti-Semitic tendencies of certain Iraqi Arab nationalists, especially some members of the Al-Muthanna Club. Theirs was not an elaborate Nazi-style racial doctrine. Most of these nationalists simply accused Jews of supporting Zionism or the British – despite the fact that many Iraqi Jews were anti-Zionists. The ultranationalists who were furthest to the right and sympathetic to Nazism found the distinction between Jews and Zionists harder to draw, since the Jews who were both anti-British and anti-Zionist were usually Communists.

The Palestinian nationalists' failure to distinguish between Jews and Zionists was generally much more 'natural' than the Iraqis', inasmuch as the Palestinian Arabs were confronted with a Yishuv which defined itself as representative of world Jewry and in which anti-Zionist Jews constituted only a tiny minority. Palestinians generalized about 'the Jews' in much the same way as Jews in Palestine under the British mandate generalized about 'the Arabs'. Indeed, the term 'the Arabs' was in much wider use, inasmuch as pro-Zionist Arabs, or Arabs who were not anti-Zionist, represented a much lower proportion of Arabs as a whole than anti-Zionist or non-Zionist Jews did of Jews as a whole.

The fact remains that the most radical representative of secular Arab nationalism in Palestine, the Istiqlal (independence) Party, had so enlightened an attitude toward the Jews that Baruch Kimmerling and Joel Migdal, in their book, *The Palestinian People*, single it out for praise. Discussing the role that the new party, founded in 1932, played in the wave of struggles that preceded the great 1936 'revolt', they explain:

> The party was forthright in proclaiming that the British, not the Jews, should be the primary targets of action – in some cases, Palestinians even organized contingents of guards to protect Jews and their property during demonstrations. In fact, during this period, while the British were firing at Arab demonstrators and breaking into offices of the Muslim-Christian Associations, not a single Jew was attacked in urban protests.[152]

Akram Zu'aytir was one of the best-known Istiqlal Party leaders, an important regional figure who exercised, successively, official functions in Palestine, Iraq and Syria, before becoming an eminent Jordanian politician in the 1960s and 1970s. He played a pivotal role in the emergence of Pan-Arab nationalism in Iraq and was one of the founders of the Al-Muthanna Club.

It was not easy for Zu'aytir to get used to the differences between the indigenous Arab Judaism of Iraq and the largely immigrant Judaism of his native Palestine. In a diary entry for 31 March 1938, he recounts what happened when the Iraqi nationalist deputy 'Ali Mumtāz al-Daftari, who was accompanying him on a political action tour for Palestine, took him to the home of a friend:

> Discussing our mission in the presence of the master of the house, I started to denounce British policy and the hypocrisy of the Jews, their conspiracy, and the need to engage in continuous action to combat and defeat them. At this point, Mr. 'Ali Mumtāz turned to me and said: 'But the master of the house is not one of them; the fact that he's a Jew doesn't mean that he's also a Zionist! And he agrees with everything you just said!' He then turned toward our host, who smiled and said: 'Everything you say is right. I beg you not to suppose that I consider your remarks about the Jews offensive, for I believe that the Zionist Jews are going to bring a catastrophe down on the heads of all the world's Jews.' I fell silent, because in attacking the Jews, I had failed to distinguish between Zionists and Jews! I had impugned all the Jews of the Arab countries. When we got up to go, 'Ali Mumtāz teased me, saying: 'I propose that we now go to

see the doctor. Who can say whether the man poisoned the coffee after your abominable, devastating attack on the Jews!'[153]

Kedourie reports this anecdote, quoting extracts from it, in support of his statement that 'One particular consequence of the disturbances in Palestine and of the Nazi war against the Jews was that the distinction between Jew and Zionist disappeared in Arab nationalist discourse.'[154] He adds: 'The anti-Jewish campaign, spearheaded by people like Zu'aytar [sic], spread in the Arab world in ever-widening ripples.'[155]

For Kedourie, the anecdote was (1) damning evidence of the validity of the charge that Zu'aytir put himself in the vanguard of the 'anti-Jewish campaign' and (2) proof that the distinction between Jews and Zionists 'disappeared from Arab nationalist discourse' beginning in the 1930s. Is this really the case?

Let us take a closer look. A member of the Iraqi parliament who shares Zu'aytir's Arab nationalist views takes him to a friend's house without feeling any need to inform him that that friend is a Jew. Zu'aytir launches into a harangue about Palestine in which he attacks Jews across the board. The parliamentarian thereupon points out that his friend is Jewish and admonishes him that being a Jew by no means entails being a Zionist. Zu'aytir falls into an embarrassed silence and the deputy makes gentle fun of him.

In fact, this anecdote might well be cited to make a point exactly opposite to Kedourie's, whose essay focuses on the rupture between Muslims and Jews in Iraq. That is, it could be used to show that the distinction between 'Jew' and 'Zionist' had been clearly established by the dominant current among the Iraqi Arab nationalists exemplified by the parliamentary deputy. A few pages further on in Zu'aytir's diary, we find a direct refutation of Kedourie's allegations in a passage that Kedourie seems deliberately to have ignored:

29/7/1938 – 1st Jumāda al-Thāniya 1357: Two weeks ago, the Jewish lawyer Mr Anwar Shā'ūl (whom I knew well when I was in Iraq) wrote a letter to the newspaper *Al-'Irāq* ... Anwar, in his letter, described the pain he felt, because, he said, 'I am an Arab who grew up in an Arab country in which my ancestors have lived for centuries as pure Arabs, shared the other Arabs' joy and sorrow, enjoyed this smiling sky and breathed in these beloved breezes. I feel pain because I am an Arab proud of being an Arab, over and above [the Arabs'] just cause. I feel pain because I see that the sons of one part of the great Arab fatherland are being subjected to a harsh ordeal in connection with the resolution of problem that they have in no way contributed to creating.' Anwar attacked the states that boasted that they would 'resolve the Jewish question at the cost of the peaceful Arabs,' and condemned the plan to make Palestine Jewish at the expense of its Arab sons.

I read the letter by the Jewish poet Mr. Anwar Shā'ūl and then sat down to write a letter of my own that I sent to Baghdad. I took care to encourage him to hold to the path he had chosen and translate his words into deeds. I expressed the view that our national interests dictated that Arab Jews be encouraged to come out against Zionism and prove that our cause is a just cause, a national cause bound up with our very existence, not the fruit of religious fanaticism. He received my letter, and the Iraqi newspapers published it, with comments expressing their pleasure over it and supporting what I said in it. Shortly thereafter, it was printed by several Syrian, Lebanese, and Palestinian newspapers. I had not been expecting it to have so great an impact.[156]

And yet the same Akram Zu'aytir – a fair representative of the ideological poverty and confusion among many Arab ultranationalists – could, in a May 1939 speech at a public meeting of Baghdad's Al-Muthanna Club, cite Germany's reaction to the 'assassination by a Jew of a German civil servant working in the German Embassy in Paris'[157] as a positive example in the course of denouncing the Arab governments' failure to react to the events in Palestine. The German 'reaction' in question was, in fact, the November 1938 Nazi pogrom known as *Kristallnacht*.

Even if Zu'aytir did not intend to precipitate a pogrom against Jews in the Arab countries but, rather, to invite the Arab governments to take up positions against Britain instead of 'adopting, vis-à-vis our cause, an attitude of mediation between the English and [the Arabs]',[158] the example he chose was sinister in the extreme. It was probably to the tastes of a segment of the Al-Muthanna Club's membership, although nothing indicates that any of them ever formulated, or even envisaged, a plan to exterminate Iraq's Jews.

Yet in the essay that we took as the point of departure for the present section on the nationalists, Stefan Wild accuses Sāmi Shawkat of setting his sights on 'the annihilation of the Jews in Iraq'.[159] Wild reproduces Sylvia Haim's 1955 *sui generis* interpretation of a speech Shawkat gave in 1938. Spelling out what she claimed Shawkat had 'indirectly' implied,[160] Haim effectively made Shawkat a precursor of the 'Final Solution'. Her interpretation was unwarranted; indeed, Haim herself did not repeat it in another essay published the same year, in which she extensively cites the same speech.[161] Peter Wien, for his part, rebuts the charge that Shawkat trafficked in fascism and Nazi-style anti-Semitism (a charge that was levelled at Shawkat by his many political adversaries in his own lifetime). Wien does underscore, nonetheless, Shawkat's 'anti-Jewism', which was motivated, he says, by his anti-Zionism.[162]

However, the lack of any genocidal anti-Semitic discourse or developed anti-Semitic doctrine in the case of Shawkat and his political colleagues hardly justifies reducing their discourse to nothing but 'flirting with Fascist Imagery', to cite Wien,[163] who is sometimes inclined to bend the stick too far in the other direction in an attempt to straighten it out. That certain Arab ultranationalists active in Iraq in the 1930s cultivated a discourse with anti-Semitic overtones, even if it was bound up with the exacerbation of tensions in Palestine and was often the work of Palestinian nationalists living in Iraq,[164] cannot be considered in isolation from the general Iraqi context of the period. And this context diverged sharply from the Palestinian one, in which Jewish immigrants had acquired the character of Zionist colonial usurpers.

The anti-Semitism that found expression in Iraq made much of the socio-economic characteristics of one segment of the country's Jewish community, generalizing them and making them over into the stuff of fantasy in the same way that European anti-Semitism had, in keeping with one of the oldest mechanisms of racism and xenophobia. In that sense, the 'contradicting element' that Wien claims to detect in the typescript memoirs of Abraham Elkabir, a former high-ranking Jewish civil servant in the Iraqi state administration, is no such thing. The fact that Elkabir 'mentioned racism and anti-Semitism as reasons [for the deterioration of relations between Jews and Gentiles in Iraq], but described at length the social reasons and the unjustified nature of the allegations against Iraqi Jews'[165] is not, in fact, a 'contradicting element' – on Wien's own formulation of the matter.

Young Egypt's anti-Semitism was of the same sort. There was, however, a major difference between the Iraqi and Egyptian situations: the distinctly higher level of violence typical of Iraqi anti-Semitism. Anti-Semitic discourse in 1930s Iraq went hand in hand with an upsurge in ethnic and religious violence, which reached a new peak in 1933 with massacres in which thousands of Christian Assyrians perished in Northern Iraq. They were a late paroxysm of the Assyrian genocide perpetrated by Turkish and Kurdish Ottoman forces beginning in 1914, at the same time and in the same areas as the Armenian genocide.

The June 1941 Pogrom in Baghdad: The Farhūd

The Iraqi pogrom of 1 and 2 June 1941, which occurred in the wake of the British military intervention that overthrew the Gaylāni government late in May, was part of a tide of anti-Jewish violence that had been rising since the end of the First World War, particularly in the 1930s. It represented, however, a sharp increase in the level of violence. In the first real anti-Jewish pogrom in Iraq, Baghdad's Jews became scapegoats on whom the ultranationalists vented their frustrations, accusing them of constituting, in some way, a pro-British fifth column. This charge, together with the question of Palestine, accounts for the pogrom, according to Kedourie.[166] Esther Meir-Glitzenstein, in contrast, emphasizes the Palestinian dimension alone.[167]

Baghdad's Jewish community was caught by surprise. Hayyim Cohen raised pertinent questions about this event, twenty-five years after it occurred:

> What were the reasons behind it, and why was it restricted to Baghdad, while almost no damage, or serious harm was done in the other scores of Iraqi towns in which Jews lived? Moreover, while the *farhud* in Baghdad lasted for about thirty hours, with the participation of thousands of Moslems, some of them armed, and including soldiers and police, and the eighty thousand Baghdad Jews were unprepared for any such attack, with no means of defence, the casualties were relatively small, only some 160–180 Jews killed and a few hundred injured.[168]

The answers Cohen offers are thoroughly convincing:

> It is fairly certain that most of those who took part in the slaughter of the Jews were young men influenced by Nazi propaganda, especially soldiers, officers, policemen and members of the para-military groups. The looters and thieves, however, were mainly the uneducated, illiterate masses ... They took part in the outbreak mainly for the sake of easy gain. For this reason, they were easily dispersed when fired on, on Monday afternoon, 2 June. Moreover, had all the mobs taken part in the actual killing, the number of victims would have been far higher, especially as the Jews were in no way prepared to confront such a *farhud,* the like of which neither they nor their ancestors had ever known.[169]

Iraqi Jewish estimates generally put the number of Jews killed at nearly 180. The Babylonian Jewry Heritage Center in Or-Yehuda, Israel, however, seems to cite a figure of 129 Jewish victims, to judge by the title of a lecture by Zvi Yehuda, director of the Center's Research Institute.[170] The repression of this mass violence probably led to a still higher number of deaths among the mob, as a Jewish eyewitness to the events who later settled in Haifa indicated in an interview he gave Wien:[171] the Iraqi army turned its machine-guns on the crowd in order to defend Baghdad's rich neighbourhoods during the violence,[172] and did so again when the *Farhūd* was forcibly brought to an end. According to Meir-Glitzenstein, 'Rioting ended at midday on Monday, June 2, 1941, when Iraqi troops entered Baghdad, killed *some hundreds of the mob* in the streets and reestablished order in Baghdad.'[173]

The official report on the events naturally attempted to play down the extent of the carnage, as Kedourie points out:

> The official investigating committee reported officially that the numbers of those killed 'including Jews and Muslims' was one-hundred and thirty,[174] but one of its members later told the chronicler Hasani (who had the story confirmed by the then Baghdad chief of police) that the true figure was nearer six hundred, but that the government was anxious for the lower figure only to appear in the official report.[175]

It is instructive to see how Bernard Lewis treats these statistics. He presents the Baghdad pogrom as 'the first Axis-style attack on a Jewish community in an Arab land'. Without citing a single reference in support of his contention, Lewis claims that 'According to official sources, 600 Jews were killed and 240 injured ... Unofficial estimates were much higher.'[176] He fails to mention that this 'Axis-style attack' was the work of a small minority; that the broad mass of Iraqi Muslims disapproved of the anti-Jewish violence, as Cohen points out in his personal account, which further notes that a number of Muslims unhesitatingly went to the Jews' defence or provided them with aid, protection and shelter;[177] that the mob was violently repressed by the Iraqi army; and that families of hundreds of Jewish victims received compensation from the Iraqi government.

The attitude of many Iraqi Muslims, as described by Hayim Habousha in his account, contrasts favourably with that of European populations confronted with similar events:

1) Many Muslims opened their homes and fed and protected the Jews. It had been reported that some Muslims apologized for not being able to provide Kasher meat and/or poultry to their guests.

2) Looters in Basrah on May 1941 were stopped by a distinguished Muslim notable, Salih Bashayan, who appointed guards from his own men to protect Jewish property.

3) On June 1, 1941 pressed by the mob to oust the injured Jews from the hospital where they were treated, Jamil Dallali, the director, called the police who dispersed the hostile crowd.

4) On June 1, 1941 Dr. Saib Showkat, Dean of the Baghdad Medical College, chief of surgery and administrator of Baghdad Central Hospital entered the surgery ward and scrubbed his hands getting ready to operate. Doctors and nurses standing idly by, had no option but to follow his example. In a few hours, all patients (mostly Jews) were attended to and moved into clean beds.

When Jewish nurses reported threats of rape by Iraqi wounded officers being treated at the hospital, Dr. Showkat sent the officers to their beds and warned on the megaphone that anyone disobeying his order would be shot by him with two guns in his belt. There was no argument – everyone obeyed.[178]

Habousha's report confirms what Nissim Rejwan notes about the *Farhūd* in his 1985 history *The Jews of Iraq*:

Throughout the disturbances, with a few exceptions, Jewish homes in mixed neighbourhoods were defended and hundreds of Jews were saved by the willingness of their Muslim neighbours to protect them, in some cases at the cost of their own lives and limbs. According to one account, the spiritual head of the Shiite community in Baghdad, Sayyid Abu'l Hasan al-Musawi, helped save many Jewish lives by ordering his followers to refrain from taking part in the looting and the killing and by refusing to issue a *fatwa* (religious edict) calling on Muslims to declare holy war (*jihad*) against the Jews.[179]

These facts should be considered in conjunction with the observation that Robert Satloff makes at the end of *Among the Righteous*, a study of the fate of North African Jews in the Second World War:

At every stage of the Nazi, Vichy, and Fascist persecution of Jews in Arab lands, and in every place that it occurred, Arabs helped Jews. Some Arabs spoke out against the persecution of Jews and took public stands of unity with them. Some Arabs denied the support and assistance that would have made the wheels of the anti-Jewish campaign spin more efficiently. Some Arabs shared the fate of Jews and, through that experience, forged a unique bond of comradeship. And there were occasions when certain Arabs chose to do more than just offer moral support to Jews. They bravely saved Jewish lives, at times risking their own in the process. Those Arabs were true heroes.[180]*

Is it any wonder that such acts of solidarity were frequent in societies marked by a long history of peaceful coexistence between different religious communities? Or that they should be considered 'unexceptional' in cultures in which hospitality ranks as a moral obligation? When Satloff had occasion to speak about the results of his research before students of the University of Jordan in Amman, he was puzzled that some of them 'dismissed any acts of "righteousness" as ordinary human kindness'.[184]

Let us, returning to Iraq, note in conclusion that the worst official anti-Semitism that the country saw in the 1940s was not the work of nationalist governments but of the man the nationalists and the Iraqi populace in general hated the most: the pro-British Nūri al-Saʿīd, who threatened to expel the Iraqi Jews en masse during his tenure as prime minister in 1949. He thus accelerated the process that would culminate, after the war for Palestine, in the massive exodus – for the most part, to Israel – and dispossession of the largest Jewish community of the Arab East (nearly 135,000 Jews were living in Iraq in the late 1940s)[185] – under a government again headed, between September 1950 and July 1952, by Saʿīd.[186]

---

*   These were not exceptions. In no sense did the Muslim populations of the Maghreb rally to the anti-Semitism of the Axis powers, as Michel Abitbol has pointed out with regard to Tunisia: 'The outcome [as far as the Tunisian Muslim population was concerned] was negative when it came to the results of the incitement by French extremist movements to anti-Semitic hatred, the Arab language broadcasts on the German radio, and the rabidly anti-Jewish articles in the Paris paper *El-Rachid*.'[181] Even Norman Stillman – who does not hesitate to write, outrageously, that 'in many Arab countries, the Jews would experience a brief but bitter foretaste of what awaited their brethren in Europe'[182] – acknowledges that 'Most thoughtful Maghrebi Muslims, however, saw that under Vichy's authoritarian and racist regime they were no closer to either independence or even a greater measure of equality under the French imperium. There was, therefore, little comfort that could be drawn from the official treatment of the Jews. On the contrary, this persecution evoked a certain degree of sympathy for the unfortunate Jews and at the same time reminded the more sophisticated Muslims of their own powerlessness under colonial domination.'[183]

CHAPTER 4

Reactionary and/or
Fundamentalist Pan-Islamists

Every enduring religion has necessarily gone through a series of mutations in order to adapt to the evolution of the societies in which it exists. Islam, too, lent itself to interpretations and reinterpretations throughout its variegated history, shaped at times by modernizing reformers, at others by traditionalist conservatives, or reactionaries, or again fundamentalist counter-reformers. Who predominates in any given period depends, first and foremost, on the general development of ideologies and political 'moods' conditioned by social developments and the historical conjuncture.

It was, naturally, in the late nineteenth-century Arab society that had made the greatest strides toward modernization – urban Egypt – that the Arab Islamic aggiornamento flowered, thanks to Muhammad 'Abduh in particular.[1] The liberal Muslim Westernism of 1930s Egypt, discussed above, was a direct continuation of the reformist enterprise launched by Jamāl-ud-Dīn al-Afghāni and Muhammad 'Abduh in the closing decades of the nineteenth century, and was notably associated with men grouped around *Al-Risāla*, such as 'Ali 'Abdul-Rāziq, Ahmad Amīn, 'Abbās Mahmūd al-'Aqqād and Tāha Hussein.

Afghāni's and Abduh's opposition to Western tutelage was basically of modernist and Westernizing inspiration, so much so that doubts have been raised about the sincerity of their (especially Afghāni's) religious commitment.[2] At the same time, for Afghāni, the adventurist leading light of the international opposition to Western domination, Pan-Islamism was the most convenient banner to raise. Afghāni, whose last name, a pseudonym, camouflaged his twofold Persian-Shiite identity, intervened politically and travelled personally across a broad area that took in the Arab, Indian, Persian and Turkish regions of the Muslim world.[3]

Pan-Islamism and Fundamentalist Counter-Reformation

The Pan-Islamism Afghāni espoused from the 1880s on – the first version of which, influenced by the Young Turks, promoted Islamic unity under the Ottoman Sultan-Caliph, held up as a bulwark of Islam against the West[4] – was always susceptible to deviation towards a fanatical rejection of Western cultural modernity. Thus Muslims who were reactionary or fundamentalist, anti-Western and anti-Westernist took up the Pan-Islamist banner, allying themselves with the Arab nationalists in a struggle against common enemies. The further to the right these nationalists stood, the stronger the ties between the two currents, despite the sharp difference in their appeal: religion in one case, the nation in the other, with a hybrid Arab-Islamic nationalism at their intersection.

Pan-Islamism crystallized for a time around the question of the Caliphate, which had been jeopardized by the demise of the Ottoman Empire and was abolished outright in 1924 by the new Turkish state led by Mustafa Kemal ('Atatürk'). The movement mobilized, on the one hand, the mass of reactionary conservatives who defined the new Islamic orthodoxy of the twentieth century,[5] and, on the other, Muslim counter-reformers, the spiritual heirs of the Great Syrian (*shāmi*) Rashid Rida (Muhammad Rashīd Ridā). Rida was born in 1865 in Tripoli, a city that the French mandatory authorities made part of Lebanon in 1920. He was initially a disciple of Abduh's, pushing his reformist enterprise – after Abduh's death in 1905 and especially from the 1920s on – in the direction of a fundamentalist counter-reformation.[6] By 'counter-reformation' I do not mean the traditionalist, strictly conservative rejection or reversal of reform but rather a reformation (possibly a profound one) with a reactionary objective, reminiscent of the Catholic Counter-Reformation in response to the Protestant Reformation. Given its fundamentalist inspiration, Islamic counter-reformation was far more reactionary than its sixteenth- and seventeenth-century Catholic predecessor, a development the more paradoxical in that the Islamic version seems to have emerged as a mutation from the reformist movement itself rather than being, as in the Christian case, the product of a frontal assault on it.

This mutation, engineered by Rida, explains the double meaning of what is known as Salafism (*salafiyya*). The term originally designated the Islamic reformation movement that took its inspiration from 'the venerable ancestors' (*al-salaf al-sālih*), emphasizing their spirit of innovation and undertaking to reinterpret the religious canon accordingly. Yet it eventually came to designate literalist, fundamentalist adhesion to the legacy of early Islam. If we had to name an Arab equivalent of the Slavophile pendant to Westernism – to recall the Russian dichotomy discussed above – it would be this Pan-Islamism of a fundamentalist bent. As Andrzej Walicki said of the classic Slavophilism of the 1840s, it was 'not so much an ideological defense of an existing tradition, as a utopian attempt to rehabilitate and revive a lost tradition'.[7]

The development of Rida's thought brought him closer to the Puritanical doctrine known as Hanbalism and especially to that of its Wahhabi adherents, who had conquered the Hejaz under the lead of the Āl-Sa'ūd (the House of Sa'ūd) and promoted an interpretation of Islamic doctrine that makes early Islam look like a model of liberalism in comparison. Rida's fundamentalist turn manifested itself above all in his defence of the Wahhabis and the Saudi monarchy. He published a number of articles on both in the review *Al-Manār*, his sounding-board from its foundation in 1898 to his death in 1935.

The long article that opens the twenty-seventh volume (April 1926) of the review – to which Rida was careful to put his signature rather than leaving it unsigned or signing in the name of the review, as he often did – announced with great fanfare what he presented as 'a great, truly great event: the Hejaz has been conquered by the one and only Sunni-Islamic Salafi state, and the cradle of Islam has come under its control'. Rida even detected in this development signs heralding the fulfilment of the prophecy.[8] In his articles he tirelessly reiterated – rebutting the many Muslim detractors of the new Saudi regime, from the Hashemites, the Saudi's Sunni rivals, through the modernist or moderate Muslims little inclined to wax enthusiastic over unpolished, ultra-Puritanical Bedouins, to the Shiites – that the Wahhabis were the best Muslims: they had kept faith with the teachings of Ibn Hanbal, acknowledged as one of the four legitimate schools of Sunni Islamic jurisprudence, and also with those of the best-known of Ibn Hanbal's disciples, Ibn Taymiyya.

At the confluence of Rida's and the Saudis' doctrinal and political influences emerged a profoundly reactionary, fundamentalist, fanatical Pan-Islamism. Its fanaticism was directed not only against non-Muslims, but also against non-Sunnis, and it incorporated a distinct Arab chauvinism. The Wahhabi monarchy of the Saudi Abdul-Aziz ('Abdul-'Azīz), known as Ibn Saud – a Hanbali, Salafi monarchy – became, from its foundation in 1926,[*] the main if not indeed sole support for this reactionary Pan-Islamism, a rallying

---

[*]   The Kingdom of Hejaz was proclaimed in Jan. 1926, after Abdul-Aziz, chief of the Āl-Sa'ūd, and his Ikhwān (Brothers) conquered the country. The following year, it was renamed the Kingdom of Hejaz and Nejd and, in 1932, the Saudi Arabian Kingdom (*al-Mamlaka al-'Arabiyya al-Sa'ūdiyya*). The Western name for it makes 'Saudi Arabia' the only country in the world named after a ruling family.

point for both advocates of the new Sunni orthodoxy and partisans of the fundamentalist counter-reform.

In the 1920s, Egypt saw the emergence, from the ideological matrix elaborated by Rashid Rida, of the first modern political movement based on a fundamentalist Muslim plan to establish an 'Islamic state'.[9] Rida's disciple Hassan al-Banna, who attempted to follow in his late master's footsteps by continuing the publication of *Al-Manār* in 1939–40,[10] founded the Society of Muslim Brothers in 1928 (Jamāʿat al-Ikhwān al-Muslimīn), which Rida himself had been on the point of joining shortly before he died, according to Banna.[11] The Muslim Brotherhood would become the spearhead of fundamentalist counter-reformation and reactionary Pan-Islamism in the Arab world.

The importance of the Saudi monarchy to the history of both the Arab world in particular and the Muslim world in general, and consequently to world history, has been badly underestimated. The new monarchy constituted a turning-point; its political and ideological influence has proved much more enduring than that of, say, Nasser's Egypt. The creation, in 1926, in the heartland where Islam was founded and its two main Holy Places are located, of a state based on the most fundamentalist interpretation of the religion ever to have existed contributed decisively to advancing the Islamic counter-reform. As Rida wrote in hailing the birth of the Saudi monarchy, 'Islamic reformation now possesses an armed state that fights heresies' (*al-bidaʿ*).[12] The Wahhabi monarchy provided reactionary Pan-Islamism with a permanent strategic base and put the resources of a state at its service – resources that were initially modest but subsequently, thanks to oil, immense. Needless to say, the new kingdom's close and enduring ties with the United States go a long way towards explaining the curtain of silence drawn, with American complicity, around the basic features of the Saudi state, the most obscurantist, anti-democratic and misogynous in the world.[13]

During its very first year, in June and July 1926, the Saudi monarchy organized an international Islamic conference in Mecca 'ostensibly for consultations about the Pilgrimage and related matters, but really in order to obtain international Muslim legitimation of [Abdul-Aziz's] conquest of the Holy Places and his rule over them'[14] – a 'legitimation' that was hardly to be taken for granted. King Abdul-Aziz charged Rida with convening the conference on his behalf, drafting the conference protocol and, finally, writing the king's opening address; in other words, he entrusted the programming to Rida and Rida alone. The conference was, however, undermined by the opposition of the leaders of the Indian Khilafat, the brothers Muhammad and Shaukat Ali, to the kind of government that the Saudi dynasty had established over Islam's Holy Places.[15] They demanded that the Hejaz government take republican form and that its president be elected by the conference,[16] and they denounced the destruction of Shiite tombs and other sacred monuments by Ibn Saud's Wahhabis – acts similar to the ones perpetrated by the Taliban after their victory in Afghanistan seventy years later.

In the end, the Mecca conference had only limited success as far as legitimisation was concerned; Egypt itself did not recognize the new state for another ten years. Yet with both Muhammad Rashid Rida and Muhammad Amin al-Husseini, the Grand Mufti of Jerusalem, in attendance, it marked an important moment in the crystallization of reactionary Arab Pan-Islamism and the association of its leaders with the new Wahhabi state.

The privileged relations that the Saudi monarchy established with the United States beginning in the 1930s attest that, from the start, its passionate anti-Westernism was not political but cultural. In contrast, the kingdom always opposed the Zionist colonization of Palestine, especially because Jerusalem is the third most important of Islam's Holy Places: in the first years of the Islamic revelation, it was the city towards which Muslims turned when they prayed (*qibla*), although it was later replaced by Mecca. For the Pan-Islamic movement, the question of Jerusalem and, therefore, of Palestine in general was a major concern, becoming increasingly acute from the 1920s on, especially after the violent riots triggered by the 1929 conflict over access to Jerusalem's Wailing Wall (the Al-Burāq or Western Wall).

The Religion of Islam and the Jews

Because both 'orthodox' reactionaries and fundamentalists adhere to the letter of the Koran and Hadith,[17] we have to preface an examination of their relationship to Nazism and the Holocaust by asking whether Islam's sacred texts encourage anti-Semitism. It is well known that the Jews (*al-yahūd*) are repeatedly vilified in the Koran, in accordance with the evolution of the Prophet's relations with the Jews of the Arabian Peninsula, even if their status as Abrahamic monotheists earned them a right to the Muslims' protection, making them, like Christians, dhimmis (*ahl al-dhimma*).

Nevertheless, as Norman Stillman emphasizes in the *Encyclopaedia of Islam*, Jews have, in the basic texts of Islam, 'none of the demonic qualities attributed to them in medieval Christian literature, neither is there anything comparable to the overwhelming preoccupation with Jews and Judaism (except perhaps in the narratives on Muhammad's encounters with Medinan Jewry) in Muslim traditional literature'.[18]

'The fact that the Jews shared their *dhimmī* status with the far more numerous and conspicuous Christians and Zoroastrians,' Stillman adds,

> mitigated and diffused any specifically anti-Jewish sentiments into a broader prejudice against the *ahl al-dhimma*. Furthermore, Jews did not have to bear the onus of suspicion that was harboured toward some of the Christian communities and that grew from the period of the Crusades onward, that they were friendly toward the European powers and a potential fifth column ...
>
> Mediaeval Muslim theologians devoted only a very small part of their polemics against other religions and doctrines to Judaism. There is nothing in Islam comparable in quantity and rarely in sheer vitriol to the *Adversus Judaeos* literature of the Church.[19]

Bernard Lewis confirms this in his book *The Jews of Islam*: 'For Muslims, [hostility to the Jews] is not part of the birth pangs of their religion, as it is for Christians. It is rather the usual attitude of the dominant to the subordinate, of the majority to the minority, without that additional theological and therefore psychological dimension that gives Christian anti-Semitism its unique and special character.'[20] It was thus very naturally by way of Christianity, Lewis continues, that the European anti-Semitism of the last decades of the nineteenth century reached the Islamic lands of the Ottoman Empire.

> One reason for this was certainly [the Christians'] increased openness to influences from Europe, including the precept and practice of European anti-Semitism; another was the educational and economic revival that was beginning among Ottoman Jews in the second half of the nineteenth century, and which confronted Christian merchants with competition from a quarter they had been accustomed to discount.[21]

Yet the situation of the Jews in the Arab countries of the Middle East and North Africa at the turn of the twentieth century was 'very much better' than that of Iranian Jews, thanks to 'the prevalence, at that time, of liberal ideas and aspirations among the political class'.[22] Stillman, in his voluminous work *The Jews of Arab Lands in Modern Times*,[23] attributes the deterioration of Arab–Jewish relations to two factors. The first was their divergent responses to Western penetration, which in the Arabs' perception led to servitude, in the Jews' to emancipation. The second and more important was the exacerbation of tensions in Palestine, especially after the 1929 riots.

Stillman himself shows, however, that the first of these two factors affected Christians as much as, if not more than, Jews, putting aside the fact that the

Christians were, generally speaking, more Westernized than Jews everywhere in the Arab world (with the exception of colonial Algeria, where 'native Israelites' were granted French citizenship by the Crémieux Decree as early as 1870). That there was no deterioration in Christian–Muslim relations even remotely comparable with the one between twentieth-century Christian and Muslim Arabs, on the one hand, and Jews on the other suffices to show that it is the second factor, the Palestinian factor, that explains the rise of anti-Judaism and a concomitant anti-Semitism in the Arab world. As Lewis has rightly emphasized, 'For Christian anti-Semites, the Palestine problem is a pretext and an outlet for their hatred; for Muslim anti-Semites, it is the cause.'[24]

The elements of anti-Judaism that the Islamic scriptures inevitably contain – inevitably, in view of the historical rivalry that pitted the three great Abrahamic religions against one another – can perfectly well be surmounted by mutual respect of the kind that prevailed among Christians, Muslims and Jews in the Arab countries in the modern period until the twentieth century – or like that which has essentially reigned there between Muslims and Christians since. However, Islamic fundamentalism, because of its attachment to the letter of the holy scriptures and its desire to imitate early Islam – the profound anachronism that has the most fanatical Muslim fundamentalists living, in their imaginations, in the first century of the Hegira – perceives religion as the prime mover of the world, as if humanity had never emerged from the Middle Ages.[*] The fundamentalists therefore see the relations between Islam and the other religions as a prolongation of the alternation, characteristic of Islam's earliest period, between war and peace or conflict and alliance, as circumstances and the requirements of Islamic expansion dictate.

This underlying attitude is the reason why Islamic fundamentalism has perceived the Palestinian conflict as a war of religion between Jews and Muslims (with their Arab Christian allies). The common denominator between this perception and anti-Semitism is essentialization of the enemy. Whereas anti-Semites regard Jews as members of a 'race', fundamentalists regard them as members of a faith. The difference is that Islamic fundamentalism is not racist, at least at the doctrinal level, because Islamic proselytism is, in its desire

---

[*] This explains why Samuel Huntington's thesis about the 'clash of civilizations' has had such resounding success with fundamentalists, whether Muslim or of other faiths: Huntington postulates a world in which religions determine the contours of geopolitical blocs.

to convert all human beings, universalistic. The Nazi notion of the subhuman (Untermensch) is foreign to it.

Rashid Rida

Sylvia Haim has pointed to the contrast between the turn-of-the-century emergence of an anti-Semitic literature in Arabic, imported from Europe by Christians, and the firm 1898 condemnation of European anti-Semitism, in connection with the Dreyfus Affair, by none other than Rashid Rida, the very man who would later become the father of modern Arab Islamic fundamentalism. This condemnation appeared in *Al-Manār*, Rida's mouthpiece and 'perhaps in its day the most widely read Arabic publication in Muslim lands'.[25]

The same year, Rida called on Arabs to take an example from the resurrection of the Jewish *umma*.[26]* Although he had perceived the Zionists' objectives in Palestine before many others, he nevertheless called, until 1914, for an accommodation with them so as to benefit from the European Jews' wealth and knowledge, on condition that they not try to take over Palestine or establish their state there.[27]

Yet Haim also notes in her essay – in passing, with a view to emphasizing Rida's pro-Jewish stance – that he defended the Jews the more harshly to condemn Egypt's Christian Copts: he preferred the descendants of 'the prophets of God' to those of 'the Pharaohs, the enemies of God'.[28] Neville Mandel, for his part, shows how the understanding between Muslim Arabs and Jews, as Rida conceived it, could only come about in opposition to Christian Arabs[29] – a position he abandoned in 1914, when he concluded that the Zionists would never renounce their plan to found a state.[30]

Hazem Saghieh observes that Rida's defence of the Jews at the time of the Dreyfus Affair was tied to his aversion for the West, both Christian and secular.[31] Rida harboured however far more animosity towards the French than the English for whom, despite everything, he expressed respect. To round off this portrait, let us add that he would, in the end, 'mak[e] anti-Shī'ism a major trait of his school',[32] after passing through a stage in which he admired the Shiite ulemas of Persia and their political role. The panegyric, already cited, in which he hailed the emergence of the Saudi monarchy in 1926 included a fierce indictment of the Shi'ites[33] – who were outraged by the Wahhabis' destruction of their tombs. Reading this text today, one can hardly shake off the impression that it belongs to our own time, so closely

---

*   *Umma* designates the community of the faithful in Islamic religious terminology.

does it resemble the anti-Shiite and anti-Persian diatribes churned out by Sunni fanatics in US-occupied Iraq, for example in its accusation that the Shiite Arabs are Iranian agents. Rida would repeatedly take the Wahhabis' side, even while continuing to distinguish 'moderate' Shiites and 'rejecters'[34] (*rāfida* or *rawāfid*),[*] a distinction that sometimes led him to argue in a more conciliatory tone.[35]

In sum, Sheikh Rashid Rida, far from rejecting xenophobia and religious sectarianism, fully embraced both, reproducing an essentially medieval mentality; he was genuinely reactionary in the sense that he projected a return to a vanished Islamic past, including an Arab Caliphate. His stance on the Jews and the Palestinian question changed, of course, between the days of the Dreyfus Affair and his death in 1935. At the turn of the century, he regarded the Zionist enterprise in Palestine as nothing more than a tool Britain was using to consolidate its domination of the region – a view still evident in the article he wrote in response to the September 1928 events in Jerusalem, a prelude to the crisis that broke out the following year.[36]

Rida explains in this article that the Jews had been used during the First World War by 'the English', who promised them Palestine in order to win their support and then settled them there in large numbers in order to provoke a *fitna* (a term usually reserved for internecine struggles between Muslims) between Jews and Arabs. A year later, he even revealed that he had gotten wind, on the eve of the 1897 founding congress of the World Zionist Organization, of steps that the Zionists had taken to obtain the Ottoman government's permission to colonize Palestine, adding that he had met on his own initiative with the Zionist movement's representative in Egypt in order to warn him of the consequences of an enterprise of the sort.[37] The Arabs would form armed bands of Bedouins to combat such an attack on their territory, he had told the Zionist representative,[38] before adding this friendly piece of advice: 'If the Jews wish to settle in large numbers in the Arab countries (Palestine and other countries as well) and live there in freedom and security, they would do better, in their own interests, to come to an understanding about means and ends with the Arab leaders themselves; I think that that is possible ... '[39]

After the First World War, when the Balfour Declaration began to be put into practice, Rida – again, on his own witness – held talks with Zionist leaders in Egypt and Palestine, including an exchange with Chaim Weizmann

---

[*]   This pejorative term, often used by Wahhabis and Sunni extremists to designate the Shiites, evokes the opposition to the caliphate of Abū Bakr al-Siddīq and his two successors by the partisans of ʿAli bin Abi Tālib.

himself, the president of the World Zionist Organization, who considered coming to Cairo to meet with him. Rida believed that he had aroused Weizmann's interest in such an agreement between 'the Arabs and their Hebrew cousins' but 'the exchange on this subject was broken off; the Zionists were counting on the English forces to reinstate them as the owners of Israel, each of the two partners trying to dupe the other'.[40]

Rida's discourse on the Jews underwent a sharp change in the late 1920s. The long two-part article that he published on the Palestinian question after the 1929 riots gave a new twist to elements already present in his more circumstantial article of the previous year; this time, he accentuated the anti-Jewish line. Rida drew on various sources, combining assertions that reflected the Muslim tradition the most hostile to Jews (whereas he had only recently availed himself of the most pro-Jewish strand in that tradition) with shameless borrowings from the most hackneyed commonplaces of the European anti-Semitism of the day. Among these commonplaces was the fantasy of the all-powerful Jewish conspiracy made popular by the worldwide dissemination of the famous Russian anti-Semitic forgery known as *The Protocols of the Elders of Zion*, which Rida did not cite, although it plainly had a pervasive influence on his text.[*]

According to Norman Stillman, the first Arabic version of the Russian fabrication – or, rather, of the French translation of it released in 1921 – appeared in 1925.[42] Translated by a Maronite priest named Antūn Yammīn, the work was published in Cairo, as is attested by documents attached to a request that the Lebanese Jewish community addressed to the French mandatory authorities in a bid to have the text banned in Lebanon.[43] The translation that appeared, as Daphne Tsimhoni reports,[44] in January 1926 in the Jerusalem (Eastern) Catholic review *Raqīb Sahyūn* (*The Observer of Zion*) was probably Yammīn's. Bernard Lewis misidentifies the *Raqīb Sahyūn* publication as the first Arabic translation of *The Protocols* in his 1986 *Semites and Anti-Semites*, adding that the text was not issued in Cairo for another 'year or two'.[45] He has not emended the subsequent editions of his book, despite what Stillman reported in 1991.

Stefan Wild's repetition of the same mistake is more serious. In a 2002 article citing Lewis's book[46] – which he probably in his turn took to be 'scrupulous,' thus returning the compliment that Lewis had paid him – he

---

[*]   Partly plagiarized, this pamphlet was written by a certain Mathieu Golovinski in Paris in 1900–1, according to the Russian historian Mikhail Lepekhin. It was commissioned by the ultra-reactionary, Orthodox head of the Russian political police in France with the intention of influencing the Czar.[41]

puts forward the surprising, if not fantastical, hypothesis that if the anti-Semitic forgery hardly circulated in Arab countries before 1948, the reason was that it had been translated by Christians; its first translation by a Muslim appeared only in 1951.[47] Wild seems not to have considered the obvious explanation: the intense exacerbation of the Palestinian conflict in 1948, the year of the Nakba and first Arab–Israeli war, and its impact on the market for anti-Semitic literature among the Arabs.

That said, the dissemination of anti-Semitism in the Arab world cannot be measured only by the circulation of *The Protocols of the Elders of Zion*, no more than it can be in the West. The absurdities contained in this pamphlet have circulated much more extensively than the pamphlet itself, for they were taken up by the European press and various Arabic publications. Rida made a decisive contribution to this proliferation in his 1929 *Al-Manār* article, which, as his fullest statement on the Jews and the Palestine question, is worth pausing over. It offers the prototype of what was to become Islamic fundamentalism's standard discourse on the Jewish question, developed in particular by the Wahhabi movement and the Muslim Brotherhood.

'The Palestinian Revolt: Its Causes and Consequences'[48] begins by describing the Jews as the most headstrong of all the world's peoples and the one most inclined to practise mutual assistance (*'asabiyya*). The Jewish people, Rida says, refuses to be assimilated into other peoples when it finds itself in the minority and refuses to coexist with them when it is dominant, since the Torah exhorts Jews to extirpate the peoples they conquer. God sent them prophets to guide them and granted them the privilege of being the first to receive his revelation; yet they rebelled against Moses and killed a number of their prophets after him, lapsing into idolatry and plundering others' property by means of usury. God punished them, taking their kingdom away from them and subjecting them to persecution by Christians, until some were able to benefit from the protection and good treatment of Muslims.

After the Jews were expelled from Spain together with the Muslims, they took revenge on the Catholic Church by spreading the freethinking they had learned from Ibn Rushd (Averroes) throughout Europe. Freemasonry is a Jewish invention and one of the tools the Jews use in their bid to re-establish a Jewish state and rebuild Solomon's temple in Jerusalem: the name 'Freemason' refers to the construction of the temple. The Western banking system is also a Jewish invention; it constitutes the means by which the Jews have succeeded in exerting decisive influence over the capitalist countries. The Jesuits, their sworn enemies, were able to combat them in the Catholic countries, but the Jews managed to defeat the Orthodox Church by diffusing atheism in

Russia and then establishing Bolshevism there, just as they managed to make Muslim Turkey an atheist country. (The allusion is to the Freemasons' role in the Young Turk movement.[49])

The Jews are trying to found their religious state in Palestine to pave the way for the arrival of the Messiah, for whom they have been waiting for thousands of years. In fact, this Messiah is the Anti-Christ; he will be killed by the true Messiah, Jesus ('Īsa bin Mariam), whom Muslims and Christians await. Notwithstanding the theological accord between Muslims and Christians, the Jews have succeeded in using the Christian states against the Muslims. (Note the shift in perspective between this text and its predecessor.) Tired of their endless wait, and under the influence of freethinkers sceptical of religious eschatology, the Jews have founded the Zionist movement in order to make their dream come true.

The Jews are the more tenacious today because they have become more powerful than ever; they are now 'the guardians of the temple of money, the main idol of the great nations that they have chained to its worship'. Thanks to their financial clout, they have acquired 'the means with which to diffuse propaganda that stands facts on their head and disguises evil as good'. Their economic and political power, however, is not backed up by military might, which is why they rely on the force of the British state.

Rida emphasizes that the Jews are competent in the financial sector, but not in agriculture or the military arts – a theme dear to the heart of a number of Zionist theoreticians as well, for whom changing this state of affairs was one reason to colonize Palestine. Rida, in contrast, regards it as unalterable. The Jews are too fond of life, he argues, citing the Koran, whereas the Arabs are both more numerous and steeled by battle. Moreover, Britain will seek to avoid antagonizing all the Arabs and all the Muslims. In prematurely opening hostilities, the Zionists have made a serious mistake.

Rida begins the second part of his article[50] with praise for the English, whom he clearly prefers to all other colonial powers, especially the 'Latin' countries, for the relative respect that they show the peoples they rule and for their pragmatism in this regard. It is not because of the Balfour Declaration that the English have taken the Jews' side in Palestine – how many promises, he exclaims, have they made and broken, especially to the Arabs, in the course of the (First) World War! – but because the Jews now seem more powerful than the Arabs, who will have to make a show of their strength (which is superior to the Jews') if they are to induce Britain to change its attitude.

The English and French, Rida continues, waged a skilful propaganda campaign during the World War, portraying themselves as champions of the freedom and independence of the nations. Thus they fooled the American president, Wilson, who came to their aid, and also the German socialists who rebelled against their government. The Arabs fell into the same trap and paid dearly for it, even if the domination imposed on them wears the aspect of a temporary 'mandate'. The injustice of which the English are guilty in Palestine is worse than all others, because it consists in implanting a new people with diverse origins in a country at the expense of its indigenous population. As the English are, however, 'closer to reason and virtue', it remains possible to convince them of the Arabs' legitimate rights and bring them to modify their government's policy.

The Arabs and the peoples from whom they are descended once represented the most advanced civilization in the world. Islam was able to extend its empire at an extraordinary rate because the Arabs were the most just and most merciful of conquerors. (Rida cites Gustave Le Bon to this effect.[51]) Their star began to fall when the religious precepts and the principle of consensus, on which the Prophet Muhammad based the state he founded, were betrayed after the death of 'Ali, the last of the four orthodox caliphs; at this point, a hereditary dynastic power was established, sowing division among the Arabs. The Persians opted for Shiism to enfeeble them. Thus it was, Rida explains, that barbaric peoples such as the Tatars and their Turkish and Berber cousins were able to bring parts of Islam's empire under their sway, ultimately ushering in its decline and defeat. The Turks even sought to substitute 'their barbaric language' for the Arabic of the Koran, and ended up rejecting both the Koran and its language.

Only the heartland of the Arab and Islamic world, the Arabian Peninsula, managed to resist domination by non-Arabs. The only two genuinely independent Arab kingdoms are to be found there – the Kingdom of Hejaz and Nejd and the Imamate of Yemen. The Palestinian question, however, the catalyst of an Arab awakening, has inspired a great movement of solidarity among the Arabs and all Muslims. The Jews' financial resources must be countered with the Arabs' natural resources: the mineral wealth of their vast territories, but also their great numbers as well as those of the other Muslims. It is to be hoped that the English will take note of the situation and bring about a shift in their leaders' policies.

The irreligious Jews are counting on Britain to win back Solomon's kingdom and its Temple, but the religion and interests of the English will eventually put them on the side of the Arabs, Muslim and Christian alike. The religious Jews are counting on what their prophets have prophesied, but these prophecies are ambiguous and depend on the coming of the

Messiah; the Messiah, however, has already come, although the Jews have not acknowledged him. Muhammad's prophecies spell things out more clearly: he warned that, when the Anti-Christ came, the Jews would join him in combating Muslims and Christians, but would go down to defeat. Rida cites a hadith of Muhammad's which he would repeatedly evoke from 1928 on, a hadith related to the prophecy: 'The Jews will fight you and you will be led to dominate them until the rock cries out: O Muslim! There is a Jew hiding behind me, kill him!'

In 1933, Rida issued his first fatwa on the Palestinian question, forbidding all Muslims to sell land to Jews in Palestine, since such sales represented betrayal of Islam and the Arab nation and complicity in the Zionist conquest.[52] That same year, a question about the Jews with a plainly anti-Semitic ring was addressed to him by an Arab living in Berlin; it obviously reflected the new Nazi authorities' views (despite the fact that the brief extract from the question published in *Al-Manār* did not directly refer to them). Rida's fatwa expanded on the above themes, in particular the idea that God had used the Jews' 'financial power, trickery, and secret intrigues (such as Freemasonry)' to wreak vengeance on the European peoples who had perverted Christ's message.[53]

In this way, Rida adds (surprisingly enough), the Jews weakened Christianity and thus allowed Islam to survive; had they not, the Crusaders would have defeated Islam, while the civilization of which it was the vehicle would not have been able to flourish in the East or Andalusia and go on to penetrate the West. The Europeans continue to make poor use of the achievements of civilization and to exterminate each other; the Jews, using Bolshevism in Eastern Europe and capitalism in Western Europe, are plotting against them. With the help of money and science, they have undermined the power of the papacy that oppressed them, and, by means of Communism, sapped that of the Czars. They also helped the Young Turks sap the power of the 'Turkish Caliphate'– in this instance, in hopes of conquering Palestine.

A typically Nazi theme appears here. The Jews are said to have undermined Germany in the (First) World War by spreading the 'poison of revolution' in the German army and navy and using their financial power and deceitfulness to push the United States into entering the war on the side of Germany's enemies, and then by trying to spread Communism in Germany at war's end. Their bitter opposition to Germany is not a sign of God's vengeance, as in the case of Russia and the Latin countries, but a service rendered England in exchange for its promise to cede them Palestine. But while 'the Latin and Germanic peoples' have begun to take revenge on the Jews, the Anglo-Saxons continue to support them. Should Britain allow them to realize their project in Palestine, however, it will precipitate both their downfall and its own, for that will arouse the Arabs' ire and accelerate the Arab renaissance.

This line of argument sheds light on the commentary, with apocalyptic connotations, that Rida wrote in the guise of an afterword to two reports published in *Al-Manār* in 1934 on the problems that Hitler's government was causing the Catholic and Protestant churches in Germany.[54] Here he describes the 'Germanic people' as 'the most advanced of the peoples of Europe and the whole world in the secular sciences and the arts of civilization' and explains that 'its government is trying to free itself of this falsified religion' at odds with science, the church's great power notwithstanding. The power of 'its new Nazi government' will prove stronger, like that of the Russian Communist and Turkish governments, which got the better of more solidly anchored religions in their countries.[55]

In sum, although Rida could not endorse Nazi doctrine, because it was obviously incompatible with his own ideology – from a religious Muslim standpoint, it would have been far more natural for him to express solidarity with the churches in their conflict with irreligious Nazism, as Muslims of the Westernizing liberal current did – he nevertheless legitimized his sympathy for Nazism by treating it as the instrument of God's will, sweeping aside heresies and false beliefs, corrupt versions of Islam among them, and thus clearing a path for the ultimate triumph of the Muhammadan revelation. One should note, however, the difference between Rida's rather benevolent attitude towards Nazism, an enemy of the Jews that also was asserting its domination over the Christian Churches, and the vituperation he directed against Kemalism and Russian Communism, both of which he saw as outright enemies of Islam in the territories under their control. This crucial difference is key to understanding the sympathy, paradoxical from a strictly religious standpoint, that Islamic fundamentalists generally felt for Nazism, both in the Nazi period and later.

In one of the last texts he wrote, in 1935, Rida reiterates his ideas on the Jewish and Palestinian questions, calling with increased urgency on Muslim Arabs to follow the Jews' example by uniting so as to focus the considerable power at their disposal, drive a wedge between the English and the Jews, and defeat the Jewish foe. He repeats the main leitmotif of fundamentalist Islamic doctrine on the Palestinian question and all other conflicts with enemies of Islam: 'If we want to save our homeland and *umma* from Jewish domination by means of the moral power of religion, we shall have to take the path traced by our ancestors [*salafīna*], who defeated the Jews in the first epoch [of Islam] and expelled them from the Arabian Peninsula.'[56]

In Rida's final text on Palestine, published four months before his death, he came to the defence of two 'mujahidin leaders' (*al-zaʿīmayn al-mujāhidayn*): his close friend Shakib Arslan, and Muhammad Amin al-Husseini, his 'friend and disciple'.[57] Both had come under attack in Palestine as the result of an incident discussed in the following pages. Rida pays a ringing tribute to Husseini, praising God for having favoured Palestine with a leader as brilliant as the Grand Mufti, who had succeeded in acquiring Pan-Islamic stature.[58] Rida died in August 1935 and thus did not live to see the 1936 revolt in Palestine, the intensifying persecution of the Jews in Germany, or the Second World War and the Holocaust. His two close friends witnessed all those events at first hand.

Shakib Arslan

Shakib Arslan, a Druze and a (feudal) emir from Lebanon, was four years Rida's junior. He survived Rida by more than a decade, dying in 1946, and observed the aforementioned events from Switzerland, where he was living at the time. Arslan resembles a fictional character patterned after a historical type, the international political adventurer who, in the course of an eventful life, cultivates relations with very different or even antagonistic political parties; the gamut of his relations ran from the Communists to the Nazis. Forever in debt, he was an aristocrat whose income had dwindled away as a consequence of the World War. He was reduced to soliciting subsidies from wealthy patrons and governments.

Arslan was an imitator of Afghāni's:[59] a Sunni by religious and political choice[60] who initially defended Islamic unity in the framework of the Ottoman Empire. He supported the Young Turk centralists who took power in Istanbul in 1913 so unreservedly that he opposed Arab struggles for autonomy, drawing heavy fire as a result, from Rida among others.[*]

After the demise of the Ottoman Empire, to be sure, Arslan underwent a

---

[*]   In an important 15 May 1935 letter to Rida, Arslan contended that his Arab detractors had been wrong, since he had forewarned them that 'the result of [their] secession from Turkey would be to enable the English and French to divide up the Arab countries between themselves, while enabling the Jews to seize Palestine'.[61] This is a specious argument, implying that if the Arabs had demonstrated solidarity with the Turks, the Turks would have been able to keep their Eastern Empire – which is patently untrue, to say nothing of the way it obscures the growing, increasingly unbearable oppression to which the Turks were subjecting the Arabs.

conversion, supporting the Arab world's struggles for independence against the colonialisms of Christian Europe. Yet even as a champion of Arab nationalism he was primarily motivated by Pan-Islamism.[62] Hence his eminent role in rallying support for independence struggles in the Maghreb: Arab nationalism would have sown divisions between Arabs and Berbers, whereas Islam united them in their opposition to French colonialism.

Like Rida, Emir Arslan became an ally of the Saudis. Ibn Saud even granted him Saudi citizenship, thus resolving his problems in obtaining travel documents, exacerbated by his tense relationship with the French colonial authorities in Lebanon.[63] Invited to the 1926 Mecca conference – inevitably, since Rida issued the invitations – Arslan, although unable to attend, was elected a member of the standing committee it created. He paid his first visit to the Saudi kingdom in 1929, making his pilgrimage to Mecca at the same time. In the Saudi king Abdul-Aziz, whom he met in Jeddah, he 'found his hero for the Arab future'.[64] He became a slavish admirer, expressing the desire that the sovereign come to rule the whole of the Muslim world and continuing to venerate him to the end of his life – not least as a result of Abdul-Aziz's financial aid.*

Arslan lived in Europe, mainly Geneva, from the end of the First World War to the end of the Second, not returning to Beirut until shortly before his death in 1946. He was thus an eminently suitable middleman between the Pan-Islamist movement and the fascist powers. As William Cleveland has summed up the matter, 'he played a central role in orchestrating the interplay between German and Italian desires for a new world order and the Arab search for independence,' in the process becoming 'enmeshed in a situation too complicated for him to manage until, in the end, he lost the flexibility which had given him a certain strength'.[66]

Beginning in the very first years of the fascist regime in Italy, Arslan cultivated contacts with Mussolini, whom he met a number of times in hopes of obtaining his support for Arab causes in the Middle East, while pleading in vain for an Italian accord with the Libyan nationalists.[67] He refrained from publicly criticizing Italy until its brutal repression of the

---

*   In recounting his first, 1929 encounter with Abdul-Aziz, at which Arslan was present, Fawzi al-Qāwuqji, whom Arslan brought to the Hejaz to help train the Saudi monarchy's army, makes no bones about his contempt for the king; he depicts him as infatuated with himself and suspicious by nature. Abdul-Aziz initiated Arslan into his vision of the world in the Bedouin dialect of the Najd; Qāwuqji assures us that Arslan understood not a word of what he said. The king lavishly praised the English, justifying his collaboration with them and thus profoundly disappointing Qāwuqji.[65]

Libyan independence movement peaked in the early 1930s, forcing him to denounce, vociferously, 'the Italian atrocities' and to call for a mobilization against Rome. Even then, however, he kept up his contacts with Mussolini through a common friend.

The anti-Italian outcry in the Muslim and Arab world led Mussolini's regime to take conciliatory measures in Libya after its bloody suppression of the rebellion there. Rome counted on Arslan, and by 1933, the Emir was already pointing to 'the changes in the way [Italy] ruled' Libya. In February 1934, he went to Rome, where he met with the Duce. Worse, Arslan acted as an accomplice to the Italian invasion of Ethiopia that began in October 1935. He tried to convince the Arabs to back the aggression or, at least, remain neutral, on the pretext that the Italians were more favourably disposed towards the Muslims than the Ethiopians were, as their good treatment of the Muslims of Eritrea supposedly showed. Thus he promoted Mussolini's efforts to present himself as the 'protector of Islam' – the same Mussolini who told Chaim Weizmann and Nahum Goldmann that he was a Zionist.[68]

Arslan's reputation sank to a new low with the scandal touched off by a letter he wrote to Mufti Amin al-Husseini, in which he stated that, in exchange for Mussolini's support for the Arab cause in Palestine, he had promised to carry out a pro-Italian propaganda campaign among Arabs. A facsimile appeared in April 1935 in *Al-Jāmiʿa al-Islāmiyya*, a newspaper published by the Palestinian opposition to the Mufti.[69] The Emir reacted strongly, denouncing the letter as a fake: the handwriting, he protested, was not his, and the text contained spelling mistakes that he was incapable of making. Ultimately, he succeeded in turning public opinion back against his Palestinian detractors by accusing them of working for the English and the Jews. His many articles to this effect also sought to justify his attitude towards Rome. Nonetheless, after carefully studying his letter to the Mufti, Zāhir al-Hasnāwi, a professor of history in Libya, maintains that 'there is no reason to call its authenticity into question': the original was probably dictated to someone who recopied it, which would explain both the handwriting and the misspellings.[70]

Radio Bari, an Arabic-language station created by the Italian fascist regime in 1934, began broadcasting a daily news bulletin in Arabic in April 1935 that from time to time included pro-Italian declarations by Arslan. Against the backdrop of the atrocious campaign that Mussolini's Italy was waging in Abyssinia, Arslan's declarations once again tarnished his reputation. His support of Italy, sharply at odds with his championship of anti-colonialism, fuelled suspicions that he had been bought off by Rome. William Cleveland nevertheless affirms that the Italian and German subsidies he received went almost exclusively to funding his political activities; in his private life, he was in dire financial straits.[71] He certainly could have 'sold out', and at a high price: he had refused a Saudi ambassadorial post offered by King Abdul-Aziz. Thus his stance was fundamentally determined by his political vision, accompanied by a measure of *Realpolitik*.

Arslan found it easier to justify his relationship with Germany, which was not in conflict with the Arab world. Since the First World War, he had cultivated relations with Berlin, to which he proudly called attention; he sought to develop them after Hitler's accession to power. However, as we have already noted, the Nazi government's reluctance to antagonize London and Paris initially made it extremely careful in its relations with the colonial powers' Arab enemies. Thus Arslan, who travelled to Berlin in 1934 in hopes of being granted an interview with Hitler, was not received by any ranking Nazi.[72] The situation changed later, but Berlin found more important Arab interlocutors than Arslan, whom it considered Rome's creature.

Arslan never became a Nazi, and for good reason: he was a Pan-Islamist and, although never particularly devout, espoused an ideology similar to the fundamentalist vision of his friends Rashid Rida and Abdul-Aziz – a situation that was well understood and accepted by both Berlin and its Muslim allies. Thus Arslan's 1935 critical review of Alfred Rosenberg's book *The Myth of the Twentieth Century*, which appeared in *La Nation arabe*, a French-language journal that he published in Geneva for a mainly Maghrebi readership, flowed easily from his pen. The very title of the review indicates its friendly intentions toward the Nazi state: 'Germany has Nothing to Gain from Such Manifestations: What Harm have Muslims and Asians Ever Done Germany?'[73] Here Arslan criticised Rosenberg for having come out in favour of maintaining a British presence in India and the Suez as a European bulwark against Asians and Muslims.

Similarly, when he wrote in *La Nation arabe* in 1938 that the Arabs did not need National Socialist doctrine in order to oppose foreign domination, and that Islam, because it was not a racial doctrine, authorized Jews and Christians to maintain their faith, he was simply stating the obvious. Cleveland is being inordinately indulgent when he cites these declarations in order to distinguish Arslan's positions from anti-Semitism,[74] while relegating to a note his discussion of the Emir's public support for the theory of a Jewish world plot.[75] (This will hardly surprise anyone familiar with the articles that Arslan's mentor, Rida, turned out on the same subject.)

Cleveland again displays unwarranted indulgence when he cites the December 1939 letter Arslan wrote to Nūri al-Saʿīd denying that he was pro-

Hitler.[76] So does Basheer Nafi when he cites the same letter as evidence that the Emir, in urging the Iraqi prime minister to adopt a position of neutrality in the Second World War, was expressing his own attitude.[77] Would Arslan, a skilled tactician, have declared to the very pro-British Nūri al-Saʿīd that he supported Hitler and asked al-Saʿīd to do the same? No objective beyond convincing the Iraqi prime minister not to side with London could have been envisaged by the man who had held it necessary to conclude an alliance with Mussolini without first demanding his withdrawal from Libya – the man who, after being the first major Arab statesman to pay a visit to Berlin (Radio Berlin announced the visit) three weeks after the outbreak of the war,[78] wrote to Amin al-Husseini in November 1942 urging him to declare his support for the Axis[79] (at a time when the Mufti was still trying to barter his official backing for certain advantages).

The year Cleveland's book was released, 1985, also saw the appearance of Wild's essay 'National Socialism in the Near East', which I have repeatedly cited. Its chief interest lies in its detailed review of Arabic translations of *Mein Kampf*. Copiously quoting extracts from documents in the Nazi archives, Wild reveals that Arslan set out to translate the National Socialist bible into Arabic in 1938, at the request of the Reich's Ministry for Propaganda and People's Enlightenment. Berlin found the existing Arabic translations poor – none of them had been authorized, and all had been censored or studded with glosses on the anti-Arab passages that were not to the Nazis' liking. The translation project was never realized, apart from an initial sample,* because of the prohibitive costs of publishing the book in Germany.[80] But in 1941, the Nazi Minister of Propaganda agreed to finance Shakib Arslan's journal, *La Nation arabe*, and authorized the Emir to publish it in German-occupied Paris.[81] Publication was, however, suspended during the war, while Arslan continued to turn out articles for the Nazi Arabic-language propaganda organ, *Barīd al-Sharq* (Courier of the East).[82]

In view of these heavily compromising facts, how should we evaluate Arslan's constant assurances that he had no illusions about Germany's imperialist ambitions? We might take, by way of example, his letter of November 1939 to Daniel Guérin, an anti-colonialist on the French far left,

---

*   While the extracts reproduced by Wild confirm that the Ministry had considered entrusting Arslan with the task with the help of a German Orientalist, they do not themselves prove that it was Arslan who translated the sample passage from the book. Wild categorically attributes the translation of this sample to Arslan. Does he do so because of other documents he may have consulted? If so, he should have cited them.

who cited the letter in 1954 to show that colonial leaders who appeared to be collaborating with the Axis 'were simply taking advantage of an existing situation in the interests of their movements'.[83]

Guérin's remark illustrates the abiding tendency of those who have made the admirable decision to put themselves 'at the service of the colonized' to abandon critical thinking when dealing with the victims of imperialism – especially those of their own country.[84] The same might be said of Cleveland's contention that 'for Arslan, friendly contact with the Axis was a natural extension of his efforts to exert pressure on Britain and France'.[85] Arslan could of course make that claim, but what is this Pan-Islamic anti-colonialism worth when it could accommodate collusion with an Italy that had imposed a brutal colonial yoke on Muslim Libya? Was that a 'natural extension' of anti-colonialism? Above all, is such collusion ever 'natural'? The question merits consideration, for the argument that 'my enemy's enemy is my friend' has all too often served to excuse the worst sort of compromise with, and even acceptance of, infamy.

'My Enemy's Enemy': Alliances of Convenience, Affinity and Complicity

A distinction must be made between those who acted in accordance with their calculated interests, provisionally, while keeping their distance from fascism, and those who, advertising their ideological convergence with Rome and/or Berlin, seriously bound themselves to the Axis powers. One cannot lump together fighters for independence such as the Westernizing Tunisian leader Habib Bourguiba – who, albeit freed from a French prison in 1942 on orders from Berlin and subsequently received with honours in Rome, acted within the limits of anti-colonialist logic, taking pains to avoid any real accommodation with the fascists[86] – with a Shakib Arslan, to say nothing of an Amin al-Husseini. Yet Husseini's invocation of the Arab adage 'Your enemy's enemy is your friend'[87] has often been quoted to precisely that end.

An overwhelming majority of liberal pro-independence activists, a majority of progressive nationalists, and all Marxists – in a word, all those Arabs who shared an allegiance to the values of political liberalism that issued from the Western Enlightenment, particularly the idea of human rights (even if, in the case of the Stalinists, this allegiance did not extend to the Soviet Union itself) – rejected Nazism and alliances with Hitler's Germany in the name of those values. For the most part, they regarded Britain as the lesser of two evils. Even during Moscow's 1939–41 accommodation with Berlin, Arab Communists made no apology for Nazism. Rather, they regarded the Stalin–Hitler pact as an 'alliance with the devil' – just as, after 1941, the alliance of Moscow with Washington and London generally failed to induce partisans of either side to wax enthusiastic about the regimes of their respective allies.

This is what certain Arab authors ignore. Philip Mattar summarises – without approving it – their argument about Husseini: 'He cooperated with Germany for political opportunism – the same reason Winston Churchill and Franklin D. Roosevelt cooperated with the despot Stalin. It was Churchill, after all, who said he would ally with the devil himself against Hitler.'[88] Note that Churchill's statement implies that Hitler was worse than the devil: only those fanatical enough to believe that Zionism was worse than Nazism could see an alliance with Hitler against the Zionist movement in Palestine as legitimate. Moreover, while it may be necessary to strike an alliance with the devil under certain circumstances, it is never legitimate to become the devil's advocate, and even less so to present the devil as an angel. Therein lies the difference between an alliance of convenience and full complicity.

Some Arabs unflinchingly threw in their lot with the Axis and took up the cudgels for them. They belonged to either nationalist or Pan-Islamist circles, the latter twisting the principles of Islam with the help of theological lucubrations of the sort Rida engaged in. Aside from straightforward emulators of Nazism, such as the Lebanese SSNP and Young Egypt, it was fundamentalist Pan-Islamism that exhibited the greatest affinity with the fascist states, Germany in particular. The affinity's rationale is plain: the common enemy was not Britain, as is too often believed, but the Jews.

The best illustration of this affinity is that bastion of reactionary Pan-Islamism, the Saudi monarchy. As Qāwuqji observed with regret in 1929, King Abdul-Aziz had nothing but respect and admiration for Britain. Moreover, the monarchy's role in dampening the Palestinian rebellion of 1936 at London's request is well known.[89] Ibn Saud was irritated by the subsequent decision of the Higher Arab Committee, headed by Husseini, to boycott the Royal Commission that London had dispatched to Palestine, in response to the British refusal to halt Jewish immigration. November, the King sent the Mufti a dry note reiterating his appeal for a compromise, on the grounds that his policy was motivated not only by his friendship for the British government but also by Palestinian interests.[90]

Of course, Abdul-Aziz's deference to London was not brought on by ideological affinity. It was dictated by his fear of England and his awareness that the Saudis' Hashemite rivals were in Britain's service, meaning that the British might always support a Hashemite military expedition to win back the

Hejaz.[91] When London showed signs of weakness in 1937–8 against the Axis, Ibn Saud, encouraged by Shakib Arslan, undertook to establish relations with Rome and Berlin. He recognized, in the process, Italy's annexation of Ethiopia and negotiated arms contracts with Germany and Italy – very quietly.[92]

The extensive publicity given to the 17 June 1939 meeting between Hitler and King Abdul-Aziz's special envoy, Khalid al-Hud al-Gargani, which had been touted as an indicator of German–Saudi rapprochement, actually helped bring it to an end. For, in order to deflect London's ire, Abdul-Aziz, who proclaimed his kingdom's neutrality when the Second World War broke out, had to abandon the idea of welcoming a German diplomatic delegation to his kingdom in 1940. The monarch was, moreover, wise enough not to bank on an Axis victory; indeed, he even expected the Axis to go down to defeat, so greatly did he respect British power.[93] Yet he could still ask the Mufti, in his Berlin exile in 1942, to inform his 'two friends' (Germany and Italy) that he had broken off relations against his will and continued to have only the warmest feelings for them.[94] Most important, the 1938 discovery, by American firms, of commercially exploitable oil deposits in the Saudi kingdom initiated its rapid transformation into a privileged ally of the United States, and then a de facto American protectorate – a status that will, it seems, endure until the last barrel of oil has been extracted from the Saudis' underground reserves.

In any event, the German–Saudi rapprochement, however episodic and brief, was more than a product of opportunism pure and simple. It foundered, in fact, as a result of the balance of forces on the Arabian Peninsula and worldwide. Otherwise, the alliance might have been cemented by the ideological affinity between Nazism and an Islamic fundamentalism situated at the intersection of Wahhabism with Rashid Rida's grand historical theories. Witness the minutes of the 1939 meeting between Hitler and the king's emissary:

> During the ensuing conversation, the Führer stated that we entertained warm sympathies for the Arabs for two reasons: 1) because we had no territorial aspirations in Arabia, and 2) because we had the same enemies. After some further statements, he added: 3) because we were jointly fighting the Jews. This led him to discuss Palestine and conditions there, and he then stated that he himself would not rest until the last Jew had left Germany.[*] Khalid al Hud observed that the Prophet Mohammed, who,

---

[*]   The Führer did not deem it useful to point out that, until then, he had incited German Jews to emigrate to Palestine; indeed, as I have noted, agencies of the Reich had gone as far as to help the Zionist organizations get around British restrictions on Jewish immigration.

apart from having been a religious leader had also been a great statesman, had acted in the same way. He had driven all the Jews out of Arabia ...

The conversation was then continued at the tea-table. The Führer referred to the strong predilection which he had always had for the Arab world, gathered from his reading, since his childhood. The idea, introduced by Khalid al Hud into the discussion, was enlarged upon, namely what would have become of Europe if Charles Martel had not beaten back the Saracens, but if the latter, imbued with the Germanic spirit and borne along by Germanic dynamism, had transformed Islam in their own fashion. The Führer described this line of thought as very remarkable.[95]

The fact remains that this new attempt to forge a unity based on the elective affinity between the Wahhabi ethic and 'the Germanic spirit' was stillborn. The Wahhabi kingdom could find affinities with Nazi Germany in the anti-Semitic realm, but there were none to be found in the two states' respective attitudes toward religion. With the United States, the Saudis lost the affinity of anti-Semitism but gained one rooted in the religiosity of both countries, as I have argued elsewhere.[96] The monarchy's American protector consistently demonstrated 'respect' for Wahhabi Puritanism, the more so as it knew that this religious obscurantism, Christian equivalents of which have always existed in the United States, was a basic pillar of the Saudi monarchy. The material interests of the Saudi dynasty, however, weighed more heavily than all ideological affinities: the clearer it became that the monarchy possessed considerable wealth in the form of oil deposits, the more this wealth became an object of others' envy and, consequently, the more the monarchy's sense of its vulnerability grew. It was above all for this reason that the Saudi dynasty chose to put itself under the protection of the most powerful state in the world, in a relationship of vassal to suzerain from which the American overlord has reaped and continues to reap immense profits.

The only disagreement between President Franklin D. Roosevelt and King Abdul-Aziz during their historic 14 February 1945 meeting on the USS *Quincy* in the waters of the Suez Canal involved the Jews.[97] Roosevelt tried to appeal to what his advisers must have told him about the king's attachment to Bedouin custom; Abdul-Aziz, for his part, limited himself to stating the Arabs' official position as defined by the newly created Arab League. Roosevelt, after bringing up the terrible fate of the Jews of Central Europe, explained that he considered it his responsibility to find a way of rehabilitating the survivors, and asked the king for suggestions. Ambassador William Eddy reports the comical dialogue that ensued:

Ibn Saud's reply was prompt and laconic: 'Give them and their descendants the choicest lands and homes of the Germans who had oppressed
them.'

F.D.R. replied that the Jewish survivors have a sentimental desire to
settle in Palestine and, quite understandably, would dread remaining in
Germany where they might suffer again.

The King said that he had no doubt the Jews have good reason not to
trust the Germans, but surely the Allies will destroy Nazi power forever
and in their victory will be strong enough to protect Nazi victims.[98]

Roosevelt was lying – pretending not to know that the vast majority of the
Jewish survivors would gladly have given up their 'sentimental desire to settle
in Palestine' in exchange for the chance to settle in the United States. The
president repeatedly returned to the attack while Ibn Saud began to lose his
patience. Yet he could not risk retorting, as Mussolini had done not long
before, that if the American president was so deeply concerned about the
survivors' fate, he had only to offer them the hospitality of his own country.
'The King's final remark on the subject was to the effect that it is Arab
custom to distribute survivors and victims of battle among the victorious
tribes in accordance with their number and their supplies of food and water.
In the Allied camp there are fifty countries, among whom Palestine is small,
land-poor and has already been assigned more than its quota of European
refugees.'[99]

Although the German–Saudi rapprochement was short-lived, two great
friends of the monarchy who remained its friends to the end of their days
went down the road with the Axis powers all the way to their defeat – and
their guilt was greater than that of those whom these regimes had fascinated
from a distance. Living in Europe, Shakib Arslan cannot be exonerated on
grounds of ignorance, as Stalinists who lived outside the USSR can be.
Amin al-Husseini's criminal complicity was greater still, because his active
collaboration with the Axis powers went much further than that of any of
their ranking Arab supporters, Gaylāni not excluded. Gaylāni considered
himself the leader of an Iraqi government in exile that was primarily caught
up in a conflict with Britain; he chose, as he saw it, between two imperialist
states that were both Iraq's enemies, throwing in his lot with 'the lesser
evil'. Husseini was a megalomaniac who presented himself as the leader of
the whole Islamic world, locked in struggle with the English but, first and
foremost, with 'the Jews'. In his years in Europe, he entered into the Nazis'
criminal delirium about 'the Jews', as it burgeoned into the greatest of all
crimes against humanity. There can be no reducing the monstrousness of

that crime and by equating Zionists with Nazis one makes no distinction between colonialist usurpation of a territory and the racist extermination of whole populations.

When 'my enemy's enemy' is much worse than 'my enemy' from the standpoint of humanity as a whole, there can be no striking a pact, no matter what the pretext. This is a fundamental humanist precept. Montesquieu put it admirably: 'If I knew [there was] something useful to my country, but prejudicial to Europe, or useful to Europe and prejudicial to the human race, I would regard it as criminal.'[100]

Amin al-Husseini: The Grand Mufti

Muhammad Amin al-Husseini stands near the top of the contemporary demonology's hit parade. One consequence is that the number of books about him – to say nothing of those in which he figures somewhere – is altogether disproportionate to his historical importance. What is more, not a single one of these books commands a scholarly consensus. Let us look at the actual course both of his career and of his reputation.[101]

Husseini completes the quartet of the leading personalities of reactionary Arab Pan-Islamism in the 1930s and 1940s, but he was a generation younger than Rashid Rida, King Abdul-Aziz and Shakib Arslan. After finishing school in 1912, he moved to Cairo, where he studied for two years with Rashid Rida. In 1914 the war forced him to break off his studies. He then moved to Istanbul, where he received a military education, after which he served as an officer in the Ottoman Army until 1916. Husseini never again took up his Islamic studies. His incomplete education, along with his temperament, explains why he never became a doctrinaire adherent of his teacher Rashid Rida's fundamentalist Pan-Islamism, even if he was later elevated to the rank of a religious dignitary. Until Rida's death, Husseini accepted his counsel on doctrinal questions; thus, when Rida issued a fatwa in 1933 forbidding the sale of land to Jews in Palestine, Husseini and the Palestinian ulemas issued a similar fatwa the following year. When political interests required that he violate Hanbali-like orthodoxy, at the risk of offending the Wahhabis, Husseini did not hesitate. His cooperation with Shiites is one example; his 1936 fatwa recognizing Syria's Alawites as Muslims is another.

In 1921, the mandatory authorities appointed the young Husseini Mufti of Jerusalem (*Mufti al-Diyār al-Qudsiyya*), a post they had begun calling Grand Mufti (*al-Mufti al-Akbar*) during the tenure of Husseini's predecessor in order to emphasise that he outranked the country's other muftis.[102] With colonialist presumption, they had arrogated to themselves the final say on appointments of Muslim religious dignitaries, which under the Ottoman Empire-Caliphate had been the prerogative of the *Shaykh al-Islām*. Husseini was also named head of the Islamic Supreme Council, created by the mandatory authorities late that same year, reinforcing his pre-eminence over Palestine's ulemas.

Barely twenty-six, lacking the requisite religious education (muftis were expected to be well-versed sharia scholars, since the supreme responsibility of issuing fatwas fell to them), convicted in absentia to ten years in prison by the mandatory authorities for his role in the 1920 riots and then granted amnesty, Husseini was not even one of the three leading candidates, elected by the representatives of Palestinian Islam, from whom, according to the usual Ottoman procedure, the mufti was supposed to be chosen. His only qualification was that he belonged to a leading Palestinian family and was the late mufti's brother. By an irony of history, the young Husseini owed his appointment to the very Zionist British High Commissioner for Palestine, Herbert Samuel, who had been one of the architects of the 1917 Balfour Declaration. As if to point the paradox, Husseini's clan had waged a smear campaign against his rival, suggesting that he had sold out to the Zionists.[103]

In retrospect, to be sure, it appears that Samuel did the Zionist movement an inestimable service. At a time when what the Palestinians needed was a unifier, they were given a sower of discord, the first of an unbroken series of calamitous leaders who have led the Palestinian national movement from defeat to defeat down to our own day. This translates in the fact that each new leader has had a low opinion of his predecessor.

In his memoirs, Ahmad Shuqayri (al-Shuqayri) – who would be named to head the Palestine Liberation Organization (PLO) when it was created in 1964 – mentions the 1934 death of Mūsa Kāzim al-Husseini, the former mayor of Jerusalem and the first true leader of the Palestinian national movement under British domination, the last Palestinian leader to command the support of all Palestinians. In this, he differed sharply from the Mufti: 'People wept a lot over Mūsa Kāzim', Shuqayri writes, only to add at once, 'whereas Hajj Amin made a lot of people weep.'[104] Mūsa Kāzim al-Husseini, the father of the Palestinian leader 'Abdul-Qādir al-Husseini, was one of several leading members of the Mufti's own clan whom he had alienated.

In his early career Muhammad Amin al-Husseini was not an extremist though.[105] A member of the upper circle of Palestinian dignitaries, he had long sought an understanding with the British colonial administration, on the advice of the Saudi king, Abdul-Aziz, whom he first met at the 1926 Islamic conference in Mecca. They had in common both Pan-Islamism and rivalry with the Hashemites, especially with Emir Abdullah of Transjordan, the future king of Jordan. Husseini was, however, like the immense majority of Palestinian Arabs, radically opposed to the Zionist colonization of Palestine.

In 1931, Husseini, in collaboration with the Indian Shaukat Ali, organized a General Islamic Conference in Jerusalem that considerably enhanced his personal prestige.[106] Like the Saudi monarch in 1926, he asked Rashid Rida to write a preparatory text and help put together the list of participants. Rida later expressed reservations about the way the conference had been organized, probably to placate his irritated Saudi friends, who did not take part;[107] he lamented the way his 'friend and disciple', the Mufti, frustrated both his attempt to bring Muslims together – including the Egyptian government and Al-Azhar, Sunni Islam's main religious educational institution, both of which boycotted the conference – and his effort to unite the Palestinians, notably the Husseinis and their political rivals, the Khalidis and Nashashibis, whom the Mufti regularly accused of selling out to the Zionists.

Though the Jerusalem conference was the Mufti's hour of glory, it was followed by the emergence of secular pro-independence and Arab nationalist groups in the country who openly challenged the Mufti's leadership of the national struggle but never succeeded in wresting his position of pre-eminence from him. Bayān Nuwayhid al-Hūt has shown how 'the Arab political movement in Palestine, overall, struck down a new path, dispensing with the participation of the religious leaders as a necessary, important element of its own leadership'. Thus, she adds, 'the political parties operating openly in the 1930s were in no sense constructed on a religious basis and no longer accorded political priority to Hajj Amin's religious rank; from this point on, they addressed him exclusively as a politician'.[108]

One of them was the Party of Arab Independence (Hizb al-Istiqlāl al-'Arabi), which came into being – or, rather, was resurrected – after a meeting of Arab nationalists and pro-independence activists convened on the periphery of the 1931 Islamic conference. Its foundation was officially proclaimed on 2 August 1932 in a declaration that denounced 'narrow-minded personal and familial politics', a barely veiled allusion to Amin al-Husseini's leadership.[109] The Istiqlal Party, as it was widely called, advocated unification of the Arab countries, initially under the lead of King Faisal of Iraq (who died in 1933). The conflict between the Istiqlal and the Mufti was bitter from the start; the party attacked the Mufti for his conciliatory attitude towards the mandatory authority and also for his nepotism.[110]

The British government was indeed generous to the Supreme Islamic

Council presided over by the Mufti. In 1932 and 1934, it signed two accords with him that guaranteed the Council substantial financial support.[111] Kimmerling and Migdal stress the fact that in the same period the Mufti, unlike the Istiqlal, strove to channel the anger of Palestinian Arabs toward the Jews rather than the British.[112] The Istiqlal played an important part in radicalizing mass protest, but it was soon thrown into disarray and then dealt a severe blow by British repression of the Palestinian national movement: nine of its eleven leaders were imprisoned and four were deported.[113] The Mufti's partisans, for their part, proclaimed the creation of the 'Palestinian Arab Party' in 1935. A majority party, it too was secular; in fact, four of the sixteen members of its leadership body were Christians.[114]

'Izz-ul-Dīn al-Qassām

Another major event helped radicalise the Palestinian struggle in this period: the creation of a secret society whose leader, Sheikh 'Izz-ul-Dīn al-Qassām, a Muslim preacher from Syria, launched a guerrilla war in 1935 with twelve of his comrades.[115] Qassām studied theology at Cairo's University of Al-Azhar from 1896 to 1904, when the institution was under Muhammad Abduh's influence. He probably knew Rashid Rida. But he did not owe his later ideas to either Rida or Abduh. Although his father was a Sufi and he himself shared the mystic dimension of the Sufis' faith, Qassām developed a severely puritan, ascetic conception of Islam that fully justifies his reputation as a Wahhabi. The sheikh first exhibited his religious intransigence in his own birthplace of Jableh (Jebla), a Sunni village on the Syrian coast. Abdullah Schleifer recounts his singular, sinister way of demonstrating the idea that the failure to pray was tantamount to death: '[Qassām] encouraged his disciples to grab a villager who did not pray, put him in a coffin, and carry him around Jebla.'[116]* This enforcement of religious practice reached such a point, Schleifer comments, that 'the women would go out into the market unveiled on Friday at noon, certain they would encounter no man on the streets, since every male in Jebla was at prayer.'[118]

Qassām formed a militia in his village, educating it in conformity with his religious standards. He did not, however, join the anti-Ottoman struggle for independence, probably for the same Pan-Islamist reason motivating Shakib Arslan. His first military exploits targeted Alawites, the majority

---

* Schleifer goes on: 'The incident also illustrates how al-Qassām's insistence on piety was accompanied by good humour.' This comment is so incongruous that it might seem to be intended ironically; its author is, however, altogether serious.[117]

in his Syrian province of Latakia. Thereafter, he led armed actions against the French. Forced into exile in Haifa in 1921, Qassām allied himself in the ideological struggle with another Syrian exile, the Salafi Sheikh Kāmil al-Qassāb, a Damascene friend of Rida, Arslan and Husseini. He espoused the fundamentalist Wahhabi objective of creating an Islamic state with a constitution based on the Koran.[119]

Much more radical than Husseini, by virtue of both his religious fanaticism and his xenophobic populism – a difference heightened by the contrasting social origins of the aristocratic mufti and the plebeian sheikh – Qassām set about creating a clandestine armed organization as early as 1925. The gradual shift in the nature of his activities is one indication of the radicalization of the Palestinian struggle in general and its Islamic component in particular, beginning with the 1929 events connected with Jerusalem's Western/Al-Burāq Wall. From 1929 on, Qassām's secret organization carried out armed actions for several years without being exposed. On the other hand, the sheikh openly preached jihad, joining the Istiqlal in pressuring Husseini even while occasionally also cooperating with the Mufti's partisans. Qassām finally opted for insurrection in November 1935: according to Muhsin Sālih,[120] he made this decision only after an illegal arms shipment to the Zionist movement was discovered in the port of Jaffa,[121] creating a sensation among the Arab population.

'Izz-ul-Dīn al-Qassām was, in many respects, a precursor of today's Jihadists, a man for whom death as a *shahīd*, a martyr of Islam, represented the supreme consecration.[122] He chose death over surrender at the end of a battle with colonial troops on 20 November 1935 that, at 13 against 400, he had no chance of winning. His death made him a national hero, thus fulfilling his lifelong faith in the power of example. The homage the Hamas movement paid him more than half a century later, naming both its armed branch (specializing in suicide operations) and its rockets after him, was an appropriate tribute: like Qassām, these actions are symptomatic of both the exasperation of the Palestinians and the ineffectuality of the means some of them resort to.

Qassām was replaced by Sheikh Farhān al-Sa'di, who commanded the armed operation that the group carried out on 15 April 1936,[123] triggering a chain of events that culminated in the 1936 Palestinian uprising. According to Bayān Nuwayhid al-Hūt, the operation had been intended to sabotage the political negotiations being conducted by the dominant Palestinian leadership around the Mufti and thus to touch off an armed confrontation.[124] Akram Zu'aytir provides a detailed description of the 15 April event; it speaks volumes about the Qassāmists' fanaticism and political benightedness, as well as the anti-Semitic affinities between Wahhabi-type fundamentalism and Nazism.

It was 8.30 p.m. Cars were being stopped at a barrier made of barrels on a mountain road in the Nablus region. The barrier was under the surveillance of three armed men: one kept an eye on the road, another held the passengers of stopped vehicles in his gun sights, and the third relieved them of their cash. Then they asked their victims if there were Englishmen or Jews among them. The driver of a truck and his passenger, both Jews, were shot on the spot. Also present was a man who 'proved to the band that he was a German, a Hitlerite, and a Christian, swearing on Hitler's honour that he was telling the truth. The three men released him ... "for Hitler's sake" ... with thirty-five pounds sterling in his pockets.'[125]

Two days later, Zionist Revisionists killed two Arabs. Arab passers-by were also attacked at the funeral of one of the 15 April victims.[126] The fateful spiral of violence had been set in motion. In the following years, the Qassāmists played a major role in the operational command of the Palestinian revolt,[127] distinguishing themselves in particular by their frequent executions of Palestinian Arabs accused of collaboration with the British or the Jews. They were careful to obtain a fatwa from an ulema close to their movement for each execution.[128] Kimmerling and Migdal underscore, in this connection, the anti-Christian bent of the Qassāmists' exhortations and violent acts.[129]

Amin al-Husseini and the 1936–1939 Arab Revolt in Palestine

Although the Istiqlal was a party in decline, some of its members, beginning with Akram Zuʻaytir, played a decisive role in the formation of the 'national committees' that sprang up from April 1936 onwards to urge the Arab Palestinian population to strike. What soon became a general strike rapidly escaped the control of the existing parties and leaders. As with all mass movements, those taking part naturally had sharply diverging levels of political education, a good many had none at all, a circumstance for which Palestinian leaders bore the blame. Zuʻaytir describes an incident that illustrates well these woeful shortcomings. It took place in Tulkarm during a street demonstration. 'A car drove by; one of the passengers, wearing a Western-style hat, was attacked by the demonstrators. He shouted "Heil Hitler!" in the direction of the demonstrators and raised his arm in the Nazi salute, then hoisted the Nazi flag over his car, while the crowd cheered him.'[130]

First there are the ignominy of applauding Nazism (which in 1936 was anti-Semitic without being anti-Zionist) and the stupidity of failing to perceive that anti-Semitism is, in general, Zionism's most powerful 'propelling force'. Then there is ignorance as to the difference between Jews and Zionists and between the varying factions of the Zionist movement – distinctions crucial to the Palestinian struggle itself, which could and should have sought an alliance with the Jews of the Yishuv opposed to a 'Jewish state'.[131] Above all the incident bears witness to the Palestinian leaders' silence about two important facts that would have inclined the demonstrators in Tulkarm, had they understood them, to rough up the Nazi rather than cheer him: first, the collusion of Nazis and Zionists in organizing the immigration of German Jews to Palestine; second, the Nazis' scorn for all colonised peoples, Arabs included.

No Arab capable of reading a European language and interested in finding out the truth about Nazism could have ignored the content of *Mein Kampf*:

> The hopes of an epic rising in Egypt [are] chimerical. The 'Holy War' ... would soon be brought to an end under the fusillade from a few companies of British machine-guns and a hail of British bombs.
>
>   A coalition of cripples cannot attack a powerful State which is determined, if necessary, to shed the last drop of its blood to maintain its existence. To me, as a nationalist who appreciates the worth of the racial basis of humanity, I must recognize the racial inferiority of the so-called 'Oppressed Nations,' and that is enough to prevent me from linking the destiny of my people with the destiny of those inferior races.[132]

The Arab population of Palestine would doubtless have detested Hitler had it known the real content of his doctrine. But it was not informed by those who wielded the greatest influence, the Mufti above all. On the contrary: its leaders concealed the reality of the matter, presenting Nazi Germany as an ally long before Germany saw these leaders in the same light. Was this attitude the result of stupidity or criminal calculation? The German Consul General in Jerusalem, the pro-Zionist Heinrich Wolff, was convinced that the explanation lay in the Palestinian leaders' stupidity:

> Palestinian Arab leaders lost little time in making known their positive assessment of events in Germany in 1933 ... The Mufti informed Wolff that Muslims in Palestine and elsewhere were enthusiastic about the new regime in Germany and looked forward to the spread of Fascism throughout the region. Wolff also relayed the Mufti's support for the aims

of Nazi Jewish policy, particularly the anti-Jewish boycott in Germany, and a pledge of similar efforts against the Jews throughout the Islamic world. [The Mufti and other sheikhs asked] only that German Jews not be sent to Palestine. Thus, there seems to have been some awareness among Arabs in Palestine that Germany might in fact be a source of their problems ... Nevertheless, Wolff concluded in his annual report for the year 1933 that the Arabs were too politically naive to recognize and fully accept the link between German Jewish policy and their problems in Palestine.[133]

The Mufti certainly knew about the existence of the Haavara agreement between the Zionist movement and Nazi Germany by October 1933, since his political journal, *Al-Jāmi'a al-'Arabiyya*, had denounced it on 10 October.* On 15 July 1935, *Al-Jāmi'a al-'Arabiyya* even denounced 'Germany's concrete participation in the Judaization of Palestine'.[135]

While Wolff saw nothing but naïveté in the Mufti's attitude, the Mufti was, in fact, Machiavellian rather than ingenuous. Consideration of his positions as a whole leads to a different interpretation of his attitude towards the Nazi regime and explains why leaders including Rashid Rida, Shakib Arslan, the Qassāmists and Amin al-Husseini himself closed their eyes to the direct relationship between Nazism and Zionism. Indeed, this interpretation even explains their favourable attitude towards Hitler's Germany, the ideological incompatibility between Pan-Islamism and National Socialism notwithstanding. The explanation lies in the hatred for the Jews that obsessed these two distinct worldviews, one religious and the other racial, both of which essentialized the enemy. Hostility towards Britain did not yet provide the common ground between Pan-Islamism and Nazism that it would a few years later. In 1933, Husseini betrayed no hint of hatred for the British, who were, at the time, showing him special generosity. For that matter, Germany itself was not then hostile to Britain.

Overwhelmed by the radicalization of the Palestinian people's struggle in 1936, the dominant Palestinian parties formed the Higher Arab Committee

---

* 'According to the latest news reports, the Zionist association and the German government have reached an agreement for the purpose of organizing the emigration of those German Jews who wish to leave for Palestine. This agreement has led to the breakdown of the campaign against Germany carried out by the Jews of the whole world, since Zionist Jews now see that their interests require that they keep quiet and promote German exports to Palestine rather than boycotting them after concluding this agreement with the German government, which has brought them major advantages ... In the wake of this agreement, then, it is no longer in the Zionists' interests to boycott German products in Palestine, since that would cost them the immigrants' capital.'[134]

(HAC), which brought both partisans and adversaries of the Mufti together under his leadership. Yehoshua Porath has described the turn that led the Mufti and his Supreme Islamic Council to invest the Arab revolt with a religious character beginning in June 1936, on the pretext that the motivation of the Jews in Palestine was first and foremost religious,[136] in conformity with Rida's interpretation. However, the HAC continued to negotiate with London and its representatives behind the back of the masses. It wanted to put a stop to their uprising, as London was urging it to do, but lacked the courage to call for a halt in the absence of concessions from the mandatory power. Thus it 'began to contact the rulers of Iraq and Saudi Arabia and suggested that they should publish an appeal to the Palestine Arabs to call off the strike and the disorder. The HAC drafted the text of an appeal which stressed the national ties of the Arab rulers to Palestine and which implicitly promised the fulfillment of the Palestinian Arabs' demands.'[137] *

The strike came to an immediate end, to the dismay of the radical nationalists of the Istiqlal movement. Zu'aytir, who had played a pivotal role in organizing the struggle, was shocked by his compatriots' reaction to the news of the Arab monarchs' appeal. 'The tears sprang to my eyes,' he writes. 'I felt pity for my people! I was saddened by these suddenly cheerful men who, delighted by the news, were trembling with joy! This nation had made a great effort, measured in human lives and material goods. It had accomplished miracles. It had astounded the world with its fervent revolt and extraordinary strike. But, to see it carried away by joy and gaiety, one might have thought that it had realized its aspirations!'[138] He concluded that struggles without resolute leadership are doomed to failure.

Ahmad Shuqayri, who was close to the Istiqlal, came to the same conclusion. He perceived the events as a 'struggle between two generations: that of the First World War, which had followed the Allies, putting faith in their sincerity and counting on them to keep their promises, and ours, the younger generation, victims of the Allies' promises, trickery, and deceitfulness, first and foremost Britain's. The result of the struggle was that the first generation prevailed over the second; Britain and its friends were thus able to bring the strike and revolt to an end.'[139]

Before long, however, the situation deteriorated again. On 7 July 1937, the British commission chaired by Lord Peel – with whom the Mufti and the HAC had finally met, after King Abdul-Aziz and his Hashemite counterparts had

---

*   The negotiations with Ibn Saud were conducted thanks to the mediation of the Salafi Sheikh Kāmil al-Qassāb, with whom 'Izz-ul-Dīn al-Qassām had collaborated earlier.

admonished them for their boycott – published its famous recommendations, including the proposal that Palestine be partitioned between the Zionists and King Abdullah of Transjordan. The Jewish state was generously accorded nearly three-quarters of the country's coastal zone as well as the North and Galilee. (The Zionists were still unsatisfied, although they approved the plan for tactical reasons.) Arab opposition, in both Palestine and elsewhere, was virtually unanimous. Even Rāghib al-Nashāshībi, the leader of the opposition to the Mufti and a friend of both the British and Abdullah, expressed his opposition, leading to a deterioration of his relations with the king.[140]

The Peel Commission's partition plan, although it was disavowed by the British government, confirmed the British ruling elite's inclination to grant the Zionists a 'Jewish state' in Palestine. This development triggered a new radicalization of the Arab struggle against the mandatory government, as well as opposition to the project on the part of Hitler's Germany. The Reich thus abandoned the reserve it had hitherto maintained so as not to irritate London, even while continuing to encourage Jewish emigration to Palestine. Such emigration would help make Germany *judenrein* (literally, 'clean of Jews'); a Jewish state, in contrast, would provide 'the Jews' with access to international institutions.[141] Germany's opposition to the partition of Palestine was the real point of departure for the Mufti's collaboration with Berlin. On 16 July, Husseini went to see the new German Consul General in Jerusalem, Hans Döhle, in order to assure him of his sympathy for Nazi Germany and inform him of his decision to dispatch a personal envoy to Berlin to maintain secret contact with the authorities of the Reich.[142]

The Palestinian Arabs had been preparing to resume hostilities ever since the interruption of their uprising in 1936 – the more actively since the Zionists, too, had been gearing up for a new round in the conflict.[143] It was, however, London's repressive measures that were mainly responsible for the new wave of revolt. The British authorities blamed the anti-British agitation on the Mufti, making him their 'scapegoat', as a historian of the period has clearly perceived.[144] They even attempted – unsuccessfully – to arrest him on 17 July, the day after he paid his visit to the German Consul General. The Mufti found sanctuary in the Al-Aqsa Mosque, where he remained sequestered under British siege for three straight months – an episode similar to Ariel Sharon's sequestration of Yasser Arafat in the 'Muqāt'a' in Ramallah between 2002 and 2004. The mandatory authority thus succeeded only in reinforcing Husseini's stature as a leader, at his rivals' expense.

In reaction to a new upsurge of violence, the mandatory authority went so far as to ban the HAC on 1 October, arresting those of its members whom it managed to take by surprise and deporting them to the Seychelles Islands. On 3 October, the Mufti, still in his sanctuary, issued a declaration calling for an end to the strike. On 12 October, he succeeded in fleeing in disguise, going first into Arab and later into European exile. 'This flight decreased Amīn al-Husayni's influence inside and outside Palestine since it was regarded as an act of cowardice,' remarks Yehoshua Porath, who also points out that it was nevertheless followed by a resumption of large-scale violence.[145] London cast oil on the flames by intensifying its increasingly brutal and bloody repression. The period saw more than 3,000 deaths, 146 executions by hanging and 50,000 arrests leading to 2,000 stiff prison sentences; 5,000 homes and businesses were demolished and long curfews were imposed (running to 140 days in Safed).[146]*

The Mufti, in exile first in Lebanon and then in Iraq, was at pains to restore his reputation and reassert his leadership. He had by and large played a moderating role for as long as he remained in the country; now that he found himself outside it, he set out on a campaign of nationalist one-upmanship, becoming as intransigent as the Qassāmists. In the process, he dragged the Palestinian national movement into its most serious historical error – which contrary to an often expressed opinion did not consist in rejecting the partition plans. Acceptance of such plans would have been a dishonourable surrender. What people could allow a minority of settlers and refugees who had immigrated to its country, most of them within the past few years, to establish their own state on part of its territory?

The major historical error of the Palestinian national movement was rather its rejection of the British White Paper of 17 May 1939, after a comfortable majority of Parliament in London had approved it. This new document rejected the idea of partitioning Palestine and creating a separate Jewish state there; the British government declared itself in favour of limiting Jewish immigration to Palestine to 75,000 annually for the next five years and of creating an independent Palestinian state within a decade, to be governed jointly, on a proportional basis, by Arabs and Jews. The White Paper aroused vehement opposition from the Zionist movement, for perfectly understandable reasons: the Zionists mobilized all their means and allies to

---

*   Half a century later, the Israeli state, confronted with the Intifada, would reproduce this gamut of repressive measures in the West Bank and Gaza, utilizing the legislative arsenal of the mandate, with one difference: condemnations to death by hanging, which had become impossible as a result of the 1954 abolition of the death penalty in Israel (except for crimes against humanity), gave way to 'extrajudicial executions' or 'targeted killing'.

counter it and, from this point on, radicalized their operations against the mandatory authority in Palestine.

Much less understandable was the rejection of the White Paper by the HAC, speaking in the name of the Palestinian Arab national movement. Though it may well have reflected the profound mistrust of the majority of the Arabs of Palestine for the mandatory authority, it was due, above all, to Husseini. Bayān Nuwayhid al-Hūt cites accounts by the participants to show that 'a majority of the members of the Higher Arab Committee had approved the White Paper after discussing it in detail at a special meeting held in Qurnāyil (the Mufti's place of residence in Lebanon), but the Mufti rejected it because of the ambiguity of certain of its clauses'.[147] The dean of the Istiqlal Party, 'Awni 'Abdul-Hādi, himself a member of the HAC, wrote in his notebooks: 'I must say that I was among those who proposed that we approve the White Paper, because I thought it impossible that the British government go any further to accommodate the Arabs. In politics, the task is to distinguish what is possible from what is not; the policy that consists in taking what one can, even while demanding more, is preferable to sterile obstinacy.'[148]

Even the very nationalistic Akram Zu'aytir, in exile in Baghdad, considered the White Paper 'the most important result of our great revolt, which lasted three years',[149] although he feared that the British government might not keep its new promises. After hesitating for some time, he rallied to the HAC's official position, in the belief that it might, paradoxically, prove a means of constraining London not to break its pledge. Formed at the beginning of the second phase of the revolt, the 'Central Committee of the Jihad', on which Zu'aytir sat, was in close communication with the Mufti and the commanders in the interior of the country;[150] it categorically rejected the White Paper. Husseini 'used the rebels' opposition as his main argument during the HAC's deliberations', Porath explains, adding that 'the rebel pressure seems to have exactly suited Amīn al-Husayni's personal motives'.[151] The most powerful of these motives, according to Porath, was that London maintained the Mufti's banishment, thus ruling out the possibility that he might participate in the new process as the Palestinians' leader.

The evolution of the Mufti's attitude confirms Philip Mattar's critique of 'the ahistorical assumption by most authors that the Mufti's behavior and actions were static throughout his political career'.[152] There were, Mattar argues, 'two distinct phases': the 'Palestine phase', during which he behaved like a traditional leader, a scion of a leading Palestinian family that was conservative by virtue of its social position and collaborated with the established authorities; and the 'exile phase', during which he displayed intransigence and collaborated with the Axis powers. This observation holds even if, as we have seen, there is greater continuity in the Mufti's positions towards the Axis than Mattar implies. That said, Mattar provides a deft summary description of the Mufti's leadership:

> During the first period, even though he understood the ominous threat of Zionism to Palestinian national existence, the Mufti cooperated with the British mandatory government of Palestine and rejected methods of national self-defense at a time when such methods may have helped his cause ... The Mufti was largely passive, and the Yishuv experienced two crucial decades of growth, increasing from 50,000 in 1917 to 384,000 in 1936.
>
> After the Arab Revolt was put down by the British, the Palestinians were considerably weakened. But instead of prudently recognizing this reality ... he shifted to a policy of active and futile opposition and rejection ... In short, moderation during the Palestine phase and rejection during the exile phase contributed to the ultimate defeat of the Palestinians.[153] *

Amin al-Husseini's Exile and Collaboration with Rome and Berlin

The failure of the 1941 Iraqi adventure reinforced Amin al-Husseini's image as a grand organizer of defeats. On 9 May 1941, the Mufti sounded a call for jihad against the English over Iraqi radio, in terms that plainly betrayed both his self-infatuation and his illusions about the extent of his moral authority over the Muslim world: 'I invite all my Muslim brothers of the whole world to the Jihad in the way of God, for the defence of Islam and its territory against its enemy. O Faithful, obey and respond to this call.'[156] Up to then, he had served as the Gaylāni government's *éminence grise*.[157]

There is no better indication of the limits of his religious influence than the feeble reaction to his call. Of course, some Arabs – Syrians in particular – rallied to the Iraqi side against the British. But they were mostly secular

---

* For an appraisal of the Mufti's record from a 'Jihadist' standpoint, see the 1988 work by Muhsin Sālih. Sālih laments the absence of an 'Islamic methodology based on the Jihadist movement'; had such a methodology been applied, in his view, the Mufti would have resigned his official functions in order to devote himself to the armed struggle, and would have adopted a more Islamic orientation than the one created by his ambition to become the leader of all Palestinians, whatever their religious affiliation.[154] Sālih thus seems to deplore the fact that Amin al-Husseini energetically opposed the exactions to which the Qassāmists subjected the Christians and Druze.[155]

nationalists who would have joined the struggle even if the Mufti had never existed. In the space of ten years, Husseini had plummeted from the peak of his prestige at the 1931 Jerusalem Islamic Conference to disgrace in the eyes of the intellectual elite as a result of his political zigzagging. The Iraqi debacle forced him further into exile; to the end of the war, he basically divided his time between Berlin and Rome (at their considerable expense).

He became his two hosts' Arab/Muslim collaborator par excellence, even if his megalomania and taste for intrigue led to friction with both them and other exiled Arab leaders. He contributed heavily to radio propaganda broadcasts to the Muslim world. The Germans and Italians also called on his services when they attempted to create Arab units from volunteers already living in Europe and Arab prisoners-of-war who had served in the Allied armies.

The meagre results say a great deal about both the Arabs' support for Nazism and the Mufti's influence. In May 1942, when a German victory still seemed very possible, the Wehrmacht's Arab unit counted a mere 130 men. When the Italians tried to organize an Arab Legion with its own flag and commanders by recruiting volunteers from Arab prisoners-of-war turned over to them by the Germans, the result was an even greater fiasco. Berlin had transferred some 250 POWs to Rome, captured from the 9,000 Palestinians serving with the British forces.[158] Only eighteen agreed to serve in the Legion, and of these only eight ultimately remained; 'The main force operating here', Hirszowicz writes, 'was the strong aversion the Arabs felt for Italy, because of her well-known colonisation plans.'[159] That explanation may be too hasty, given that these Palestinian troops had fought for Britain, the colonial oppressor in their own country. In any case they were unmoved by the exhortations of the 'Grand Mufti of Palestine' to rally to fascist Italy's struggle against 'the English and the Jews'.

Overall, according to the calculations of the American military historian Antonio Muñoz, 6,300 soldiers from Arab countries served in various German military organizations. Of these 1,300 came from Palestine, Syria and Iraq, the rest from the countries of Northern Africa, from Egypt to Morocco.[160] Muñoz also reports that just as many soldiers from Arab countries served in the forces of France's Vichy regime.[161] A great many more Arabs and Berbers fought in the Allied ranks. They ranged (proceeding from East to West) from the aforementioned 9,000 Palestinians enlisted in the British army to the hundreds of thousands of Maghrebis mobilized by the French forces in

1939–40 and, after the 1942 Allied landing in North Africa, by the Free French forces – impressive numbers that colonial ingratitude chose to forget.*

The fate of the hundreds of Arab prisoners interned in the Nazi concentration camps, incidentally, is even less widely known. According to an estimate by Gerhard Höpp, whose untimely death prevented him from completing his research on these 'forgotten victims' of Nazism, there were 1,500 of them.[163] Of the 450 individuals identified by Höpp, it proved possible to establish that 248 were natives of Algeria, 27, of Morocco, 22, of Tunisia, and a dozen of the Middle East (four of them Palestinian).[164] Some were simply victims of Nazi racism; others were political prisoners, left-wing resistance fighters arrested on 'Nacht-und-Nebel' orders.[165] Many of these men died in the concentration camps, such as Mohamed Bouayad, who was born in Rabat, Morocco, on 13 March 1904 and interned on 25 April 1944. Reproduced in facsimile by Höpp, Bouayad's prisoner's identity card, probably filled out by a French-speaking Red Cross worker when a registry of the prisoners was drawn up after the liberation of the camp, bears the mention 'Dcd [an abbreviation for décédé, 'deceased'], 24-4-45 Mauthausen (chambre à gaz).'[166] Thus Bouayad was murdered a mere eleven days before the Mauthausen camp was liberated on 5 May 1945.

To return to the Mufti: his appeals to the Arabs of the Middle East or

---

* Belkacem Recham gives a synthetic account of Maghrebi contributors to the Allied war effort. 'The mobilization in Northern Africa made it possible to form, from September 1939 to June 1940, fourteen fighting divisions numbering 340,000 troops; they consisted of officers who were almost all Europeans and enlisted men who were, in their majority, natives of the region. By 10 May 1940, when the German offensive was launched, eight of these divisions had been stationed on the French front ... In the June 1940 calamity suffered by the French army, more than 85,000 men were killed, 5,400 of them North Africans; another 1,800,000 were taken prisoner, including, according to the Governor General of Algeria, Yves Chatel, 90,000 Muslims, 60,000 Algerians, 18,000 Moroccans, and 12,000 Tunisians. These men were interned in Frontstalags (prisoner-of-war camps located in France) scattered throughout the occupied zone; they were accompanied by a handful of French officers in supervisory roles ... According to the figure most often cited, 233,000 Muslims from the Maghreb were serving in the French army in 1944. Jacques Frémeaux estimates that, from 1943 to 1945, the forces provided by the three countries of North Africa totalled between 200,000 and 250,000 men, 120,000 to 150,000 of them from Algeria alone.
  Evaluations of the casualties suffered by the French army from the Tunisian campaign to the German surrender on 8 May 1945 range from 97,000 to 110,000 killed, wounded, and missing in action. If we rely on the figures provided by the Historical Service of the French army (SHAT), then the army sustained a total of 97,715 casualties; 11,193 of those killed and 39,645 of those wounded, or 52% of the total, were Muslims.'[162]

North Africa produced no tangible effects; his final exhortations found the same pitifully feeble echo as the declarations of a 'Thousand Year Reich' already in its death agony after fewer than twelve years of existence. A call broadcast by the Mufti on 17 December 1944 may serve as an example. It culminated in this vain exhortation: 'I call on all Muslims and on all Arabs in the world to carry out their duty toward their nation and countries by struggling together with these upright friends against the tyrannical common foe until the final triumph, which none can doubt, since victory belongs to the god-fearing.'[167] We might also cite Husseini's multimedia appeal of 23 January 1945, complete with fliers, inciting the Arab soldiers among the Allied forces to desert: 'Arab soldiers, you should not be helping your enemies: turn against them, abandon their lines, and go over to the side of your German friends.'[168]

Nevertheless, the SS Handschar and Kama divisions, created in Bosnia in 1943 with almost exclusively Muslim recruits (together with a handful of Catholics native to the region), seem to indicate that the Mufti had greater influence among his co-religionists outside the Arab world. The photograph of Husseini reviewing a detachment of these troops is omnipresent in the copious literature demonizing the Mufti, which is often aimed not just at him but at all Muslims. The facts are not well known. The neo-conservative writer Stephen Schwartz has disinterred certain truths about these divisions that are too often glossed over:

> In Bosnia, the infamous Bosnian *Waffen SS* units played no role in the removal of Jews on their territory, which was carried out by Germans and Croats ... They were reluctant to participate in such actions, having enlisted in the *Waffen SS* on the mistaken belief that such service would resemble that of the Bosnian gendarmerie under the Habsburg empire. They were sent by the Germans to France for retraining. There they mutinied against their Nazi officers and attempted to join the French Partisans, the only known example of a *Waffen SS* rebellion. By 1944, most of them had joined the Yugoslav Partisans. In addition, the Bosnian Muslim clerics issued three declarations publicly denouncing Croat-Nazi collaboration-ist measures against Jews and Serbs: that of Sarajevo in October 1941, of Mostar in 1941, and of Banja Luka on November 12, 1941.[169]

The Nazis solicited the Mufti's help in countering the dissuasive effect of these fatwas. Husseini's primary motivation in this case was not anti-Semitic but, rather, Islamic and defensive; in his memoirs, he emphasizes that his goal in helping create the Handschar and Kama divisions was to enable Muslim

Bosnians to defend themselves against Mihailovic's Serbian Chetniks, who had liquidated some 200,000 of them.[170]* He was, however, lying in 1945–6 when he assured the authorities in France, where he went after leaving Germany, that he had had no hand in organizing Bosnian SS divisions against the Allies,[172] a fight that had nothing to do with self-defence. That said, the Handschar Division was known not for anti-Jewish atrocities but for anti-Serbian reprisals. Indeed, as a general rule, the Balkan Muslims were much more favourably disposed toward the Jews than were their Christian neighbours. That was also the case, Schwartz emphasizes, in Albania: 'while it is true that the Albanian *Waffen SS* Skanderbeg division turned some 210 Jews in Kosovo over to the Nazis, not one Jew was handed over in Albania itself, which was the only country [in continental Europe] to come out of the second world war with a larger Jewish population than it had at the beginning of the war.[173] (Albanian Muslims have been honoured as 'righteous Gentiles' at Yad Vashem in Israel.)

In his memoirs, the Mufti proudly takes credit for organizing the participation of '200,000' Muslims – Azeris, Bosnians, and others – to fight for the Axis, and for training imams in Dresden under the auspices of the *Waffen SS* to serve as their chaplains.[174] The Mufti's ambition, however, had been to provide a much more significant Arab contribution to the fascist states' war effort. He makes a great deal of the memoranda that he sent the German Foreign Minister in November 1942 and January 1943, proposing that the Axis powers 'liberate' the Arab countries of the Maghreb, defined as Morocco, Algeria and Tunisia – to the exclusion, of course, of Libya, which was under Italian domination† – and unite them in a single Maghrebi state

---

* What then happened offers an excellent demonstration of the inanity of concluding pacts with manifestly unjust forces in pursuit of just causes. Faced with the growing strength of Tito's Communist partisans, the Nazis allied themselves with the Chetniks and provided them with arms and ammunition; this allowed the Serbian troops to resume their persecution of the Bosnian Muslims. The Mufti, who acknowledges these facts in his memoirs, claims that he lodged a protest with the German military command, which, he assures us, proceeded to supply Mihailovic's men with the kind of defective ammunition that made their weapons unusable![171]

† Here is one more instance of the double-talk the Mufti used to try to justify himself after the fact. Aware of fascist Italy's terrible oppression of the Libyans, he explains in his memoirs that he repeatedly informed the 'Italian leaders' of his distress (there is no indication that he ever directly broached the subject with the Duce). He further claims that he raised the problem at a banquet in his honour organized by an official of the Italian Foreign Ministry, who assured him that Rome had been led astray by the English and French, who had reserved the best territories in the region for themselves, and that the Italians had found only 'bullets and sand' and the hatred

associated with the Axis by treaty. This state was then supposed to raise an army of 2,500,000 soldiers, or 10 per cent of the three countries' 25 million inhabitants, to fight alongside the Axis powers, while simultaneously depriving the Allied armies of their soldiers from the Maghreb, who would surely desert to the new force en masse.[176]

The real content of the Mufti's 18 November 1942 and 16 January 1943 memoranda – sent, respectively, to the German ambassador to Italy and the German foreign minister in Berlin – is less farfetched than those self-justifying memoirs suggest.[177] In fact, he promised the Nazi authorities 'only' half a million battle-tested soldiers from the Maghreb. Even this more modest promise must not have seemed credible to them, since the Mufti's plan was simply ignored. The diplomat Curt Prüfer was charged with answering him and met with him on several occasions. According to the Mufti's account, Prüfer declared that Germany was interested only in Europe and that its European allies would not accept the creation of a unified Maghrebi state, because they feared Islam more than Communism – haunted as they were by the prospect of a new Muslim invasion![178]

Amin al-Husseini and the Jewish Genocide

In addition to the indirect complicity in Nazi crimes that Husseini's collaboration with Hitler's Germany implies in and of itself, he was and still is accused of direct complicity in the Jewish genocide. When this charge is levelled in responsible fashion, it is based mainly on his anti-Semitic radio harangues on behalf of the Axis, and also on letters he wrote to the authorities in an attempt to block all Jewish immigration to Palestine when the 'Final Solution' was in full swing. Two other accusations are often made, although they have not been proved and probably never will be: that the Mufti had ties with Adolf Eichmann; and that he visited Auschwitz. Both are founded on highly dubious evidence given by a single person at the Nuremberg trials; and, at all events, they add nothing of a qualitative nature to the indictment against the Mufti.

Let us first examine the more complicated question of the Mufti's letters. In his memoirs, he discusses his 1944 efforts to dissuade Axis governments from allowing the emigration of Eastern European Jews to Palestine:

---

of the Muslims in Libya; Italy would rectify the situation after the war in a way that would satisfy the Arabs.[175] Since he was no fool, one can only conclude that the Mufti took his readers for idiots.

We combated this enterprise by writing to Ribbentrop, Himmler, and Hitler, and, thereafter, the governments of Italy, Hungary, Rumania, Bulgaria, Turkey, and other countries. We succeeded in foiling this initiative, a circumstance that led the Jews to make terrible accusations against me, in which they held me accountable for the liquidation of four hundred thousand Jews who were unable to emigrate to Palestine in this period. They added that I should be tried as a war criminal in Nuremberg.[179]

He discusses this question again later, at length, producing facsimiles of letters to Ribbentrop, Himmler and the Hungarian Foreign Minister, as well as some of the responses, adding:

In certain European countries, these memoranda had positive results that advanced the Palestinian cause, but they stirred up a storm of protest from the Zionists and led them in 1947 to lodge a complaint against me with the United Nations in which they claimed that hundreds of thousands of Jews were unable to emigrate to Palestine because of my memoranda, perishing as a result ...

In fact, when I sent these memoranda to the authorities in the German Reich and the aforementioned states, my intention was not to bring about the extirpation of the Jews, but, rather, to prevent a flood of aggressive Jewish immigration that sought to inundate Palestine and empty it of its native inhabitants, as in fact occurred later with the help of Great Britain and the United States of America.[180]

There can be no doubt that the Mufti's primary motivation was to block Jewish immigration to Palestine, an objective about which, as he never fails to note, Palestinian nationalists were unanimous.[181] However, its legitimacy varied enormously with the context. It was certainly legitimate when it was addressed as an appeal to the British mandatory authorities, especially when it accompanied demands for them to drop their hypocrisy and provide the refugees a haven in Britain and the British Commonwealth or the United States. It had no legitimacy whatsoever when addressed to Nazi authorities who had cooperated with the Zionists to send tens of thousands of German Jews to Palestine and then set out to exterminate the Jews of Europe.

The Mufti was well aware that the European Jews were being wiped out; he never claimed the contrary. Nor, unlike some of his present-day admirers, did he play the ignoble, perverse and stupid game of Holocaust denial. He could engage in trickery when justifying his betrayal of causes that he professed to defend to his Arab compatriots, but his amour-propre would not allow him to justify himself to the Jews. In his memoirs, he consoles himself as only a rabid anti-Semite could, gloating that the Jews had paid a much higher price than the Germans. The figures he cites are remarkably close to contemporary estimates: 'Their losses in the course of the Second World War represented more than thirty percent of the total number of their people, whereas the Germans' losses were less significant when measured against their population, not exceeding eight to ten percent.'[182]*

Statements like this, from a man who was well placed to know what the Nazis had done and who had no desire to worsen his own situation by exaggerating the crimes of his partners, constitute a powerful argument against Holocaust deniers. Husseini reports that Reichsführer-SS Heinrich Himmler, for whom he felt nothing but admiration and affection, told him in summer 1943 that the Germans had 'already exterminated more than three million' Jews:

> I was astonished by this figure, as I had known nothing about the matter until then. Himmler asked me on this occasion: 'How do you plan to resolve the Jewish question in your country?' I answered: 'All we want is to see them go back to the countries they came from.' He responded: 'We will never let them return to Germany.'[185]

Thus, in 1943, Husseini knew about the genocide. How could he not, given that he moved in the highest circles of the Third Reich and that no one could have suspected him of harbouring the least sympathy for the Jews? For that matter, why would Himmler have hidden the 'Final Solution' from him when – drinking tea with the Mufti again in the summer of 1943 – he let him in on a secret that, according to Husseini, he had shared with only ten Reich leaders: namely, that Germany would have an atomic bomb in three years' time?[186]

The letters on the immigration of Jews to Palestine that Husseini reproduces in his memoirs date, in the case of the letter sent from Rome to the Hungarian minister (an identical copy of which was sent to the Foreign Ministers of Bulgaria and Romania, also members of the Axis) from 28 June 1943, in the case of the letters to Ribbentrop and Himmler, from July 1944. In his own account, however, the Mufti dates the letters to the Eastern European ministers to 1944.[187] This is a patent error, as is shown by the facsimiles that the Mufti himself includes in his book, which are consistent with the

---

* Raul Hilberg estimates the number of Jewish victims of the Nazi genocide at 5.1 million.[183] The number of Jews when the Nazis came to power is estimated at 15.3 million.[184]

documents assembled by Höpp.[188] The encounter with Himmler that the Mufti describes took place after the letters were written: namely, on 4 July 1943, as is attested by a photograph of the two men together that the Nazi leader dated and dedicated to Husseini, who responded in a 30 July letter thanking the Reichsführer-SS for the 'memento of our first meeting'.[189]

It would nevertheless appear that the reason the Mufti confused the dates in retrospect is that he made a second appeal to the governments of Eastern Europe in 1944, as another facsimile document in his memoirs would seem to indicate: the 25 July 1944 response by the Hungarian royal envoy to Berlin. Here, the Hungarian confirmed receipt of the Mufti's letter *of 22 June 1944* 'about obstructing the Jews' emigration to Palestine'.[190] Husseini remarks – in his memoirs, again – that he received identical responses from the other governments to which he had written. (These June 1944 letters have not been included in the collection of documents from the Mufti's years in exile published by Höpp, although Höpp's is the most complete collection of such material available to this day.)

In any event, when we bear in mind that, as was well known by then, most of the Nazi concentration camps were in Poland, we can find little ambiguity in the words the Mufti used when writing to the Hungarian minister in June 1943:

> I ask your Excellency to permit me to draw your attention to the neces-sity of preventing the Jews from leaving your country for Palestine, and if there are reasons which make their removal necessary, it would be indispensable and infinitely preferable to send them to other countries where they would find themselves under active control, for example, in Poland, in order thereby to protect oneself from their menace and avoid the consequent damage.[191]

The allusion to Poland is, unambiguously, a reference to the concentration camps: how could it have been otherwise? On the other hand, it is improbable that, in June 1943, in Rome, before leaving for Berlin and meeting Himmler, the Mufti knew that the majority of these concentration camps were death camps: Auschwitz-Birkenau, Belzec, Chelmno, Majdanek, Sobibór and Treblinka.

Edgar Ansel Mowrer, who was eager to accuse the Mufti of direct complicity in the Nazi genocide when he learned that Husseini had 'fled' from Paris, reproduced parts of the French letters to the Hungarian and Romanian Foreign Ministers in the *New York Post* of 13 June 1946. The letters had been found in the Mufti's archives in Oybin, Germany, and Bad Gastein, Austria.

They bore the plainly visible date of 28 June 1943. Yet Mowrer dated these letters to the 'Balkan governments [*sic*]' to 1944, commenting on them as follows: 'To anyone who, like Haj Amin, knew that Poland had been set aside as the extermination hell of European Jewry, this meant sending the Balkan Jews, including children, to certain and horrible death.'[192] In his turn, Maurice Pearlman cited Mowrer in the indictment of the Mufti that he published in 1947 with the hope of gaining the attention of the British government, without noticing the error in the dating of the letter.[193] Pearlman would be followed by numerous other authors who throw accuracy to the winds in their desire to denigrate the Mufti and, in the process, all Palestinians, Arabs, 'Islamists' or even Muslims.

This more precise information is not, to be sure, intended to exculpate Amin al-Husseini for his criminal complicity with the Nazis. To recommend that the Jews of the countries in question be sent to concentration camps in Poland – even on the assumption that these were merely internment camps – was a great deal more than a request that they not be sent to Palestine. Coming from a leader of the Palestinian national movement, such a request might have been defended as legitimate: the recommendation that the Mufti in fact made was abominable. Moreover, it is probable that he would have made the same request even had he known that the Nazis were carrying out their 'Final Solution'.

Similarly, there is little ambiguity in the insinuations the Mufti made when he asked Himmler to prevent Egyptian Jews living in Germany from emigrating to Palestine in exchange for Germans interned in Palestine. He reminded the Reichsführer-SS of the terms of the telegram Himmler had sent him in November 1943, on the twenty-sixth anniversary of the Balfour Declaration: in it, Himmler had affirmed that 'since its inception, the National Socialist movement has inscribed the struggle against world Jewry on its banners'. The Mufti reminded him of the German declaration published on the same occasion, affirming that 'the annihilation [*Vernichtung*] of the so-called Jewish National Home in Palestine is an inalterable component of the policy of the Grossdeutsches Reich.'[194]

Remarks that Himmler made in conversation with the Mufti in summer 1943 throw a singularly chilling light on the fate that Husseini expected was in store for the Jews of Palestine and the other Arab countries in the wake of an Axis victory. It was this hope that motivated him to collaborate with Nazism. He justified his stance in his memoirs in remarks intended for his Palestinian and Arab compatriots:

In Germany, I strove to make whatever modest contribution I could for
the good of our Palestinian cause, as well as that of the other Arab countries and a few more Muslim countries. I also called on all those devoted
to the Palestinian and Arab causes to collaborate with Germany, not for
Germany's sake, nor out of a belief in the principles of Nazism, which I
do not endorse and have never considered endorsing, but because I was
persuaded, and still am, that if Germany and the Axis had carried the
day, no trace of the Zionists would have remained in Palestine and the
Arab countries.[195]

The sequel to these remarks leaves no doubt that by 'the Zionists' the Mufti
meant the Jews *tout court*. This is indicated by the satisfaction with which he
evokes the fear that came over the Jews of Egypt as Rommel's troops advanced
on the country in 1942.[196]

Husseini was, however, telling the truth when he said that he did not
embrace National Socialist doctrine. He did not, at any rate, embrace it in its
entirety. His attempts during his exile in Rome and Berlin to give Nazism a
patina of Islamic respectability are hardly convincing.[197] His efforts to induce
the Nazis to try to seem more acceptable to Muslims go a long way toward
revealing the hypocrisy of his speeches on the profound affinity between Islam
and Nazism as well as his aristocratic contempt for his coreligionists.

For proof, one need only examine the memorandum he sent to the
Information Service of the German Ministry of Foreign Affairs in November
1942, offering very detailed advice on how German propaganda should address
Arabs in general and North Africans in particular.[198] He attains the height
of ludicrousness when he declares that the Führer should be presented in
sharp contrast to Franklin D. Roosevelt (repeating the standard anti-Semitic
allegations about Roosevelt's Jewish ancestry):[199]

It is imperative that Hitler's speeches be published, especially the passages
that underscore his belief in God and victory, as well as the phrases he aims
at the British and their appalling treatment of the Arabs ... Furthermore,
it should be very clearly stated that he does not drink wine or smoke and
is not a glutton. On the contrary: he leads a simple life and personally
directs battles against Satan's henchmen and the enemies of the Merciful
on various fronts.[200]

The hypocrisy of Husseini's attempt to build up the image of an Islam-friendly
Axis combating Islam-unfriendly Allies was equally flagrant when, on 5
February 1943, he sent the German foreign minister a copy of the instructions

regarding respect for the Muslims' religion and customs that had been given to American soldiers who had landed in Northern Africa. The Mufti urged the armies of the Axis powers to take them as a model.[201]*

In point of fact, the Jewish question aside, there were, all in all, fewer doctrinal affinities between the Mufti and the Nazis than between the Nazis and another partisan of alliances with the 'enemy of one's enemy', the Indian nationalist Subhas Chandra Bose, the former president of the Indian National Congress. Bose's relations to Hitler's regime had, moreover, a good deal in common with those of the Arab leaders exiled in Berlin. In particular, Bose had, like them, taken note of the narrow limits of Hitler Germany's 'anti-colonialism'.[203] It is, however, undeniable that the Mufti espoused the Nazis' anti-Semitic doctrine, which, as we have already seen, was easily compatible with a fanatical anti-Judaism cast in the Pan-Islamist mould.

In his radio speeches, Husseini exploited his religious authority as Grand Mufti to underscore the ostensible identity between Islamic and National Socialist approaches to the Jewish question. This discourse, based on an extremely tendentious and highly selective utilization of the Islamic corpus, blotted out a heritage of several centuries of coexistence. It makes no distinction between Jews and Zionists, and is, down to Husseini's eulogy of the Final Solution, perfectly consistent with Nazi anti-Semitism.

There is also a startling harmony between the Mufti's vision and the Islamophobic interpretation of Islam as an intrinsically racist religion. I shall simply give a single enlightening example here, the speech he delivered on the 2 November 1943 anniversary of the Balfour Declaration:

> The immoderate egoism inherent in the Jews' nature, their contemptible belief that they are God's chosen people, and their claim that everything has been created for their sake and that other people are beasts that they can use to their own ends, together with the treatment they mete out to others on the basis of this belief – all this has caused them no end of problems. These character traits make them incapable of keeping faith with anyone or of mixing with any other nation; they live, rather, as parasites among the peoples, suck their blood, steal their property,

---

*   Nothing illustrates the hypocrisy in the relationship to the Arabs that the Nazis maintained through al-Husseini better than the fact that they had to convince themselves – Hitler not excepted – that the Mufti had 'Aryan' blood in his veins, as his red beard and blue eyes supposedly showed. They had to do so in order to be able to accept him as a trustworthy ally, something no pure-blooded Arab could have been, since the Arabs belonged to an inferior race.[202]

pervert their morals, and yet demand the same rights that the native inhabitants enjoy ...

It is the duty of Muhammadans in general and Arabs in particular to set themselves a goal from which they must not deviate, which they must pursue with all their strength. This goal is to drive all Jews from Arab and Muhammadan countries. This is the sole means of salvation; it is what the Prophet did thirteen centuries ago ...

Germany is also struggling against the common foe who oppressed Arabs and Muhammadans in their different countries. It has very clearly recognized the Jews for what they are and resolved to find a definitive solution [*endgültige Lösung*] for the Jewish danger that will eliminate the scourge that the Jews represent in the world.[204]

On returning to the Arab world after the Axis defeat, Husseini initially limited himself to echoing his master Rashid Rida's views on the Jewish question. In 1954, he responded to questions from the newspaper *Al-Masri* in Cairo, where he was then living, and subsequently published his answers in a brochure. He fell back on the religious explanation of the Jews' motivations that Rida had put forward, while maintaining his enthusiasm for Hitler. He denounced the 'long-standing conspiracy hatched by the Jews and colonialism' to expel the native inhabitants from Palestine in order to 'transform it into a religious, political, and military center for the Jews of the whole world, and to reconstruct the Jews' temple, known as Solomon's temple, on the site of the blessed Al-Aqsa mosque'. And he stressed that this 'world Jewish center' was merely the bridgehead for an attack on the entire Arab world.[205]

Then, at the end of his life, in the memoirs that he wrote in Lebanon between 1967 and his death in 1974, the Mufti, repeatedly citing Hitler, once again took up Nazi notions of a world Jewish conspiracy – operating with the help of Jewish socialists and capitalists from Karl Liebknecht and Rosa Luxemburg to the Rothschilds – united in the desire to do Germany harm.[206] He deployed the whole anti-Semitic arsenal, the *Protocols of the Elders of Zion* not excepted,[207] to justify the Nazis' ('the Germans'') hatred of the Jews. He even legitimised the Final Solution, by referring to the 'scientific' evaluation provided by Alfred Rosenberg's Institute for Research on the Jewish Question (Institut zur Erforschung der Judenfrage) as to whether the Jews were capable of reform. The Führer himself put this question to the Institute, which, unsurprisingly, answered that they were not. Deeply impressed by this institution, which he had visited, the Mufti selected one of his assistants to spend some time there and produce an Arabic version of its bulletin.[208]

Amin al-Husseini, Architect of the Nakba

The Mufti's anti-Semitism and collaboration with the Nazis are beyond all serious question, as we have seen. But does it then follow that his political line, inspired by these premises, is the main reason for the 1948 Nakba, and that, in some way, the Palestinians 'got what they deserved' because they rallied behind his leadership? This is a common Zionist or pro-Israeli argument. Thus the causal line leading from the Mufti to the Nakba deserves closer examination; unsurprisingly, the reality is much more complex. The fact is that, even before the 1948 Nakba utterly discredited him, Husseini's reputation had reached a low ebb in Arab and even Palestinian political circles with the defeat of the Axis. Fawzi al-Qāwuqji reports in his memoirs that the Egyptian liberal minister Muhammad 'Ali 'Allūba exclaimed, upon learning in 1947, during the partition crisis, that the Mufti had arrived in Beirut: 'This man has never gotten mixed up in any business without making things worse ... Lord protect us!'[209] Even Husseini's chief Palestinian political lieutenant, Jamal al-Husseini, whom the Mufti had put at the head of his Palestinian Arab Party, had become critical of him in private by 1946.[210]

True, the Palestinian population nevertheless continued to regard the Mufti as its leader, since no alternative had emerged. As with Yasser Arafat after him, Husseini continued, notwithstanding an endless series of defeats, to find a source of popularity in the very fact that his people's enemies demonized him. His failure was, however, patent. Bayān Nuwayhid al-Hūt, the leading Palestinian historian of her people's pre-1948 national movement, has drawn up a balance sheet of the Mufti's activity during the Second World War. In a clear, strikingly honest manner – one that stands in stark contrast to the manifestly apologetic blindness with which she seeks to refute the 'Zionist accusations' levelled against the same Mufti[211] – she blames him for forging 'strategic ties to the Axis, whereas the Zionist movement, in contrast, even when it collaborated with Nazism and also Fascism, did so very differently ... concluding nothing more than a tactical alliance for the purpose of ensuring, as best it could, Zionist interests in the event of an Allied defeat'.[212]

Nonetheless, the Mufti continued to engage in nationalistic one-upmanship with his Palestinian and Arab interlocutors. On 17 July 1947, he sent a letter to the Arab Foreign Ministers in anticipation of their scheduled Beirut meeting with the UN Special Commission. After arrogantly criticizing 'certain Arabs' for giving approval to the 1939 British White Paper (and then, with very peculiar logic, explaining that it had not been implemented because they had approved it), he called on them to abjure all 'flexibility and moderation' and to demand 'a state in which those Palestinian Jews living in Palestine when it was occupied by the British [1917], as well as their descendants, will participate, without the other Jews present in Palestine, whom the Arabs regard as an intrusive Jewish community that has entered the country against its inhabitants' will'.[213]

In October 1947, Jamal al-Husseini, after boycotting the UNSCOP, appeared as the Mufti's spokesman – officially, as vice-president of the Higher Arab Committee – before the UN ad hoc committee on Palestine. His line of argument, inspired by his superior, was pitifully weak: fully endorsing the biblical-racial logic of the Zionist movement, he explained that the Jews from Eastern Europe were descendants of the Khazars and therefore had no connection to Palestine,[214] as if being a remote descendant of the Jews expelled from Palestine nearly 2,000 years earlier would have conferred a certain title to the country on European Jews. We have already seen that the Arab governments took no account whatsoever of the Mufti's injunctions, declaring before the UN commissions that they were in favour of a settlement that would encompass all the Jews in Palestine (see Chapter 1, above).

Confronted with the fait accompli of the UN vote for partition, should the Mufti not have proceeded, as a temporary expedient – even while rejecting the principle informing this unjust resolution – to create an Arab state on that part of Palestinian territory that the international organization had designated for the purpose? Such was the view of Salah Khalaf, better known by his pseudonym, Abu Iyad, a co-founder, with Yasser Arafat, of Fatah, and a central leader of the PLO until his assassination in 1991: 'The partition plan of 1947 was certainly unjust in principle. But why didn't the Palestinian leaders accept a temporary solution just as the Zionists did, which would consist of founding a state on the portion of the national territory assigned by the United Nations ?'[215]

Abu Iyad put the question to the Mufti shortly before the latter's death, and reported his answers in his memoirs: 'Although plausible, Hajj Amin's justifications didn't strike me as entirely convincing. ... In short, although Hajj Amin and his companions did have a strategic vision of Palestine's future, they were sadly lacking in the qualities necessary to make tactical concessions.'[216]

Abu Iyad's retrospective tactical flexibility here is obviously mandated by the flexibility he was looking forward to showing when he made this comment: the leadership of the PLO, which he incarnated together with Yasser Arafat and the other heads of Fatah, had a few years earlier opted for the tactic of making concession after concession that was to culminate in the Oslo Accords. His judgement contrasts sharply with Arno Mayer's assessment:

> Could any Palestinian or Arab leader have accepted [in 1948] that 60 per cent of the mandatory Holy Land would be turned over to a minority of about one-third of the population to form a state in which close to half its inhabitants would be Arab Palestinian? And what of the prevalent suspicion that the Zionists would never abandon their reach for the whole of Palestine? If a Jewish majority in an expanding Jewish state were to be secured, that could only entail the expulsion of legions of Arab Palestinians.[217]

The attitude of the Arab states would certainly have been different if Britain had supervised enactment of the UN partition plan before withdrawing its troops, instead of criminally washing its hands of the tragedy that it had directly created. Nasser quite rightly pointed this out in 1955:

> It was not the Arabs who prevented the realization of the plan in 1947 and incited the Palestine conflict, but rather the British ... when they withdrew in 1947, they left face to face on the lines of partition fixed by the United Nations, the Zionists, who were actively arming themselves, and the Arabs, who were simple, unarmed peasants. This was to offer all of Palestine to Zionism, and it was against the factual violation of the spirit of partition that the Arab states took up arms in 1948.[218]

Moreover, as Simha Flapan observes, it was less Amin al-Husseini's role that was decisive than Ben-Gurion's. Flapan even raises doubts as to the real popularity of the Mufti and his partisans:

> For all of its public posturing, however, the [HAC] did not enjoy massive popular support, and when, in the wake of the UN resolution, the mufti of Jerusalem called for volunteers for his Army of Sacred Struggle, the majority of the Palestinian Arabs declined to respond. In fact, prior to Israel's unilateral Declaration of Independence, many Palestinian leaders and groups wanted nothing to do with the mufti or his political party and made various efforts to reach a *modus vivendi* with the Zionists. But Ben-Gurion's profound resistance to the creation of a Palestinian state significantly undermined any opposition to the mufti's blood-and-thunder policies.[219] *

---

*   Let us also note the part played by King Abdullah of Transjordan, in collusion with

At the stage that the evolving conflict reached after 1945, with the accumulation of defeats under Husseini's disastrous leadership, the only path still open to the Palestinians, if they were to avoid the catastrophe, the Nakba, was to shake off the political influence of this disreputable individual once and for all and, as I have already suggested, seek an understanding with the Jewish partisans of a binational state on the basis of the programme formulated by the Arab governments in 1946. This was not the path taken: Husseini's compromising shadow, his execration of the Jews and his obstinate attachment to a line of conduct that consisted in impotently raining imprecations down on the heads of his adversaries, continued to loom large over the Palestinian national movement until its debacle.

Even after the Nakba, the Mufti and his collaborators intransigently maintained their demand that the Jewish immigrants leave Palestine. The representative of the Higher Arab Committee, Henry Cattan, speaking in November 1948 before the UN General Assembly at the Palais de Chaillot in Paris, declared that

> the Arabs and the Jewish citizens of Palestine should be able to live together in a united Palestine under a democratic constitution. It [is] consequently necessary to provide for the return to their countries of origin of all the terrorist Zionists who have entered the Holy Land. The arms they [have] smuggled in must be confiscated and reparations must be paid for the damage they [have] caused. Without such a solution, there can be no peace in the Middle East, since the Arabs will continue to fight until the foreigners illegally installed in Palestine are defeated.[221]

Amin al-Husseini's Divergent Legacies

The Mufti continued to defend inconsistent positions to his dying day. In 1954, after reiterating his anti-Jewish stance and lavishly praising King Saud, Abdul-Aziz's successor on the Saudi throne, he affirmed his desire to 'arrive at an understanding with America on the basis of common interests'.[222] Following the Arab defeat in 1967, he warned that any notion of creating a Palestinian state in the West Bank was to be avoided.[223] After he began collaborating with his former enemy, the Jordanian monarchy, his closest collaborator, Emil al-Ghūri, participated in the government of Jordan,

the Zionist leaders, in aborting all plans for an Arab Palestinian state in 1948, as well as the cacophony reigning among the Arab states. [220]

maintaining his participation despite the massacres of Palestinians that the monarchy perpetrated in 1970.

In his biography of Husseini, Zvi Elpeleg – who served, in the course of a long career, as the Israeli military governor of the Triangle, Gaza, the West Bank and Southern Lebanon and as Israeli Ambassador to Turkey before retiring from public office to pursue academic research – provided a good description of the situation at the Mufti's death in 1974:

> Haj Amin's death did not leave a vacuum in the Palestinian camp. The PLO leaders had for some time constituted the national leadership, and since the end of the 1960s they had succeeded, better than any previous leadership, in uniting the Palestinians ...
>
> The memory of Haj Amin disappeared from the Palestinian public consciousness almost without trace. No days of mourning were set aside in his memory. His name was not commemorated in the refugee camps, and no streets were named after him. No memorials were built in his memory, and no books written extolling his deeds ...
>
> Haj Amin, who more than any other Palestinian had borne the burden of leadership, and who had dedicated his long life to his people, became, at the end of his life and after his death, a symbol of defeat. His achievements have been lost to oblivion; and the Palestinians have tried to repress the failures that characterised the end of his career, along with his memory.[224]

Since the Intifada, the irresistible rise of Hamas in Palestine in the wake of the resurgence of Islamic fundamentalism throughout the region has led to the production of a few hagiographic texts about the Mufti. By and large, however, events have confirmed a situation that Elpeleg observes in his biography:[225] the sharp contrast between the embarrassed silence surrounding the memory of Amin al-Husseini and the glorification of such 'heroes' or 'martyrs' of the struggle for Palestine as 'Abdul-Qādir al-Husseini or 'Izz-ul-Dīn al-Qassām. It is Qassām, not the Mufti, who serves Hamas as its 'positive hero' – a circumstance the more striking in that the Muslim Brothers, from whose Palestinian branch Hamas emerged, steadfastly treated the Mufti during his lifetime as the legitimate leader of the anti-Zionist struggle.[226]

Amin al-Husseini and Hassan al-Banna, the founder of the Muslim Brotherhood, had been friends since the 1920s. When Said Ramadan, Banna's son-in-law, set about creating the basic structures of the Palestinian branch in 1945, his father-in-law insisted on the need to act in concert with the Mufti.[227] The Muslim Brothers did in fact operate with the Mufti's blessing and benefited from his popularity, shored up by British and Zionist hostility toward him. Ramadan transmitted the Mufti's greeting to an immense crowd during the sermon he delivered at the Al-Aqsa Mosque in Jerusalem in September 1947, before he was forced to flee Palestine to avoid arrest by the mandatory authorities.[228]

As for the Muslim Brothers's discourse on the Jews, it was, like their discourse in general, not free of contradictions. The Brothers echoed, quite naturally, Islamic religious attitudes on Palestine and the Jews, with the anti-Jewish twist that Rida added when he began mining this vein.[229] They rejected the distinction between Jews and Zionists. They contended that the creation of a Zionist state in Palestine would transform the Jewish communities in the Arab countries into a 'Zionist fifth column'.[230] Writing in 1948, one of their main leaders, Muhammad Sālih al-'Ashmāwi, called it a 'fact' that could not be 'challenged or denied' that 'every Jew is a Zionist'.[231]

Nevertheless, in a September 1945 address to the general assembly of the Brotherhood's leading members, Hassan al-Banna expressed – furtively, to be sure – an idea of which the Mufti of Jerusalem would certainly have disapproved, although it was in harmony with the official line of the Egyptian government and the Arab League: 'There can be no doubt about the fact that we feel great sympathy for the suffering Jews, but this does not mean that they should obtain justice by committing an injustice against the Arabs.'[232] Still, when, in 1946, the Muslim Brothers waged an energetic campaign to get the Mufti out of France, where he had been placed under house arrest, and secure his admission to Egypt, they 'asserted that he had not committed any errors and that all he had done was to perform jihad'.[233]

Today, at the time of writing, there is only one article about Amin al-Husseini on the Egyptian Muslim Brotherhood's website – a short biography which simply affirms that during the Second World War the Mufti supported the Axis against the Allies 'because he wanted Germany to help him put an end to the British occupation'.[234] He does not feature any more prominently in the publications of the Palestinian Hamas. Outside these religious-political circles, if the frequency of references on the internet is any index of fame, it is worth noting that a Google search conducted in October 2008 turned up ten times more results for 'Amin al-Husseini' on English than on Arabic pages. The proportion was reversed in the case of 'Abdul-Qādir al-Husseini.

By the immediate post-war period, Zionist and pro-Zionist sources were already blowing the Mufti's case out of proportion. Raul Hilberg points to one example: 'In all the sessions of the American Jewish Conference and its interim committees [in 1946], no proposal was put forward for the trial of any specific individual or category of individuals save one: the ex-Mufti of Jerusalem.'[235] What motivated this disproportionate interest was obviously not a desire to see the Mufti pay for his crimes, but the wish to exploit his dismal reputation in the eyes of the Allied governments in the battle for Palestine.

After the creation of the state of Israel, the Mufti was converted into a heavy-calibre argument for the Zionist/Israeli anti-Arab and anti-Palestinian propaganda campaign. He even played a role in the 1961 trial of the Nazi war criminal Adolf Eichmann. Citing David Ben-Gurion, Hannah Arendt points out in her *Eichmann in Jerusalem* that 'one of the motives in bringing Eichmann to trial was to "ferret out other Nazis – for example, the connection between the Nazis and some Arab rulers"'.[236] This objective was not attained, for, as Arendt notes, Eichmann exculpated the Mufti more than he incriminated him.[237]

According to Tom Segev, the wall devoted to Husseini's relations with the Nazis in the Yad Vashem Memorial museum in Jerusalem leaves the impression that 'there is much in common between the Nazis' plan to destroy the Jews and the Arabs' enmity to Israel'.[238] Peter Novick, for his part, notes that the article on the Mufti in the four-volume *Encyclopedia of the Holocaust*,[239] published in association with Yad Vashem, 'is more than twice as long as the articles on Goebbels and Göring, longer than the articles on Himmler and Heydrich combined, longer than the article on Eichmann – of all the biographical articles, it is exceeded in length, but only slightly, by the entry for Hitler'.[240]

According to Novick, this lack of all proportion is due in part to the most effective of the standard Arab arguments about the relationship between Israel and the Holocaust: 'The claims of Palestinian complicity in the murder of the European Jews were to some extent a defensive strategy, a preemptive response to the Palestinian complaint that if Israel was recompense for the Holocaust, it was unjust that Palestinian Muslims should pick up the bill for the crimes of European Christians.'[241]

Meir Litvak and Esther Webman of the Moshe Dayan Center for Middle Eastern and African Studies at the University of Tel Aviv admit as much, after a fashion, in *From Empathy to Denial*, their recent book about post-1948 Arab reactions to the Holocaust:

> Husayni's war-time collaboration with Germany, which was raised in the Nuremberg trials, served Zionist efforts to undermine the image of the Palestinian national movement in the early post-war years. His actions

positioned them no longer as 'reluctant bystanders' in the Holocaust, as they saw themselves, but as collaborators, a status which the Arab discourse and historiography on the Holocaust vehemently opposed.[242]

Litvak and Webman promote the kind of confusion according to which a common ethnic identity determines a common ideological identity: their apparent candour paves the way for the attacks that follow. It is 'the Palestinian national movement' in its entirety that, thanks to the actions of one man, is supposed to have acquired the shameful status of direct 'collaborators' in the Holocaust. The authors do, however, admit that the Palestinian debate on the Mufti's conduct during the Second World War 'was heavily influenced by the ambivalence with which Arab, particularly Palestinian, historiography viewed Husayni as the person responsible [for] the 1948 defeat'.[243]

Let us take a closer look at this putative ambivalence, extended once again to take in a vast group defined in ethnic terms, even though that group is, politically speaking, extremely diverse. Consider the Arab-American historian Philip Mattar, who, albeit president of the Palestinian American Research Center,[244] does not mince words when it comes to the Mufti. According to Litvak and Webman, Mattar has 'conceded' that the period Husseini spent in Germany was the most 'controversial' of his career, but they hasten to add that he also says the whole business has been 'distorted' and blown out of proportion.[245]

They also provide a summary of the judgement that Salah Khalaf, alias Abu Iyad, pronounces on the Mufti. But let us first examine for ourselves what this leading member of the PLO actually says. After pointing out that the Palestinians have to conclude alliances with governments whose interests coincide with theirs, Abu Iyad goes on: 'This principle was falsely applied by Hajj Amin al-Husayni when he rallied to Nazi Germany during the Second World War, thereby committing an error which we vigorously condemn.'[246] He nevertheless rejects the idea that the Mufti was a 'Nazi sympathizer', recounting a conversation that took place shortly before the Mufti's death in which he underscored his conviction that, if Germany had won the war, it would have granted independence to the Palestinians. Abu Iyad continues:

> I told him that such calculations were a bit naive when one considers that Hitler placed the Arabs in fourteenth place, *after* the Jews, in the hierarchy of 'races' on our planet. If Germany had won, it would have instituted a far crueler occupation than the one known under the British mandate.
> Haj Amin in any case was not a Nazi, any more than the Palestinian leaders who supported Great Britain during the war were agents of

imperialism. The pro-British faction was quite simply betting on an Allied victory and hoped through their support of Britain to wrest their country's independence, which after all was the primary and sacred goal of all the struggles waged by the Palestinian people since the First World War.

Those who have tried to promote the belief that the Palestinian nationalists were agents of Nazi Germany conveniently forget that thousands of our compatriots fought in the British army. Even today, Fatah's best military instructors were trained in the British army. Ironically, General Wagih al-Madani, the first commander-in-chief of the Palestine Liberation Army constituted in 1965, was a classmate of General Moshe Dayan in a British military school in Palestine.[247]

Here is how Abu Iyad's reasoning is transformed in Litvak and Webman's account: 'Hajj Amin was not a Nazi, just as those leaders who supported the British were not imperialist, Khalaf concludes, *thereby placing both choices on the same moral ground*.'[248] Let the reader judge the good faith of this pronouncement. Their presentation of the opinions of other Palestinian historians and commentators of the period is in keeping with their presentation of Khalaf's. If they are to be believed, 'The only writer who advocated a principled position against Husayni was 'Azmi Bishara'[249] – who, they hasten to add, did so 'in an article directed to European and Israeli audiences', implying that this sole condemnation of the Mufti's collaboration with Nazism was produced for external consumption and thus reflects no credit on the Palestinians.

Pace Litvak and Webman, Husseini has been severely criticized in countless texts from the Arab left in general and the Palestinian left in particular, especially in the wake of the political radicalization that swept the region in the aftermath of the June 1967 defeat. To cite one example among many, drawn from a brochure of the Popular Democratic Front for the Liberation of Palestine, *written in Arabic*, that was widely distributed in the late 1960s:

> The orientation to Nazi Germany diminished the prestige of the Palestinian struggle in the international arena, just as it drained this struggle of the emancipatory content that it had had at its beginnings. The basic reason for this orientation was neither shortsightedness nor political manœuvring, despite what many history books maintain, but, rather, the nature of the Palestinian leadership, which, by virtue of its class affiliation, could not go to the masses and militate among them in order to liberate their potential ...

Hajj Amin al-Husseini's relationship to Nazi Germany thus helped provide Zionism with an occasion to cast the Palestinian struggle as one that

1) is convergent with Nazism and fascism
2) lends support to the anti-Semitic movement that was led by Hitler. This 'tactical' collaboration reflected utter ignorance of the racist, colonialist nature of the Nazi movement.[250]

Litvak and Webman at least make nods toward candour and objectivety – indeed, they claim to 'empathize' with the Arabs. This cannot be said of the flood of hate-filled anti-Arab and anti-Muslim texts churned out since the 11 September 2001 attacks, in the context of a new Islamophobia that forms the pendant to the 'new anti-Semitism' identified by Bernard Lewis and pilloried in all the texts in question. Amin al-Husseini is a favourite target of these writers, who, generally speaking, subscribe to a historical grand narrative that leads straight from the Mufti to Osama bin Laden. (Earlier, it came to a halt with Arafat, as in a 1993 book by Benjamin Netanyahu that Idith Zertal has analysed.[251])

The most recent document of this sort, at the moment I write, is a book by two Americans, David Dalin and John Rothmann, that bears the eloquent title – eloquent for the insight it provides into the authors' mental universe – *Icon of Evil*.[252] The book, whose cover is adorned with the inevitable photograph of the Mufti's meeting with Hitler, emphasizes

the unbroken continuity from generation to generation, an unbroken chain of terror from Adolf Hitler, Haj Amin al-Husseini, Sayyid Qutb, and Yasser Arafat to Hamas's founder and spiritual leader, Sheikh Ahmad Yassin, Sheikh Omar Abd al-Rahman, and Ramzi Yousef, who planned the World Trade Center bombing of 1993, to Osama bin Laden and Mohammed Ata, to Ahmed Omar Saeed Sheikh, the Pakistani Muslim terrorist who planned the kidnapping and murder of U.S. journalist Daniel Pearl, and to Iranian president Mahmud Ahmadinejad.[253]

The orientation of Dalin and Rothmann's book, its cover emblazoned with high praise from Dov Zakheim and Douglas Feith, two members of George W. Bush's administration, Daniel Pipes and other neo-conservatives and Israel champions, is clear: it is a compilation of clichés of anti-Palestinian, anti-Muslim and anti-Arab propaganda, drawn, with rare exceptions, from secondary sources – if not from sources at third or fourth hand – all of them in English. To cite just a few gems culled at random from the opening pages: Husseini, who was nearly forty-six years old in 1941, is twice said to have waited 'for much of his adult life' to meet Hitler, although it is highly unlikely that he had so much as heard of him before 1933, that is, eight years earlier.[254] In 1929, he is supposed to have called for 'a campaign of jihad against the British, the Jews, and the West',[255] whereas we have seen how keen he was until the mid-thirties to appease the British. Sayyid Qutb, whose ideological radicalization and first political-theoretical writings date from after 1948, is supposed to have had 'a profound ideological influence' on a whole gamut of individuals, including 'al-Husseini and al-Banna'.[256] (Banna was murdered in 1949, before Qutb joined the Muslim Brothers' movement.) Young Egypt, we are told, elaborated its anti-Semitic programme 'under the emerging leadership of Gamal Abdel Nasser and Anwar Al Sadat', at the same time as 'the pro-German Ba'ath Party in Syria'.[257] 'With the exceptions of Ibn Saud of Saudi Arabia [*sic*] and Abdullah of Jordan, no leader of the Islamic Middle East opposed Hitler and supported the Allied cause.'[258]

Tom Segev was engaging in euphemism when he described it, in a review for the *New York Times*' literary supplement, as being 'of little scholarly value.'[259] Well aware that he had to justify reviewing it at all, when large numbers of incomparably more serious books that criticize Israel are passed over in silence, Segev concluded with this incongruous argument: 'In spite of all this, the book is worth noticing, as it belongs to a genre of popular Arab-bashing that is often believed to be "good for Israel." It is not.'

A few months earlier, there appeared, also in the *New York Times*, a review of another book in the same category, as its title suggests: *Jihad and Jew-Hatred: Islamism, Nazism and the Roots of 9/11*, by the German writer Matthias Küntzel.[260] The original version of the book, published in 2002, was widely criticized in Germany, as the author reports in the preface to the English edition, for being 'political propaganda'.[261] Like Dalin and Rothmann, Küntzel is an 'expert' on Islamic questions who does not know Arabic. His book, like theirs, is a fantasy-based narrative pasted together out of secondary sources and third-hand reports; it aims to demonstrate that there is a direct line of descent from Amin al-Husseini and Hassan al-Banna through Gamal Abdel-Nasser to Osama bin Laden. The *New York Times* assigned the task of reviewing it, as it would Dalin's and Rothmann's book, to a writer capable of criticizing Israeli government policy without being accused of hostility towards Israel. The review, by *Atlantic journalist* Jeffrey Goldberg, notes:

Küntzel marshals impressive evidence to back his case, but he sometimes oversimplifies ... In his effort to blame Germany for Muslim anti-Semitism, he overreaches. 'While Khomeini was certainly not an acolyte of Hitler, it is not unreasonable to suppose that his anti-Jewish outlook ... had been shaped during the 1930s,' Küntzel says, citing, in a footnote, an article he himself wrote. He also oversimplifies the Israeli-Arab conflict. Jews today have actual power in the Middle East, and Israel is not innocent of excess and cruelty.[262]

Shortly after Küntzel's book was released in Germany, there appeared, in the United States, a direct precursor of Dalin and Rothmann's, with the same photograph of the meeting between Hitler and the Mufti on its cover. Written by Chuck Morse, a journalist and an unsuccessful Republican candidate for Congress, it is entitled: *The Nazi Connection to Islamic Terrorism: Adolf Hitler and Haj Amin al-Husseini.*[263] Morse presents the same historical scenario, running from the Mufti to contemporary 'Islamic terrorism' by way of a long string of leading personalities of Arab nationalism, indiscriminately demonizing the Palestinian national movement while defending himself against the charge of being anti-Arab and Islamophobic on the grounds that he acknowledges the existence of a minority of 'enlightened', albeit powerless, Arabs and Muslims. Morse does not pull his punches:

> The Nazi Holocaust against the Jews of Europe did not end with the collapse of Nazi Germany in 1945, but rather the program of Holocaust has continued against the Jews of Israel. Hitler's crematoria have been replaced by human bombs, programmed to blow themselves up for the sole purpose of killing as many Jews as possible ...
>   Nazi style anti-Semitism continues its grim goose-step across the Arab and Islamic landscape as Arab and Muslim nations promulgate, through their media outlets, their public institutions, and their schools, the same hateful and demented anti-Jewish conspiracy theories, as did Hitler.[264]*

Let us cite, finally, a fourth work symptomatic of this spate of post-September 11 publications, a 2006 book by Klaus-Michael Mallmann and Martin Cüppers, *Halbmond und Hakenkreuz: Das Dritte Reich, die Araber und Palästina* (The Crescent and the Swastika: The Third Reich, the Arabs and Palestine).[265] Its title, too, sums up an entire programme.† What would be

---

*   Morse brings his book to a close with a 'Prayer for the State of Israel' by 'The Chief Rabbinate'. The back cover displays a photograph of himself speaking at the National Synagogue, the oldest orthodox synagogue in Washington, DC.

†   The same title had already been used for a documentary broadcast on German

the reaction to a work (such works no doubt exist) titled *The Star of David and the Swastika*?

Mallmann's and Cüpper's book is, however, more serious than the three just discussed (it would be hard to be *less* serious). It is not one more grand narrative that sets out from the Mufti in order to arrive at Hamas or Al-Qaida via Nasser and Saddam Hussein, but a history of German–Arab relations under Nazism based on the German archives and a medium-length bibliography that presents a mixture of scholarly works and propaganda. It suffers from the handicap common to the other three books: its authors have no knowledge of Arabic.

The book contains gross errors, due in particular to the authors' unfamiliarity with the Arab dimension of their subject. One striking example: in the book's epilogue, the authors affirm that the Saudi King Abdul-Aziz accorded 'Āli al-Gaylāni exile and go on to say that 'Even when the Iraqi monarchy was overthrown in July 1958, so that [Gaylāni] could even have gone back home, the former prime minister did not return to his native land. Rather, he spent the last years of his life on the Arabian Peninsula, without ever again setting out to make a public political intervention directed at Baghdad.'[267] Had they simply consulted the article on Gaylāni in the *Encyclopedia Britannica*, they would have discovered just how far they were from the mark:

> Afterward he lived in exile in Saudi Arabia and Egypt, returning to Iraq only in 1958 following the revolution that overthrew Iraq's Hāshimite monarchy. In December of that year, Gaylānī was implicated in a plot against President 'Abd al-Karīm Qāsim and was later imprisoned and sentenced to death. In 1961, however, he was released from prison by a special amnesty and soon after settled in Beirut, where he lived out his days.[268]

Moreover, Mallmann and Cüpper's flagrantly anti-Arab prejudice makes their book as much a work of propaganda as the other three.

The illustrations in *Halbmond und Hakenkreuz*, which also sports the inevitable picture of the Mufti's meeting with Hitler on the cover, are reminiscent of the television reports that Edward Said often criticized, in which the only suffering one is allowed to see in the conflict between

Israel and Palestine is that of Jewish Israeli women at the funerals of Israeli victims. The first illustrations show the body of 'a pedestrian shot to death by Arab terrorists' on a stretcher being put in an ambulance marked with a Star of David, and a woman sobbing in front of the coffin of her 'Jewish [husband], murdered by Arab terrorists'.[269] The only time that Gamal Abdel-Nasser is mentioned, in the course of the inevitable allusion to Young Egypt – presented, with the usual clichés, as the primary inspiration for the Free Egyptian Officers – it is stated that it 'is, among other things, well known that he enthusiastically read and promoted *The Protocols of the Elders of Zion*'.[270] Backing up this tendentious presentation of Nasser is a reference, in a note, to non-specialist or straightforwardly anti-Arab works on the subject of both the Egyptian leader and Young Egypt, on a pattern common to all four of these books: the multiplication of references to sources that are themselves unreliable seeks to give the reader an impression of scholarly rigour.

Mallmann and Cüppers's scholarship, for its part, makes no distinction between anti-Semitism, anti-Zionism and even anti-imperialism.[271] This kind of scholarship is blind to nuance and unaware of what it means to put facts in context. Francis Nicosia quite rightly points out in the conclusion of his review of the authors' book in *Holocaust and Genocide Studies*: 'Indeed, the danger here may be to simplistically equate Arab leaders with their Nazi contemporaries, Arab nationalism with National Socialism, and Arab hatred of Jews with the historically and culturally rooted antisemitism in modern Germany and the rest of Europe.'[272] The inability to draw these elementary distinctions is particularly alarming in the case of writers from Germany. Nicosia provides, in a few edifying lines, basic pointers on what would be needed to remedy the failure to put 'Arab hatred of the Jews' in context, using Zionist sources:

> Zionist sources provide necessary and important context. Chaim Weizmann's pronouncement at the Paris Peace Conference in 1919 that the aim of Zionism was 'to make Palestine as Jewish as England is English' sent an unambiguous message to the Arab majority in Palestine. Vladimir Jabotinsky rejected any compromise with the Arabs over the absolute necessity of a Jewish majority and state in Palestine while arguing, as Walter Laqueur has written, that 'the Arabs loved their country [Palestine] as much as the Jews did. Instinctively, they understood Zionist aspirations very well, and their decision to resist them was only natural.' David Ben Gurion's 1938 statement 'I support compulsory transfer. I don't see anything immoral in it,' certainly heightened Arab fears.[273]

This indispensable contextualization of Arab attitudes toward Jews and the Holocaust makes all the difference between a legitimate, reasoned denunciation of those who do indeed deserve to be condemned – bearing in mind, of course, that Arab attitudes were very diverse and that many were irreproachable, if not, indeed, commendable – and the kind of indiscriminate demonization that inevitably leads to anti-Arab racism and Islamophobia.

PART II

THE TIME OF THE NAKBA

Arab Attitudes to the Jews
and the Holocaust from 1948 to the Present

Prelude

The 1948 Nakba catalysed a series of political transformations in the Middle East, inaugurating a historical dialectic chiefly structured around the Arab–Israeli conflict. Up to this point I have offered a synchronous study of the main ideological currents in Arab politics during the 1930s and 1940s. The following pages, in contrast, are organized chronologically; they concentrate exclusively, or almost exclusively, on the particular ideological current that dominated each major period.

If what follows is both less extensive and less detailed than the previous chapters, it is in part because the foundations of the various ideological currents – the basis for their differing attitudes to the Holocaust – were essentially laid between the end of the First World War and the end of the Second. Furthermore, Arab attitudes towards Nazism in the 1930s and 1940s have come in for a great deal of attention; the result has been a considerable mass of counter-truths twisting reality in one direction or the other and requiring exhaustive treatment. In addition, a study of the six decades since 1948 as extensive and detailed as that of the two decades before that watershed year would exceed the bounds of a single volume.

Israeli writings on Arab attitudes to the Holocaust since 1948 are, unsurprisingly, polemical. The most recent and the bulkiest work on the subject, the book by Meir Litvak and Esther Webman already discussed, is by no means an exception to this rule, although the authors declare that they have 'tried to maintain, as much as possible, a dispassionate approach'.[1]

Litvak's and Webman's most illustrious predecessor in the enterprise of cataloguing Arab attitudes, Yehoshafat Harkabi, died in 1994. A student of Arabic who became one of the outstanding Israeli experts on the Arab world, Harkabi, a former general, headed the Israeli army intelligence between 1955 and 1959 before turning in his stripes for an academic career. His book, which began life as a doctoral dissertation completed on the eve of the June 1967 war and was first published in Hebrew the following year, was not focused exclusively on the Arab reception of the Holocaust, but surveyed Arab attitudes towards Israel and the Jews in general.[2]

Harkabi was honest enough to acknowledge the problem inherent in any assessment of Arab attitudes by a Zionist: 'How can an Israeli be objective, since he is not indifferent to the subject or the results of his research, as he himself is saturated with memories and emotions associated with the conflict?'[3] Harkabi was especially sensitive to the tendency to apply a double standard: 'I had to suspect myself of being alert in criticizing the Arab attitude and eager to discover its faults, hidden motives and weaknesses, while, on the other hand, being insensitive in examining the Zionist and Israeli attitude. I was much troubled by these problems.'[4] He was worried to the extent that he felt the need to include an appendix on 'the problem of subjectivity'.[5] His book nevertheless leaves the reader with the powerful impression that he raises such doubts for the sole purpose of establishing the objectivity of his approach, whereas his whole approach is clearly in conformity with a logic of war that is simply an extension of Harkabi's military career, in a country where the frontiers between the military and the academic (or, for that matter, the political) are among the most highly permeable in the world. Yet the sincerity of Harkabi's self-questioning was confirmed when, in 1986, he published *Israel's Fateful Decisions* which pleaded for a peace settlement based on dialogue with the PLO and withdrawal from the territories that Israel occupied in 1967.[6]

In *Arab Attitudes to Israel*, Harkabi was still striving to convince himself that peace with the Arabs was impossible, as he confirms in his 1970 afterword: while protesting that he has not presented the 'Arab attitude' as unalterable, he nevertheless affirms that, in fact, it has not changed.[7] The sharp limits on the empathy that he claims to feel appear nowhere more clearly than in his perception of the Arabs. Although the book intermittently draws the indispensable distinctions between different families of thought in the Arab world (while arbitrarily excluding the Communist movement from consideration), it ultimately trades in an unjustifiable amalgam of Arab attitudes.

Indeed, despite the plural *Attitudes* in the book's English title, the singular holds undisputed sway in the text itself – and, for that matter, in the original Hebrew title of the dissertation: *Emdat Ha-'Aravim be-Sikhsukh Yisrael-'Arav* (The Arabs' Attitude – or Stand – in the Israeli–Arab Conflict). Harkabi's book is not an examination of various ideological tendencies among the Arabs but, rather, an examination of the different 'conceptual elements' contained in 'Arab ideology'. That is, Harkabi proceeds as if these elements were so many building blocks that come together to produce one and the same 'attitude' – notwithstanding their more than heterogeneous, indeed, blatantly contradictory character. He explains this away in his chapter on the transition 'from ideology to attitude':[8] 'the Arab attitude' is itself a tissue of contradictions, according to him, inasmuch as inconsistency, even irrationality, is, in the Arab world, in abundant supply.

The most systematic critique of Harkabi's monolithic approach to analysis of the Arab world prior to his transformation into a dove, was elaborated by an academic of Iraqi background, Nissim Rejwan, a researcher at the Truman Institute of the Hebrew University of Jerusalem and one of the most accomplished Israeli specialists in Arab culture.[9] Rejwan takes issue with Harkabi in particular for his decisive contribution to forging the idea of 'the emergence and growth [among the Arabs] of a new center of anti-Semitism, superseding and in some ways surpassing the old European center'.[10] He firmly criticises Harkabi's 'cardinal mistake': 'that he chooses to speak of one, collective Arab "attitude" or "stand"' while 'such a uniform attitude had never existed in reality'.[11]*

Yet, more than forty years after Harkabi, Israeli monitoring of Arab positions appears to have made little progress, except, perhaps, in the aggravation of tendencies denounced by Rejwan. Litvak's and Webman's 2009 book provides the best illustration, the more so as it is the first book comparable to Harkabi's to appear since his dissertation was completed in 1967. The authors seem to think that their predecessor underestimated Arab

---

* It was probably in response to the criticisms of his very reductive presentation of the 'Arab attitude' that Harkabi included, in the 2nd edn, a supplementary section, 'Three Concepts of Arab Strategy', which looks at Arab attitudes, in the plural.[12] Yet, here again, Harkabi aims to put his compatriots on their guard against illusions about the moderate school among the Arabs that advocates political resolution of the conflict with Israel. He sees this school's attitude as identical to that of the school that seeks to liquidate Israel through a combination of military pressure and internal erosion. Anwar al-Sadat is one of his explicit targets here. Thus Harkabi was even more suspicious of the Arabs than Menachem Begin, who received the Egyptian president in Israel a year later, in 1977, before concluding the Egyptian–Israeli peace treaty with him in 1979. Ten years later, Harkabi seemed to provide a refutation of his own earlier contentions that: 'The ceaseless debate between Arab radicals and moderates is the best guide to understanding Arab positions, and the vehemence of the terms in which it is expressed demonstrates that the divergence is not over trivial details. The very existence of the debate disproves the conception, widespread in Israeli circles, that all Arabs share a common goal – the destruction of Israel – and that any differences among them are merely tactical.'[13]

anti-Semitism, to judge by Meir Litvak's declaration at a 2003 conference at the Jerusalem Center for Public Affairs:

> Harkabi thought that Arab anti-Semitism was the result of the Palestinian conflict and that if a political solution for it could be found Arab anti-Semitism would weaken. Perhaps that was true 30 years ago. Today anti-Semitism has become an integral part of the intellectual and cultural discourse of the Arab world. Much of Arab society believes it and it is much harder to uproot than was the case 30 or 40 years ago.[14]

The problems in the book immediately make themselves felt in its long introduction: 'Even Arab intellectuals,' write Litvak and Webman, 'who assailed Nazism, did not admit or denounce the Nazi genocide against the Jews, charging Zionism with cynically using the Holocaust or inventing it as a means of financial and psychological extortion.'[15] First, to say that there were no anti-Nazi Arab intellectuals who denounced the Jewish genocide is to utter a gross untruth. Second, the authors are guilty of a libellous amalgam when they lump together those who maintain that Zionism 'invented' the Holocaust with people – far more plentiful – persuaded, on the basis of evidence cited by countless Jewish and Israeli critics who are above all suspicion of Holocaust denial, that the state of Israel has exploited and continues to exploit the Holocaust for financial and political purposes.

Exactly like Harkabi, Litvak and Webman identify a variety of Arab attitudes only to claim that they converge in one and the same 'discourse': 'Consequently, we have witnessed the development of an Arab Holocaust discourse encompassing various attitudes partly inspired by those in the West, which range through a spectrum from justification to denial and projection of Nazi images onto Zionism and Israel, who had thus been transformed from victims to culprits.'[16*] This 'Arab Holocaust discourse', the two authors explain, is 'part of a broader anti-Zionist and anti-Semitic discourse which developed as part and parcel of the Arab-Israeli conflict'.[17] Thus Litvak's and Webman's fabrication of a putative 'Arab discourse on the Holocaust' rests on disparate and even contradictory elements. Like Harkabi, they assume that the incoherence resides not in their own far-fetched construct but in the Arab discourse itself:

> We would contend that the Arab discourse did not develop into one

---

* Let us note that Jews are implicitly identified with Zionism and Israel here; if they were not, it would be quite simply absurd to suggest that Zionism and Israel were victims of Nazism.

coherent narrative. Rather it is more appropriate to speak of a reservoir and a repertoire of references, arguments and images that are scattered and intertwined in the vast literature on the conflict, Zionism, Judaism, World War II, and the history of Arab attitudes toward Nazi Germany and the National-Socialist Party. This reservoir does not represent a specific intellectual trend, but rather serves Islamists, nationalists and leftists, who draw elements from it almost indiscriminately, and incorporate them into their discourse.[18]

The preceding sections of this book, showing as they do the four different major ideological currents that emerged in the Arab world in the inter-war period, confirm how outrageous it is to conflate three of these currents as a single 'Arab discourse' (the fourth current, that of the liberal Westernizers, having been omitted here for some unspecified reason).

What follows is not an inventory of all the inanities about the Holocaust that have been uttered, written, or, most frequently, simply translated from other languages in the Arab world at a rate that has been growing exponentially over the past few years. I will let others savour the perverse satisfaction of cataloguing them. Anyone with an interest in such an anthology will have no trouble finding one. In addition to the many printed sources available, of which Litvak's and Webman's book is the most comprehensive, a plethora of internet sites offer essentially the same compilation of quotations, which only testify to the alarmingly high proportion of ignorance and mindlessness among those who make public statements in the Arab world – a world governed, to its detriment, by regimes that generate just such ignorance and mindlessness.

The site par excellence belongs to the Middle East Media Research Institute (MEMRI), founded and headed by Yigal Carmon, formerly a ranking officer in the same intelligence service that Harkabi once directed. The Institute, which claims to reflect the 'reality' of the Arab world, translates its findings into English, German, Hebrew, Italian, French, Spanish, Russian, Chinese and Japanese.[19] However, MEMRI is conspicuously – even more than the two books just discussed – a function of the Arab–Israeli conflict, acting like a sub-department of the Israeli propaganda services. Launched in Washington in 1998 in order to 'inform the debate over U.S. policy in the Middle East',[20] it has no difficulty – given the substantial means placed at its disposal by private and institutional donors – selecting, translating and distributing an impressive series of articles culled from Arab and Iranian print media and the internet, as well as extracts from television programmes, all of which often contain remarks of abysmal stupidity.

If such biased inventories and anthologies are of any use beyond propaganda, it is as a barometer of the ideological and intellectual regression currently underway in the Arab world. That undertakings of this sort no more reveal the 'Arab attitude' than they do 'the reality of the Arab world' does not mean that those who compile them invent the quotations they proffer. What they do is to put manifestations of the regression on prominent display, while often taking them out of context; selected, assembled, and concentrated in a single stream, these exhibits project a deliberately distorted image of the Arab world's intellectual production. Nevertheless, as long as one keeps in mind that this material is being used for propaganda purposes, these collections may be treated as so many early warning systems: scanners that reveal the lesions in the Arab media.

Paradoxically, then, Arabs should consider these propaganda enterprises salutary – in the way that an information bulletin that your enemy devotes to your vices and defects is. Every Arab who recognizes that these anti-Semitic ravings or mindless denials of the Holocaust, far from undermining the Israeli cause as their authors intend, in fact help Israel produce anti-Arab propaganda has already taken a big step towards understanding why they are so inept.

The Nakba as seen by Benny Morris: A Symptomatic Trajectory

The history of Israeli receptions of the Nakba has yet to be written; that is certainly not our subject here. Nevertheless, a brief review of the way the Nakba's main Israeli historian portrays it may help shed light on the logic of the war of narratives now being produced. The memory of the Holocaust has become one of the direct stakes of these polemics, ever since it was elevated into one of the main Israeli arguments designed to win the West's support against the Arabs. However, as indicated in the Introduction to this book, Israeli receptions of the Nakba weigh heavily on Arab receptions of the Holocaust in a symbolic tit for tat. This warrants an examination of the way one of the most complete Israeli acknowledgements of the facts about the Nakba was eventually marred by an extremist Zionist perspective.

Benny Morris is, incontestably, the leading Israeli historian of the Nakba. He acquired this status long before publication of his most recent book, *1948: A History of the First Arab–Israeli War*,[21] an impressive compendium on what was perceived as 'a war of national independence' by one side and 'a war of colonial usurpation' by the other. Morris's first major work on what Palestinians and other Arabs call the Nakba, *The Birth of the Palestinian Refugee Problem, 1947–1949*,[22] appeared just before another Arab word naming an episode in Palestinian history made its way into the international lexicon: Intifada. In the year 1987, the last weeks of which saw the beginnings of the Palestinian uprising that peaked in 1988, the book that made Morris's reputation was published. Together with another pioneering work, Simha Flapan's iconoclastic, hard-hitting book about the same historical period, *The Birth of Israel: Myths and Realities*,[23] released the same year as Morris's, it marked the debut of what was termed, by Morris himself,[24] Israel's 'new history' or 'new historiography', before it was ranged under the more apposite rubric of 'post-Zionism'.[25]

The post-Zionist ethos was, first and foremost, a product of the trauma that the 1982 invasion of Lebanon inflicted on the conscience – the clear conscience – of a generation of Israelis born after the foundation of the state. They had been steeped, until the invasion, in the traditional ideological discourse of the Zionist establishment, of its 'right-thinking' left in particular, and the apologetic Zionist narrative about the state's creation. This myth, which held that the 'Jewish state' had been based since its inception on the noblest values of Jewish philosophical humanism, was shattered or, rather, 'deconstructed', by Israel's commitment to a programme of murderous violence that could not be justified by the presumption of legitimate self-defence or by the memory of a Holocaust the spectre of which had to be conjured away at all costs. Six years after the invasion of Lebanon, this violence was reproduced in another guise with the brutal repression of the Intifada. As Morris emphasized, 'Most of [the New Historians] were born around 1948 and have matured in a more open, doubting, and self-critical Israel than the pre-Lebanon War Israel in which the Old Historians grew up.'[26]

The revelations of the Israeli 'New Historians' confirmed what Palestinian historians had always maintained about the massive expulsion of the Arab population from the 78 per cent of the territory of Palestine that the Zionist movement succeeded in seizing in 1948.[27] Acknowledging the reality of this 'transfer' – the consecrated euphemism for expulsion in Zionist jargon – Morris was still, in 1988, blunting the impact of this acknowledgement by minimizing the premeditation involved. Among the Zionist establishment's myths, as enounced and denounced by Flapan, is the claim that 'the flight of the Palestinians from the country, both before and after the establishment of the state of Israel, came in response to a call by the Arab leadership to leave temporarily, in order to return with the victorious Arab armies. They fled despite the efforts of the Jewish leadership to persuade them to stay.' In Flapan's debunking, 'the flight was prompted by Israel's political and military leaders, who believed that Zionist colonization and statehood necessitated the "transfer" of Palestinian Arabs to Arab countries.'[28] The myth itself was permanently shattered by Benny Morris. But it gave way in his book to another myth, according to which the expulsion was the result of an unfortunate combination of circumstances, most of them fortuitous.

Pressured by anti-Zionist critiques, especially those proffered by the Palestinian historian Nur Masalha[29] and confirmed by the most famous of the Israeli 'New Historians', Tom Segev,* Morris ultimately conceded that the 'transfer' had been more fully premeditated than he had at first believed. In the 2004 second edition of his book, *The Birth of the Palestinian Refugee Problem Revisited*, he acknowledged that 'pre-1948 "Transfer" thinking had a greater effect on what happened in 1948 than [he] had allowed for' and that 'the evidence for pre-1948 Zionist support for "Transfer" really is unambiguous'.[31] At the same time, however, he strove to downplay what he had been compelled to admit by minimizing the relationship between this line of thought and the course of operations in the 1948 war. A few years earlier, he had been distinctly franker: 'Without doubt, the crystallization of the consensus in support of transfer among the Zionist leaders helped pave the way for the precipitation of the Palestinian exodus of 1948. Similarly, far more of that exodus was triggered by explicit acts and orders of expulsion by Jewish Israeli troops than is indicated in *The Birth*.'[32]

Between the time when he made this affirmation, published in 2001, and the 2004 book release, Morris had undergone a political metamorphosis. To employ the sociologist Uri Ram's typology, he had abandoned post-Zionism for neo-Zionism.[33] Ram defines the difference between the two attitudes as follows:

> Post-Zionism is citizen-oriented (supporting equal rights, and in that sense favoring a state of all its citizens within the [pre-1967] boundaries of the Green Line), universal and global. Neo-Zionism is particularist, tribal, Jewish, ethnic nationalist, fundamentalist, and even fascist on the fringe.[34]

Morris's conversion dates to 2000, as he himself revealed in a 2004 *Haaretz* interview that caused a scandal.[35] The interview came in the context of the right-wing radicalization that swept over Israeli society after the summer 2000 failure of the Camp David negotiations, a radicalization triggered by

---

* 'The notion of population transfer is deeply rooted in Zionist ideology, a logical outgrowth of the principle of segregation between Jews and Arabs and a reflection of the desire to ground the Jewish state in European, rather than Middle Eastern, culture.'[30]

the provocation Ariel Sharon staged on Jerusalem's Temple Mount (*al-haram al-qudsi al-sharif*) in September of that year, which also sparked the Second Intifada bringing Sharon to power in February 2001.

Without denying the facts that he himself had helped establish, Morris began to justify what he did not hesitate to call 'ethnic cleansing'. What is more, he pointed out that the verb 'to cleanse' was omnipresent in the 1948 Zionist documents that he had examined. Like official Zionist ideologues, he based his justification on the spectre of the Holocaust, pressed into service as an all-purpose pretext: 'There are circumstances in history that justify ethnic cleansing. I know that this term is completely negative in the discourse of the 21st century, but when the choice is between ethnic cleansing and genocide – the annihilation of your people – I prefer ethnic cleansing.'[36]

Morris was altogether blind to the incongruity of his argument. It makes sense to choose 'ethnic cleansing' over genocide only if the victimizers and the victims are identical. Thus it would be possible to argue that, on balance, the 'ethnic cleansing' of Palestine, that is, the expulsion of the Palestinians, was less grave than a Palestinian genocide pure and simple, on the cynical assumption that, at all events, the end justifies the means. The ethnocentric individual who makes such a statement generally forgets that that end itself can be judged very differently, depending on the system of values chosen. He also assumes that all means are justified in the final analysis, genocide included, as was made clear by Morris's next statement: 'Even the great American democracy could not have been created without the annihilation of the Indians. There are cases in which the overall, final good justifies harsh and cruel acts that are committed in the course of history.'[37]

But in a role reversal typical of official Zionist reasoning about Palestine, in which Israeli Jews are always victims, potential if not real, the choice in 1948 according to Morris was between the expulsion of the Palestinians and the genocide of the Jews – the expulsion of the other and the genocide of one's own ('your people').

The fact that some of the Jews of Palestine felt threatened by annihilation in 1948 is past doubting. But for a historian to affirm that threat some six decades later is just bewildering. How could the Palestinians have mustered the strength to perpetrate genocide when they lacked even the strength to prevent their expulsion and were not prepared for war? The question never crosses Morris's mind, although he is better informed than most about a situation that he himself sums up in the conclusion to his most recent work, *1948: A History of the First Arab-Israeli War*:

The Yishuv had organized for war. The Arabs hadn't. The small, com-
pact Jewish community in Palestine was economically and politically
vibrant, a potential powerhouse if adequately organized and directed.
And it enjoyed a unity of purpose and a collective fear – of a new Holocaust – that afforded high levels of motivation (as well as magnetizing
international support) ...

The Palestinian Arabs, with well-established traditions of disunity,
corruption, and organizational incompetence, failed to mobilize their
resources. They even failed to put together a national militia organization before going to war.[38]

The whites in South Africa never genuinely incurred the danger of genocide
by the blacks, although there were four times as many blacks as whites. This
was not, of course, because the whole black population espoused the principles
of non-violence, but because the whites held a monopoly on military force.
The monopoly on the means of violence determines sovereignty. Thus the
Israeli Jews could have exercised sovereignty over a disarmed Palestinian
population as large as their own, or even over one superior in numbers,
depriving them of political and civic rights in a system similar to that of
South African apartheid.

In other words, the real alternative facing the Zionist leadership in 1948
was not a choice between a 'new Holocaust' of Israeli Jews and 'ethnic
cleansing' of Palestinian Arabs, but between two versions of the Zionist state:
Jewish apartheid or 'Jewish and democratic'. The second option – chosen by
the Yishuv's majority leadership for reasons of ideological compatibility –
implied both expelling the majority of the Palestinians and maintaining a
Palestinian minority within the boundaries of the Jewish state as a token of
its democratic character, as I have argued in an essay on 'Zionism and Peace'
written in the wake of the 1993 Israeli–Palestinian Oslo agreement:

As to the *plausibility* of this ideology with regard to the egalitarian universalism proclaimed in 1948, it is precisely conditioned by the existence
of an assured Jewish majority inside the *demos** – concealing the fact that
it has been constituted by the discriminatory denial to the indigenous
inhabitants of an elementary right of return. The maintenance of a minority of non-Jewish citizens inside the Israeli *demos* appears, therefore, as
the indispensable token, not to say alibi, of Zionist democracy and its
proclaimed universalism – on the express condition that this minority

---

*   *Demos*, the Greek root of the word 'democracy', means 'people'.

remains very much a minority and cannot put in question the 'Jewish-ness' of the state.[39]

The same observation also serves as an indirect response to the specious argument on which Morris, after many others, has fallen back: the expulsion was not premeditated, the argument goes, because if it had it been, it would have been total. Yet the leadership of the Yishuv pursued an objective that dictated the expulsion, *ma non troppo*[*], of the Palestinians. Morris eventually came to regret this policy:

> If [Ben-Gurion] was already engaged in expulsion, maybe he should have done a complete job. I know that this stuns the Arabs and the liberals and the politically correct types. But my feeling is that this place would be quieter and know less suffering if the matter had been resolved once and for all. If Ben-Gurion had carried out a large expulsion and cleansed the whole country – the whole Land of Israel, as far as the Jordan River. It may yet turn out that this was his fatal mistake. If he had carried out a full expulsion – rather than a partial one – he would have stabilized the State of Israel for generations.[40]

Morris here assumes, in altogether arbitrary fashion, that complete expulsion of the Palestinians would have done more to 'stabilize' the state of Israel than maintaining a minority of Arabs within its borders. Yet one can also contend that the presence of the Arab minority not only has had precious few destabilizing effects, but that it has been abundantly exploited to various ends by Israeli propaganda.[†]

The balance of Morris's comments in the *Haaretz* interview presages a logic that came to full fruition in his latest book, *1948*. Palestinian society is 'barbarian', he opined; 'Something like a cage has to be built for them.'[41] For the foreseeable future, the opposition between Palestinians and Israelis will

---

[*]   *Ma non troppo*, an Italian expression used in musical scores, means 'but not too much'.

[†]   If Morris had remained as self-consistent as he was when, in 1988, he published the book that made him famous and spent three weeks in prison for refusing to serve in the army on the occupied West Bank, then rocked by the Intifada, he could have affirmed – while sticking to the post-Zionist interpretation of the 'Jewish and democratic state' – that Israel cannot achieve stability unless it withdraws from the 1967 occupied territories. The condition for Israel's stability is certainly not a new Nakba in those territories or those of 1948, since that would only considerably heighten tension in the region and increase, by the same token, the real, long-term risk of a 'new Holocaust' – a Holocaust brought about, this time, by nuclear bombs or some other weapon of mass destruction.

remain irreducible, for it is dictated, not by circumstances, but by cultural differences:

> I think the West today resembles the Roman Empire of the fourth, fifth and sixth centuries: The barbarians are attacking it and they may also destroy it.... The Arab world as it is today is barbarian ... I think that the war between the civilizations is the main characteristic of the 21st century. I think President Bush is wrong when he denies the very existence of that war. It's not only a matter of bin Laden. This is a struggle against a whole world that espouses different values. And we are on the front line. Exactly like the Crusaders, we are the vulnerable branch of Europe in this place.[42]

This logic of implacable opposition to a dehumanized enemy – the ultimate implication of which is extermination,[*] even if that is not what Morris advocates, since, as we have seen, he prefers 'ethnic cleansing' – holds the key to the striking contradiction that runs through *1948*. In this crowning accomplishment of years of research, a book so instructive that one is ill advised to ignore it, Morris goes very far in the direction of demolishing Zionist (and Hollywood – consider *Exodus*) myths about the creation of the state of Israel. He throws a harsh light on the reality of a war in which the behaviour of the Jewish armed forces was in fact more sharply at variance with the canons of morality than that of their Arab foes:

> After the war, the Israelis tended to hail the 'purity of arms' of its militiamen and soldiers and to contrast this with Arab barbarism, which on occasion expressed itself in the mutilation of captured Jewish corpses. This reinforced the Israelis' positive self-image and helped them 'sell' the new state abroad; it also demonized the enemy. In truth, however, the Jews committed far more atrocities than the Arabs and killed far more civilians and POWs in deliberate acts of brutality in the course of 1948 ...
>
> The Arab regular armies committed few atrocities and no large-scale massacre of POWs and civilians in the conventional war – even though they conquered the Jewish Quarter of the Old City of Jerusalem and a number of rural settlements ...
>
> The Israelis' collective memory of fighters characterized by 'purity

---

[*]   This is Carl Schmitt's theorem presented the other way around: 'People who use such [genocidal] means against other people find themselves constrained to destroy these other people, who are their victims as well as their objects, morally as well. They are forced to declare the entire enemy camp criminal and inhuman, to reduce it to a complete nullity. Otherwise they would be criminals and monsters themselves.'[43]

of arms' is also undermined by the evidence of rapes committed in
conquered towns and villages ... Arabs appear to have committed few
acts of rape.[44]

The cold, hard look that Morris takes at the atrocities perpetrated by his
coreligionists in 1948 and his disillusioned acknowledgement that their
claim to a war of exceptional 'purity' simply masked the banality of one more
dirty war are both made possible by a declaration he makes at the outset:
this enterprise that the Zionists regarded 'as legitimate, indeed, as supremely
moral'[45] was even more legitimate and moral than they themselves thought.
For Ben-Gurion himself, Morris assures us, 'failed fully to appreciate the
depth of the Arabs' abhorrence of the Zionist-Jewish presence in Palestine, an
abhorrence anchored in centuries of Islamic Judeophobia with deep religious
and historical roots'.[46] Going on to cite an anti-Jewish pronouncement by
the Muslim Brotherhood, he comments: 'Such thinking characterized the
Arab world, where the overwhelming majority of the population were,
and remain, believers.'[47] The problem, consequently, resides in Islam, since
believing Muslims are ipso facto Jew-haters. This is followed by a number
of arguments of the same cast, designed to prove that the 1948 war was not
only a war between two nationalisms but also 'part of a more general, global
struggle between the Islamic East and the West, in which the Land of Israel/
Palestine figured, and still figures, as a major battlefront'.[48]

As Avi Shlaim pointed out, after noting the positive qualities of *1948* in his
review of the book in the London *Guardian*, 'the only major departure from
the evidence, and from common sense, is the stress on the jihadi character
of the two-stage Arab assault on the Jewish community in Palestine ... The
empirical evidence for this view is utterly underwhelming, consisting as it
does of a collection of random quotes.' [49] Thus Dr Morris, a historian who
has systematically defended 'the facts' and scholarly rigour based on ample
documentation, has succumbed to an ideological discourse that is all too
common in the dawning twenty-first century: a mélange of neo-conservatism
made in the USA and neo-Zionism, against a backdrop of Islamophobia.

For Nissim Rejwan, one of the best Israeli specialists of the Arab world,
ordinary Islam is far from being a doctrine that threatens Israeli Jews with
a holocaust under the aegis of a new totalitarianism. Islam itself is, rather,
precisely the reason that such a prospect is implausible in the Arab world,
in contrast to twentieth-century Europe:

Auschwitz and similar anti-Jewish horrors of World War II would have been unthinkable without the strong and uninterrupted anti-Semitic strain in the Christian tradition and culture of the West; and to the extent that this is so, the Holocaust in Europe of the 1940s must be seen as a culmination of the history of the Christian West's attitude toward its Jews. Neither their religious culture nor their historical record lends credence to the claim that the Muslim Arabs of today are capable of the kind of historical consummation that found expression in Auschwitz and other Nazi extermination camps.[50]

CHAPTER 5

The Nasser Years (1948–1967)

The Nakba dealt a heavy blow to three of the four major currents in the Arab independence movement of the inter-war years. The liberal Westernizers, who might otherwise have reaped the benefits of their successful wager on an Allied victory, suffered a mortal setback as a result of the Allies' complicity in the creation of the state of Israel. As Orayb Aref Najjar has shown in the Palestine case in a study of the editorials in the daily *Falastīn*:

> As late as 1943, *Falastin* still hoped that some good for Palestinians would come out of the war (*Falastin*, December 19 and December 24, 1943). By 1945, however, the journalists writing for the newspaper were disillusioned. For instance, one editorial compared 'overt and covert' dictatorships. It explained that, while the overt dictatorships of WW II were now defeated, the world could not mend until the covert ones were uprooted ... The newspaper editors concluded that both the British Labor and Conservative parties share the same logic of imperialism, 'and it rests on one unchangeable premise: a foundation which excuses the strong lording it over the weak.'[1]

The Arab Communists, who had profited immensely from the Soviet Union's military achievements after the turning point at Stalingrad, were considerably weakened by Stalin's political and military support for Israel. Politically motivated ingratitude was the sole reason for Israel's reluctance to admit that this two-pronged support had been of decisive importance: Israel found it hard to acknowledge its debt to a Soviet Union that had rapidly shifted from opposition to the Zionist project to support for it, only to adopt, in the end, a position of hostility to the Zionist state, when the latter chose to ally itself with the USSR's opponents during the Cold War. As Benny Morris has recently recalled:

> The Americans imposed an arms embargo on the region starting in December 1947. The United Nations imposed a wider embargo in late

May 1948, crucially affecting supplies to the Arab states, which had traditionally received their weapons and ammunition (on credit) from their former colonial masters, Britain and France ...

Once the fighting began, the Yishuv/Israel discovered another, major source of equipment. The Americans and, by and large, the Western European states refused to sell the Haganah arms. But the Soviet Union and Czechoslovakia, for a combination of reasons ... were willing to ignore the United Nations and sell arms to the Yishuv ... From late March 1948 onward, Czech arms – and additional arms from black and gray market sources – poured into Palestine/Israel, enabling the Yishuv to neutralize the Palestinian Arab militias, go over to the offensive, parry the Arab armies' invasion, and, eventually, win the war.[2]

The 1948 defeat also weakened the Pan-Islamic movement. It is true that the Egyptian and Palestinian Muslim Brothers, who had taken an active part in the armed struggle against the Zionists in Palestine, succeeded, for a time, in taking advantage of the hatred and rancour caused by the Nakba. But the defeat dealt the already floundering reputation of their Palestinian hero, Amin al-Husseini, the crowning blow; it also revealed the hypocrisy of the Saudi kingdom, the one Arab state that, like the Muslim Brotherhood, championed a fundamentalist interpretation of Islam. As Madawi Al-Rasheed has written, in an essay on the Wahhabist monarchy's role in the 1948 war: 'Over Palestine, the Saudi king demonstrated a remarkable servile attitude to the British against the rhetoric of the Jihad that was meant to defend the holy land and the Palestinians.'[3] Hence 'the Saudi regime was inevitably counted,' by Arab nationalists, 'among those regimes that "sold Palestine" to the Jews.'

The only position that the Nakba reinforced in the long run was that of the Arab nationalists. With the onset of post-war decolonization, nationalists in the colonized countries had the wind in their sails. The war for Palestine intensified the general anti-colonial hostility to the Western powers in the Arab world. It also offered a clear illustration of the need for Arab unity: Israel thus helped catalyse aspirations for unification of the region. What is more, the nationalists were not represented in any of the regimes that had been put to shame by the 1948 defeat, and they owed no allegiance to any of the Zionist state's sponsors, on either side of the Iron Curtain that had come down across Europe.

For all these reasons, Arab nationalism found it easy to identify with a Third World whose political emergence was marked by the 1955 Bandung Conference. Let us add that the Nakba – by heightening the military's resentment of the civilian authorities whom it held responsible for the defeat, absolving itself of all blame in the process – rang in the age of the coup d'état in the Arab world. Coups became the Arab nationalists' privileged route to power (despite the fact that the series of coups was inaugurated in 1949 in Syria by military men associated with the Arab nationalists' rivals in the Greater Syrian nationalist movement founded by Antun Saadeh).

By far the most important figure behind the tempestuous rise of Arab nationalism in the years following the Nakba was Gamal Abdel-Nasser; the Baath also played a major, albeit less significant, role. Underpinning this nationalist tendency was an even more motley combination of influences than the one that had shaped it during the preceding period, from liberal or illiberal Westernism (the emblematic figure of the latter being, of course, the founder of the new Turkey, Mustafa Kemal, although Arab nationalist military rulers refused to acknowledge his profound influence) to Islamic fundamentalism, from right-wing ultra-nationalism to Marxism-Leninism.

The group of Free Officers who overthrew the Egyptian monarchy in 1952 provides the best illustration of the composite nature of post-war Arab nationalism. As has already been emphasized in Part I, it brought together followers of nearly all the currents previously discussed.[4] But, as James Jankowski recently pointed out, quite rightly, 'The impact and meaning of such contacts should not be exaggerated ... By and large, the officers were their own men.'[5] It should be added that Nasserism did not spring whole, like Athena, from Nasser's brain: it was an ideology under construction during the eighteen years that its leading spokesman – a man with a great thirst for knowledge, as his biographers emphatically affirm – was in power. Thus the increasingly leftward tilt of Nasserism, which grew into 'Arab socialism' in the 1960s, like the concomitant radicalization of other variants of Arab nationalism, went hand in hand with the growing influence of Communist ideas, which the nationalists' public declarations patently echoed.

Nor should we overestimate the role that the Nakba played in shaping Arab nationalist currents in the 1950s, Nasserism in particular. Although Nasser attached great importance to the Palestinian question, he himself explicitly disassociated the 1952 'Revolution' from the shock of the 1948 defeat. His 1954 manifesto, *Philosophy of the Revolution*, attributed the Revolution primarily to specifically Egyptian conditions. Quoting an account published in the *Jewish Observer* by the Israeli officer Yeruham Cohen,[*] with whom he had been in contact during the 1949 cease-fire negotiations, Nasser even admitted that the Zionists' success in their struggle against the British[6] had

---

[*]   An Arab-speaking native of Yemen, Captain Yeruham Cohen had been named to his post by General Yigal Allon, responsible, at the time, for the Negev front.

fascinated him – just as it had fascinated Michel Aflaq, the founder of the Baath, in the same period.*

Cohen, for his part, got the impression, from his exchanges with Nasser, that the Egyptian leader understood the Jews' struggle against the British in Palestine and envied them for it. He wrote in the 30 January 1953 *Haaretz* that

> It was obvious that he understood and approved our struggle against the British. He was well acquainted with the combats of the Haganah and, on the basis of the Zionist struggle against the English, was making an effort to understand the possibilities offered by a mobilization of the masses in a resistance movement ... Without a doubt, he envied us.[8]

'Throwing the Jews into the Sea'?

Laura James has pointed out that, initially, Israel was a secondary preoccupation for the men who carried out the Egyptian putsch:

> Before the revolution, the question of Israel was not a high priority for the Free Officers. Nasser is said to have told a CIA representative [Miles Copeland] that the conspirators' enemies were 'our own superior officers, other Arabs, the British and the Israelis – in that order'. Their problematic neighbour was not mentioned in the revolutionary charter, which focused on expelling the British and fostering domestic development ...
>
> 'The idea of throwing the Jews into the sea is propaganda,' Nasser told Richard Crossman in December 1953.[9][†]

It was not just in Crossman's presence that Nasser repudiated the idea of 'throwing the Jews into the sea'. The Gamal Abdel-Nasser Foundation's website, created in collaboration with the Bibliotheca Alexandrina,[10] contains

---

*   See 'The Baath Party' in Ch. 3 above. It is interesting to compare these facts with Bernard Lewis's interpretation of the impact of the Nakba: 'The shock of defeat in 1948 was especially humiliating in that the victors were not the mighty imperial powers but the Jews, familiar as a tolerated minority. Defeat at their hands was especially galling, and led to the overthrow by violence of most of the regimes held guilty of allowing it to happen.'[7]

†   Richard Crossman (1907–74) served as a Labour MP in the British House of Commons before taking a post as a cabinet minister. In 1945–6, he was a member of the Anglo-American Committee of Inquiry on Palestine. After Clement Attlee's Labour government, and, in particular, Foreign Secretary Ernest Bevin rejected the Committee's proposal to allow 100,000 Jews among the post-war 'displaced persons' to emigrate to Palestine, Crossman became one of Labour's fiercest supporters of the Israeli state.

1,359 declarations and transcriptions of speeches or interviews by the founder of modern Egypt. This electronic resource makes it considerably easier to analyse Nasser's discourse. There one finds an address delivered by *Bikbachi* (colonel) Abdel-Nasser before Alexandria's Palestine Club on 13 December 1953 – the same month that he made Crossman's acquaintance. In it, the future president offers an ironical comment on the Arab attitude during the period when the Zionist plan was being translated into action under the British mandate: 'At our meetings and in our speeches, we said we were going to throw the Jews into the sea, and felt reassured after every speech. Then we all went back home.'[11]

Jean Lacouture reports witnessing a similar incident. Early in 1954, when Nasser and two other leaders of the new regime paid a visit to the University of Cairo, the Free Officers were booed by students, who demanded weapons with which to liberate the Suez Canal and Palestine. Salah Salem, a member of the Revolutionary Command Council, answered the students: 'When we were your age, we, too, demanded to be given weapons so that we could throw the Jews into the sea! But it was the Jews who threw us out!'[12]

One of the central themes that Nasser hammered in his early writings and speeches was that the principal enemy was Britain; the British, not the Jews, were primarily responsible for the Arabs' loss of Palestine. In the 13 December 1953 speech just cited, Nasser went on:

> Who urged the Jews on, encouraged them to occupy Palestine, and defeated the Arab people? It was England. It was England that was the problem, the foremost calamity. We forgot this, and said 'the Jews'; but when we were fighting in Palestine, England prevented us from receiving weapons, whereas the Jews received weapons from all quarters ... Arab leaders forget the primary cause of our defeat, England, and say Israel and the Jews. They are afraid to say England.

This was a recurrent theme of Arab nationalism in its revolutionary phase, in which it sought to subvert Arab regimes subservient to the West. While these regimes strove to turn the resentment of the Arab populations against Israel, if not the Jews *per se*, the Arab nationalists identified imperialism as the enemy to be combated before all others, and simultaneously identified its local lackeys as targets. The main enemy of the Arab nation to which Nasser points in his 1954 manifesto is accordingly not Zionism but (British) colonialism:

It is a single region. The same circumstances, the same factors ... even the same forces, united against all of it.

And it was clear that the foremost of these forces was imperialism.

Even Israel itself is but a result of imperialism. For if Palestine had not fallen under the British mandate, Zionism would never have been able to muster enough support to realize the idea of a national home in Palestine. The idea would have remained a mad dream, incapable of being fulfilled.[13]

Even after the Egyptian leaders' anti-Zionism had become more radical – following the Israeli army's bloody 28 February 1955 raid on Gaza (then under Egyptian rule) and, above all, the Tripartite (British–French–Israeli) Aggression launched on Egypt in October–November 1956 in reaction to its nationalization of the Suez Canal – the main enemy was still, in Nasserism's view, imperialism. Zionism and reactionary Arabs were always considered its creatures. Nasserism thus never seriously and fundamentally embraced the fantasy of an omnipotent international Zionist movement controlling even the United States:

> By May 1967, therefore, on the eve of the Six Day War, the enemy from Nasser's point of view was threefold. 'Imperialism' was represented by the USA and her 'lackey' Britain. They led the 'West' ... [which was] viewed as the staunch political ally and arms supplier of its own creation, 'Zionist' Israel, formulaically described as the 'imperialist base in the heart of the Arab homeland.' Since the 'Arab reactionaries' were also supported by imperialism, they and Israel 'cannot by any means be two conflicting sides but must be two co-operating sides, even if that co-operation is through a middle-man.' There was no question of who was in charge, however. Imperialism was 'the origin and the source of planning'; the others were 'only satellites spinning in the US orbit and following its steps.'[14]

Nasser's stock criticisms of Israel were generally based on democratic principles. He repeatedly declared that religious discrimination[15] was at the foundation of the Zionist state, which he called belligerent and expansionist, referring to both Ben-Gurion and the increasing electoral success of the Herut, the heir to Jabotinsky's Revisionism.[16] As for a solution to the Israeli–Palestinian problem, Nasser first alluded to it in a 1 March 1953 declaration in which he criticized the United States for supporting the creation of Israel while ignoring 'the Arabs' right to live with the Jewish minority in harmony and peace within the frontiers of a single state'.[17]

This underlying attitude, which he maintained over the years, involves, to be sure, a fundamental error: it underestimates Zionism's success in forging a national entity (something well understood by both Arabs and Jews who drew up pre-1948 plans for a binational Palestine) while assuming that the national dimension of the Israeli entity can be converted back into a religious one. It has nothing to do, however, with expelling the Jews and even less to do with extirpating them. Arab nationalism's proclaimed objective in the 1950s and 1960s – to 'destroy', 'liquidate' or 'bring down' (*al-qāda' 'ala* was the expression most commonly employed until 1967, according to Harkabi) Israel,[18] or, to use the then consecrated term, the 'Zionist entity' – was directed exclusively at the institutions of the Zionist state created by force of arms in 1948; Israel's Jewish population was not the target, just as the South African National Congress's struggle to 'destroy the apartheid state'* did not target the country's white population.[19] Michel Aflaq, the Baath Party's founder and ideologue, expressed the same idea in 1957. Aflaq even held that the rise of Arab socialism constituted a guarantee for the Jews living in Arab countries:

> It is the Israeli state entity that endangers the Arab nation, not the presence of a Jewish minority in the Arab fatherland ... The rapid progress of the Arab struggle for socialism allays the Jewish minority's apprehensions about the impossibility of peaceful, equitable coexistence with the Arabs, just as it neutralizes or blunts the weapon employed by international Zionist propaganda to win the sympathy of the free peoples and popular classes for Israel as a state that supposedly constitutes a refuge for an oppressed, refined, advanced people. Finally, the fact that the Arabs have continued to remain humanists in the international arena while co-operating with other peoples to secure peace and socialist progress for all the world's peoples, as well as their policy of positive neutrality, have helped eliminate the causes of racist and religious fanaticism in the world and simultaneously fostered the integration of the Jewish minority in the European countries, thus undermining the justifications for Israel's existence.[20]

Thus it is no wonder that relations between Cairo and Ahmad Shuqayri were heavily strained after Shuqayri made an inflammatory speech in Amman on the eve of the 1967 War. While he did not literally call for throwing the Jews

---

*   The preamble to the ANC's 1991 Constitution states that 'the ANC has emerged to lead the struggle of all democratic and patriotic forces to destroy the apartheid state and replace it with the united, non-racial, non-sexist and democratic South Africa in which the people as a whole shall govern and all shall enjoy equal rights.'

into the sea, as he was accused of doing, in substance he made much the same demand, if not, indeed, worse.[21] His declaration reflected the position of the Higher Arab Committee, headed by Amin al-Husseini, which Shuqayri had joined at the end of the Second World War; it conceded the right to remain in Palestine only to those Jews already resident before the British mandate, demanding that all others return to their countries of origin. After a stint as the Saudi kingdom's ambassador to the UN, Shuqayri was installed as the leader of the Palestine Liberation Organization by the League of Arab states when, in 1964, the PLO was created in Jerusalem (then under Jordanian rule). From June 1967 on, he cultivated a politics of permanent one-upmanship vis-à-vis the Nasser regime, especially after Cairo accepted UN Security Council Resolution 242 in November of that year.[22] This rivalry, of course, did not prevent Israeli propaganda from attributing Shuqayri's remarks and positions to the Nasser regime.

Nasser's vision of a just solution to the conflict never changed; witness his 8 February 1970 response to two American journalists who asked him on what conditions Israelis and Arabs could peacefully coexist:[23]

> There are two fundamental points here. The first is complete withdrawal of the Israeli invaders from the [post-1967] occupied territories. The second is the solution of the Palestinian problem. Palestinian leaders have said, for example, that they are prepared to live in Palestine with the Israelis as they are today; they meant that the Jews, as they are today, should live with Muslims and Christians. The Israelis, however, are determined to rid themselves of the Palestinians and establish their state on the basis of Judaism. They interpret Judaism as not only a religious belief, but also a form of nationalism, and this complicates the problem. I do not know what would happen if we decided to base our state on Islam, while others based theirs on Christianity, and still others on Buddhism. There would be acts inspired by fanaticism everywhere.[24]

The demonstration of Israel's 'conventional' military superiority, however, as well as the certain knowledge, from 1968 on, that Israel had the atom bomb, ultimately persuaded Nasser of the folly of a strategy aimed at resolving the Palestinian problem by defeating the Zionist state on the battlefield. He was, consequently, all the more firmly convinced that Israelis themselves had to pressure their state into making a radical change of course and finding a peaceful solution to the Arab–Israeli conflict. In one of his last public speeches – delivered on 23 July 1970, the eighteenth anniversary of the Egyptian Revolution, two months before his death – Nasser put out a message of hope, invoking recent protests against the occupation organized by Jews in Israel itself:

> In Israel, there are demonstrations in Tel Aviv and occupied Jerusalem; in Israel, there are, today, young people who perceive their leaders' racist fanaticism, aimed at bringing about a state of permanent war; in Israel, there are people who put no faith at all in talk to the effect that the Arabs want to slit the Jews' throats and throw them into the sea, because they remember that Jews have lived alongside us for thousands of years here and have never suffered massacre or persecution; they know that the reason for the predicament in which we find ourselves today is the fact that Israel has invaded Palestine, expelled the Palestinian Arab people from its land, denied the rights of the people of Palestine, and decided to enact a policy of brute force aimed at terrorizing the Arab people by killing women and children.[25]

Nasserism and Anti-Semitism

From the day Nasser became president until the day he died, Israeli propaganda energetically denounced the Egyptian leader as an anti-Semite – an insult systematically cast in the teeth of anyone opposed to the state of Israel. Elie Podeh, head of the Department of Islamic and Middle Eastern Studies at the Hebrew University of Jerusalem, has shown how Nasser was demonized by Israel's leaders, beginning with Ben-Gurion, and how their aspersions were circulated by the country's mass media.[26]

This diabolical image of Nasser was constructed on the basis of several grotesque analogies: Nasser = Hitler; *Philosophy of the Revolution* = *Mein Kampf*; the 1958 Syrian–Egyptian Union = the 1938 *Anschluss*; the alliance between Nasser and Khrushchev = the Hitler–Stalin Pact; and so on. And of course a conciliatory stance of any kind towards Nasser's Egypt elicited cries of *Munich* and *appeasement*. The frenzied use of this analogy and of 'the Holocaust as propaganda', in Tom Segev's phrase,[27] exacerbated by both increased Israeli and international sensitivity to the question of the Holocaust in the wake of the 1961 Eichmann trial, naturally peaked during the crisis leading up to the June 1967 war.

Those who levelled the charge of anti-Semitism against Nasser and Arab nationalism as a whole sought to underpin it with supporting evidence from documentary sources. The main culprit was none other than General Yehoshafat Harkabi, who, in a 1965 article in the Israeli daily *Maariv*, reported some of the results of his research on the 'Arab attitude' and the 'new anti-

Semitism'. The Education Department of the Israeli army distributed the general's article to the troops,[28] and his book became one of the Israelis' favourite weapons in the propaganda war. The speciousness of his line of reasoning is made immediately evident by the way he denounces 'the identification of Zionism with Judaism': he conflates failure to draw a proper distinction in speeches and writings, which is frequent, with explicit rejection of this distinction, which is far more exceptional.

Like most Arabs who lived during the period of the British mandate over Palestine, Nasser often used 'the Jews' to designate the Israelis. The nationalists' refusal to recognize the state of Israel after 1948 made them uncomfortable with the term 'Israeli'; the terms 'Jews' and 'Arabs' had long been the everyday designations for the two communities living in Palestine under the mandate. Yet Harkabi's all but certain awareness of this usage did not prevent him from making the unwarranted assertion that the confusion between Jews and Zionists was, as a rule, deliberate:

> Arab writers and leaders repeatedly emphasize that they bear no hostility to the Jews but only oppose the Zionists. However, this distinction is not maintained, and Zionism and Judaism are often used as synonyms, a denunciation of Zionism leading naturally to a denunciation of the Jews. It is not a matter of confusing 'Jew', 'Zionist' and 'Israeli' in the flow of speech or writing, in the same way as even Israelis do not always preserve the distinction; the identification is deliberate.[29]

Let us first note that Harkabi feels no need to make any distinctions among 'Arab writers and leaders' based on the political currents to which they belong. That makes him guilty of the same sin for which he is excoriating his adversaries. It is also not true that the confusion between Jews and Zionists was always 'deliberate' (and many Arab writers and leaders did draw the distinction). The failure to distinguish between 'Jews' and 'Zionists' is undeniably frequent in the Arab world – as it also is in Israel, something Harkabi all too hesitantly acknowledges. At the same time, *pace* Harkabi, many of those who habitually refer to the Israelis as 'the Jews' very deliberately distinguish between Jews and Zionists when they are expressing themselves in considered fashion.[*] Note these remarks of Nissim Rejwan's upon the publication of Harkabi's book in Israel:

> Harkabi gives me the feeling that he wants to eat the cake and have it.

---

[*]   For an example, see the anecdote related by the Palestinian Arab nationalist Akram Zu'aytir, Chapter 3 above, 'Arab Nationalism and Anti-Semitism'.

He himself, as a Zionist, would not really make any distinction between Zionism and Judaism, Israeli and Jew – but he asks the Arabs to do so, and the trouble is that even if they do so, he would not agree; he would still call them anti-Semites since, as is often said here [in Israel], you cannot draw the line between Zionism and Judaism.[30]

Since its inception, Zionism has been calling itself 'the movement for national liberation of the Jewish people'; it has been identifying itself with Judaism and Jewishness; it has practically appropriated the Jewish Bible, the Talmud and the whole of Rabbinic Judaism and made them its own; and it has turned Abraham, Moses and the Prophets into the first Zionists. After 1948, Israel – the consummation, however partial, of Zionism – defined itself in such a way and promulgated laws and regulations of such a nature that it virtually turned all the 90 percent of Jews living outside its borders into Israeli 'nationals.' Who are we, then, to accuse Arabs of anti-Semitism when all they have done is fallen right into the ideological trap which the Zionists set for them?[31]

In fact, the distinction between Jews and Zionists had been firmly established by the official ideology of Nasser's Egypt. Nasser himself expressed it in words and even deeds, despite accusations that his regime persecuted the country's Jews during the 1950s, before the overwhelming majority of them chose exile. A contemporary observer has described the chain of events:

In the past, [Nasser] had encouraged harmony among non-Islamic groups; with monotonous regularity, the Grand Rabbi and leaders of the Coptic Church had been produced at major official functions. With apparent regret, Nasser authorized two trials against Jews, one involving espionage for Israel and the other 'Zionist cooperation with local Communists.' Foreign criticism notwithstanding, both cases appeared bona fide and the distinction between Jew and Egyptian seldom was made publicly. Although Nasser received unfavourable publicity from abroad when two persons convicted of spying were executed, it should be noted that the same penalty previously had been inflicted upon Muslims convicted of espionage.[32]

The two Egyptian Jews executed in 1955 had, in fact, taken part in a large-scale terrorist operation. Joel Beinin describes it as follows:

In July 1954, Israeli military intelligence ordered an espionage network of Egyptian Jews it had formed three years earlier to launch Operation Susannah – a campaign to firebomb the main Alexandria post office, the

United States Information Service Library in Cairo, the Cairo train station, and several movie theaters in Cairo and Alexandria. The saboteurs
(today they would be called terrorists, especially if they were Arabs or
Muslims acting against Israel or the United States) were quickly apprehended and brought to trial in December 1954.[33]

None of these circumstances prevented Israel and its allies from orchestrating
an international campaign presenting the trial and executions as anti-Semitic
acts perpetrated by a proto-Nazi regime. Operation Susannah, directed
from a distance by Israel – which, let us note in passing, has a long record
of state terrorism in the Middle East – made the Egyptian Jews' situation a
precarious one, inducing many to leave the country, for Israel in particular.
This development was of course not something that the Zionist authorities
were inclined to deplore. The subsequent Israeli participation in the 1956
attack on Egypt dealt a fatal blow to the Jewish community in Egypt, which
had already shrunk by a quarter as a result of the 1948 war:

> In response to the British–French–Israeli attack on Egypt on October 29,
> 1956, Egypt took harsh measures against its Jewish community. About
> 1,000 Jews were detained, more than half of them Egyptian citizens.
> Thirteen thousand French and British citizens were expelled from Egypt
> in retaliation for the tripartite attack, among them many Jews ... The
> government nationalized the assets of all British and French citizens, and
> Jews holding those nationalities were affected in that capacity ...
>
> The military proclamation seizing Jewish property [the military had
> sought to justify it by saying that it was a protective measure designed to
> prevent capital flight] was rescinded on April 27, 1957, and the property
> of Jews who were not British or French citizens was returned. By then,
> the Jewish community was crippled beyond restoration.[34]

The years following the Nakba saw the exodus of the great majority of the
Jews from the Arab world. Between 1948 and 1976, the number of Jews
living in Arab countries of both the Middle East and the Maghreb plunged
from 856,000 to 25,870,[35] and continued to fall in the decades thereafter. In
1948, the Jewish community of Egypt (75,000) was the fifth largest, after
those of Morocco (265,000), Algeria (140,000), Iraq (135,000) and Tunisia
(105,000).[36] Michel Abitbol, professor emeritus at the Hebrew University of
Jerusalem and himself a native of Morocco, has summed up the controversy
about this exodus:

> As might be expected, opinions vary as to the precise reasons for these

departures. For nationalist Muslims, the responsibility for them lay essentially with foreign agents – European colonial circles, Zionist militants,
Mossad agents, or the representatives of international Jewish organizations – who, by means of provocation and propaganda, had made Jewish
life in any form impossible in Muslim lands. For the Zionists, in contrast,
what had convinced the Jews to pick up and leave was the general feeling
of insecurity caused by nationalistic agitation and the repercussions of
the 1948 defeat.[37]

If there does exist a clear case of Arab responsibility for a massive Jewish
exodus, it is not that of 1950s–1960s Arab nationalism, with its socialist,
anti-imperialist bent, but, rather, that of monarchist Iraq under British
domination. Here the exodus went hand in hand with acts of despoliation
– whatever the truth may be about still controversial allegations attributing
attacks on Jewish life and property to the Zionists.[38] Yet the fact remains that
the victims resented both the Iraqi government and the Zionists.[*]

The only argument for Nasser's anti-Semitism that merits truly serious
consideration is the reference to the *Protocols of the Elders of Zion* that he
made in an interview he granted an Indian journalist on 28 September 1958.
The Egyptian president asked his interviewer:

> I wonder if you have read a book called 'Protocols of the Learned Elders
> of Zion'; it is very important that you should read it. I will give you a copy.
> It proves beyond the shadow of a doubt that 'three hundred Zionists, each

---

[*]   Yehouda Shenhav reports the following facts: 'In January 1952, about half a year
       after the official conclusion of the operation that brought Iraq's Jews to Israel, two
       Zionist activists, Yosef Basri and Shalom Salah, were hanged in Baghdad. They had
       been charged with possession of explosive materials and throwing bombs in the city
       center. According to the account of Shlomo Hillel, a former Israeli cabinet minister
       and Zionist activist in Iraq, their last words, as they stood on the gallows, were "Long
       live the State of Israel." It would have been only natural for Iraqi Jews in Israel to
       have reacted with outrage to news of the hanging. But on the contrary, the mourning
       assemblies organized by leaders of the community in various Israeli cities failed to
       arouse widespread solidarity with the two Iraqi Zionists. Just the opposite: a classified
       document from Moshe Sasson, of the Foreign Ministry's Middle East Division, to
       Foreign Minister Moshe Sharett maintained that many Iraqi immigrants, residents
       of the transit camps, greeted the hanging with the attitude: "That is God's revenge on
       the movement that brought us to such depths." The bitterness of that reaction attests
       to an acute degree of discontent among the newly arrived Iraqi Jews. It suggests that
       a good number of them did not view their immigration as the joyous return to Zion
       depicted by the community's Zionist activists. Rather, in addition to blaming the
       Iraqi government, they blamed the Zionist movement for bringing them to Israel
       for reasons that did not include the best interests of the immigrants themselves.'[39]

of whom knows all the others, govern the fate of the European Continent and that they elect their successors from their entourage.'[40]

That Nasser mentioned the *Protocols* is itself evidence of the increased diffusion – hardly surprising – of this Russian forgery in the region in the aftermath of the Nakba.* It is also, and above all, evidence of the ignorance and lack of cultivation characteristic of nationalist circles, from which not even a nationalist of the first rank such as Nasser was exempt. It is true that heads of state are not selected on the basis of general knowledge tests, in Egypt or anywhere else for that matter. Nevertheless, that Nasser could in 1958 have been so ignorant of the history of this text is quite simply disgraceful.

Yet nothing but ignorance – compounded by the desire to impress on the Indian journalist a sense of the Zionist adversary's omnipotence – is to blame here. Those who fabricated and distributed the *Protocols* in Europe had patent anti-Semitic designs. They sought to whip up popular hatred of the Jews both as imaginary scapegoats for the evils of the dominant economic order and, given the high proportion of Jewish activists and intellectuals in the ranks of the far left, as real participants in the movements that challenged that order. Those who disseminated the *Protocols* in the Arab countries after 1948 were seeking an excuse for the Arab states' shameful, all too real defeat at the hands of the Zionist movement, and also an explanation for the Zionists' success in gaining the support of the victorious Allies. The Tripartite Aggression of 1956 had only heightened their bewilderment. Nasser believed he had discovered the key to the collaboration between the two main West European powers and Israel in the *Protocols*.

Certain mitigating factors should, however, also be noted. First, Nasser's remarks in that 1958 interview – made when he was probably under the influence of his recent reading of the Russian forgery, published in April 1956 by the Egyptian information services[41] – are very much at odds with the basic line of Arab and Nasserite nationalism of the period, which, as we have seen, considered Israel an imperialist tool and did not subscribe to the opposing, anti-Semitic vision. Second, this was the only mention Nasser ever made of the *Protocols* in his eighteen years in power; he was most likely informed soon after the interview that the document was spurious.

Finally, and most important, it must be noted that Nasser – like most of those who distributed and read the *Protocols* in the Arab countries at the time – thought the document was the product of a *Zionist*, not a *Jewish*, conspiracy.

---

*   See Chapter 4 above, section on 'Pan-Islamist Reactionaries and Fundamentalists: Rashid Rida'.

Harkabi, who devotes several pages in his book on the 'Arab attitude' to the dissemination of the *Protocols*,[42] expatiates on the unsigned introduction to the Egyptian edition. He thinks that it was written by a German; he probably had in mind the Nazi professor Johann von Leers, a virulent anti-Semite and a friend of Amin al-Husseini's who had found refuge in Cairo in the mid-1950s and taken a post with the Egyptian information services. Harkabi's final argument to this effect is precisely that the introduction – which Nasser apparently did not read or to which he gave no credit – explicitly attributes the document to Jews, not Zionists:

> The argument [of the Introduction] that the Protocols are the product not of Zionism but of Jewry as a whole also represents a Nazi line, for the Arabs' tendency to concentrate the attack on Zionism, as the source of evil, would lead them to insist on their Zionist provenance. In most Arab books, indeed, it is emphasized that they are minutes of secret delibera-tions at the Zionist Congress, and even of a secret speech by Herzl.[43] [This statement is followed by thirteen references to works in Arabic.]

This distinction is not minor. There is a qualitative difference between a delusive, anti-Semitic approach that believes, or seeks to make others believe, that the leaders of the Jews or the 'Jewish race' are conspiring against the rest of the world, and an equally delusive but not racist approach that seeks consolation by mobilizing a conspiracy theory to explain Zionist successes both in creating a state more powerful than all its Arab neighbours put together and in garnering Western European support for its unjust cause. Yet this distinction does not seem to have occurred to Harkabi, who concludes his consideration of the *Protocols* by posing a reductive alternative that is delusive in its turn: 'Did the Arabs simply seize on the Protocols as a valuable asset in their propaganda against Israel, or did they, perhaps, feel in their heart of hearts that the Protocols fitted in with the Arab objective of liquidating and destroying the Jewish State?'[44]

The general's intellectual heirs, Meir Litvak and Esther Webman, give the correct answer when they write that the *Protocols of the Elders of Zion* 'acquired widespread popularity in the Arab world, as it provided a reasonable explanation for the Zionist phenomenon and its successes in the Middle East'.[45] On the other hand, they do not make the necessary distinction between the anti-Semitic and anti-Zionist reading of the Russian forgery. One has to have clearly understood these two aspects of the Arab nationalists' relationship to it to make an accurate judgement of their dominant attitude – which differs from the dominant attitude of fundamentalist Pan-Islamism, whose reading of the *Protocols*, initiated by Rashid Rida, I have already explored.

The Eichmann Trial, Reparations, Comparisons and Holocaust Denial

Nasser's relationship to the Holocaust naturally holds a place of honour in the indictments demonizing him. The first of his allusions to the Holocaust, or, rather, its consequences, came in the course of a 26 January 1958 press conference before American journalists. Echoing Arab liberalism's favourite argument, he affirmed that he understood the necessity of 'finding a solution to the problem of the Jewish refugees who fell victim to Hitler'. However, he added: 'We understand this humanist vision, but there exists another human problem as well: that of the Arabs who have lived in Palestine for centuries.'[46]

Nasser returned to this line of argument on 2 February 1970, a few months before his death. Addressing an international congress of parlementarians, he declared:

> Immediately after the Second World War – after the leading position in the Western world went from Britain to the United States of America – the Zionist movement gained a new source of support and a new master, passing from London's hands to Washington's. Washington had committed itself to supporting Zionism on the pretext of saving the Jews, victims of Nazism.
>
> Thus it appeared that it was incumbent on the Arab nation – which has never in the course of its history perpetrated the crime of persecuting Jews – to pay the full price for their persecution, to pay with its territory and blood. In reality, this was only a facade thrown up to hide the truth; for the United States – heir to Britain's hegemonic position – has made all the objectives of this hegemony its own. This holds especially for the Arab world, which others have always sought to threaten, dismember, and bleed white.[47]

Nasser never expressed any admiration for Hitler. The only one of the Free Officers who did was none other than Anwar al-Sadat, the man the furthest to the right in the group that made the 1952 Revolution. But even in his case, it should be pointed out, the object of his admiration was the Führer's nationalism, his 'faith in his country and people', not his Nazi ideology or his anti-Semitism. Sadat's declaration, copiously cited in anti-Arab propaganda literature, was published on 18 September 1953 in the Egyptian weekly

Al-Musawwar, which had invited a number of personalities to write a letter to Hitler. Litvak and Webman take note of his remarks, of course, but put them honestly in context:

> The other respondents, among them three former ministers, expressed reservations and aversion toward Hitler's deeds, although none of them referred to his anti-Jewish policies. Ihsan 'Abd al-Qudus, editor of the left-wing weekly *Ruz al-Yusuf*, was the boldest. There was no place [for] dictators in the free world, he said, and reminded Hitler of his responsibility for the death of millions, for the gas chambers and bloodbaths, and sent Hitler back to his hiding place.[48]

References to the Jewish genocide in Nasser's statements naturally occur most often in connection with the issue of the reparations that the German Federal Republic paid to the state of Israel.[49] Litvak and Webman devote a chapter in the relatively objective first part of their book to Arab reactions to these payments in the early 1950s,[50] summing them up as follows:

> References to the Holocaust in the mainstream [Arab] discourse were indirect, and did not dispute its being a historical fact. Nor was Germany's right to compensate Jews on a personal basis denied, but Israel's right to represent and receive reparations in the name of those Jews was rejected out of hand. A large part of the discussion about the agreement evolved around its political aspects and implications for the balance of power between Israel and the Arab states. The assertion that the Arab refugees were more entitled to compensation, which implied an equation between the suffering of the Palestinians and the suffering of the Jews under Nazi persecutions,[*] also seemed to stem from political considerations rather than from an intention to minimize the Holocaust.[51]

The Arabs were nevertheless profoundly irritated by Israel's political exploitation of the Eichmann affair, both in the aftermath of the kidnapping, from Argentina, of the Nazi official who had been in charge of deporting Jews to the death camps, and during his trial in Israel, which was held in defiance of calls from all quarters, including the United States and Israel itself, for an international court.[52] Tom Segev offers an admirable description of the uses to which the trial was put:

---

[*]   Contrary to what this sentence gives us to understand, the Arab contention was not (and, as a rule, never has been) that the Palestinian refugees had a better right to German reparations than the Jewish victims of Nazism. It was, rather, that they had a better right to them than *the state* of Israel – which is, patently, very different.

Ben-Gurion had two goals: One was to remind the countries of the world that the Holocaust obligated them to support the only Jewish state on earth. The second was to impress the lessons of the Holocaust on the people of Israel, especially the younger generation ... The trial, he said, could unmask other Nazi criminals and perhaps, also, their links with several Arab rulers. He claimed that the anti-Zionist propaganda coming out of Egypt was anti-Semitic and inspired by the Nazis. 'They generally say "Zionists," but they mean "Jews,"' he maintained. This led to the obvious conclusion that the enemies of the State of Israel were the enemies of the Jewish people and that supporting Israel was equivalent to fighting anti-Semitism.[53]

Idith Zertal's assessment is equally acute:

> The transference of the Holocaust situation on to the Middle East reality, which, harsh and hostile to Israel as it was, was of a totally different kind, not only created a false sense of the imminent danger of mass destruc-
> tion. It also immensely distorted the image of the Holocaust, dwarfing the magnitude of the atrocities committed by the Nazis, trivializing the unique agony of the victims and the survivors, and utterly demonizing the Arabs and their leaders. The transplanting of one situation into the other was done, before and during the trial, in two distinctive ways: first, by massive references to the presence of Nazi scientists and advisers in Egypt and other Arab countries, to the ongoing connections between Arab and Nazi leaders, and to the Nazi-like intentions and plans of the Arabs to annihilate Israel. The second means was systematic references –
> in the press, on the radio, and in political speeches – to the former Mufti of Jerusalem, Haj Amin El-Husseini, [who] was depicted as a prominent designer of the Final Solution and a major Nazi criminal.[54]

The affair of the former Nazis who had found a haven in Egypt was much ballyhooed in the media, in the context of the campaign that sought to portray the Nasser regime itself as Nazi. It is, of course, true that a number of important Nazi officials took refuge in Arab countries after the German defeat or in the 1950s; some of them fled to Egypt. However, with the exception of Alois Brunner, Adolf Eichmann's assistant, who ultimately fled to Syria, no known war criminals of the Nazi regime or, at least, no Nazi with major responsibility for the genocide were among these refugees.

It should also be borne in mind that Egypt's record in this respect was no worse than the United States's and, in particular, the CIA's dealings with former Nazis, including war criminals. The issue has been well documented since the relevant archives were opened to the public.⁵⁵ The CIA's official historian, Kevin Ruffner, has himself summed up the indictment that the agency faces as follows:

> CIA, and its predecessor organizations ... employed German intelligence personnel as sources of information. Afterward, the CIA sponsored the new West German intelligence service, an organization under the control of officers of the defunct German general staff. The ranks of the organization sheltered many officers of the German SS and SD whose loyalty to the new West German Government remained in doubt ...
>
> CIA evacuated Nazi war criminals [among them Klaus Barbie] and collaborators through 'rat lines' in southern Europe, allowing them to escape justice by relocating them incognito in South America.⁵⁶

Many Nazi war criminals, to say nothing of countless former Nazis who had not had a direct hand in war crimes, were co-opted by institutions of the German Federal Republic, with which the state of Israel, under Ben-Gurion, established close cooperative ties – the same Federal Republic that, thanks to its financial transfers to Israel, played a crucial role in securing the Zionist state's development and consolidation. Documents that have recently been made public in the United States confirm one of the most sordid aspects of the Eichmann trial: the efforts to cover up the fact that the West German chancellor, Konrad Adenauer – who had become a personal friend of Ben-Gurion's and was the architect of the German reparations payments to Israel, where he was received with all the honors in 1966 – had a national security adviser, one Hans Globke, about whom Hannah Arendt had, in 1961, already said all that needs to be said:

> It is one thing to ferret out criminals and murderers from their hiding places, and it is another thing to find them prominent and flourishing in the public realm – to encounter innumerable men in the federal and state administrations and, generally, in *public* office whose careers had bloomed under the Hitler regime.⁵⁷

One such case was brought to the attention of the court, that of Dr. Hans Globke, one of Adenauer's closest advisers, who, more than twenty-five years ago, was co-author of an infamous commentary on the Nuremberg Laws and, somewhat later, author of the brilliant idea of compelling all German Jews to take 'Israel' or 'Sarah' as a middle name. But Mr. Globke's name – and only his name – was inserted into the District Court proceedings by the defense, and probably only in the hope of 'persuading' the Adenauer government to start extradition proceedings. At any rate, the former *Ministerialrat* of the Interior and present *Staatssekretär* in Adenauer's Chancellery doubtless had more right than the ex-Mufti of Jerusalem to figure in the history of what the Jews had actually suffered from the Nazis.[58]

Arab reactions to the Eichmann trial also are the subject of one of Litvak's and Webman's chapters.[59] It reveals, naturally, a broad spectrum of opinion. As one might expect, they have culled a large number of appalling commentaries on the trial from the Arab press. The worst, published on 31 May 1960, in the Saudi daily *Al-Bilād*, is an abominable commentary by a certain Hilmi Abu-Ziyād bearing a title that congratulates Eichmann for having murdered five million Jews.[60] Bernard Lewis, after mentioning the 'mixed' commentaries in the Arab media, cites this obscene article – and this article alone – labelling it a 'fairly typical hostile response'.[61]

Litvak and Webman criticize Lewis for this stratagem. They also criticize other 'Jewish and Israeli scholars' – among them Harkabi and Robert Wistrich, another professional of the anti-Arab propaganda war, as well as Hannah Arendt[62] – for having, 'based on a small number of articles and cartoons repeatedly quoted, and on Arab propaganda against the trial', engaged in 'distortion' by failing to present 'the entire scope and the nuances of the discourse about the trial and the Holocaust'.[63] Their use of the term 'Arab discourse' in the singular to cover so broad a range of positions appears in this instance more clearly absurd than anywhere else.

With respect to Egypt in particular, Litvak and Webman acknowledge that 'The justification of the Holocaust and regret that the annihilation had not been completed was a marginal theme and even absent from Egyptian writing on the trial.'[64] They pay particular attention to two Egyptian intellectuals of the Nasserite left, Lutfi al-Khūli and Ihsān 'Abdul-Quddūs – the only two well-known intellectuals mentioned in their chapter and, in fact, the only people mentioned who occupied leading positions in the intellectual life of both their own country and the Arab world in general. An editorial of 12 April 1961 that Lutfi al-Khūli published in *Al-Ahram*, Egypt's most prestigious daily, is cited at length a few pages earlier. Invoking revolutionary anti-colonialist and anti-racist principles in the name of a collective 'we', Khūli, one of the many Communist intellectuals co-opted by the Nasserite power elite after the regime's socialist turn, forthrightly declares that he rejects everything that Eichmann and Nazism represented.[65]

Litvak and Webman nevertheless deplore the fact that Arabs who thought along these lines seized the occasion of the Eichmann trial to underscore the magnitude of Israel's crimes against the Palestinians.[66] Yet that Arab intellectuals should have done so is all the more understandable in view of the way Israel exploited the trial: the two authors would have done well to express their indignation over the Israeli comparisons between the Arabs and the Nazis that brought Arab anger to the boiling point.

Subsequently, when German reparations took the form of arms shipments to the state of Israel (as the German press revealed in 1964), Nasser, in his exasperation, was driven to what would be more accurately labelled outrageous exaggeration of Israeli crimes (stemming from his desire to denounce Zionism as a criminal enterprise) than mitigation of Nazi crimes. In the course of an interview with West German media on 20 February 1965, on the eve of a visit to Cairo by the East German president Walter Ulbricht meant as a gesture of protest against the Federal Republic, Nasser said that Egypt

> was surprised and pained upon learning that Ben-Gurion and the former German Chancellor Konrad Adenauer had reached an agreement whereby the Germans were to deliver two hundred tanks, fifty airplanes, two hundred armored reconnaissance vehicles, and hundreds of cannon for the purpose of killing us. We can only regard this as an act of aggression toward us, since Israel uses these weapons to kill us. We consider Ben-Gurion to be our enemy number one: he has killed as many Arabs as Hitler killed Jews.[67]

Nasser did not repeat this preposterous exaggeration in the address he made four days later in honour of his East German guest. Instead he was careful to keep his distance from Nazism:

> It is sometimes imagined – or so, at any rate, people say – that our admiration for the German people is informed by a sympathy for Nazism, because Nazism fought Great Britain, which was then our enemy, and persecuted the Jews, whose state, Israel, is our enemy today. Neither reason is valid.
>
> Our war against British colonialism took place for reasons different from those that spawned the contradiction between it and Nazism. Our fight was a fight for freedom, not a struggle for domination; we demanded the independence of the colonies, not a division of the colonial spoils. Our war against Israel is not racist in its inspiration, but is the continuation of our war against colonialism, because it is colonialism which has exploited racism and transformed one of the heavenly religions into a nationalism,

and then impelled that nationalism to engage in aggressive adventures that promote colonialism's designs for domination and exploitation.[68]

In one of his major public speeches, delivered a few days later, on 8 March 1965, Nasser returned to the theme of German reparations:

> Over the past ten years, Israel has received 3,700 million dollars from Germany, that is, more than a million dollars in aid every day ... *Bakshish* ... Well, then: why does West Germany give these funds to Israel, to the exclusion of the rest of the world? Were the Jews the only ones to suffer at German hands? The Jews suffered at German hands ... The Czechs suffered at German hands ... The Yugoslavs suffered at German hands ... The French suffered at German hands ... There exist, then, attempts and pressures to strengthen Israel economically.[69]

Nasser drew up a double indictment in the open letter, cited by Harkabi, that he wrote in May 1965 to the chancellor of the German Federal Republic, Ludwig Erhard. Israel, he said, was exploiting the Holocaust in order to appropriate part of the Arabs' territory. Furthermore, the Arabs were being made to pay in Germany's stead, while Germany assuaged its conscience at their expense by arming and financing Israel:

> Zionist racism exploited the sufferings of the Jews under the Hitlerite regime in order to execute a terrible plot against the Arab nation and tear off part of their territory in order to establish a national home in Palestine ... Through the disaster inflicted on it, the Arab nation served as a scapegoat for the German conscience.[70]

The rejection of anti-Semitism resurfaces in a 31 August 1965 speech in which Nasser celebrated Arab friendship with the Soviet Union and affirmed that the Arabs' 'hostility to Israel was not racist in its inspiration ... In the whole history of our region, there has never been anti-Semitic hostility toward the Jews living in our country; the very foundation of Israel, however, is the aggressive racism that colonialism has exploited.'[71]

He took up the same theme in a 25 January 1969 address before a conference in support of the Arab peoples held in Cairo:

> Has Arab history ever witnessed anti-Semitism or persecution of the Jews? Is it not true that the Jews have, in the course of their history, never experienced greater tolerance than that they enjoyed on Arab soil? Were the Arabs not among the peoples who felt the greatest sympathy for the

Jews because of the persecution they suffered as a result of Nazi racism and its methods? The question that immediately arises in connection with the foregoing is: should the Arabs have to endure the consequences of the Nazis' persecution of the Jews, paying for it with one of their fatherlands? And [should they have to suffer because of the fact] that Zionist racism borrows all its thinking and methods from Nazi racism? Are human beings capable only of learning from their executioners and becoming copies of them that are worse than the originals, and a shameful repetition of them in their thoughts and deeds? Has history ever known the Arabs to be aggressors? Were they the aggressors in 1948? Were they the aggressors in 1956, in collusion with certain great powers? Were they the aggressors in 1967?[72]

In a public address on 1 May 1970, however, Nasser once again indulged in flagrant exaggeration, citing a UN Commission of Inquiry that, he said, had come to the conclusion that Israel 'practiced forms of torture against the Palestinian Arab people worse than those Hitler practised against the German Jews in the Second World War'.[73]

These rhetorical excesses obviously had their origins in a game of tit for tat. Yehoshafat Harkabi, himself engaged in demonizing Nasserism and, consequently, especially cognizant of the symmetrical nature of the accusations involved, is relatively unforthcoming about the equation of Zionism with Nazism: he devotes only two pages of his 500-page book to it.[74] His intellectual successors, Litvak and Webman, however, dedicate an entire chapter to the subject.[75] But the objectivity they start by striving for has diminished by the time they reach this point in their book.

They set out by acknowledging that the method of comparing the enemy with Nazism became, after the Second World War, 'the ultimate verbal weapon of delegitimization'.[76] They cite the British Prime Minister Anthony Eden, who, on the eve of his country's 1956 attack on Egypt, compared Nasser with Hitler. Yet they studiously avoid mentioning that Nasser himself had already been compared with Hitler in Israel and that the comparison continued to be made there much more systematically than in Britain or France (Israel's two partners in the Tripartite Aggression of 1956), although those were the Western countries in which it was most frequently drawn. Such selective amnesia paves the way for an accusation whose anguished tone rings false: 'Arab writers were probably aware of the particular painful effect of such an equation on the Israeli psyche, in view of the past suffering of the Jews under the Nazis. They sought to deprive the Jews of their human dignity by equating them with their worst tormentors.'[77]

On what grounds can Israeli writers criticize their Arab counterparts (the great majority of whom are poorly informed about the Holocaust) for comparing Zionism to Nazism, when the Israeli media and Israeli political leaders (who know a great deal about it) have never hesitated and still do not hesitate to compare Arab political forces – from Nasserism to the Baath and the various governments it has spawned to the Lebanese Hezbollah – to Nazism? How many Muslim leaders – from Nasser to Arafat to Saddam Hussein to Mahmoud Ahmadinejad – have been denounced in Israel as 'new Hitlers'?

Litvak's and Webman's guiding assumption, like that of many others who hurl accusations at the Arabs, is that the comparison of Zionism to Nazism in 'Arab discourse' is a 'trivialization' of Nazism and the Holocaust, if it does not, indeed, amount to anti-Semitism and Holocaust denial. Why does the same stricture not hold for the comparisons to Hitler and Nazism with which Israeli and pro-Israeli sources indiscriminately bombard Muslim leaders? Why is it a heinous show of bigotry for an opponent of Israel's to compare Menachem Begin with Hitler but a mere polemical exaggeration when the comparison comes from the principal founder of the state of Israel? For, as Tom Segev has noted, 'Long after the grisly details of the Holocaust became known, Ben-Gurion compared Menahem Begin to Hitler.'[78]

The only admissible evidence against Nasser with regard to the charge of Holocaust denial is an interview he accorded Gerhard Frey, a far-right German politician who was nostalgic for Nazism. The interview was published on 1 May 1964 in the *Deutsche National-Zeitung und Soldaten-Zeitung*, a weekly founded and directed by Frey, in the midst of a public debate in Germany about reparations payments. It is not available on the Gamal Abdel-Nasser Foundation website, and it is unlikely that it was submitted to the Egyptian president for approval before it was released. The progressive American journalist I. F. Stone found a copy of the German weekly in Athens airport during a stop-over on his way to Israel, translated extracts from it, and published them in his own bulletin. Among them was a statement in which Nasser raises doubts about the figure of six million Jewish victims.[79] Harkabi cites it in his book (in the English translation of which the name of the German politician is misspelled 'Frei').[80] Bernard Lewis also cites it,[81] as do countless other anti-Arab sources, including, most recently, Litvak and Webman.[82] It is also often quoted by Holocaust deniers intent on claiming Nasser for their camp. Here is this ubiquitous sentence, placed in context:

Frey: These stories [about the German reparations to Israel] are justified with reference to the murders of the Jews.

Nasser: But no one takes the lie about the six million murdered Jews seriously, not even the simplest soul here [in Egypt]. How is it in your country?

Frey: No one denies the fact that Jews were murdered, and every decent human being deeply regrets it. But most Germans have long since understood that numbers are being bandied about abusively here.[83]

It is quite plausible that Nasser believed the figure of six million Jewish victims had been purposely inflated, the more so as his official intellectual confidant and collaborator, Mohamed Hassanein Heikal, cultivated and continues to cultivate such notions. In 1998, Heikal agreed to write a preface to the Arabic edition of the book written by French Holocaust denier Roger Garaudy, *Les Mythes fondateurs de la politique israélienne*, in which Garaudy argues that the real figure is closer to one than to six million. He further contests the notion of a Nazi genocide of the Jews, or even genocidal intent on the Nazis' part.[84]

In his preface, Heikal affirms that he has been following the battles around the question of the Holocaust ever since reading *Far and Wide*, a book by the (racist and anti-Semitic) British writer Douglas Reed that he dates to 1947. (In fact, it appeared in 1951.) Without calling into question the Holocaust itself (a term that Heikal uses and Garaudy rejects), he reviews the reasoning that led Reed to estimate the number of Jewish victims at no more than 400,000. Heikal pronounces only indirectly on this question and does not assess Garaudy's theses, although he expresses admiration for his courage, adding:

> This is, in any case, a dreadful figure – enough not only to torture the European conscience, but that of all humanity. Nevertheless, the Jews were not the ones to sacrifice the most victims to the Nazi inferno; the Germans themselves sacrificed more, like the Russians, Poles, and Gypsies. (And then there were the Palestinians, who were blameless, but were forced by the Zionist movement to atone for the guilt that weighed on German and European consciences. It fell on them to pay that debt with compound interest many times over, and to pay with their native homeland of Palestine itself, their history, land, people, and future!)[85]

Thus it was probably under Heikal's influence that Nasser questioned the generally cited figure of six million Jewish victims of the Nazi genocide in 1964. This lead him both to a polemical exaggeration of the number of Arab victims of the Nakba and, a year later, to the declaration that Israel had 'killed as many Arabs as Hitler killed Jews'. Yet what holds for the *Protocols of the Elders of Zion* holds here as well: Nasser never again called the figure of six million into question. It is quite possible that his 1964–5 statements and the reactions they aroused (perhaps including reactions from his new East German friends) led to criticism from his advisers – the Communists in particular – and that he took note of that criticism.

CHAPTER 6

The PLO Years (1967–1988)

Israel's crushing victory over its Arab neighbours in June 1967 demonstrated the exhaustion of Arab nationalism's progressive potential – a potential even easier to make out against the contrasting backdrop of the historical regression now underway. The limits of Nasserite nationalism resided above all in the dictatorial nature of the regimes it inspired. After 1967, Arab nationalism developed in different directions. In the Middle East, Nasser's death, in 1970, brought on the end of the Nasserite regime; under Sadat, Egypt lost no time joining the camp of the Arab autocracies allied with the United States. In Syria, the same year, the radical faction of the Syrian Baath was swept from power by Hafez al-Assad, whose dictatorship was socially conservative and pragmatic in its foreign policy.

Two new variants of Arab nationalism attest the movement's political and ideological degeneration. One was the ferocious dictatorship of the competing wing of the Baath Party in Iraq, which, even before it came to power in July 1968, did not hesitate to exploit anti-Semitism, mobilising it as part of a strategy of ultra-nationalist one-upmanship vis-à-vis all other political forces.[1] The other was the dictatorship of Muammar al-Gaddafi, a self-proclaimed disciple of Nasser's who took power in Libya in September 1969 and whose reign has oscillated between tragedy and farce ever since.

Westernizing liberalism proved unable to replace the dictatorial Arab nationalism that had managed to destroy it to a large extent before it sank into a period of protracted degeneration after 1967. Liberalism was all the less able to take over once the June 1967 war had radicalized anti-imperialist passions in the region. Fundamentalist Pan-Islamism recovered much of its strength, but was still handicapped by the reputation it had acquired over the previous decade and a half as a tool of the United States and the Americans' Saudi allies. A leader of Hamas (founded by the Muslim Brotherhood's Palestinian branch) would note years later that 'as a result of the two-decade long campaign by

'Abdel Nasir against the Brotherhood, religion became something foreign in our countries; anyone who called for a return to Islam was accused of being a reactionary, a conspirator, and an agent' of the reactionary Arab regimes and the United States.[2]

The regimes favoured by Washington did indeed promote Islamic fundamentalism after 1967, thus helping to establish the conditions for its massive resurgence a few years later – to their own cost. Like the Sadat regime in Egypt, many Arab governments allied with the Saudis and the Western powers gave the fundamentalists free rein, in the universities in particular, in hopes of countering the left-wing radicalization of the years following the Six-Day War.

Both the traditional Communist left and a new left made up of radicalized factions that had emerged from the Communist and nationalist movements were indeed growing rapidly throughout the region. With the exceptions, however, of South Yemen, a poor, peripheral country in which a nationalist force that had mutated into a Marxist-Leninist organization took power in 1969, and the Sudan, an equally poor country in which the Communist Party fell victim to a wave of murderous repression in 1971, no Marxist organization had enough support to take power or was prestigious enough to impose its ideology at the regional level.

What most clearly set the political tone in the region for the next two decades in everything with regard to the Israeli–Palestinian question was the tempestuous rise of Palestinian nationalism, manifested above all in the growth of armed organizations active among the Palestinian refugees. Guerrilla formations gained control of the Palestine Liberation Organization in 1969. Like the Egyptian Free Officers' nationalism, the Palestinian national movement stemmed from several tendencies, ranging from Islamic fundamentalism to Marxism; but it was dominated at the ideological level by just two of them, which converged and competed at the same time. Both went beyond the Arab nationalism of the preceding period and sought to learn from its failure. One was a liberal nationalism of Western inspiration. The other was a left-wing nationalism inspired by a Marxism-Leninism independent of Moscow.

The latter current, which advocated following the Vietnamese and Cuban roads, split into two organizations: the Popular Front for the Liberation of Palestine (PFLP) and the Popular Democratic Front for the Liberation of Palestine (PDFLP, later the DFLP). The liberal nationalists, for their part, were co-opted by the ideological institutions of the Movement for Palestinian National Liberation – Fatah, led by Yasser Arafat. Arafat's movement heavily dominated the Palestinian armed resistance and produced an ideology for external consumption that soon found itself at variance with the reality of its internal organization, which reproduced many of the vices of the authoritarian Arab regimes.

Fatah's leaders, however, shook off all doctrinal rigidity, adapting their views to the evolving needs of their cause in a way that reflected both a learning process and *Realpolitik*. The PLO itself, though hardly democratic internally, nevertheless developed a sufficiently pluralist framework to lend credit to its intelligentsia's liberal claims. These two major ideological tendencies generated the official discourse of the PLO, which held the position of the political avant-garde in the regional confrontation with Israel.

The Programmatic Redefinition of the Palestinian Position toward the Jews

The 1964 PLO Charter, adopted when the organization was founded in Jerusalem with Ahmad al-Shuqayri as its president, was implicitly informed by an ultra-nationalist logic conceived on the model of Algerian independence. That is, it implied the departure – or, in the Palestinian case, the expulsion – of all those who were not native to Palestine:

> Article 6: The Palestinians are those Arab citizens who were living normally in Palestine up to 1947, whether they remained or were expelled. Every child who was born to a Palestinian Arab father after this date, whether in Palestine or outside, is a Palestinian.

> Article 7: Jews of Palestinian origin are considered Palestinians if they are willing to live peacefully and loyally in Palestine.[3]

In 1968, the Palestinian National Council (PNC) of the PLO, which had by then ridden itself of Shuqayri (he resigned in December 1967) and come under heavy pressure from the Palestinian armed organizations, redefined the term 'Jews of Palestinian origin' more precisely, stripping it of its ethnic Arab dimension and replacing it with a territorial one. That is, it made a transition from a right based on blood ties to one based on residence. Simultaneously, the political conditions laid down by the old definition disappeared. Article 7 was replaced by a new article, which became Article 6 when Articles 4 and 5 were combined: 'The Jews who had normally resided in Palestine until the beginning of the Zionist invasion are considered Palestinians.'[4]

In a sense, the new formulation could be interpreted even more restrictively than its predecessor, which left room for doubt as to whether and to what extent the term 'Palestinian' included Jews. Only Jews who had resided in Palestine before the 'Zionist invasion' – a reference to the year 1917, according to the accompanying explanations – were now defined as Palestinian.[5] Far from progress, this was a return to the position put forward by Amin al-Husseini in 1947.[*] Thus the first reaction to the bitter Arab defeat of 1967 was greater nationalist rigidity. It would, however, soon be transcended.

In February 1969, the Palestinian armed organizations completed their takeover of the PLO. With Nasser's blessing, Arafat became its president. Fatah had already announced, in January 1969, its new conception of the liberation of Palestine and the solution to the Israeli–Palestinian conflict in a declaration issued at an international conference in Cairo in support of the Arab peoples. Essentially identical to Nasser's, this declaration represented a step forward for Fatah, an organization that had been founded by former members of, or sympathizers with, the Muslim Brothers:[6]

> We are fighting today to create the new Palestine of tomorrow; a progressive, democratic and nonsectarian Palestine in which Christian, Muslim and Jew will worship, work, live peacefully and enjoy equal rights ... Our Palestinian revolution still stretches its welcoming hand to all human beings who want to fight for, and live in, a democratic, tolerant Palestine, irrespective of race, color or religion ... This is no utopian dream or false promise, for we have always lived in peace, Muslims, Christians and Jews in the Holy Land. The Palestinian Arabs gave refuge, a warm shelter and a helping hand to Jews fleeing persecution in Christian Europe, and to the Christian Armenians fleeing persecution in Muslim Turkey.[7]

It was no longer a question of 'throwing the Jews into the sea' but of creating a state open to all the inhabitants of Palestine, native or immigrant, regardless of their 'race, color, or religion'. Similarly, in February 1969, the main left-wing organization of the Palestinian armed struggle, the PFLP, headed by George Habash, which was then in a period of transition from the Nasserism of its pre-1967 years to Marxism-Leninism, drew up a programme for a democratic state that, to a certain extent, revived ideas that had been developed by Marxists in the period of the British mandate:

> The aim of the Palestinian liberation movement is the establishment of a national democratic state in Palestine in which the Arabs and Jews can live as equal citizens with regard to rights and duties ...

[*] See 'Amin al-Husseini, Architect of the Nakba' in Chapter 4 above.

> Israel has carefully portrayed our war against it as a racist war aiming at the destruction of every Jewish national and throwing him into the sea. The aim behind this is the gathering together of all Jewish nationals and their mobilization for a war of life and death. A basic strategy in our war against Israel should aim at exposing such a falsification, and addressing the exploited misled Jewish masses and pointing out the contradiction between their interest in living peacefully, and the Zionist movement and the ruling forces in the state of Israel. Such a strategy will ensure for us, alongside the growth of the progressive armed resistance and the [clarification] of its identity, the widening of the gap in the contradiction which objectively exists between Israel and the Zionist movement, on the one hand, and the millions of exploited and misled Jews, on the other. [8]

This formula for a democratic state that was further described, on occasion, as secular (though not necessarily in the sense of the strict separation between religion and public affairs that *laïcité* implies to the French) was adopted by Fatah in its turn. Like Nasser's similar position, it neglected the reality of the national – not merely religious or confessional – character of the Jewish Israeli population. Like the rest of the Arab nationalist movement, the Fatah of 1969 refused to acknowledge the existence of a *national* Israeli entity, relegating the Israelis to the status of a population of Jewish faith living on occupied Palestinian territory. The notion of a democratic state envisaged the transformation of Israeli Jews from a colonial Zionist population into a non-Zionist religious community enjoying equal rights in a secular Palestine.

In a long June 1969 interview conducted by Lutfi al-Khūli and published in the prestigious left-wing Egyptian monthly *Al-Talīʿa*, of which Khūli was the founder and editor-in-chief, Salah Khalaf (alias Abu Iyad), the Fatah leader most deeply marked by left culture, explained the meaning of this notion of a democratic state in the name of his movement. Mixing, with a certain ideological incoherence, disparate (Marxist, Nasserite and religious) elements, Abu Iyad underscored the need to distinguish between Zionists and Jews, adding that the 'democratic Palestinian state' would grant citizenship to both anti-Zionist Jews and Jews willing to repudiate Zionism as contrary to humanism – whether they had arrived before 1948 or not. [9]

A founder of the organization that had achieved hegemony within the PLO thus effectively disavowed the PLO Charter by abandoning the stipulation about the required length of Jewish residence in Palestine that the recently revised PLO Charter contained. This was combined with the return to a politically conditioned notion of citizenship that was not likely to reassure Israelis, Abu Iyad's intentions notwithstanding. Fatah's Westernizing intellectuals were, however, now given carte blanche to elaborate the idea of a democratic state, which became an integral part of the PLO leadership's discourse, a sign of the positive evolution of Palestinian nationalism.

On 20 November 1969 and on 1 and 19 January 1970, the English-language biweekly *Fateh* published three essays on Jews and the democratic state, under the pseudonym Mohammad Rasheed. Collected in a pamphlet, they marked a decisive stage in the development of official PLO thinking. They are worth quoting at length, for they contain a remarkable critique of Palestinian nationalism and the ambiguities of a certain anti-Zionism, while also testifying to an effort to understand the enemy in human terms:

> In their misery, humiliation and despair the Palestinians learned to hate the Jews and everything connected with their enemy.
>
> Few sophisticated leaders, and most propagandists took pains to differentiate between Jews and Zionists. We are not anti-Jewish, we are anti-Zionists it was repeated. 'We are Semites and Jews are our cousins ... ' they stated. They sounded so unreal and phony saying, 'some of our best friends are Jews ... '
>
> We are against the state of Israel, it was claimed. But the distinction was lost on the suffering 'refugees' who were told by the Israelis that all Jews were Zionists anyway ...
>
> Reading of the 'Protocols of the Elders of Zion' became fashionable, anti-Semitic literature developed by European racists in a completely different context – i.e. where the Jews were the victims – became quite popular. This wave of bitterness, hate and utter confusion spread to other Arabs. It helped Zionist pressure and propaganda designed to secure the departure of thousands of Arab Jews from their homes to join the ranks of the occupying enemy.[10]
>
> The majority of those who came over to Palestine were fleeing German concentration camps and were told that they are a people without land – going to a land without people ...
>
> Further, it was discovered, new Jewish immigrants as well as old settlers were told by the Zionist machine that they had to fight to survive, that the only alternative to a safe 'Israel' was a massacre or at best a little sinking boat on the Mediterranean Sea. Even Arab Jews – called oriental by the Zionists – who were discriminated against in 'Israel' by the European Zionist oligarchy had to accept the argument and fight for what they considered to be their very survival.[11]

The people of the Book, the men of light, the victims of Russian pogroms, of Nazi genocide, of Dachau and other Polish concentration camps shut their eyes and ears in Palestine and changed roles from oppressed to oppressor. This is THE Jewish dilemma of modern times.[12]

The last of the three essays, which is about the question of the state, explicitly rejects any notion of distinguishing among Israelis according to the date of their arrival in Palestine. It advocates a 'democratic, nonsectarian' Palestine with Arabic and Hebrew as the two official languages. Yet it expressly rejects a binational state in favour of equality of rights for all citizens without recognition of any collective identity, religious or national. These three essays represented the most advanced thinking ever produced in Fatah circles about the attitude to be taken towards the Jews. They were not, however, released in Arabic, as the Palestinian writer Elias Sanbar, a member of the PNC, emphasises in his account of the genesis of the idea of a 'secular, democratic' Palestinian state:

> [The idea was] to earn our 'passport' and achieve the status of a revolution-ary movement, and to get rid of the characterization, which was pejorative at the time, as a 'nationalist' movement. This is why the leadership of the resistance, already equipped with an impressive degree of pragmatism, asked a little group of intellectuals among its members, professors in fact at the American University of Beirut, to write a coherent text. The group – coordinated by Nabil Shaath, now a minister in the Palestinian Authority – went on to publish a long essay in 1969 *in English* – evi-dence that the work was aimed first of all at a foreign audience – in the semi-underground journal *Fateh,* which the movement's Information Department was then publishing in Beirut. Somewhat later the Fatah cell in Paris, which I belonged to, took on the task of spreading the French translation of the text ...
>
> Thus we see that this founding text on the future of the Palestinians and Israelis was never published in Arabic, the language of those it pri-marily addressed. On the contrary, perceived as a weapon in the struggle, it was aimed at the outside world, in order to show it in a way that the Palestinian movement, so often belittled, had its own original 'theoreti-cal reflection'; in order to reduce to silence all those who were accusing the Palestinians of wanting to drive the Jews into the sea; and equally to reassure the friends who were constantly asking, 'What will you do with the Jews if you liberate your country?'[13]

Sanbar went on to affirm that the proposal to establish a democracy became, nonetheless, 'a central demand of the whole of Palestinian society'.[14] Yet the relatively advanced thinking of these essays continued to be reserved for outsiders, diminishing their self-critical import. The proposal did, however, bear witness to the ongoing maturation of the Westernizing Palestinian intellectuals, whose contributions the PLO leadership had solicited. These intellectuals would have a clear impact on the organization's ideology, even if some disparity between their discourse and that of the leadership remained a permanent feature of the organization.

In the years immediately following the June 1967 war, only the PDFLP, led by Nayef Hawatmeh, defended a solution to the conflict that, however minimally, took the existence of two national communities into consideration. The PDFLP was a splinter of the PFLP that had been joined by survivors of the radical Iraqi left, then a target of the new Baathist government's bloody repression. Protected by a Fatah intent on weakening Habash's PFLP (perceived, in this period, as the main rival of Arafat's organization), the PDFLP was for some time the Palestinian organization with the closest affinities to the Marxism of the international new left that had emerged in 1968. It soon, however, evolved into the group that stood closest to Moscow. In its initial, radical phase, it submitted a draft resolution to the sixth session of the PNC, held in Cairo in September 1969, calling for 'the establishment of a popular democratic Palestinian state in which Arabs and Jews would live without discrimination, a state opposed to all forms of national or class oppression that will grant Arabs and Jews the right to develop their respective national cultures'.[15]

This draft resolution did not go so far as to explicitly recognise an Israeli right to national self-administration that would coexist with Palestinian self-determination after the overthrow of the oppressive Israeli state by joint Palestinian–Israeli struggle. Hawatmeh, however, put forward such a perspective in an essay on the democratic solution of the Palestinian problem published in the 12 January 1970 issue of the Beirut weekly *Al-Hurriyya*. He envisaged a federal structure for the future state in Palestine, confirming a binational perspective by citing the examples of Czechoslovakia and Yugoslavia. His essay paid tribute to anti-Zionist and anti-imperialist Israeli organizations, referring by name to the Arab-majority Communist Party Rakah and the Jewish-majority Israeli Socialist Organization (best known by the name of its publication, *Matzpen*). But his invitation for them to join the Palestinian armed struggle betrayed a logic still marked by a nationalist vision of territorial liberation rather than an internationalist vision that included change within Israeli society.

The PDFLP's position was nonetheless the most advanced at the time as far as the repudiation of narrow nationalism and the recognition of the reality of Israeli nationhood was concerned. It was also the one that attracted the fewest supporters. Indeed, since the ultra-nationalist current was so powerfully represented in the Palestinian ranks, it was hard to find support even for the plan for a democratic Palestinian state that intellectuals of the current dominating Fatah and the PLO elaborated from 1969 on; its advocates constantly had to provide its opponents with proof of their nationalism.

Thus the third and last of the essays that appeared under Rasheed's signature culminated in a polemic against the programme's Arab and Palestinian detractors which pointed out that a democratic Palestine would necessarily have a Palestinian Arab majority.[16] Nabil Shaath publicly complained, in February 1971, that the attacks on the programme for a democratic state had been 'so virulent ... as to force other organisations into defensive positions'. He added that they had made it impossible to amend Article 6 of the Charter, 'thus giving the Zionists a windfall opportunity to attack the democratic state on the basis of Palestinian inconsistency and tactical manoeuvring'.[17]

The PNC ultimately adopted the programme for a democratic Palestinian state in March 1971, at a time when the decimation of the armed Palestinian organizations in Jordan was nearing completion. To accommodate the maximalist nationalist positions that still largely held sway, the resolution of the PNC's eighth session began by categorically ruling out a state that would be established in only part of Palestine – an idea then emerging within the PLO that would find its first explicit champion in the DFLP before being officially adopted in stages, beginning at the PNC's twelfth session in 1974.[18] The resolution passed at the eighth session of the PNC declared:

> The Palestinian armed struggle is neither a racial nor a sectarian struggle against the Jews. That is why the future state in the Palestine liberated from Zionist colonialism will be the democratic Palestinian state, where those wishing to live peacefully in it would enjoy equal rights and obligations within the framework of the aspirations of the Arab nation to national liberation and complete unity, with emphasis on the unity of the people on both banks of the River Jordan.[19]

Yehoshafat Harkabi had an easy time of it portraying these resolutions and programmes as nothing more than plans to liquidate the Israeli nation, since all, without exception, were based on the destruction of the Zionist state, the return of the Palestinian refugees, non-recognition of Israeli nationhood and the inclusion of Palestine in a perspective of regional Arab unity.[20] At the time, Harkabi remained wilfully blind to the considerable progress this approach represented, from the standpoint of peace, for a people made up entirely of refugees in involuntary exile, most of them living in conditions of dire poverty, and natives who had remained on their land under military occupation – a people to whom Israel offered no choice but to renounce all its rights.

Transposing the Image of the Holocaust: the Battle of Comparisons with the Nazi past

The 1967 war severely exacerbated tensions in the Middle East and unleashed an unprecedented intensification of the battle for Western public opinion. The Holocaust, which had again become a focus of international attention after the Eichmann trial, naturally found its way to the centre of the conflict. In the months preceding the Six-Day War, Israel had invoked it more than ever before, with an eye to mobilizing support both domestically and abroad. Peter Novick explains in his 1999 study *The Holocaust in American Life*:

> As is well known, the spring of 1967 was a dramatic turning point in American Jews' relationship to Israel ... The great majority of American Jews, including many who had not previously shown the slightest interest in Israel, were in a state of high anxiety, and plunged into a flurry of rallies and fund-raising. In fact, Israel was hardly in serious peril. Shortly before the outbreak of war in June, President Lyndon Johnson's intelligence experts debated whether it would take a week or ten days for Israel to demolish its enemies. But this was not the understanding of American Jews, for whom Israel was poised on the brink of destruction – and it is our perceptions of reality, not the reality itself, that shape our responses.[21]

This situation only heightened Arab exasperation, which found expression from 1967 onward, in the best cases, in emphatic reiteration of the classic argument by those who had never had the slightest sympathy for Nazism and were not in the least reluctant to acknowledge the tragic scope of the Holocaust. There is a good example of this reaction, at the junction of Marxism and liberal Westernizing nationalism, in a statement by Lotfallah Soliman, who in his youth had been a member of the Egyptian Trotskyist group.* It appeared in a 1967 special issue on the Israeli–Arab conflict of *Les Temps modernes*, the review edited by Jean-Paul Sartre:

> The Jewish Holocaust concerns us *only in the precise measure* that we are concerned by the universal: Hiroshima, for example, or the genocide of

---

*   See Chapter 2 above.

the red-skins, or anti-black racism in the United States or South Africa. Since we did not participate in any way whatsoever in the Holocaust, neither actively nor *by our passivity*, we have no guilt complex at all, nor do we labour under any sense of guilt.[22]

This attitude lies at the root of many Arab writers' apparent indifference to, or silence about, the Holocaust. They do not regard the Shoah as their problem and hold – quite wrongly – that to speak out at length on the subject would be to fall into a Zionist trap. As a Palestinian journalist from Bethlehem who was born in a village razed by the Zionist forces in 1948 explained to David Shipler (chief of the Jerusalem bureau of the *New York Times* until 1984),

> I think the Arabs are aware of what happened in the Holocaust, and they intentionally disregard it. They don't want to talk about it. They minimize it. Because the Holocaust to them represents the case which made the Jews establish their state on their land. But if you talk to them on an intellectual basis, they would say, 'We condemn what the Nazis did to the Jews.' At the same time they would say, 'We are not responsible for that, we are not the ones who massacred the Jews, so why do we pay the price?'[23]

Shipler cited these remarks to underscore his own sense that 'It is impossible to see Jews as victims when you are being victimized by them, even where your suffering has no parallel to theirs. And the defenses you set up to screen out the suffering of your enemy are quite effective, it seems.'[24] This observation calls for two remarks: first, that the suffering of one's enemies – more precisely, the suffering of the forebears of some of one's enemies (Israelis of European origin, in this case) – is harder to see when it has taken place in the past while one is suffering at their hands in the present; and second, that it is by no means impossible to acknowledge this past suffering – just hard.

Of course, in many cases Israel's frenzied invocation of the Holocaust has prompted a visceral reaction from the most ignorant and/or backward Arabs. They either deny the reality of the Jewish genocide, which they write off as a myth put into circulation by a conspiracy, or, worse still, they sanction Hitler's crimes, occasionally adding that he should have finished the job. A much more frequent stance charges Israel with exaggerating the scope of the genocide for purposes of political blackmail and financial extortion. A detailed inventory of such abominations for the decades following June 1967 may be found in Litvak and Webman's book. However, the most common attitude, far from passing over the Holocaust and the horrors of Nazism in silence, accuses Israel of imitating or reproducing them and, sometimes, of going one better than the Nazis – an accusation that reflects the propensity for overemphasis and exaggeration that informs a good deal of political statement in the Middle East. The following passage by the renowned Palestinian poet Mahmoud Darwish provides a good illustration. It comes from one of his prose works, published in the early 1970s, and accurately reflects the *Zeitgeist*:

> It is not the duty of Jews alone not to forget the Nazi massacres. All those whose conscience is not dead and all those who love liberty commemorate them together with the victims of Nazism and draw the lessons they have to teach, especially when the historical similarity between Nazism and the racist movements resurfaces in today's world. However intense the hostility between Israelis and Arabs, no Arab has the right to feel that his enemy's enemy is his friend, for Nazism is the enemy of all the world's peoples. That is one thing.
>
> However, Israel's insistence on venting its resentment on another people ... is quite another. One crime cannot be made up for by another. One cannot make up for the Holocaust by demanding that Palestinians and other Arabs pay for crimes that they have not committed. Israelis boast to the whole world that they are the historical champions of those who emigrate in search of refuge, to the point of having transformed this characteristic into a quality and a privilege. But those who have a sense of what it means to emigrate in search of refuge have become wholly incapable of recognizing that sense in others. It is not overly severe to say that the Israeli Zionists' behaviour towards the original people of Palestine resembles that of Nazism towards the Jews themselves.[25]

There is, however, an enormous difference between invoking Nazism as the supreme abjection in order to stigmatize an adversary, even by means of wild exaggeration, and denying the Holocaust or, even worse, endorsing Nazi crimes. Anyone of good faith is capable of distinguishing between Arab silence about – or even outrageously offensive references to – the Holocaust motivated by anti-Zionism and Holocaust denial motivated by anti-Semitism.

Litvak and Webman do not make these distinctions. One of their most frequently recurring ideas is the 'uniqueness' of the Holocaust – a notion that (the specificity of any historical phenomenon aside) has come in for severe criticism from many Jewish (and even many Israeli) intellectuals, who question the philosophical implications of this putative uniqueness. The co-authors' reasoning takes the form of the following syllogism: (1) any comparison involving Nazism and the Holocaust calls the uniqueness of the

Holocaust into question; (2) calling the uniqueness of the Holocaust into question is tantamount to denying it; therefore (3) any Arab who compares Zionism to Nazism, or the suffering inflicted on the Palestinians to the Holocaust, is a Holocaust denier and, consequently, an anti-Semite. That line of argument is what allows them to make a statement as outrageous as this one: 'Denial has been the most pervasive theme in the Arab Holocaust discourse since the 1950s, with the aim of delegitimizing Zionism and Israel. Therefore, it has appeared in all Arab countries and among all political trends with varying nuances.'[26]

I have already underscored the ethnocentricity of Litvak and Webman's approach. It must, however, be recalled that, after 1967, Arafat and the PLO replaced Nasser and Nasserism as targets for the supreme invective of Israeli media and political propaganda – that is, comparison to Hitler and Nazism. Here again, the Arab riposte that compared Zionism to Nazism was tit for tat. Either one condemns this kind of polemical excess, beginning with one's own camp (as some Israeli writers, such as Idith Zertal, and some Arab writers have indeed done), or one awards oneself a monopoly on legitimate symbolic violence in exploiting the Holocaust on the grounds that one is an Israeli or a Jew.

As I noted in the Introduction, the Six-Day War radically altered Israel's image in the West. It ceased to be a state threatened by extinction (even if this image was pure sham, especially since the Tripartite Aggression on Egypt in 1956) and became a conquering state that had occupied, with its troops and armoured vehicles, territories that it was not able this time to annex and assimilate as it had in 1948. For the great majority of Palestinians in the West Bank and Gaza had learned the lessons of history: they refused to abandon their homes and land and flee beyond the borders of their territory, for fear that they would be prevented from returning. While only a minority across the globe called the territory conquered in 1948 'occupied Palestine', the term 'occupied territories' was the universal name for the 1967 conquests from the beginning.

This radical transformation of Israel's image led many to turn back on Israel itself, like a boomerang, the comparison to Nazism and the Holocaust that Israeli propaganda had abused during the Six-Day War. In a 1969 book, Saul Friedländer described this reversal of Western public opinion in psychological terms:

> The passive attitude of vast segments of the Western world's population in the face of the destruction of the Jews during the Second World War

engendered, after the cessation of hostilities, a profound malaise and, often, a severe, always latent bad conscience, which the creation of the state of Israel did not suffice to allay ... It was in this psychological climate that, in May 1967, a new massacre of Jews seemed to be looming on the horizon. This was too much for the conscience of the West; Europeans and Americans in massive numbers rallied to Israel's cause. But then came the surprising Jewish victory.

The whole world watched as Jewish [*sic*] tanks rolled down the roads of the occupied territories, and witnessed the pitiful exodus of Arab refugees. The reversal was abrupt: the remorse that had been accumulating for twenty years ebbed away. In the consciousness of the West, June 1967 cancelled the import of the Holocaust. Now Jews, identified with the victorious Israelis, were strong and cruel. The victims were the others.[27]

This last contention is an obvious exaggeration, designed to explain and denounce the apparition of a 'new anti-Semitism' that had penetrated even the West. Disguised as anti-Zionism, it happily identified Israelis with Nazis: 'it was the Israelis – and thus, by identification, the Jews – who, now, were branded Nazis'.[28] It is true that this new anti-Semitism has emerged in the form depicted by Friedländer. However, its importance has once again been blown up out of all proportion: those who, in Europe, trade in the equation 'the Israelis = the Jews' were, and fortunately remain, a tiny minority. Why, then – to repeat myself – should it for so long have been tolerated when the Egyptians and Palestinians – and by extension, sometimes explicitly, the Arabs – have been called Nazis in both Israel and Europe?

Exorbitant comparison for exorbitant comparison: how is it that likening conquered peoples, whose lands have been occupied and who have been uprooted and reduced to refugee status, to the Nazis is less shocking than likening an occupying army that has conquered territory from four neighbouring countries to the Nazis? Which is the more grievous breach of the respect due to the memory of the Holocaust's victims: comparison of the state that claims their legacy with that of the Nazis, or the conduct of that state as an expansionistic conqueror that has, by putting entire populations under its thumb, elicited this galling comparison? We must also draw a distinction here between the identification of the Zionists with the Nazis when it is made by Europeans – citizens of countries that were actively or passively responsible for the Holocaust and who can, for that reason, be legitimately suspected of anti-Semitism – and the same identification when it is made by people oppressed by the Israelis in the form of an invading, occupying army.

By the same logic, when a Jewish or Israeli intellectual compares Zionists or the Israeli army to the Nazis, it is extremely unfair automatically to charge the speaker or writer with anti-Semitism. The reason is not, of course, that Jews cannot be anti-Semitic* but rather that the indignation that some Jews feel upon seeing their noble conception of the Jewish heritage perverted by the state that lays claim to being Jewish is deeply honourable and cannot in the least be labelled anti-Semitic. Indeed, a few pages later in his book, Friedländer reports this moving testimony by an Israeli officer renewing his ties with 'what is best in the Jewish spiritual tradition':

> It was hard for me to be part of an occupying army, a victorious army, a powerful army, says Menahem in *Ein-Ha-Horesh*. And I understood, all of a sudden, what the Second World War and the Holocaust were as I was coming back up the road from Jericho to Jerusalem, while the refugees were going down it in the opposite direction ... I completely identified with them. When I saw the children that their parents were carrying in their arms ... I could almost see myself being carried by my own father.[29]

As usual, some will attempt to disqualify such remarks by invoking 'that all too familiar *jüdischer Selbsthass*, Jewish self-hatred, the imbeciles' eternal argument against those who wander, however short a way, from the tribe's beaten paths', as Pierre Vidal-Naquet wrote in a spirited tribute to his late friend Marcel Liebman.[30] An active adversary of the Holocaust deniers, Vidal-Naquet cites the following passage written by Liebman in 1973:

> The long trail of horror and suffering that marks the passage of human history and lines up the Treblinkas and Auschwitzes as it passes by does not lead to the *kibbutzim,* military or not, but rather to the concentration camps where the Palestinian people is vegetating and dying, plundered and negated by the Israelis and by the auxiliaries that Israelis have found in the Arab camp. And if it must be said briefly: some Jews declare their solidarity with the Palestinians, not in spite of their own origin, but *because* of their origin and a certain logic that their origin induces in their view. This logic leads them, almost by definition, to take the side of the oppressed: in this case the Palestinians, the Jews of the Middle East.[31]

The 1967 war revived traumatically intense memories of the Nakba. The rise of the new PLO in its wake went hand in hand with the emergence of a new Arab intelligentsia shaped by both the painful defeat and the worldwide

---

* This argument, obviously, is not worth twopence, like, for that matter, the claim that an Arab cannot be an anti-Semite because he or she is a 'Semite'.

radicalization of the young that arrived on the shock wave of the year 1968. The principal cohort in this new Arab intelligentsia – influenced by Marxism, liberal Westernizing nationalism, or some combination of the two – was made up of Palestinians, most of them active in the institutions of the PLO. Edward Said became their standard-bearer with the 1978 publication of his *Orientalism*. The global wave of radicalization created a context more favourable to the Palestinians and more receptive to their arguments. As a result, the battle for Western public opinion among the contending narratives of Zionists and anti-Zionists, Israelis and Arabs, widened considerably in scope.

After 1967, on the initiative of this new intelligentsia, Arabs began to stand the Holocaust problem on its head. The innovative element was not the designation of Zionists as Nazis (that went back a long way) but, rather, of Palestinians as 'the Zionists' Jews'. The Zionist state's own victory and its vainglorious triumphalism were turned back against it by Arab intellectuals who had been permanently immunized against the bloated rhetoric of pre-1967 revanchist Arab nationalism and had perceived the ideological benefits to be reaped from laying claim to the Palestinians' actual status as *victims* – victims of a Zionism that could be denounced, first and foremost, as racist, like South African apartheid. This comparison was considered far more relevant and more persuasive than the comparison to Nazism.

One of the high points of this counter-offensive in the international arena, staunchly backed by the Soviet Union, came on 10 November 1975, when the UN General Assembly adopted, by a majority of 72 to 35, with 32 abstentions, a resolution declaring that 'Zionism is a form of racism and racial discrimination.'[32][*] Despite the blatant hypocrisy of several states that voted for the resolution while themselves engaging in forms of racial discrimination, the argument became all the more compelling as Israel established ever closer ties with Pretoria down to 1987. It was soon a matter of common knowledge that the Israeli state, which claimed to be the antithesis of Nazism and to embody the highest moral values, had forged shameful links with the apartheid state, including military collaboration, especially in the nuclear field.[33][†]

In April 1976, as if to confirm the UN resolution six months after its

---

[*] As if it were a litmus test indicating the change in political conditions that followed the collapse of the Soviet Union, this resolution was officially revoked by the General Assembly on 16 Dec. 1991, by a vote of 111 in favour and 25 against, with 13 abstentions. Fifteen countries did not take part in the vote.

[†] This historical fact is worth keeping in mind today, when Israel is making a great deal of noise over the possible acquisition of nuclear weapons by Iran.

adoption, Yitzhak Rabin's Israeli government received an official visit from South African Prime Minister, John Vorster, one of the fiercest defenders of segregation and one of the worst leaders that the South African Republic had ever had. Vorster had been, in his youth, an enthusiastic supporter of Nazi Germany and a member of the pro-Nazi Afrikaner terrorist organization Ossewabrandwag; this had earned him a stint in prison from 1942 to 1944 and then travel restrictions until war's end.

Three major events during the period under consideration in this section would considerably bolster the Arab struggle to invert Israel's image and contest its ownership of the Holocaust. The first was the 1977 assumption of power in Israel by the heirs of the Zionist far right, united in the Likud under the leadership of Menachem Begin. In his youth, Begin had headed the Revisionist terrorist organization Irgun; he was a man whom Ben-Gurion had compared to Hitler in 1963[34] and who was known for his frenetic exploitation of the memory of the Shoah in domestic Israeli debate. 'The Holocaust was, especially throughout Begin's term in office, a cornerstone of the basic creed of the State of Israel and the policies of its government,' Tom Segev has noted.[35] Unsurprisingly, Begin made exorbitant use of the comparison to Nazism and the exploitation of the memory of the Holocaust. As Segev remarks,

> He often compared Yasir Arafat to Hitler, referring to him as a 'two-legged beast' – a phrase he had used, years earlier, to describe Hitler. Begin further compared the PLO's Palestinian National Covenant to *Mein Kampf*. 'Never in the history of mankind has there been an armed organization so loathsome and contemptible, with the exception of the Nazis,' he liked to say.[36]

Identification of the PLO with Nazism peaked with the invasion of Lebanon engineered by Begin and Ariel Sharon in June 1982 – the second major political event to have a profound impact in the battle of the comparisons. As wielded by Begin, such comparisons could border on the grotesque: witness his declaration to his cabinet, in justification of the Israeli troops' imminent invasion of Lebanon, that 'the alternative is Treblinka.'[37] This time, the boomerang effect was enormous.

The Israeli army's siege and blockade of West Beirut, beginning in June 1982, prompted comparisons with episodes of the Nazi occupation of Europe – even in Israel. This was especially true after the September 1982 massacres at Sabra and Shatila.[*] The eminent scholar and philosopher Yeshayahu Leibowitz, who considered himself a Zionist, went so far as to describe the invasion, in the daily *Yedioth Ahronoth*, as 'Judeo-Nazi policy'.[38] The historian Israel Gutman, a veteran of the Warsaw uprising and a concentration camp survivor, the general editor of the *Encyclopedia of the Holocaust* and chair of Yad Vashem's scholarly advisory board, staged a sit-in near the entry to the memorial to protest against the war.[39] Personal accounts such as the one published in *Haaretz* by Shlomo Shmelzman, another survivor of the Warsaw Ghetto and the camps, wreaked havoc with Israel's image. Shmelzman, who undertook a hunger strike to protest against the war, also at Yad Vashem (although he was ultimately prevented from carrying it through by the Memorial's directors), wrote:

> In my childhood I have suffered fear, hunger and humiliation when I passed from the Warsaw Ghetto, through labor camps, to Buchenwald. Today, as a citizen of Israel, I cannot accept the systematic destruction of cities, towns and refugee camps. I cannot accept the technocratic cruelty of the bombing, destroying and killing of human beings.
>
> I hear too many familiar sounds today, sounds which are being amplified by the war. I hear 'dirty Arabs' and I remember 'dirty Jews'. I hear about 'closed areas' and I remember ghettos and camps. I hear 'two-legged beasts' and I remember 'Untermenschen.' I hear about tightening the siege, clearing the area, pounding the city into submission and I remember suffering, destruction, death, blood and murder ... Too many things in Israel remind me of too many other things from my childhood.[40]

David Shipler has delineated the circumstances that impelled these protesters to make use of the terrible comparison. His explanation also applies to the Arabs' use of similar comparisons:

> For an idealistic old veteran who imagined his country forsaking its ideals, the Holocaust became the only container large enough to hold the grief and the guilt, the only metaphor atrocious enough to accommodate the shame ... Nothing else seemed sufficient to capture their deep agony and anger. They recognized the differences, of course; they were trying to measure not the objective events in Lebanon but their feelings about what they, their army, had done there.
>
> Just as Shimon Avidan, the famous brigade commander from 1948, sat

---

[*]   These massacres were not perpetrated by the Israeli troops but by their allies among the Lebanese Christian militias, under the Israeli army's supervision in a zone under its control. This fact hardly lessened the enormous damage to Israel's image.

on his kibbutz during the war and saw, flashing in front of his memory, the photograph of the Warsaw Ghetto that Begin kept on his desk, so younger warriors kept seeing images from Nazi Europe.[41]

The comparison of besieged Beirut (I was there throughout the siege) with the Warsaw Ghetto, made by more than one Israeli, was, to be sure, excessive – but much less so than Begin's comparison of Beirut and Berlin, with which he sought to legitimize the siege of the Lebanese capital. He offered the analogy in response to concerns Ronald Reagan had expressed over the fate of the civilian population: 'I feel as a Prime Minister empowered to instruct a valiant army facing "Berlin," where, amongst innocent civilians, Hitler and his henchmen hide in a bunker deep beneath the surface.'[42] As the former Israeli Foreign Minister Abba Eban wrote in *Yedioth Ahronoth* in July 1982, 'with Mr. Begin and his cohorts, every foe becomes a "Nazi," every blow becomes an "Auschwitz."'[43] The memory of the Holocaust served Begin to justify his actions and ward off criticism from abroad, as Segev explains:

> A few weeks after the war began, Begin responded to international criticism of Israel by repeating a premise that his predecessors had shared: after the Holocaust, the international community had lost its right to demand that Israel answer for its actions. 'No one, anywhere in the world, can preach morality to our people,' Begin declared in the Knesset. A similar statement was included in the resolution adopted by the cabinet after the massacres in Sabra and Shatila, the Palestinian refugee camps on the outskirts of Beirut.[44]

In 1982, Arafat paid Begin back in kind by accusing him of wanting, like Hitler, to carry out a 'Final Solution' of the Palestinian problem. Shortly after leaving Beirut that year, he told his biographer Alan Hart, somewhat more soberly:

> You know, Alan, it is not really my way to compare the Israelis or some Israelis with the Nazis. I don't think it really serves any purpose to speak in such a way. But I have to tell you something from deep inside me. When I think over the tactics, the strategy and the firepower the Israelis have used to try to liquidate my poorly armed and mainly unarmed refugee people, a people with justice on their side, I think it is fair to say that the Israelis, certain Israelis, have behaved like Nazis, are Nazis in their minds. Let us suppose for the sake of argument that you are Hitler. You give the order to liquidate a people who happen to be Jews by killing them in gas chambers. Now let us suppose that I am Begin or Sharon. I give the order

to liquidate a people who happen to be Palestinians by bombing and strafing their refugee camps and by dropping cluster and fragmentation bombs among them. Am I really any different from you, any better than you, because I am liquidating a people by more conventional means, more acceptable means? What is the crime ... is it liquidating a people or the means by which a people is liquidated?[45]

The reasoning is obviously specious. It is certainly not the method used (gas chambers or fragmentation bombs) that marks the difference between the Nazi genocide of the Jews and the Roma and the war crimes committed by the Israeli army over the years or by the US army in Vietnam or the Soviet army in Afghanistan; it is the attempt to wipe out an entire population, not because it represents an obstacle or a threat or resists the imperialist or expansionist projects of the aggressor state, but simply to satisfy a desire to annihilate born of racial or ethnic hatred.

Arafat was right about one thing, however: there is nothing to be gained by using comparisons of this sort. Most of the time they are simply a means of venting rage. To detect an act of Holocaust denial in every Palestinian or Arab comparison of Israel's actions and the Nazis' is not only to ignore the equally frequent use of such comparisons by Israelis or Jews intent on disparaging Arabs or other Israelis – or on condemning Israeli actions; it is also, and more fundamentally, to display a lack of the empathy that is indispensable to correctly interpreting the behaviour of others. Understanding of this sort is what an Israeli officer exhibited in an exchange with David Shipler, who had expressed his indignation over the slogan 'Ansar is Auschwitz' used by a Palestinian prisoner in the Ansar detention camp which the Israeli army had set up in Southern Lebanon: "The officer said he didn't blame the Palestinians. They were merely wielding the best weapon they could find to attack Israel, he said, and he would do the same if he were in their position. That is how the game is played, he explained: It is a war of emotion and propaganda, not only of guns.'[46]

The third of the major political events affecting the battle of the comparisons was the 1987–8 Intifada, which the Arab media called 'the revolution of the stones' to underscore the fact that the Palestinians restricted themselves to throwing stones at the armoured vehicles of the occupying army. The Intifada contributed to the degradation of Israel's image in the world as well as at home and undermined the morale of the Israeli army, which found itself repressing demonstrations by civilians, many of whom were often women and children.

The occupation could no longer be portrayed as benign, as nineteenth-century colonial occupations could be painted in colonizing countries with no access to information about the form they actually took. It was widely recognized as an occupation maintained by brute force and marked by the war crimes that such a repressive situation inevitably implies. Avi Shlaim put it well:

> The biblical image of David and Goliath now seemed to be reversed, with Israel looking like an overbearing Goliath and the Palestinians with the stones as a vulnerable David ... Within a short time of the outbreak of the uprising, Israel's standing sank to its lowest ebb since the siege of Beirut in 1982.[47]

CHAPTER 7

The Years of the Islamic Resistances (1988 to the Present)

Until its expulsion from Beirut in 1982, the PLO served as a sort of counterweight to the failure of Arab nationalism demonstrated in 1967 by the simultaneous defeat of nationalist ideology's two main bastions, Egypt and Syria. The crushing of the armed Palestinian resistance in Jordan in 1970–1 and the blow that Israel later dealt it in Lebanon combined with internal dissension to seriously diminish its role as an ideological avant-garde in the region. In the meantime, a radiant new star had appeared in the Middle Eastern firmament: the Islamic Republic of Iran, born of the 1979 revolution.

The decline of left-wing Arab nationalism and the old and new discrediting of Communism and liberal Westernism had opened up a space in which the only ideology that had not been undermined by recent history (because it had been relegated to the margins) was able to become the preferred channel of protest against Israel and the United States. That ideology, Pan-Islamic fundamentalism, was already in the ascendant because the United States, with the support of the Saudi monarchy, had made it a favoured weapon in the struggle against nationalism and Communism, a policy that reached its height during the 1979–89 war against the Soviet occupation of Afghanistan.

Israel's invasion of Lebanon sparked the formation of the Lebanese Shiite Hezbollah (officially established under that name in 1985) and the Islamic Resistance that it led. Israeli repression of the Intifada catalysed the creation, starting from December 1987, of the Palestinian Sunni Movement of Islamic Resistance, better known by its acronym, Hamas. The Soviets' departure from Afghanistan in 1989 was widely regarded as a triumph of the Afghan Islamic resistance. This culminated in the turn of Osama bin Laden and his terrorist network, Al-Qaeda, against their former allies, the United States and the Saudi monarchy. Bin Laden had been particularly shocked by the massive stationing of US troops on Saudi territory after Iraq's August 1990 invasion of Kuwait. The 1991 war against Iraq brought Arab national resentment to the boiling point, fostering the resurgence and expansion of Islamic fundamentalism as a privileged vehicle for Arab anger.

The increasing Islamization of popular, political, social and national forms of protest went hand in hand with the Islamization of Arab societies, reflected in changes of dress that everyone could see – more an unprecedented type of expansion of religiosity than a mere 'return' of religion. Life in the Arab world, as elsewhere in the Muslim world, continues to be affected by this historical phenomenon, which must be viewed as a regression – not because Islam is more retrograde than other religions (*pace* the Islamophobes) but because the renewal of religion's grip over politics and society runs counter to the development of humanity from the Enlightenment on: it would be a regression no matter what the religion in question.

Jewish Israeli society witnessed a similar regression in this period. It was marked by the ascension of Orthodox and fundamentalist Judaism in the wake of the exhaustion of the 'socialist Zionism' of the Yishuv and the first decades of the state of Israel. Michel Warschawski has offered a perceptive analysis of this phenomenon:

> Non-religious Zionism is pathetically incapable of offering a secular and democratic alternative project to the one defended by the religionists. There is not and never has been a truly secular current in Israel, armed with a social outlook in which religion does not play an essential role.[1]

> However, because the Zionist platform could not or did not want to be secular, its revolution ran out of steam in less than two generations, allowing its antithesis to develop in the swamp of its contradictions ... In fact, the social program that has been developed over the last generation within that part of society that is called 'the other Israel' clearly harks back to the past: 'Revive the glorious past' is the electoral slogan of the Shass Party, which succeeded in galvanizing hundreds of thousands of Jews of Arab culture ...

> The religious world, which increasingly sets the tone for this part of Israeli society, went through a hardening process that saw different branches of Judaism absorbing the most fundamentalist aspects of their rivals: Sephardic Judaism (of the Arab and Mediterranean world), traditionally moderate and tolerant, adopted the intransigent fundamentalism of the Judaism originally from Lithuania, and Western Judaism, generally more resistant to mysticism and superstition, acquired a taste for amulets and rabbinical miracle-makers.[2]

Ever since Ygal Allon, the main architect of Israel's system of control over the West Bank, gave his approval to the fundamentalist rabbi Moshe Levinger's attempts to establish a Jewish community in the heart of Arab Hebron – as Simha Flapan reminded us[3] – Jewish fundamentalism has spearheaded the colonization of the occupied territories. It played this role after the 1993 Oslo Agreement, contributing massively to the doubling of the number of settlers in the space of a decade. In Gaza and the West Bank (not including East Jerusalem), the settler population went from 116,300 in late 1993 to 231,800 by late 2003, an increase due in roughly equal measure to the influx of new settlers and an exceptionally high birth rate[4] – three times higher than within Israel's 1948–67 borders.[5] One of the most compelling comparisons with Nazism was drawn in connection with the settlers in Hebron. And it came not from an irresponsible ignoramus but from one of the leading Israeli and international specialists in contemporary German history, Professor Moshe Zimmerman of the Hebrew University of Jerusalem. Zimmerman made his remarks in a 1995 interview with the newspaper *Yerushalayim*:

> It is obvious that we, from every aspect, have a better 'pretext' for many of our actions. Yet there is also a monster in each of us, and if we continue to assume that we are always justified, that monster can grow. Therefore, we Jews are obliged to always hold the German example before our eyes. Already today I am addressing a phenomenon which is growing: there is an entire sector in the Jewish public which I unhesitatingly define as a copy of the German Nazis. Look at the children of the Jewish Hebron settlers: they are exactly like the Hitler Youth. From infancy they are pumped with ideas that all Arabs are bad, of how every Gentile is against us. They are turned into paranoids, they think [of] themselves as a master race, they are exactly like the Hitler Youth. There is a very dangerous tendency of lenience towards that sector.[6]

The pursuit of colonization at a time when the Palestinians were hoping to see the settlements dismantled was the main reason for their rapid disenchantment with the Oslo Peace Agreement. It was accompanied by a new round in the spiral of violence in the occupied territories, as a result of which the 'peace process' ran permanently aground. The year 2000, which saw the final retreat of the Israeli army from the Lebanese territory it had occupied in 1982 – a retreat that took on the cast of a debacle and carried Hezbollah's prestige to new heights – also saw the outbreak of the Second Intifada, also known as the Al-Aqsa Intifada after the Jerusalem mosque that is Islam's third holy place. Ariel Sharon had insisted on going to the Esplanade of the Mosques in

Jerusalem, accompanied by a heavy escort, a deliberate provocation staged in the confident expectation that the explosion it was certain to bring on could only heighten his popularity in an Israeli society that had been inexorably sliding to the right since 1967.

Sharon, condemned in 1983 by a commission of inquiry headed by the president of the Israeli Supreme Court for his indirect personal responsibility in the massacres at Sabra and Shatila – to say nothing of his very direct personal responsibility in the invasion of Lebanon, which reached its tragic climax with the massacres – was brought to power by a majority of Israeli voters in February 2001. He had never made a secret of his opposition to the Oslo Accords or his desire to see Israel annex a substantial part of the territories on the West Bank it had occupied in 1967. Yitzhak Rabin, too, had thrown his support behind this 'unilateral separation' after the Oslo process foundered. As early as 1994, Rabin had ordered construction of the barrier surrounding the Gaza Strip, before Sharon began construction of the wall separating the portion of the West Bank annexed de facto by Israel from the rest of the territory and its population.

In 2005, the authors of an Israeli-American study of textbooks used in Palestinian schools under the Palestinian Authority deplored the image of Israel they purveyed:

> Israel's image is wholly negative: It has been an occupying entity since 1948, exclusively responsible for the Palestinian Catastrophe of that year and the source of violence. Israel shells schools, arrests and tortures people, demolishes Palestinian houses, blocks roads, oppresses the Palestinians – including by means of the 'racist annexation and separation wall', steals Palestinian land and water, strives to destroy Muslim and Christian holy places, tries to impoverish the Palestinians and destroy their agriculture and economy, maltreats its own Palestinian citizens, etc.[7]

All this, unfortunately, is literally true; these authors might consider that reality must change in order to bring about changes in the reigning image of it. The situation has, alas, deteriorated still further in the twenty-first century. In the name of the 'war on terrorism' declared in the wake of the 11 September 2001 attacks, George W. Bush's administration, the most right-wing administration in the history of the United States, and Ariel Sharon's government, the most right-wing government Israel had ever had until then, threw themselves like twin cannon into parallel wars: the invasion of Afghanistan in 2001 and Iraq in 2003 on the one hand, and a second invasion of the West Bank in 2002 on the other. Hatred throughout the region rose to a fever pitch. The occupation of Iraq, carried out against the backdrop of a low-intensity civil war between Sunnis and Shiites, generated a fourth Islamic resistance movement in what the Bush administration dubbed the Greater Middle East.

The banners of preceding struggles, on which the adjectives 'national', 'popular', and 'socialist' were inscribed, have vanished almost without a trace; their place has been taken by the standards of Islamic fundamentalist movements. At the same time, anti-Semitism, in both its traditional and Islamized variants as well as its Holocaust-denying corollary, has grown spectacularly in Arab political statements and Arab media. Israeli and pro-Israeli propaganda in general have observed these developments with great satisfaction: the Middle East Media Research Institute (MEMRI) delights in collecting public expressions of them.

Hezbollah, Hamas and Islamized Anti-Semitism

Amal Saad-Ghorayeb's *Hizbu'llah: Politics and Religion* offers a subtle, thoroughgoing analysis of the discourse of the Lebanese 'Party of God'. In Saad-Ghorayeb's chapter on its attitude to the Jewish question, she shows, even while acknowledging declarations distinguishing Jews from Zionists, that this distinction is 'purely academic': 'That the overwhelming majority of Jews happen to be Zionists, by Hizbu'llah's reckoning, only highlights the Judaic origins of Zionism and greatly facilitates the close identification between two doctrines which are perceived to be equally iniquitous.'[8]

Although Saad-Ghorayeb draws an indispensable distinction between religious anti-Judaism and racial anti-Semitism, she nevertheless concludes – in view of the party's demonization of the Jews and its adherence to the theory of a universal Jewish plot against God and the human race – that 'the anti-Judaism of Hizbu'llah is as vituperative against Jews, if not more than, conventional anti-Semitism.'[9] On the question of the Holocaust, Hezbollah has taken up all the classic theme of European Holocaust denial over the years: that the Holocaust is a myth fabricated by Jews/Zionists, who have enormously exaggerated or invented outright the story of the slaughter when they did not themselves help perpetrate it.[10]

As for Hamas, it is common knowledge that the Movement of Islamic Resistance began life as the armed wing of the Palestinian branch of the Muslim Brothers. It is important to recall that the development of the Brotherhood in the occupied territories, with the financial backing of the Saudi and Jordanian monarchies, was fostered by Israel, which until 1988 saw it as an antidote to the PLO – as Ze'ev Schiff and Ehud Ya'ari have explained in their book *Intifada*:

> The Israelis were quite willing to overlook the seamier side of the Brotherhood's doctrine calling for the destruction of Israel – once conditions were right. But above all, what made the movement so appealing to them was its rivalry with the PLO. Sheikh Yassin [the movement's main historical figure] never concealed his distaste for Arafat. 'Pork eaters and wine drinkers' is how he dismissed the PLO leadership, and he had special contempt for the leftists because they violated the precept (hallowed by every pious Muslim [this is an interpretation peculiar to Schiff and Ya'ari]) that 'a woman's voice is indecent.' Being a prudent man, he was careful to explain that the PLO was not evil, merely misguided; the yardstick for judging Arafat, like every other Muslim, was not nationalist fervor but religious piety. Hearing these comments as signs of strong discord in the Palestinian camp, Israel was only too happy to let the 'prayermongers' thrive.[11]

Hamas's Charter, published on 14 August 1988, is a document on which a good deal of ink has been spilled.[12] Articles 7 and 22 in particular represent a condensed version of the Islamized anti-Semitic ravings cultivated earlier by Rashid Rida, in the years just before his death in 1935. One need only compare these articles with the description of Rida's views above[*] to see that they are in full harmony. What is more, Article 32 quotes *The Protocols of the Elders of Zion*. Nazism is repeatedly linked with the Jews (meaning the Jews of Palestine: 'The Nazism of the Jews has been extended to women and children, they terrorize one and all' – Article 20), Zionism and Israel, with the obvious intention of making the insult as offensive as possible, as in the preposterous expression, 'this cruel Nazi-Tartar invasion' (Article 32).

Studies of Hamas have, however, noted that its terminology and conceptions have evolved, and that it has introduced a distinction between Jews and Zionists. Khaled Hroub, in the English edition (2000) of *Hamas: Political Thought and Practice*, his first book on the subject, cites an interview with the leaders of the movement published in its official organ, *Filastin al-Muslima*, that begins by defining a non-Zionist Jew as a Jew who does not endorse certain ideas – which are not specified in Hroub's citation.[13]

In the original (1996) Arabic version of his book, however, Hroub, one of the movement's most knowledgeable students, reproduces the paragraphs that precede and explain this definition. The Hamas leaders draw a distinction

---

[*]   See 'Rashid Rida' in Chapter 4 above.

between Judaism, 'a falsified religion of which their [*sic*] literature is full of racism and aggression toward others, under the slogan of the promised land and the promise, which God supposedly made them, that they could take control of it,' and Zionism, 'which represents the racist entity in interaction with aggressive Jewish thought'.[14] This distinction did not represent real progress, inasmuch as Article 31 of the Charter had already emphasized, notwithstanding its anti-Jewish and anti-Semitic rant, that 'disciples of the three religions, Islam, Christianity, and Judaism, can coexist in security and confidence in the protective shadow of Islam'. Hroub, taking his hopes for realities, considerably overestimated Hamas's ideological evolution toward a stance transcending anti-Judaism and anti-Semitism.

Writing at about the same time, Khālid Abul-'Amrayn, another very competent student of Hamas and a member of its external leadership from 1986 to 1995, emphasizes that 'Contrary to other patriotic Palestinian forces, the movement has made no distinction between Jews and Zionists; from its standpoint, all Jews are enemies of God and murderers of the prophets who suck human blood and are to blame for corruption and degeneration everywhere. The Jews living on the soil of Palestine are all enemies, whatever the party they belong to or the ideas they espouse, because all are living illegally on other people's land.'[15]

Abul-'Amrayn's diagnosis was corroborated in a well-informed collection of essays by Palestinian and Jordanian academics (to which Hroub, too, contributed), one of which concludes that Hamas distinguishes between Judaism and Zionism in theory but considers the distinction difficult to uphold, because Judaism is now as much a form of nationalism as a religion.[16]

Helga Baumgarten, in a remarkable overview of the movement published in German, does not deny the evidence of anti-Semitism in its discourse but points to tangible signs that the Charter may eventually be amended.[17]

The Hamas sympathizer most critical of its anti-Semitic statements, because he is keenly aware of the harm it has done to the movement's image, is the Palestinian-British intellectual Azzam Tamimi. In February 2006, Tamimi told the *Jerusalem Post* that a revision of the Charter was underway: 'The whole language [of the new document] will be changed to political language ... All that nonsense about *The Protocols of the Elders of Zion* and conspiracy theories – all that rubbish will be out. It should have never been there in the first place.'[18]

Tamimi has said the same thing in his English-language book *Hamas: Unwritten Chapters*, in which he discusses the question at greater length:

When it was drafted [in 1988], the Charter was an honest representation of the ideological and political position of Hamas at that moment in time. Hamas had emerged from the Ikhwan (the Muslim Brotherhood), and the Charter was a reflection of how the Ikhwan perceived the conflict in Palestine and how they viewed the world ...

Until the beginning of the second Intifada in September 2000, very little debate had taken place within Hamas on this issue, despite the fact that much of the criticism levelled against the movement has involved references to the Charter.[19]

He further explains that the leadership has finally become aware of the harm done by the Charter, thanks especially to 'consultations conducted in Beirut and Damascus from early 2003 until the end of 2005' which culminated in 'the commissioning of a draft for a new Charter'.[20] The process was suspended after Hamas's January 2006 victory in the Palestinian legislative elections, because its leaders wanted to avoid creating the impression that they were yielding to pressure. Tamimi even provides details about the contents of the new Charter, giving his readers to understand that he was personally involved in drafting it:

It is anticipated that ... the new Hamas Charter will be cleansed from the ludicrous claim that there is Jewish conspiracy. It will instead emphasise the racist nature of the Zionist project, explaining that many Jews are opposed to it. The idea that not every Jew is a Zionist is already widely accepted by the Islamists, who previously believed this was a myth invented by Palestinian secular nationalists.[21]

The *Jerusalem Post* reporter who interviewed Tamimi by telephone in February 2006 sought to confirm what he told her by interrogating leading figures in Hamas:

Recently elected Hamas leaders in Gaza and the West Bank, who said they knew nothing about plans for a new charter, did not rule out changing it.

'This is a very special issue which would be addressed by the highest level of Hamas,' Sheikh Yasser Mansour, No. 5 on the Hamas national electoral list, told the *Post* by phone from his home in Nablus. Mansour added that, in principle, 'it is true that we could discuss changes. The charter is not the Koran.'

That sentence was repeated by other Hamas leaders interviewed by the *Post*.

Sheikh Salah Abu Rukbeh, recently elected from the Hamas list to the council of Gaza's Jabalya refugee camp, believes that the charter could ultimately be changed to recognize Israel.

'It will be very easy to change the charter if Israel changes its stance about the Palestinians,' he said. 'We are ready to change our charter, but is Israel willing to recognize a Palestinian state? Until now it hasn't. The PLO recognized Israel and changed its charter but Israel did not give us anything.'[22]

The same reporter did not, however, have any trouble finding recent remarks of an anti-Jewish or anti-Semitic nature emanating from the Palestinian movement; sources that specialize in monitoring Arab media, such as MEMRI and its many counterparts, have a plethora of examples of this kind at their disposal. Yet while there can be no doubt that anti-Jewish, anti-Semitic and Holocaust-denying expressions still emanate unceasingly from Hamas circles, the fact remains that the movement has evolved on this question and can evolve still further. Jeroen Gunning stresses this possibility, even as he acknowledges that Hamas leaders 'undermine their position by using inflammatory quotes and espousing anti-Semitic themes'.[23] He opens his own study of the movement with a judicious critique of the analysts who treat it as if it were static and incapable of change.[24]

Indeed, quite as undeniable as the anti-Semitic expressions in Hamas's public statements is the considerable evolution of its political conceptions. Recent programmatic documents, while remaining faithful to its ultra-nationalist religious perspective, carefully avoid crude anti-Semitism. Witness, for example, both the electoral programme on which Hamas campaigned in the January 2006 Palestinian legislative elections[25] (that it took part in them at all was already proof of a major shift in stance) and the long self-description published on its information agency's website in September 2006,[26] a document that presumably anticipates the new Charter.

This capacity for change is what distinguishes mass movements with a broad social base, such as Hezbollah and Hamas, from sects, big or small, cut off from the real life of society. That both movements adhere to fundamentalist doctrines naturally puts limits on their ideological development, but the gap between the unalterable core of their political-religious doctrine and their real political positions can widen, in the same way that social-democratic and Communist parties evolved away from Marxism. In reality, these massive organizations are anything but monolithic, encompassing attitudes that range from the most unbending dogmatism to the most flexible pragmatism. The general rule (which, like all general rules, admits exceptions) is that the professional guardians of religious doctrine tend to be the most rigid, while the political leaders tend to be the most flexible.

When we consider Lebanese Shiite fundamentalism, for example, we observe a clear difference between the discourse of Ayatollah Muhammad Hussein Fadlallah and that of Hezbollah's Secretary General, Hassan Nasrallah. Fadlallah continues to multiply anti-Jewish declarations based on conspiracy theories, as in his February 2008 letter to the Danish Prime Minister protesting against the republication of the controversial caricatures of the Prophet Muhammad in the Danish press as a gesture of defiance after one of the cartoonists involved received death threats. In his letter, the ayatollah announced his altogether arbitrary conviction that 'Jewish circles manipulated by agencies with links to international Zionism endeavor constantly to complicate relations between Muslims and Christians, and between the Islamic world and Western states',[27] utterly unaware that such attempts to incite 'Christians' and Westerners against the 'Jews' could only elicit revulsion.

Conversely, the anti-Jewish and anti-Semitic statements in Hassan Nasrallah's discourse have decreased over the years, providing undeniable proof that he has gone through a learning process. As with Nasser earlier, if to a lesser extent, there are intellectuals in the Hezbollah leader's entourage who are capable of making the right distinctions and repudiating anti-Semitic and Holocaust-denying bluster as both erroneous and detrimental to Hezbollah's cause. Nasrallah, the most pragmatic of all the leaders of the movements spawned by Islamic fundamentalism, is quite capable of taking advice. Thus if, in 1998, he could attack 'the murderers of the prophets, the grandsons of apes and pigs' – the kind of anti-Semitism in which MEMRI delights[28] – MEMRI itself bears witness to the decline of such declarations in his discourse!

Since the Thirty-Three-Day War that Israel waged against Lebanon and Hezbollah in summer 2006, Nasrallah has adopted the political premiss championed by Nasser and his comrades: Israel, he has stated, is a 'tool' of the United States – as opposed to the thesis that Israel 'manipulates' the United States, although the latter had just been bolstered by John Mearsheimer and Stephen Walt's famous attempt to show that their country's Middle Eastern policy is dictated not by its 'national interest' (some would say 'imperial interest') but by the excessive influence of the pro-Israel lobby.[29]

On 29 July 2006, in an international appeal issued in the midst of the war, Nasrallah accused the Bush administration of urging Israel to pursue the fighting; more than ever, he stressed, 'Israel appears as a compliant tool for the realization of an American plan and an American decision.'[30] He repeated the argument a few months later in a speech delivered at the end of the mourning period (*Arbaʿin*) of Ashura 2007, speaking of 'the [American] military outpost known as Israel, which is usurping Palestinian territory'.[31]

Thanks to the indispensable dose of pragmatism without which organizations such as Hamas and Hezbollah could not have attained their present size and played the roles they now play, they can learn to leave their Islamized anti-Semitism behind, or at least to mute it, and to repudiate such inanities as the theory of an international Jewish plot or Holocaust denial – ideas that are not an inherent feature of Islamic fundamentalism but have left a deep stamp on it as a result of the confrontation with the Zionist movement in Palestine. The evolution of Rashid Rida's attitude towards the Jews and even the Zionists offers a good illustration.

Yehoshafat Harkabi, in the book on the 'Arab attitude' that he wrote when he was still a hawk, was honest enough not to categorize anti-Semitism as an ancestral trait of the Arab or Muslim 'mind', although countless other writers increasingly do just that. Rather, Harkabi writes:

> It should be stated with the utmost emphasis that Arab anti-Semitism is not the cause of the conflict but one of its results; it is not the reason for the hostile Arab attitude toward Israel and the Jews, but a means of deepening, justifying and institutionalizing that hostility. Its rise is connected with the tension created as a result of Zionist activity, and especially of the traumatic experience of defeat, the establishment of independent Israel and the struggle against her. Anti-Semitism is a weapon in this struggle. It is functional and political, not social: it presents the Jews mainly as a political, not a social threat ... Hence it describes the Jews, not as passive, shrinking parasites, but as aggressors. Unlike Western Christian anti-Semitism, it is not the result of generations of incitement which have created an archetype in the popular consciousness, although there are elements in Islam on which anti-Semitism could build.[32]

As many writers have pointed out, there is a crucial difference between the German or French anti-Semitism of the late nineteenth and early twentieth centuries (to say nothing of its present-day remnants) and anti-Semitic statements of the kind proffered in the Arab world over the past few decades. The former is a pathological fantasy that scapegoats the Jews as a way of venting social frustrations for which 'the Jews' are in no sense responsible, even if anti-Semites always manage to find individuals of Jewish origin to serve as symbolic targets for their loathing of 'plutocracy' or 'cosmopolitanism'. In contrast, the anti-Semitic statements now heard in Arab countries are fantasy-laden expressions – due, as a rule, to cultural backwardness – of an intense national frustration and oppression for which 'the Jews' of Palestine in their majority as well as Israel, the 'Jewish state' they founded, must in fact be held responsible.

One cannot equate the anti-Semitism called forth by an occupying army that declares its allegiance to a 'Jewish state' and has perpetrated war crimes in Palestine and Lebanon with the anti-Semitism based, for example, on the notion that 'the Yids' were to blame for German or French military defeats with which Judaism had absolutely nothing to do. To take a similar example from another domain, one cannot equate the anti-white racism that took hold in the 1960s among militant black groups in the United States with the early twentieth-century racism of white American farmers who attributed the inexorable decline of their socio-economic conditions to hapless black victims they hunted down and lynched.

From Garaudy to Ahmadinejad: Reactive Exploitation of the Memory of the Holocaust

The further Israel's image deteriorated in Western public opinion as a result of the Lebanese war and the Intifada, the more Israel and its unconditional supporters in Europe and the United States – see Peter Novick's admirable *The Holocaust in American Life*, published in 1999 – felt the need to shore up the legitimacy and untouchability of the 'Jewish state'. It was in this context that the political exploitation of the memory of the Holocaust reached its height, accompanied by a deluge of literary and audiovisual productions that added a new dimension to the uniqueness of the Shoah: no genocide in history has received so much attention, a circumstance that has sharply exacerbated the 'competition of the victims'.

This exploitation of the Holocaust spawned its epigones: other predatory states saw that the Israeli formula might prove useful to them as well. Untold new Hitlers have sprung up since the end of the Cold War, leading to an alarming trivialization of Nazism and the Holocaust. The elder George Bush went so far as to pronounce Saddam Hussein 'worse than Hitler' in 1991;[33] his son fell back on the same comparison eleven years later.[34] The analogy of Hitler/Jews/Allies and Milosevic/Kosovars/Nato was employed without reserve during the 1999 war in Kosovo, provoking even the indignation of Claude Lanzmann:

I might point out ... that the phenomenon of automatic comparison is something new: intellectuals did not fall back on this allusion to the Shoah in the worst periods of the Algerian war, when the fighters of the FLN were being murdered or tortured in droves and vast areas were being depopulated. The same applies to the Vietnam War, when villages by the hundreds, forests, and rice paddies were being laid waste by napalm. Even during the war in Biafra, which saw the emergence of the practice and ideology of humanitarianism, people abstained from making comparisons with Nazism ...

These constant references to the Holocaust are a way of silencing all discourse. A gag rule. No more debate.[35]

This observation is very much on the mark. Lanzmann certainly did not have Israel in mind, yet the 'gag rule' to which he points here is, in fact, the primary objective of the Zionist state's exploitation of the Holocaust, as Idith Zertal has emphasized: 'By means of Auschwitz – which has become over the years Israel's main reference in its relations with a world defined repeatedly as anti-Semitic and forever hostile – Israel rendered itself immune to criticism, and impervious to a rational dialogue with the world around her.'[36] Zertal's diagnosis is confirmed by Avraham Burg, who has served as president of the Jewish Agency and World Zionist Movement, vice-president of the World Jewish Congress, and president of the Knesset. Burg goes even further in his exploration of the way Israel utilizes the memory of the Holocaust:

For us, every killing is a murder, every murder a pogrom, every terror attack an anti-Semitic act and every new enemy a Hitler. Behind every danger lurks a new holocaust. We, and many of our leaders who incite us, believe that almost everyone wants to destroy us. By feeling so threatened by shadows that will attack us at dawn, we have become a nation of attackers ...

We always want a stronger army because of the Shoah, and more resources from other countries' taxpayers, and an automatic forgiveness for any of our excesses. We want to be above criticism and attention.[37]

Vidal-Naquet described the function and result of this 'daily exploitation of the great massacre by the Israeli political establishment' in his turn:

The genocide of the Jews abruptly ceases being a historical reality, experienced existentially, and becomes a commonplace tool of political legitimation, brought to bear in obtaining political support within the country as well as in pressuring the Diaspora to follow unconditionally the inflections of Israeli policy. Such is the paradox of a use that makes of the genocide at once a sacred moment in history, a very secular argument, and even a pretext for tourism and commerce.[38]

Is it any wonder, then, that Israeli exploitation of the memory of the Holocaust has triggered a sharp rise in the reactive exploitation of the Holocaust in the Arab countries? The reasons why Israel's public-relations use of the genocide has intensified – namely, the war crimes that have led to the deterioration of its image – are the very same reasons that have brought Arab resentment to a fever pitch. The intellectual barriers standing in the way of negative uses of the Holocaust are naturally much lower in the Arab world than in Israel and the West, not only for obvious political reasons but also because knowledge about the Holocaust is far less widely diffused in the Arab countries.

In recent years, two affairs have provided the occasions for Holocaust-denying proclamations in Arab countries: one associated with Roger Garaudy, the other with Mahmoud Ahmadinejad. The first exploded in the headlines in 1996, when Garaudy, a convert to first Catholicism and then Islam who was once the French Communist Party's 'official philosopher', was brought to trial in France on charges of denying the Holocaust and fomenting racial hatred. Thereafter, he became one of the most prominent standard-bearers of Holocaust denial and anti-Semitism. The accusation against him was based on a book mentioned above, *Les Mythes fondateurs de la politique israélienne*, released in 1995 by a publisher that was a centre of Holocaust denial. Garaudy's book echoes the deniers' basic theses, sharply underestimating the number of Jews who fell victim to the genocide and denying that the gas chambers were used to put people to death. The general context of the book, a mélange of criticisms of Judaism and criticisms of Zionism, is one of manifest anti-Semitism.

Garaudy was tried under the 'Gayssot Law' – named for the Communist member of the National Assembly who proposed it in 1990 – which makes it a punishable offence to deny the existence of crimes against humanity recognized as such by the 1945 6 Nuremberg International Military Tribunal. It is controversial in France itself, where it has been challenged by prestigious historians, including Vidal-Naquet, who was noted for his own writings against Holocaust deniers, whom he called 'assassins of memory'.[39]

As if to prove the law's opponents right, Garaudy's trial turned out to be very profitable for him, both financially and otherwise. His book, which, had it not caused a scandal, would probably have remained known only to insiders (like the vast majority of Holocaust-denying publications), acquired extraordinary fame and was widely circulated, somewhat like a samizdat text. Garaudy was able to portray himself as the victim of a violation of the right to free speech perpetrated by those who (as his defenders inevitably contended) feared a free discussion that would unveil the truth they had been trying to hide. This is, of course, a fallacious argument, since the claims of the Holocaust deniers are freely expressed outside the handful of countries where they are banned by law. They have, moreover, been dissected and refuted time and again.[40]

Because Garaudy had converted to Islam, he was already an exemplary figure for those looking for confirmation of Islam's superiority to Marxism confirmed. His trial and conviction were the final steps on the way to his beatification in the eyes of Muslim fundamentalists, Arab ultra-nationalists, anti-Semites and others; but he was also lionized by large numbers of nationalists eager to demonstrate their solidarity with this victim of 'Zionist propaganda'. All of them sang his praises, if in different keys, before a public that was largely ignorant of the facts and primarily motivated by animosity towards Israel. Needless to say, his book was immediately published in Arabic – first in Beirut in 1996, then in Cairo in 1998 with, as we have seen, a preface by Mohamed Hassanein Heikal.

Garaudy went on a triumphant tour of several Arab countries. He was the guest of nationalists in Lebanon and Jordan, of the Syrian minister of information and of the ministers of culture in Qatar and Egypt. In Egypt, he was received by the Grand Imam of the Al-Azhar mosque and the rector of the university associated with it, Sunni Islam's main theological institute; he was also warmly welcomed by the Iranian authorities. The wife of the president of the United Arab Emirates gave him more than double the amount he had had to pay in fines in France. He was very frequently quoted in or interviewed by the Arab media, and is still cited there as an authority on Zionism and the Holocaust. A considerable number of Arab intellectuals have declared their solidarity with him – a few in the name of freedom of speech, but many others because they endorse his beliefs. [41]

Garaudy's reception in the Arab world was, in a word, a calamity. It was symptomatic of a problem that went much deeper than Holocaust denial: namely, the intellectual regression that has been underway in the Arab countries for several decades now, brought on by the decline of the educational system, the curtailment of intellectual freedoms (which, when they are tolerated here and there by the governments, are snuffed out by ever more powerful religious authorities) and the stultification of whole populations by television – which, even in the best of cases, is a reflection of the surrounding mindlessness, and more often than not makes it worse.

I shall limit myself to one revelatory example: a book about the historical context of Garaudy's trial published in Beirut in 1998. It purports to be a 'scholarly work'; the cover proclaims that the author holds a doctorate.[42] Also on the cover is a composite Nazi and Israeli flag, with a blue Star of David on a black swastika at its centre. Reciting all the stock themes of the literature of European anti-Semitism and Holocaust denial, the author situates Garaudy's trial at the point where French 'Christian Zionism' and German 'Nazi Zionism' intersect with Israeli 'Jewish Zionism'.

All this would be of merely pathological interest if the author had not included, in an appendix, an anthology of declarations and essays published in Lebanon and a few other Arab countries in support of Garaudy and his claims. Here we find position statements by religious dignitaries such as Muhammad Hussein Fadlallah (then not yet an ayatollah), the head of Lebanon's Supreme Islamic Shiite Council, and the Mufti of Syria, as well as by the Writers' Unions of Lebanon, Syria and Jordan and the Syrian and Arab bar associations. Also reproduced in the appendix are the minutes of a meeting of jurists, politicians and journalists held in Beirut in January 1998 in solidarity with Garaudy, together with several articles by various other figures, among them a Lebanese minister of technical and professional education.[43]

Even the Arab doyen in the field of Jewish and Zionist studies, Abdelwahab Elmessiri, who has unquestionably amassed great knowledge of these subjects after working on them for decades, saw fit to dedicate his 1997 book on Zionism and Nazism to Garaudy (under his Arabized name of *Rajā' Jārūdi*), citing him in the epigraph as well.[44] Elmessiri's book, too, boasts a preface by Mohamed Hassanein Heikal. It is based on extracts from a work that would be published two years later, the *Encyclopedia of Jews, Judaism, and Zionism*, of which Elmessiri was the general editor and principal author.[45]

Elmessiri devotes at least as many pages to the Jews' collaboration with the Nazis as he does to the Holocaust; a good part of the Holocaust section is, moreover, given over to a denunciation of its exploitation by Zionists. He does not call the reality of the Jewish genocide into question, and he concedes that the gas chambers were used to put people to death, although he tends to downplay matters. This nod to probity, however, does not prevent him from describing works by such Holocaust deniers as Paul Rassinier, Arthur Butz and Robert Faurisson as 'scholarly studies' of 'controversial subjects'.[46] Similarly, he offers a number of arguments to the effect that *The Protocols of the Elders of Zion* is a forgery, yet describes the affirmation that it is false as a mere 'viewpoint' he happens to share.[47]

Arab intellectuals, however, did not grant Garaudy unanimous acclaim. Several of the most important Arab dailies published acerbic critiques of the writer and his Arab partisans – often the same newspapers that published the Holocaust deniers' articles. Such columnists as Samir Kassir, Hazem Saghieh and Joseph Samaha, who are especially sensitive to the damage that the enthusiastic Arab reception of Garaudy has done to the Palestinian cause in Europe (where they have all lived for some time), braved the climate of ultra-nationalistic intimidation and distinguished themselves in the polemic against Garaudy's admirers.

A number of Arab intellectuals rose up to condemn both Garaudy and the acclaim he had received. The most prestigious was Edward Said, who wrote several essays on the controversy; the main one was published in English in *Al-Ahram Weekly* on 25 June 1998 and in Arabic five days later in *Al-Hayat*, a well-known pan-Arab daily based in London. Besides condemning Garaudy, Said denounced the ideological regression in the Arab world.

> There is now a creeping, nasty wave of anti-Semitism and hypocritical righteousness insinuating itself into our political thought and rhetoric ... The history of the modern Arab world – with all its political failures, its human rights abuses, its stunning military incompetences, its decreasing production, the fact that, alone of all modern peoples, we have receded in democratic and technological and scientific development – is disfigured by a whole series of out-moded and discredited ideas, of which the notion that the Jews never suffered and that the Holocaust is an obfuscatory confection created by the elders of Zion is one that is acquiring too much, far too much, currency.
>
> Why do we expect the world to believe our sufferings as Arabs if (a) we cannot recognise the sufferings of others, even of our oppressors, and (b) we cannot deal with facts that trouble simplistic ideas of the sort propagated by bien-pensant intellectuals, who refuse to see the relationship between the Holocaust and Israel? Again, let me repeat that I cannot accept the idea that the Holocaust excuses Zionism for what it has done to Palestinians: far from it. I say exactly the opposite, that by recognising the Holocaust for the genocidal madness that it was, we can then demand from Israelis and Jews the right to link the Holocaust to Zionist injustices towards the Palestinians, link and criticise the link for its hypocrisy and flawed moral logic.
>
> But to support the efforts of Garaudy and his Holocaust-denying friends in the name of 'freedom of opinion' is a silly ruse that discredits us

more than we already are discredited in the world's eyes for our incompetence, our failure to fight a decent battle, our radical misunderstanding of history and the world we live in. Why don't we fight harder for freedom of opinion in our own societies, a freedom, no one needs to be told, that scarcely exists?[48]

This line of argument was criticized on the grounds that it sought to establish a trade-off – mutual recognition of the Jewish and Palestinian tragedies. Yet Said laid down no conditions for recognition of the Holocaust; he merely treated it as a prelude to the Palestinian and Arab demand for Israeli recognition of 'Zionist injustices'. Meir Litvak and Esther Webman nevertheless upbraid him for falling 'into the trap of instrumentalization [of the Holocaust] by connecting the recognition of the two tragedies'.[49] One can only be astounded by the ethnocentric complacency that leads two Israeli authors to criticize a Palestinian for explaining that if his compatriots do not acknowledge the suffering of others, they cannot demand that others acknowledge theirs. Compare Litvak and Webman's reaction to the remarkably clear manner in which Hazem Saghieh posed the problem:

> In principle, the demand for reciprocity should not exist, in the sense that a humanist position should not be made to depend on what one obtains in politics. But, when all is said and done, human beings are human beings: that is, they stand under the influence of their conditions, contingencies, and priorities, and they make exchanges with others. Thus reciprocity can, at least initially, prove useful, or even indispensable.
>
> It is Israeli intellectuals' duty to talk about the Palestinian tragedy (the 'new historians' who have revised the historiography of the war of 1948, together with other books and writings, are luminous in this regard).
>
> It is Arab intellectuals' duty to talk about the Holocaust and spread knowledge of it.[50]

In January 1998, the Palestinian negotiators in the Oslo process – among them several liberal Westernizers allied with the PLO – advised Arafat to visit the Holocaust Museum in Washington, DC, as part of a more comprehensive plan that sought, among other goals, to undo the damage wrought by the Garaudy affair. The planned visit, organized by the American negotiators from the State Department, Dennis Ross and Aaron Miller, was, however, aborted by the refusal of the Museum's directors to receive the Palestinian leader as a VIP: they said he would have to attend like any ordinary visitor. This refusal caused controversy in the United States itself, and in the face of the public protests the Museum's directors changed their position, while still insisting that Arafat would not be received as a head of state. Although he did not reject the invitation, the Palestinian leader ultimately postponed what would have been a humiliating visit.

Thus an important occasion to educate Arab public opinion on the Shoah was lost.[51] This debacle reinforced the arguments of the Muslim fundamentalists and the ultra-nationalists who accuse Arabs prepared to acknowledge the full tragedy of the Holocaust of 'servility'. Arafat sought to make up for the missed occasion by visiting the Anne Frank House in Amsterdam three months later, on 31 March 1998. This is how Reuters reported the event:

> Palestinian President Yasser Arafat said on Tuesday he was deeply moved by a visit to the cramped rooms where Jewish teenager Anne Frank hid from Nazi occupiers during World War II.
>
> 'A sad story. A very sad story,' Arafat told reporters as he left the narrow house on Princes Canal where Anne and her family hid for over two years in claustrophobic and squalid conditions. 'This is what I worked on with my peace partner Rabin so it would not happen to our children and the next generation,' he said, referring to slain Israeli Prime Minister Yitzhak Rabin.
>
> Earlier, at a news conference, Arafat pledged to pass on his impressions of the Anne Frank house to fellow Palestinians.[52]

This visit, which had obvious symbolic importance even if a visit to the Washington museum would have been more 'spectacular', received very little coverage in the Western media. In Israel, however, it provoked considerable controversy[53] – a circumstance that did not prevent Litvak and Webman from shrouding it in silence while reporting a mass of infinitely less important facts. The speech delivered by Mahmoud Darwish on the fiftieth anniversary of the Nakba, 15 May 1998, had a similarly didactic purpose. According to the Arabic-language *Review of Palestinian Studies*, this 'Call by the Palestinian People' was drafted by a fifty-member committee representing all Palestinian political forces and tendencies with the exception of Hamas and Islamic Jihad. On the question of the Holocaust, the Call declares:

> If we have a moral obligation both to accept the Jewish narrative of the Holocaust as it stands, without getting involved in discussions of the statistical treatment of the crime, and also to express greater compassion for the victims, we also have a right to demand that the children of the

victims acknowledge the condition of the Palestinian victims and their right to life, emancipation, and independence.[54]

Sheikh Jamāl Mansūr, a leader of Hamas, is among those who seem to have understood and appreciated this Call. His reaction to the proposition made in April 2000 by Anīs al-Qāq, a Palestinian Authority official, to include the history of the Holocaust in Palestinian and Arab school curricula was among the most measured and anti-Nazi of all those catalogued by MEMRI:

> 'It is not fair to deny the Holocaust or to diminish the importance of the persecution that the Jews have suffered. We must clearly condemn it and stand by the oppressed – whoever they may be – and against the oppressor.' However, Sheik Mansour explained that the problem is with 'the West, which takes a rigid stance when it comes to the history of the Jews with the Nazis and forces all of the governments and peoples to teach one history of the Holocaust. In addition, the West uses Zionist historians in order to establish this [narrative] and turn it into an axiom, which no one is allowed to question.
>
> 'At the same time,' adds Sheik Mansour, 'they want us to forget all the massacres, the tens of thousands of victims, the millions of exiles, our confiscated land, our occupied land, and our blood which continues to be spilled. ... The Jews have mobilized the so-called free and civilized world in order to bow the heads of [their] victims, to [bring them to] apologize for their history and to commit to their well-being and to protect their strength in the future, and all this because of one crazy man who was an enemy to the entire world and not the Jews alone, and who murdered 20 million Russians with his own hands.'[55] *

The Arab Holocaust deniers went back on the offensive in 2001, when they tried to organize a 'scholarly' conference in Beirut with two anti-Semitic Western organizations specialising in Holocaust denial – the far-right Truth and Justice, based in Switzerland, and the neo-Nazi Institute for Historical Review (IHR), based in the United States. This attempt was foiled in large part by the outcry that it raised from a group of Arab intellectuals – including Edward Said, the poets Adonis ('Ali Ahmad Sa'īd Isbir) and Mahmoud Darwish, and the writer Elias Khoury, to mention only the most internationally renowned – who signed a petition declaring themselves 'incensed by this anti-Semitic undertaking'.[56] The petition called on the Lebanese authorities to prevent the conference from being held there

---

* Sheikh Jamāl Mansūr was assassinated by Israel, who used a missile for the task, on 31 July 2001.

– which they did after coming under international pressure. Said disavowed
the call to ban the conference, as he explained to a journalist who asked him
about it:

> I was called by phone, told that there was no time to send a copy for me
> to see, and was asked to approve the text for signature. I did, on condi-
> tion that there would be no appeal to any government concerning the
> banning of the conference ...
>
>   All I had agreed to sign was a statement denouncing the holding of
> such a conference in Beirut. To repeat, I did not ask the government to
> ban it, nor would I ever. This request was added against my wishes, and
> without my knowledge. I am deeply opposed to holocaust-deniers but
> I am equally opposed to banning by government edict everyone's right
> to free speech.[57]

A second attempt was made in Jordan a few weeks later; and was no more
successful. Jordan is the Arab country in which Holocaust deniers are the
most active, according to the IHR:

> Nowhere has recent support for revisionism been more open and ardent
> than in Jordan, where the Jordanian Writers Association (JWA) and
> numerous scholars and journalists have done much to promote aware-
> ness of Holocaust deceit. Prominent in this effort has been Dr. Ibrahim
> Alloush, who is active in the JWA and the Association against Zionism
> and Racism (AZAR).[58]

A Palestinian from Jordan, 'Allūsh specializes in ultra-nationalist, anti-
Semitic outrages and Holocaust denial, and has constructed a website for
the purpose.[59] He is one of the Western Holocaust deniers' favourite authors
and is also, of course, much appreciated by MEMRI, as well as by Litvak
and Webman, who cite his name no less than twenty times in the main
text of their book. He illustrates the profound foolishness of those Arabs
who think they are fighting Zionism by outdoing others in anti-Semitism
and Holocaust denial when in fact they are doing Zionist propaganda an
inestimable service.

Holocaust denial loomed up again in the Middle East in summer 2005,
following Mahmoud Ahmadinejad's election as president of the Islamic
Republic of Iran. A few months after his inauguration, Ahmadinejad made a
number of Holocaust-denying declarations, which were abundantly reported
and commented on in both Arab countries and international media. His
remarks turned on three points: (1) that the Holocaust is a myth – if it were

not, the Europeans would not deny those who contest its reality the right to speak out, rather than refuting their arguments; (2) that the Holocaust deniers' right to free speech is violated by the West, which at the same time defends the right to blaspheme Islam; (3) that if the Holocaust did really happen, those who are to blame for it are those who should have given and should still give the Jews land.[60]

Ahmadinejad's remarks reflect the arguments central to Holocaust denial, which has been enjoying a boom since the Garaudy scandal. They show, yet again, how legal bans on Holocaust denial backfire, undermining the credibility of European governments that otherwise sanctify the right to free speech and cite it in protecting the freedom to denigrate the Islamic faith or its symbols. The head of Hezbollah, Hassan Nasrallah, invoked this argument when he commented on the Garaudy affair in February 2006.[61] Arab and Iranian admirers of Western Holocaust deniers appear to be unaware, however, that the legal ban on the expression of their views is in force only in Israel and twelve European countries; no such ban exists in the United States or Britain.

Ahmadinejad's final argument and the one he takes the greatest pleasure in repeating is not *per se* an act of Holocaust denial, since it takes the Holocaust as its premiss, even if this premiss is always presented as an unconfirmed hypothesis. It is the idea that Europe – especially Germany and Austria, as Ahmadinejad has expressly indicated[62] – should have offered the Jews part of their territory at the end of the Second World War, rather than granting them Palestine. There is, naturally, a broad consensus, if not unanimity, around this idea in the Arab world. The notion is hardly shocking; David Ben-Gurion himself, during an October 1945 visit to Germany, suggested to General Dwight Eisenhower, then military governor of the American occupation zone, that he set up 'a Jewish state in Bavaria'.[63] Ahmadinejad's reasoning goes awry when he proposes that land in Europe or the Americas be allotted to the Jews *today* to replace the state of Israel.

But does his reasoning really go awry, or is this, rather, a deliberate provocation? There is good reason to favour the second hypothesis.[64] With his carefully placed remarks – first made in December 2005 in Mecca, where he was taking part in a meeting of the Organization of the Islamic Conference – Ahmadinejad undeniably scored points in the ideological competition between the Khomeinist republic and the Wahhabi monarchy. He garnered praise not only from Iran's natural allies, such as Nasrallah, who declared that Ahmadinejad had said what 1.4 billion of the world's Muslims think,[65] but also from the Sunni fundamentalist movement around the Muslim Brothers.

Both the leader of Hamas, Khaled Meshal, and the head of the Egyptian Muslim Brothers, Muhammad Mahdi 'Ākif, publicly endorsed the Iranian president's comments.

As in Garaudy's case, this Arab support for Ahmadinejad's remarks elicited vigorous protest from a large number of Arab columnists and intellectuals. However, the Iranian president received much less support than the French Holocaust denier had enjoyed, owing in part to nationalist or sectarian animosity towards Iran. Various articles denounced Holocaust denial as a 'sickness'. Khaled Hroub did his part to convince Muslim fundamentalists of its inanity:

> Israel and its political leaders are delighted when the leaders of Hamas, the Muslim Brothers, Iran, or any Arab or Muslim at all, make statements denying the Holocaust or adopt a discourse hostile to the Jews as members of a faith or Judaism as a religion. For all this confirms their propaganda, repeated everywhere, which has it that the Palestinians, Arabs, and Muslims want to wipe out the Jews, contrary to what is in fact going on in Palestine. On the other hand, Israel, its political leaders, and all its lobbies will be disconcerted when the naive, superficial discourse on the Holocaust and Jews in general put forth by a handful of [Arab or Muslim] leaders or intellectuals disappears for good and all. [66]

The exasperation of the Holocaust deniers' Arab detractors was increased when Tehran organized an international conference on the Holocaust in December 2006. 'Enough stupidity!' ran the title of an editorial in the left-wing Beirut daily *Al-Akhbar*, reputed to be close to the resistance led by Hezbollah. [67] The standard-bearer of the national struggle of those Palestinians who are citizens of Israel, Azmi Bishara, then a member of the Knesset (he was forced out of the Israeli parliament and into exile in spring 2007), wrote a long, spirited article on 'the ways of denial of the Nazi Holocaust' that was first published in Arabic in the 14 December 2006 *Al-Hayat* and in English a week later in *Al-Ahram Weekly*. Bishara concluded:

> Holocaust denial does not undermine the moral justifications for the existence of the state of Israel, as some imagine. What it does, however, is hand the European right and Israel a convenient enemy upon which to unload their problems. This enemy comprises Palestinians and Arabs, specifically fundamentalist Muslims, those Bush is fond of calling 'Islamic fascists.'
>
> The initial Arab reaction to the Holocaust was simple and straightforward and much more rational. The Holocaust occurred, but it was a

tragedy for which the Europeans, not the Arabs, should assume responsibility. This is the opinion that prevailed throughout the 1940s and 1950s
– the sense of normalcy that survived in all of us continues to hold it.[68]

Yet every new deterioration in the relationship between Israel and its
Palestinian and Arab neighbours blocks or undoes the progress of the counter-
offensive against Holocaust denial. The latest, terribly bloody incursion of
the Israeli armed forces into Gaza, which caused the deaths of more than
one thousand Palestinians, the great majority of them civilians, many of
them children (and the deaths of thirteen Israelis, three of them civilians),
represented a new stage in the escalation of the Israeli military's war crimes.
The appropriate word is not, however, 'escalation', but descent – a step-by-
step descent into barbarism that has continued since Begin and Sharon's
1982 invasion of Lebanon.

With the extreme exacerbation of passions that has resulted, the temptation
to vent anger on the memory of the Holocaust has only been heightened, as
has the game of competitive comparison between the Shoah and the fate of
the Palestinians – all the more so as Israeli leaders have joined the contest,
not only comparing the Palestinians to Nazis (as usual) but even threatening
them with destruction in terms borrowed from the vocabulary of the Jewish
genocide. Thus the former general Matan Vilnai, a Labour Party vice-minister
of defence in Ehud Olmert's government, declared with respect to Gaza in
February 2008: 'The more Qassam [rocket] fire intensifies and the rockets
reach a longer range, they will bring upon themselves a bigger shoah because
we will use all our might to defend ourselves.'[69] The response of the Palestinian
Prime Minister and Hamas leader, Ismail Haniyeh, was not long in coming:
'They want the world to condemn what they call the Holocaust and now
they are threatening our people with a holocaust.'[70]

Comparisons between Israel and Nazism, like their corollary, comparisons
between the Israeli army's war crimes and the Holocaust, have mushroomed
since the offensive launched against Gaza on 27 December 2008.[71] This
state of affairs is hardly surprising. Only someone possessed of unlimited
effrontery and utter insensitivity could inform those on whom the bombs
were falling, as they watched the mangled corpses of children and adults pile
up around them, that their fate was enviable in comparison with what the
Jews in the concentration camps endured. Given the atrocity of the Israeli
bombing attacks, the attempt to meet such comparisons with accusations of
Holocaust denial and anti-Semitism, or even, in some countries, to subject
them to legal prohibitions, was ludicrous.

In fact, these exorbitant comparisons are the logical antithesis of Holocaust denial, since, as I have already noted, they treat the Holocaust as the supreme horror – even if Arabs all too often conjoin such unwarranted comparisons with Holocaust denial, quite illogically, as a way of expressing their rage. Of course, neither religious fundamentalism nor ultra-nationalism is generally characterised by rational coherency. It is incoherent again when Arabs combine Holocaust denial with enthusiasm for Norman Finkelstein's vigorous denunciation of what he brands the 'Holocaust Industry' and Vidal-Naquet and others the 'Shoah Business' – which Finkelstein accuses of prospering at the expense of Holocaust survivors.* Yet Finkelstein takes pains to explain at the beginning of *The Holocaust Industry* that both his parents 'were survivors of the Warsaw Ghetto and the Nazi concentration camps. Apart from my parents, every family member on both sides was exterminated by the Nazis.'[73]

The incoherent, to be sure, are a minority. The majority of those Arabs who disapprove of Israel's exploitation of the Holocaust would never deny the reality of the event. Yet it is clear that the further Israel goes in its political and practical denial of the Nakba,[74] and the longer Israel continue to exacerbate its consequences, the more Palestinians and Arabs will be tempted to riposte by denying the Holocaust. That is, to be sure, a pitiful sort of reply; but in the face of the increasing barbarity of Israeli offensives, what can be accomplished by such symbolic initiatives as Arafat's in Amsterdam, or the Holocaust Institute and Museum in Nazareth founded by a Palestinian citizen of Israel, Khaled Mahameed?[75] Very little.

Political exploitation of the Holocaust naturally causes Arabs, more than others, the fatigue syndrome about which Didier Pollefeyt has sounded the alarm:

> 'Holocaust fatigue' refers to a phenomenon of people responding with irritation, resistance, cynicism, or indifference when the Holocaust is brought up in politics, social life, the media, educational settings, or daily conversations ... Among other things, 'Holocaust fatigue' is the result of a certain canonization of the history in the Holocaust, which

---

* As if to prove Finkelstein right, on 27 Jan. 2009 *Ynet* published an article deploring the miserable plight of 60,000 Holocaust survivors in Israel – that is, more than one-quarter of the 230,000 survivors who live there. The following statement by a survivor requires no comment: 'I have a sister who still lives in Hungary and doesn't want to come to Israel,' he said. 'She has free healthcare there, and she also gets free medication. The State of Israel was established thanks to the survivors' money, and I don't have enough money right now even for all the medications that I need. I don't even remember the last time I bought underwear and a shirt.'[72]

fixes the meaning of the Holocaust to serve certain clear or (seemingly) hidden moral, ideological, or political agendas. If these mistakes are not corrected and the memory of the Holocaust is not allowed any longer to be 'a dangerous memory' for the politics of the State of Israel, Israel itself can become a danger for the memory of the Holocaust ('a memory in danger').[76]

There is no more powerful illustration than the poll carried out in 2006 among Arab and Jewish Israeli citizens under the direction of Sami Smooha, the dean of the faculty of social sciences at the University of Haifa. *Haaretz* reported the striking results: 'In its most dramatic finding, the poll showed that 28 percent of Israeli Arabs did not believe the Holocaust happened, and that among high school and college graduates the figure was even higher – 33 percent.'[77] Of course, if there is one Arab group that is informed, if not over-informed, about the Holocaust, it is certainly the Arab citizens of Israel, exposed as they are to a school curriculum in which the Jewish genocide holds an important place.* And it is impossible for anyone living in Israel who understands Hebrew – as four-fifths of Israeli Arabs do – to avoid the constant invocation of the memory of the Shoah. Yet the poll showed that the proportion of Arab citizens of Israel who denied the reality of the event increased with their educational level. Moreover, as if to confirm the fundamentally political character of this denial, the proportion of deniers among Palestinians in Israel shot up to 40 per cent in the following two years.[79]

The key to this apparent paradox is what the Israeli officer quoted above affirmed: namely, that the 28–40 per cent of Israel's Arab citizens who deny the Holocaust are 'merely wielding the best weapon they [can] find to attack Israel'. For great moral strength is required to understand, as Joseph Samaha pointed out in 2001, that 'the Arabs will be the more capable of condemning the exploitation [of the Holocaust] to the extent that they avoid the trap that a facile, simplistic, dangerous consciousness lays for them'. And he added: 'Avoiding this trap is the only way to link the Palestinians' and other Arabs' legitimate grievance against Israel and its allies to the general humanist concern that makes them the heirs of the moral rejection of Nazi bestiality and Israeli tyranny.'[80]

---

* The Holocaust is taught in ninth grade in Arab schools in Israel on the basis of a book, translated from Hebrew, that is used in the same grade in Jewish schools. It is also taught in twelfth grade in the context of modern Jewish history, a compulsory subject. An essay by three Israeli academic specialists in education has shown that it is impossible to instruct Palestinian teachers in the Holocaust successfully without also dealing with the Nakba.[78]

Stigmas and Stigmatization

'Good sense is, of all things among men, the most equally distributed,' Descartes declares at the beginning of the *Discourse on Method*, only to add straightaway, 'for everyone thinks himself so abundantly provided with it, that even those who are the most difficult to satisfy in everything else, do not usually desire a larger measure of this quality than they already possess.' The point of his obvious irony is to reduce his first counter-intuitive, if not paradoxical, affirmation to the Aristotelian idea that man is an animal endowed with reason – which, Descartes explains, 'is by nature equal in all men'. Consequently, he goes on, 'the diversity of our opinions ... does not arise from some being endowed with a larger share of reason than others, but solely from this, that we conduct our thoughts along different ways, and do not fix our attention on the same objects. For to be possessed of a vigorous mind is not enough; the prime requisite is rightly to apply it.'[1]

The shared reason is what can allow us to transcend, with time, the ethnocentric peculiarities responsible for justice that vary from one side of a border to the other – as both Montaigne, two generations before Descartes, and Pascal, a generation after him, pointed out. It is faith in human reason that justifies the hope that what counts as truth on one side of the Green Line* or, rather, the Separation Wall, will not forever count as error on the other. Arabs and Israeli Jews have already made considerable progress towards mutual comprehension, given how extraordinarily difficult it was for them to communicate at all in the decades following the Nakba. Unfortunately, the bridges built by the humanists of the two communities have been stretched to the breaking point in recent years by the widening gulf between them: neo-Zionism and xenophobia on the one hand, ultra-nationalism and Islamic fundamentalism on the other.

---

* The 'Green Line' is the internationally recognized border that separated the state of Israel from its Arab neighbours before the 1967 war.

Of Anti-Semitism, Anti-Zionism, Philosemitism, Islamophobia and Exploitation of the Holocaust

The basic condition for all communication is the ability to understand one's interlocutor: to put oneself, in other words, in his place or in her shoes – which further presupposes the intellectual discipline to step out of one's own temporarily in order to reflect. Nothing is more inimical to dialogue than the a priori assumption that the other's being and thinking are immutable. No dialogue is possible until one acknowledges that it is existence and experience, in both their individual and collective dimensions, and not atavism of one or another stripe, that shape consciousness, including the consciousness of others. Stereotyping the other always goes hand in hand with stereotyping the self. As a rule, it is caricature of the other and idealization of the self, and only rarely the opposite.

When some Arabs write off the Jews as fundamentally perverse, claiming to find confirmation of their view in the fact that it used to be a hundred times more common in the West, they forget how Westerners once perceived Arabs and Muslims and, in all too many cases, still do. When some Arabs succumb to the collective paranoid fantasy that the Holocaust is a myth perpetuated by a vast Jewish conspiracy in order to legitimize statist Zionism, they do not stop to consider that those who have done the most to gain a hearing for the Arab cause in the West and counter the propaganda of statist Zionism are thinkers who invoke the universal lessons of the Holocaust, or that many of them are Jews, whether believers or 'non-Jewish Jews',[2] and sometimes even 'Zionists'.[3]

The bigoted notion that all Jews are Zionists has its pendant in the bigoted notion that all Arabs are anti-Semites. There are, of course, anti-Semitic Arabs, and there are more anti-Semites among the Arabs today than among any other population group – for obvious historical reasons. But does this amount to a 'new anti-Semitism' that has taken up the torch of Christian European anti-Semitism in general, and Nazi-German anti-Semitism in particular, as a plethora of authors has maintained ever since Yehoshafat Harkabi cast that thesis in systematic form and Bernard Lewis popularized it? Carrying the analogy to an absurd extreme, some authors even argue that there is a historical Arab *Sonderweg*, the successor to the German original, which makes Arabs, if not all Muslims, potentially 'willing executioners'.

That notion, which is an even greater slander of Arabs than of Germans, has achieved a certain currency in recent years, despite both Harkabi's and Lewis's insistence that the 'new anti-Semitism' is not a continuation of the anti-Jewish tradition specific to Islam (a much milder form than the tradition specific to Christianity) but rather an anti-Semitism imported from Europe and fuelled by the Palestinian conflict. Inexorably, the logic of polemic gained the upper hand. Thus was born what Mark Cohen has dubbed 'the neo-lachrymose conception of Jewish-Arab history', the emergence of which – especially after 1967 – Cohen has analysed as a myth designed to counter the myth of an 'interfaith utopia'[4] (which might be termed the 'Andalusian myth') utilized by Arab propaganda in the ideological war against Israel.

But apart from the defamatory notion of an anti-Jewish atavism that has spawned the Arabs' 'new anti-Semitism', the most important question facing us here concerns the real weight of anti-Semitism in today's Arab world. And this question brings another in its wake, which involves the very definition of anti-Semitism: how much aversion is imputable to anti-Semitism in the strict sense? Is the fantasy-based hatred of the Jews that was and still is typical of European racists, whether of the far right or the ostensible left (anti-Semitism, in the phrase commonly attributed to August Bebel, is 'the socialism of fools'), to say nothing of the genocidal Judeophobia of Nazism, the equivalent of the hatred felt by Arabs enraged by the occupation and/ or destruction of Arab lands; the expulsion/dispossession or subjugation of the populations living on them; and the war crimes committed by the armed forces of a state that declares itself a *Judenstaat*?

Does the obsessive nitpicking of Western Holocaust deniers, who spend endless hours assembling 'demonstrations' that the Holocaust never happened or was far smaller in scale than is generally claimed, that the gas chambers were used only to exterminate lice, and other inanities of the same stripe, all motivated by a pathological hatred of Jews – does this obsession have its counterpart in the reaction of the ignorant or semi-educated Arab who, seeing Israel's exploitation of the memory of the Holocaust, comes to the conclusion that it is a propaganda tool, exaggerated if not invented, and therefore swallows the 'proofs' of Western Holocaust deniers? And what shall we say about those Arabs who deny the Holocaust out of rage or as an act of bravado, as if to discharge the tensions bred by a 'Jewish state' that, in its overpowering supremacy, crushes them from on high – perfectly well aware, as they are, that Holocaust denial is painful precisely because the Holocaust was all too real?

Are all forms of Holocaust denial the same? Should such denial, when it comes from oppressors, not be distinguished from denial in the mouths of the oppressed, as the racism of ruling whites is distinguished from that of subjugated blacks? Why can some arrogate the right to cast accusations of anti-Semitism right and left while criticizing others for calling Israel or Zionism racist? Are accusations of anti-Semitism less serious than accusations of racism, or even of Nazism, so that they can be fired off without a second thought? Is it a less serious offence to define anti-Zionism as anti-Semitism than to define Zionism as racism?

Even Bernard Lewis warns, in his 1986 book *Semites and Anti-Semites*, against abusive generalizations. In his last chapter – 'The New Anti-Semitism' – he credits Harkabi's idea that the Arab–Israeli conflict has fostered an Arab version of European anti-Semitism that in turn reinforces Arab opposition to Israel. Yet Lewis, writing in 1986, after the signing of the Egyptian–Israeli peace treaty, takes pains not to implicate all Arabs or Arab governments in this 'new anti-Semitism', but only those who maintain their opposition to Israel. In the chapter he further multiplies fine distinctions and reservations, not merely out of a desire to appear objective and moderate but also because his cultivation and sophistication make it impossible for him to indulge in the excesses of anti-Arab propaganda. (Furthermore, he does not want to contradict affirmations made before his pro-Israel stance was radicalized.) In the introduction, Lewis clearly states that 'It is unreasonable and unfair to assume that opposition to Zionism or criticism of Israeli policies and actions is, as such and in the absence of other evidence, an expression of anti-Semitic prejudice. The Arab–Israeli conflict is a political one – a clash between states and peoples over real issues, not a matter of prejudice and persecution.'[5] He adds this perfectly reasonable twofold warning:

> It would be palpably unjust, even absurd, to assert that all critics or opponents of Zionism or Israel are moved by anti-Semitism; it would be equally mistaken to deny that anti-Zionism can on occasion provide a cloak of respectability for a prejudice which, at the present time and in the free world, is not normally admitted in public by anyone with political ambitions or cultural pretensions.[6]

Lewis also introduces the necessary distinction between Arab comparisons of Israeli actions to those of the Nazis – which he even finds somewhat reassuring (he acknowledges the vast difference between, on the one hand, expressing admiration for Hitler and, on the other, likening Menachem Begin to Hitler as the incarnation of evil) – and the same analogies coming from Europeans who have had first-hand experience of Nazism.[7] He goes so far as to contradict standard Israeli propaganda:

Even the frequently reiterated Arab intention of dismantling the state of Israel and 'liquidating the Zionist society' is not, in itself, necessarily an expression of anti-Semitism. In the view of most Arabs, the creation of the state of Israel was an act of injustice, and its continued existence a standing aggression. To those who hold this view, the correction of that injustice and the removal of that aggression are legitimate political objectives.[8]

Other authors who are above all suspicion of anti-Semitism express similar ideas, but with the aim of rejecting the notion of a 'new anti-Semitism'. One of the rare books offering contrasting views on the subject (among the avalanche of books that echo, in unison, the stock themes of Israeli propaganda) is a collection edited by Michael Curtis and published the same year as Lewis's; it contains an essay by Michael Marrus in which the renowned Canadian historian concludes, indirectly refuting Lewis:

> The antisemitism that persists in Western societies is not new, and it continues to feed from traditional roots. It is largely on the decline, so far as we can tell. The anti-Israel sentiment that has arisen in recent years does possess a sense of novelty, and it is, indeed, linked to some factors utterly extraneous to the conflict in the Middle East. It is conditioned by the structure of the electronic and print media, as well as by the particular rhetoric of some Jewish leaders. It is sometimes unfair, exaggerated, and defamatory. But it is neither generally antisemitic nor illuminated by that term.[9]

Marrus adds cogently: 'Every era operates in the shadow of its historical past, and it is inevitable that the great reference points of our own time – particularly Hitler and the Nazi genocide against Jews – will be used and misused to describe what people think and feel about momentous political upheavals.'[10] He cites several examples of such comparisons that have appeared in Israel itself, not only against Arab enemies but also against Jewish political opponents.

Similar refutations of the 'new anti-Semitism' theory have been put forward by a number of Jewish authors, including Brian Klug:

> To argue that hostility to Israel and hostility to Jews are one and the same thing is to conflate the Jewish state with the Jewish people ...
>
>   Mainstream Zionism set out ... to put Israel, a political entity in the here and now, at the center of Jewish identity. This was a radical departure from the 'old' Jewish idea of a Jew. The concept of 'new anti-Semitism', to the extent that it is based on mainstream Zionist ideology, is just the

other side of the coin, the obverse of this new idea of a Jew, the national Jew.[11]

Despite all such warnings, there has been an exponentially increasing identification of anti-Zionism with anti-Semitism since the Israeli invasion of Lebanon in 1982, as part of the ideological counter-offensive to the deteriorating reputation of the Zionist state. Naturally, this counter-offensive was first launched from Israel itself, by Israeli academics, among others.

A typical example, among countless others, comes from *Anti-Zionism and Antisemitism in the Contemporary World*, a book published in 1990 under the editorship of Robert Wistrich, a historian at the Hebrew University of Jerusalem, the director of the Vidal Sassoon International Center for the Study of Antisemitism, and one of the leaders in the attacks on Arab and Muslim anti-Semitism.[12] In an essay called 'Antisemitism and Anti-Zionism – New and Old', Yehuda Bauer, an eminent historian at the same university, co-founder of the same centre, and himself a staunch believer in the 'new anti-Semitism' theory, peremptorily asserts that, apart from those who reject all forms of nationalism of whatever kind, 'anti-Zionists are, whether they realise it or not, antisemites' – which will come as news indeed to the many Jews who define themselves as anti-Zionists. 'Anti-Zionism', he adds, 'is a destabilising, basically anti-democratic trend. It poses a danger to Jews and to Israel. But it is also a threat to democracy, liberalism and to all the values that make life worth living.'[13]

Extravagant? Yet this is precisely the definition of the 'new anti-Semitism' that Israel's most intransigent defenders put forward. It even obtained semi-official status when it was incorporated into the 'Working Definition of Anti-Semitism' elaborated in 2005 by the European Monitoring Center on Racism and Xenophobia (EUMC, now FRA, the European Union Agency for Fundamental Rights) in collaboration with both Jewish institutions and the Office for Democratic Institutions and Human Rights (ODIHR) of the Organization for Security and Co-operation in Europe (OSCE).

Deviating considerably from the standard definition, or even the extended one that includes Holocaust denial, the text of the 'working definition' offers examples of anti-Semitism 'with regard to the State of Israel': not only 'drawing comparisons of contemporary Israeli policy to that of the Nazis' but also 'denying the Jewish people their right to self-determination, e.g., by claiming that the existence of a State of Israel is a racist endeavor'.[14]

Let us deconstruct that last phrase. First, it postulates the existence of a 'Jewish people' in the sense of a nation made up of all the world's Jews (the

equivalent of 'the Christian nation' or the Pan-Islamists' *umma islamiyya* –
neither one a concept above criticism). Second, it grants this international
group a right to self-determination and the creation of a state – a right no
other international religious community can claim. Third, it assumes that
this right to self-determination rules out criticism of the form that the state
thus created takes. Fourth, it confuses criticism of the actually existing state
of Israel with denial of the right, making it a corollary that the state created
manu militari by the Zionist movement in Palestine is the only possible state
for the 'Jewish people'.

That is an impressive number of misconceptions for a single phrase.
That it emanates from official European institutions shows just how far
the European guilty conscience (well-earned as it is) is still invested in the
German philosemitism of the post-war period – 'an integral component
of the ideological legitimacy of the Federal Republic,'[15] in former Ben-
Gurion University Professor Frank Stern's magisterial analysis. Stern's *The
Whitewashing of the Yellow Badge* is essential for a comprehension of both
contemporary German culture and the European Union's political culture,
given Germany's central place in it. The book quotes the theologian Martin
Stöhr's definition of the 'philosemitic syndrome': 'an emotional, enthusiastic
liking of Jews or for the State of Israel, an affection indifferent to any form
of critical perspective and all exact information.'[16] Contrary to the fantasies
of those obsessed with Jewish or Israeli power, it has its origins neither in
emotional blackmail nor in intellectual terrorism carried out in the name
of the Holocaust. German post-war philosemitism is, rather, a product of
what Stern calls 'political instrumentalization of German attitudes towards
Jews and Israel'[17] – part of the price paid for the integration of the Federal
Republic into the Cold-War West. There is a perfect illustration, as well as a
good demonstration of the way philosemitism borrows from anti-Semitism
simply by standing anti-Semitic attitudes on their head* in 1966 remarks of
Konrad Adenauer's, cited by Stern, in which the retired German chancellor
justified material and political support for Israel:

> We had done to the Jews ... so much injustice, we had committed so many
> crimes against them, that somehow these had to be expiated, there had

---

* As Eleonore Sterling spiritedly wrote: 'Anti-Semitism and the more recent idolization
of the Jews have a good deal in common. Both are symptomatic of a sort of
hypothermia of complex human relationships and derive from a mental incapacity
truly to respect the "other." Jews remain foreigners for anti-Semites and philosemites
alike.'[18]

to be recompense if we wished once more to gain respect and standing among the world's nations. Moreover, the power held by the Jews, even today, especially in America, should not be underestimated.[19]

In one of the most remarkable passages in his book, Stern describes the philosemitic stereotypes operating in various registers.[20] His last chapter traces the development of German anti-Semitism and philosemitism down to the late twentieth century. He observes a decline in the latter from the late 1960s on, followed by a resurgence of public expressions of anti-Semitism, which he does not, however, conflate with criticism of Israel.[21] At the same time, Stern points to a peculiar evolution of German philosemitism:

> The function of domestic philosemitism in foreign policy became less and less important, although philosemitic stereotypes were accompanied and strengthened by a totally exaggerated public image of Israel after 1967. In the West German media, Israeli military prowess was glorified and Israelis now came to be seen as the 'Prussians of the Orient.' An Israeli military victory was celebrated by segments of the West German press as an indication of the success of the *Blitzkrieg*.[22]

Near the end of his book, Stern emphasizes that 'whenever the moral legitimation of the Federal Republic was under stress', as it was during the German unification process, 'philosemitic declarations or actions were utilized as a form of response'.[23] These two aspects of Germany's relationship with Israel – moral legitimization for itself and military complicity with its partner – were at the heart of a speech that the German chancellor, Angela Merkel, delivered before the Knesset on 18 March 2008,[24] in which she congratulated a bellicose state that occupies its neighbours' territory for sixty years of 'fighting for peace and security' and commended a country formed on the basis of the exclusion of its native Palestinians for sixty years of 'integrating immigrants into [its] body politic'.

The chancellor also emphatically reiterated, with reference to the Holocaust, the legitimizing instrumentalization of philosemitism. She explained, in this connection, that the 'unique relationship' between Germany and Israel 'has its origins in the values that we, Germany and Israel, both share, the values of freedom, democracy and respect for human dignity'. The chancellor articulated then a rather peculiar conception of democracy:

> Or how do we react when surveys show that a clear majority of European respondents say that Israel is a bigger threat to the world than Iran? Do

we politicians in Europe fearfully bow to public opinion and flinch from imposing further stricter sanctions on Iran to persuade it to halt its nuclear programme? No, however unpopular we may make ourselves, that is precisely what we cannot afford to do.

Far from acting as a brake on Germany, the weight of the Holocaust has cleared a path for its military collaboration with Israel.* An editorial that appeared in the *Jerusalem Post* on 24 August 2006 – that is, ten days after Israel called a halt to its aggression against Lebanon – hailed this extensive military assistance. It bore the title 'Germany's Transformation', and represents a high point in the exploitation of the Holocaust:

> The stance of the German government underlines a radical transforma-
> tion for that country's people. While their grandparents' generation
> perpetrated the Holocaust, and the previous generation paid for the
> Holocaust with reparations to its victims, the current generation is helping
> prevent a second Holocaust by providing the IDF with some of the most
> important defensive weapons systems in its arsenal. As far as corrective
> steps go, that's a huge one.[26]

The German state's relationship to Zionism has indeed undergone a 'transformation' – two, in fact. From 1933 to the present, it has moved from complicity to hostility both in the context of anti-Semitism, and then back to complicity, based, this time, on philosemitism. Increasingly, this philosemitism is paired, in Germany as well as the rest of Europe, with Islamophobia, the true European racism of our day. Anti-Semitism, to be sure, has not disappeared; but, among Europeans, with the exception of recent immigrants, it is confined to the margins.

The anti-immigrant racism promoted since the 1970s by European far-right movements (which in most cases are anti-Semitic as well) – to which

---

*   A report that the US Congressional Research Service published in 2007 nicely
      summarizes this complicity and the legitimization of it in the name of the Holocaust:
      'German arms played a considerable role in Israeli military victories in 1967, 1973 and
      1982 ... In 1999 and 2000, in perhaps the most high-profile German arms shipments
      to Israel since German unification, Germany financed 50% of the costs for three
      "Dolphin-class" submarines designed specifically for the Israeli navy. In August
      2006, the German government committed to deliver and finance one-third of the
      costs, approximately 1 billion Euros ($1.3 billion), for two more submarines by 2010.
      Those opposed to the most recent agreement, primarily members of the Green and
      Left political parties, cite widespread concern that Israel plans to reconfigure the
      submarines to enable them to launch nuclear missiles. Proponents repeatedly invoke
      a German obligation to defend the existence of the state of Israel.'[25]

European governments, conservative and social-democratic alike, have increasingly pandered against the backdrop of the fracturing of economies and the rise in unemployment – has, as Bernard Lewis observed more than two decades ago, gone hand in hand with a 'surge of anti-Islamic and anti-Arab feeling' in the wake of the oil crisis and the Iranian revolution. Although Lewis downplayed its import, he recognized that it 'sometimes reaches a level of nastiness which, while still permitted when discussing Arabs, is no longer acceptable when dealing with Jews. There is no Holocaust to inhibit the expression of anti-Arab prejudice; there is no anti-Zionism to provide for its sublimation.'[27]

Since Lewis wrote these lines, of course, there has been a huge increase in Islamophobia, notably after the 11 September 2001 attacks. While it is true that anti-Zionism can serve to 'sublimate' traditional anti-Semitism – although mainly in marginal cases, inasmuch as European anti-Semitism is seldom accompanied by support for the Arabs (the number of Western anti-Semites who are pro-Israeli and anti-Arab certainly outweighs the number of those who are pro-Arab) – Islamophobia has found a means of large-scale 'sublimation' in hostility to what came to be called 'Islamism' or even 'Islamo-Fascism'. The Western mass media serve up harangues on these subjects that, if the word 'Islam' were replaced by 'Judaism', would provoke an uproar and, in Europe, lead to legal prosecution.[28]

As for the 'new anti-Semitism' (some prefer to call it 'new Judeophobia') deemed to be rampant among Muslim immigrants, it remains a minority phenomenon distinct from traditional European anti-Semitism – the result of a transfer to Europe of the widespread anger in the Arab and Muslim worlds over the Arab–Israeli conflict, as indicated by the statistical correlation between the recrudescence of anti-Semitic acts and statements and Israeli offensives. Anti-Semitic tendencies among Muslim immigrants also constitute an idiotic reaction to the post-11 September 2001 wave of Islamophobia. These Judeophobic immigrants are either unaware or wilfully ignorant of the fact that Jews are often in the first ranks of the battle against Islamophobia and among the most unsparing of Israel's critics – which makes them, in their turn, targets of zealous philosemites.[29]

Israel's allies, however, include not only philosemites but also a great many anti-Semites. Adenauer's government was chock-full of former Nazis, including former members of the SS and the Gestapo, and even war criminals. The name of Adenauer's national security adviser, Hans Globke, popped up at the Eichmann trial;* even more outrageous was the sinister Theodor Oberländer, a minister responsible (all too ironically) for displaced persons, refugees and those injured in the war.[30] Members of the Israeli government knew the situation very well and readily accepted it.

This is not at all surprising. Were not Stalin and Truman the godfathers of the Israeli state? Truman, we now know, shared the typical anti-Semitic sentiments of his day. In his 21 July 1947 diary entry, he wrote: 'The Jews, I find are very, very selfish. They care not how many Estonians, Latvians, Finns, Poles, Yugoslavs or Greeks get murdered or mistreated as D[isplaced] P[ersons] as long as the Jews get special treatment. Yet when they have power, physical, financial or political neither Hitler nor Stalin has anything on them for cruelty or mistreatment to the underdog.'[31]

But then some of Israel's – and the United States' – best friends in the Arab world are rabid anti-Semites. The United States' longest-standing Arab ally, the Saudi kingdom, was from the beginning the most anti-Semitic of all the Muslim states. King Faisal, who reigned from 1964 to 1975, espoused the anti-Jewish ravings of the Wahhabis and their supporter Rashid Rida: he was probably the contemporary world's only chief of state to perpetuate the medieval blood libel when, in 1972, he accused the Jews of eating bread mixed with the blood of children.[32]

The Wahhabi monarchy was a relentless enemy of Nasser's, and even fought a proxy war against him in Yemen from 1962 to 1967. It supported the Muslim Brothers' fierce opposition to the Nasser regime in every possible way; both the monarchy and the Brotherhood considered Nasser, not Israel, their foremost enemy.[33] The most extremist of the Brothers, Sayyid Qutb – the main source of inspiration for the ideological tendency that spawned contemporary Jihadism and Al-Qaeda – certainly did. His pamphlet attacking the Jews is often mentioned. Much less well known are facts that Emmanuel Sivan has cited:

> Sayyid Qutb himself paid only scant attention to Israel, although when he did so he made ample use of his vast knowledge of the Koran to conjure up the image of an essentially depraved Judaism, an age-old enemy of Islam. All his writings on Judaism and Israel amount, however, to but one small booklet (*Our Struggle with the Jews*), assembled and published in 1970 (five years after his execution) in Jedda, Saudi Arabia.[34]

But, it will be objected, whatever Saudis' ties to the United States, they have yet to become friends of Israel, officially at any rate. True enough. It

---

*   See Chapter 5, 'The Eichmann Trial, Reparations, Comparisons and Revisionism'.

should be pointed out, however, that the Arab leader who did become one of Israel's best friends, after jettisoning the Nasserite heritage and sidling up to Washington, also happened to be a notorious Jew hater. On 25 April 1972, three months after expelling all Soviet military advisers from Egypt, Anwar al-Sadat delivered a ringing speech during the festival of Mawlid in which he attacked both Israel and the Jews in these terms:

> Today they talk about direct negotiations, although they were neighbors of Muhammad, prayer and peace be upon him, neighbors of his in Medina, and he negotiated and concluded a treaty with them. In the end, however, they proved that they are a petty-minded people, deceitful and treacherous, when they allied themselves with his enemies in order to strike him a blow in Medina, a blow from within. Thus the most marvelous thing that our prophet Muhammad did, prayer and peace be upon him, was to expel them from every part of the Arabian Peninsula.[35]

As for Mahmoud Abbas, alias Abu Mazen, the best Palestinian friend of Israel and the United States, the man whom they strove to play off against Yasser Arafat: before his rise to power he was known in Israeli propaganda literature above all for remarks denying the Holocaust in the doctoral dissertation he defended in Moscow and published in Amman in 1984.[36] The year before it was released, he wrote a preface for a pamphlet on the gas chambers by the French Holocaust denier Robert Faurisson.[37]

Is it an accident that Israel's rulers chose to sign treaties with Sadat rather than Nasser, and preferred Abbas over Arafat? Or is it a sign of elective affinities between Jew-haters and Arab-haters, whose vision of the world is the same, only stood on its head?

Of Zionism, the State of Israel, Racism, the End of Denial and Peace

In the aforementioned collection of essays on anti-Semitism under the editorship of Michael Curtis, the most surprising entry is the one by the neo-conservative American sociologist Nathan Glazer. It is distinguished by a remarkable effort to understand the real motives for criticisms of Israel while eschewing 'the easy explanation that Jews are permanently threatened by the world simply because they *are* Jews, and that anti-Zionism is [anti-Semitism's] current form'.[38]

Although Glazer rejects the accusation of racism levelled at Zionism, which he regards as 'a liberal and progressive nationalist movement',[39] he acknowledges the problem posed by the Law of Return, under which any Jew recognized as such on the basis of essentially religious criteria is automatically accorded the right to Israeli citizenship. This paradox of secular Zionism, in Glazer's estimation, explains the charge of racism, even if it does not justify it:

> There is no usable definition of the Jews aside from the religious one that defines a Jew by birth, and by conversion. The only alternative available is the truly racial definition of the Nazis ... The religious definition that prevails in Israel and is used to police those who want to enter the State and join the people creates enormous difficulties for Israelis themselves, and for many Jews wanting to settle in Israel. It is hardly surprising that it would not be easy to explain, and that Israel's enemies would seize upon it. To believe that they would really 'know' that Zionism is not racism, and Jews are not racist, would be to give them too much credit in understanding the complexities of Jewish history, Judaism, Zionism and Israel.[40]*

Glazer goes still further: he admits, in a way, the exclusive nature of Israeli society:

> In Israel we have a society in which integration is not the ideal, in which a people who once permanently lived as an endangered minority now wish to become a majority – more than a majority, they hope for a state only for Jews, free of non-Jews. *That* is the idea ... How could a community trying to create itself in the midst of another people as a majority have escaped the charge of racism? ...
>   Liberal and progressive and democratic intentions were undermined by reality. Since there was war, it was imprudent to allow Arabs to serve in the army. It was imprudent to allow them sensitive positions in administration. The way they taught their children had to be checked – one would not want them to be taught hatred of Jews. Areas of exclusive Arab settlement had to be policed, controlled, administered. How could one avoid the charge of racism? And the strain of long decades of intense preparation for war, repeated wars, inevitably produced its racist sentiments, incidents, attitudes.[42]

With a remarkable candour that contrasts strikingly with the stereotyped language of the propagandists (a candour more often encountered in texts by

---

* Compare this argument with Bernard Lewis's attempt to refute the UN resolution defining Zionism as 'a form of racism and racial discrimination' by advancing, with regard to the definition of a Jew as someone born of a Jewish mother, the far-fetched contention that 'for the racist, fathers are at least as relevant as mothers'.[41]

ultra-conservative than by ostensibly progressive writers), Glazer characterizes Israel as 'in fact a state created by Europeans, in a country inhabited by non-Europeans, and one in which the European element holds the upper hand'.[43] This provenance, he concludes, explains the elective affinities between the United States and Israel, two states 'forced to use power in what they conceive of as the national interest and the interest of the democratic world'.[44] In the space of a few pages, Glazer, an unabashed partisan of Zionism and Israel, exhibits greater understanding of the Arab critiques of Zionism and Israel as a racist ideology, state and society than any number of commentators who claim to stand above the fray.

How, indeed, is it possible to deny the obvious realities that Glazer acknowledges? How is it possible to deny the racist nature of Israeli society, at both the ideological and institutional levels, when Israeli governments have welcomed such openly racist ministers as Rehavam Ze'evi or Avigdor Lieberman, men who have advocated 'transferring' Arab-Israeli citizens in order to achieve the goal of an *araberrein* Israel? How is it possible to deny what the Israeli writer David Grossman deplored in a 4 November 2006 speech in Tel Aviv before a crowd of 100,000 gathered to commemorate the eleventh anniversary of the assassination of Yitzhak Rabin: 'This indifference to the fate of the hungry, the elderly, the sick and the disabled, all those who are weak, this equanimity of the State of Israel in the face of human trafficking or the appalling employment conditions of our foreign workers, which border on slavery, to the deeply ingrained institutionalized racism against the Arab minority'?[45]*

In 2005 Daniel Bar-Tal and Yona Teichman of the University of Tel Aviv published the results of a study of the images of Arabs prevailing in Jewish Israeli society. In spite of their care to euphemize the reality, they show in particular that the discourse of Israel's media and its political leaders harmonizes with this institutionalized racism:

> Israeli public discourse is characterized by a continuous negative stereotyping of Arabs in general and of Palestinians in particular, with use of delegitimizing labels ... The Arab citizens of the state of Israel are constantly disregarded. The media ignore this sector by not reporting its concerns, problems, discrimination, or achievements; there is a significant lack of positive reports about this minority. Instead, the media focus on

---

* Grossman was speaking only of Palestinians who hold Israeli citizenship, although almost three times as many Palestinians have been living under Israeli occupation for more than forty years in incomparably more oppressive conditions.[46]

their threat to the Jewish society, reporting mainly on events related to crime, protests, and anti-Israeli activities.[47]

A new study undertaken by Bar-Tal and Rafi Nets-Zehngut, based on a survey carried out in summer 2008 – the study is titled *The Israeli-Jewish Collective Memory of the Israeli–Arab/Palestinian Conflict* – corroborates these conclusions.[48] Akiva Eldar summarized its findings in *Haaretz*:

> Israeli Jews' consciousness is characterized by a sense of victimization, a siege mentality, blind patriotism, belligerence, self-righteousness, dehumanization of the Palestinians and insensitivity to their suffering ... Bar-Tal emphasizes that the Israeli awareness of reality was also forged in the context of Palestinian violence against Israeli citizens, but relies primarily on prolonged indoctrination that is based on ignorance and even nurtures it.[49]

According to an extensive opinion poll on relations between Jews and Arabs in Israel that was carried out in 2004 under the direction of Sami Smooha of the University of Haifa, more than 63 per cent of the Arabs feared that they would be expelled from Israel; more than 70 per cent feared violence, whether 'state violence' or 'Jewish violence'; and more than 80 per cent feared that their rights would be seriously restricted. On the other hand, more than 66 per cent of the Jews were alarmed by the Arab birth rate, and more than 71 per cent feared that the Arabs would engage in struggle or stage a rebellion.[50]

According to the same poll, nearly 85 per cent of the Arabs recognized Israel's right to exist within its 1948 borders (the Green Line) as an independent state with a Jewish and Arab population; 70 per cent were even prepared to concede Israel's right to exist as a democratic Jewish state. The overwhelming majority, however, denied its right to exist as a Zionist state, since 72 per cent considered the *Zionist* state to be racist. Only 24 per cent accepted the principle that the Israeli state had to continue to ensure the existence of a Jewish majority – as opposed to more than 96 per cent of the Jews; indeed, nearly 68 per cent of the Jews declared that, if forced to choose between Israel's democratic character and its Jewishness, they would opt for the latter. More than 80 per cent of the Jews thought that all decisions about the nature of the state and its borders should be made by a majority of the Jews, not by a majority of Israel's citizens; fewer than 66 per cent approved of the right of Arab citizens to vote in Knesset elections, and fewer than 49 per cent accepted the idea that there might one day be Arab ministers.[51]

These sad facts make it easier to recognize the courage that Avraham

Burg – the former president of the Jewish Agency and of the World Zionist Movement, vice-president of the World Jewish Congress, and president of the Knesset – showed in *The Holocaust is Over: We Must Rise from its Ashes*, his remarkably self-critical reflection on Israel and Zionism written from a humanist, anti-war perspective:

> Every state in the world determines its identity and how residents and immigrants are naturalized. In Israel the direct path to becoming a citizen, at least for the Jews, is the Law of Return ... A modern definition of citizenship, according to a genetic or religious code, is by itself an enormous ethical problem, especially for Jews.
>
> The problematic definition of a Jew according to the Law of Return – 'A Jew is a person who is born to a Jewish mother or who converted and is not of a different religion' – should be abolished, along with the old-fashioned concept of the nation-state. Israel should become the democratic state of the Jewish people which belongs to all of its citizens, and the majority will decide on its character and essence.[52]

The book, in large measure a cry of alarm at the 'creeping racism' in Israeli society, also contains these terrified and terrifying lines:

> True, we are not like Germany at the war's end and at the height of the Final Solution. But we are somewhere very close to the first stages of humanistic and cultural Germany's implosion in the face of Hitler and his henchmen, whose National Socialism shredded everything good and beautiful in what had been Germany. To my great sorrow and pain, I cannot always distinguish between the early Social Nationalism and some national theories of here and now.[53]

Burg saves the honour of one strain of Zionism. For the problem with the equation 'Zionism = racism' is its totalizing nature. There is Zionism and 'Zionism', as Martin Buber once wrote;[54] we can hardly treat all Zionists, from Avnery (Uri) to Ze'evi (to mention only contemporaries while leaving 'post-Zionists' aside), as birds of the same racist feather. While statist secular Zionism may indeed be based on the paradox of a state founded on a genetic or religious definition of citizenship, it is nevertheless indisputable that Eastern European Zionism emerged in reaction to an unbearable form of racist oppression that, ultimately, defined the Jews as a race and culminated in the Nazi genocide.

Statist Zionism thus has a twofold nature. On the one hand, it is a form of racism born of a defensive reaction that spawned the idea that Jews were incapable of living among Aryans (the anti-Semitic version) or *goyim* (the

Zionist version). As such, it is as morally excusable as the reactive racism of blacks to white racism. On the other hand, statist Zionism, once it created a *Judenstaat* in Palestine as 'a portion of the rampart of Europe against Asia, an outpost of civilisation as opposed to barbarism' – in the words of its founder, Theodor Herzl[55] – became, ipso facto, a fundamentally racist colonial movement comparable to the European forms of colonialism with which it had identified. As Maxime Rodinson wrote in 1973, 'Wanting to create a purely Jewish, or predominantly Jewish, state in an Arab Palestine in the twentieth century could not help but lead to a colonial-type situation and to the development (completely normal sociologically speaking) of a racist state of mind, and in the final analysis to a military confrontation between the two ethnic groups.'[56]

This racist state of mind may have reached a nadir when Israel, not content to crush the Palestinian people physically under a hail of bombs, and symbolically under the weight of an instrumentalized Holocaust, attempted to keep it from invoking the drama of which it had been a victim and even to prevent the very use of the term 'Nakba'. There was an official Israeli protest when UN General Secretary Ban Ki-Moon used the term in a telephone conversation with the president of the Palestinian Authority, Mahmoud Abbas, on 15 May 2008, the sixtieth anniversary of the Nakba.[57] That same day, the Israeli Foreign Minister, Tzipi Livni, declared in a solemn address: 'The Palestinians can celebrate an Independence Day if, on that day, they eliminate the word Nakba from their vocabulary.'[58]

Statist Zionism is a Janus, one face turned toward the Holocaust, the other towards the Nakba, one towards persecution endured, the other towards oppression inflicted. The obstinate insistence with which both sides fix their gaze on only one face is the source of their inability to communicate. To put the matter in the Cartesian terms with which I opened this final chapter, 'the diversity of our opinions' arises because we 'do not fix our attention on the same objects'. Yet only recognition of both of Janus's faces – of the Holocaust *and* the Nakba – can bring Israelis, Palestinians and other Arabs into a genuine dialogue.

The sole reason for guarded optimism in the increasingly tragic context of the Arab–Israeli conflict is slow but sure progress that has been made towards this mutual recognition, even if the voices pleading for it are currently being drowned out by the noise of bombs, cries and imprecations. On the Israeli side, they have already moved past the small circle of the anti-Zionists of the far left to the heart of post-Zionism and beyond. If an Avraham Burg, with his irreproachable Zionist credentials, can air admirably critical introspection, then there is a glimmer of hope. Burg turns his back on egotistical ethnocentrism: he sees the beam in the eye of his country before the mote in that of his neighbours:*

> We have taken the Shoah from its position of sanctity and turned it into an instrument of common and even trite politics. We turned the Shoah into a tool at the service of the Jewish people. A weapon, indeed; mightier than the Israeli Defense Force itself. The Shoah has become our exclusive property.[60]

> We are on the side of the Turks in their denial of the Armenian Holocaust, and we are beside the U.S. right-wingers, not knowing anything about America's original nations. We supplied arms to those who perpetuated the massacres in Rwanda and our denial reaches inside the Balkans ... In this manner Israel isolated itself from profound world processes and became a denier of other peoples' holocausts. [61]

These admirable words might almost be an echo of the essay of Edward Said's that I quoted at the outset – but an inverted echo, as is appropriate to two thinkers motivated by the same humanism yet situated on opposite sides of the wall of hatred: not the 'my tragedy is greater than yours' of the ethnocentric in both camps, but rather an ability to recognize the tragedy of others. Burg, a Jew and an Israeli, recognizes the tragedies that befell other peoples, including the Palestinians. Said, a Palestinian and an Arab, recognizes the exceptional scope of the Jewish tragedy:

> All in all though, the sheer enormity of what took place between 1933 and 1945 beggars our powers of description and understanding. The more one studies this period and its excesses the more one must conclude that for any decent human being the slaughter of so many millions of innocents

---

* Burg's book fully meets the 'real test facing Israeli and diaspora Jews' as formulated by Israel Shahak, 'the test of their self-criticism which must include the critique of the Jewish past': 'The most important part of such critique must be detailed and honest confrontation of the Jewish attitude to non-Jews. This is what many Jews justly demand from non-Jews: to confront their own past and so become aware of the discrimination and persecutions inflicted on the Jews. In the last 40 years the number of non-Jews killed by Jews is by far greater than the number of the Jews killed by non-Jews. The extent of the persecution and discrimination against non-Jews inflicted by the "Jewish state" with the support of organised diaspora Jews is also enormously greater than the suffering inflicted on Jews by regimes hostile to them. Although the struggle against anti-Semitism (and all other forms of racism) should never cease, the struggle against Jewish chauvinism and exclusivism, which must include a critique of classical Judaism, is now of equal or greater importance.'[59]

must, and indeed should weigh heavily on subsequent generations, Jewish and non-Jewish. However much we may concur, say, with Tom Segev in his book *The Seventh Million*, that Israel exploited the Holocaust for political purposes, there can be little doubt that the tragedy's collective memory and the burden of fear it places on all Jews today is not to be minimized. Yes, there were other collective massacres in human history (native Americans, Armenians, Bosnians, Kurds, etc.) And yes, some were neither sufficiently acknowledged by the perpetrators nor adequately compensated. But there is no reason at all, in my opinion, not to submit oneself in horror and awe to the special tragedy besetting the Jewish people. As an Arab in particular I find it important to comprehend this collective experience in as much of its terrible concrete detail as one is capable: this act of comprehension guarantees one's humanity and resolve that such a catastrophe should never be forgotten and never again recur. [62]

I attach no conditions to such comprehension and compassion: one feels them for their own sake, not for political advantage. Yet such an advance in consciousness by Arabs ought to be met by an equal willingness for compassion and comprehension on the part of Israelis and Israel's supporters who have engaged in all sorts of denial and expressions of defensive non-responsibility when it comes to Israel's central role on our historical dispossession as a people ... We must think our histories together, however difficult that may be, in order for there to be a common future. And that future must include Arabs and Jews together, free of any exclusionary, denial-based schemes for shutting out one side by the other, either theoretically or politically. That is the real challenge. The rest is much easier.[63]

Even if Burg has not yet fully recognized the extent to which Zionism was responsible for the Nakba, as the post-Zionists have, he has gone a long way in that direction. It is as if he were engaged in continuing dialogue with Said. His way of explaining the problem is, at the human level, convincing:

We must stand on the tallest mountain and declare clearly and loudly: we know that solving the Shoah refugee problem directly and indirectly caused the Palestinian refugee problem. Only then can we give our excuses and explanations ...

We have to admit that, post-Shoah, we valued our lives because we wanted to live after so much death. We were not sufficiently sensitive to the lives of others and to the price they paid for our salvation. Please forgive us, and together we will put an end to the unhealthy refugee mindset that torments us all. [64]

These words echo the notion of the 'original stain' of the Zionist response to
the Holocaust that the Lebanese journalist Joseph Samaha advanced more
than fifteen years ago:

> Fulfilling the national rights of the Palestinian people is the humane his-
> torical response to 'the Holocaust', for it is based on cleansing the other
> responses, the Jewish response included, of the original stain besmirch-
> ing them as a result of the fact that the Palestinian people was dispersed
> so that the Jews might be granted a 'refuge' that fulfills the role of the
> region's policeman for the benefit of foreign powers.[65]

What an enormous difference between the tone of such unilateral
acknowledgements and that of Meir Litvak and Esther Webman, for
example. After constructing their book around the faulty idea of a single 'Arab
Holocaust discourse', they discover, in their final chapter, that this discourse,
which, in fact, never existed anywhere, has become 'less monolithic and more
complex than it used to be'[66] and that its 'unanimity' (sic) 'has been broken'[67]
– only to dismiss this 'new approach' on the grounds that it is 'charged, in
different degrees, with sophisticated motifs of Holocaust denial discourse
as well as elements of relativization and political instrumentalization'. Thus,
they assert:

> The recognition of the Holocaust by Saghiya, Said, Khouri, Bishara[*] and
> others is instrumental. The persecution of the Jews is acknowledged, but
> at the same time is linked to the Palestinian tragedy and its acknowledg-
> ment by Israel and the West. The comparison between the two, either
> directly or by inference, involves by definition the minimization and
> relativization of the Holocaust.[68]

This attempt to discredit those in the opposing camp who have endeavoured
to build bridges between the populations has its equivalent in certain Arabs'
rejection of all post-Zionists as, in the end, 'Zionists'. Nonetheless, despite the
zealots on both sides of the conflict, the mutual recognition of the Shoah and
the Nakba shows great promise. One initiative in particular deserves to be
singled out for its rich symbolism: an exhibition on the Shoah that opened
on 27 January 2009, International Holocaust Remembrance Day, in the West

---

[*]   Note that Litvak and Webman cite only Christian Arabs, although there is no lack
        of Muslim Arabs who recognize the Holocaust. This is surely no accident, for one of
        the more or less explicit messages of their book is that the Arabs capable of producing
        a discourse acceptable to the West are, in fact, Christians, i.e. a structural minority
        in the Arab world, or else Muslims living in the West.

Bank Palestinian village of Niʻlīn (or Naalin) – one of the focal points of the fight against the Separation Wall, which cuts through the village's land.[69] The mutual recognition of the Shoah and the Nakba must make further progress in order to enable true communication.[70]

Yet that is not enough. It is just as essential that Arabs outside Palestine recognize their (varying) responsibility for the exodus and the despoliation of Arab Jews, as well as for the persecution of the Palestinians. I have already mentioned the appalling treatment to which the Iraqi Jews, in particular, were subjected. The wrongs that the Arab states have visited on the Palestinians are no less appalling, including massacre and subjugation by the Jordanian monarchy, and recurrent massacre in Lebanon (where the scandalous plight of the Palestinian refugees can only be called apartheid) with or without the complicity of the Syrian regime. Samaha has put it very well:

> What has happened to the Palestinian people is less terrible than the 'Holocaust,' but is terrible nonetheless. And it must not be forgotten that we, the Arabs, have helped make it happen, consciously or not, voluntarily or not. It follows that we have a moral obligation to find the specific concept defining our responsibility to the Palestinians and to conduct political and ethical examinations on that basis. Just as Europe is alarmed by any manifestation of anti-Jewish racism, because it implies, among other things, a return to its wars, conflicts, and backwardness, so it is incumbent on the Arabs to tremble before all gratuitous acts directed against the Palestinians, because such acts are the most flagrant sign, not of their attitude toward their 'brothers' and 'the members of their clan,' but of the decadence into which their own project has fallen.[71]

It is just as indispensable for Israeli Jews of European background to recognize the oppression and discrimination to which they have subjected not only the country's Palestinian citizens but also the population at the intersection of two ethnic groups: the Arab or Eastern Jews or the Mizrahim, the 'Jewish victims of Zionism,'[72] who could play the role of mediator between the opposing camps.

The two faces of Janus, in Roman mythology, look in two different directions – one to the future, the other, the past – and they are inseparable. The symbolism is clear: it is not possible to look towards a peaceful future until accounts have been settled with the past and its lessons assimilated. But in order for the efforts of those who are trying to promote mutual comprehension between Jews and Arabs to bear fruit, the violence must come to an end; only then can the political currents inspired by the universal heritage of the Enlightenment drive back, in both the Arab world and Israel, the many forms of political and religious fanaticism that, today, have the wind in their sails.

The Romans left the doors of the temple of Janus open in wartime. In the Middle East, those doors have remained wide open for more than sixty years. It is urgent that they finally be closed – forever.

Acknowledgements

This book is the result of intensive research conducted mainly in Berlin's Staatsbibliothek, the Widener Library of Harvard University and the University of London libraries – especially the library of the institution to which I belong, the School of Oriental and African Studies (SOAS). I undertook the research with no help other than from friends who helped me get access to some of the sources of information. I am grateful for their assistance. They are Bashir Abu-Manneh, D.G. Adili, Musa Budeiri, Ulrike Freitag, Israel Gershoni, Angela Klein, Paul Kleiser, Norbert Mattes, Afsaneh Najmabad, Miguel Romero and Hazem Saghieh – with my apologies to those I might have omitted.

I am also grateful to the friends who volunteered to read the original manuscript and give me their comments and suggestions, particularly Peter Drucker, who translated most of my previous books into English, and Bashīr al-Sibā'i who translated this one into Arabic. My very good friend Stephen Shalom provided extensive feedback. I also profited greatly from the knowledge of the contemporary Arab world shared by Farouk Mardam-Bey, who welcomed the original French edition of the book in the collection he edits at Actes Sud.

I am most grateful to G.M. Goshgarian, who translated this book into English and managed to do so marvellously despite having had to work, quite unusually, while I was still writing the manuscript with the book stretching far beyond the initial plan.

Last but not least, I owe a special debt to Riva Hocherman, my editor at Metropolitan, to whom Anthony Arnove kindly introduced me. Riva encouraged my work on the book from the start. She believed in the project and her interest was all the more meaningful to me because she herself is directly affected by the topic and highly knowledgeable about it. She did a wonderful job making my prose in this English version more accessible to readers: I learned a great deal from her about the economy of words. At the same time, I had to engage with her in an 'editor-author war of (downsizing the) narrative': in her role as publisher, Riva was eager to reduce the size of the book so as not to deter potential readers. We ended up with a peaceful compromise – fewer citations and subtleties than in the French original, none of the omissions being essential to the argument, of course – which will hopefully allow more readers access to this English edition. In preparing this British edition at Saqi Books, I had the pleasure of dealing with Lynn Gaspard who combined efficiency with passion for this book.

A final note, which in the case of a work on this topic is more necessary than usual: none of the persons cited above share in any way my responsibility for the opinions and errors contained in this book.

Notes

Preface

1. Marina Cattaruzza, Marcello Flores, Simon Lewis Sullam and Enzo Traverso, eds., *Storia della Shoah: La crisi dell'Europa, lo sterminio degli ebrei e la memoria del XX secolo*, 2 vols, Turin, 2005–6. Editorial advisory board: Omer Bartov, Philippe Burrin, Dan Diner and Saul Friedländer.
2. Gilbert Achcar, 'Le reazioni all'Olocausto nel Medio Oriente arabo', ibid., vol. 2, pp. 869–900. Thanks are due to UTET for allowing me to make use of this chapter here.
3. Such insinuation is what Palestinian leader and former Arab member of the Israeli Knesset, Azmi Bishara, was rightly objecting to when he rejected the association of the Arabs and the Holocaust in one phrase, although he overstated his argument in pretending that it was tantamount to associating the Indians and the Holocaust. See Azmi Bishara, 'The Arabs and the Holocaust: Analyzing the Problems of a Preposition', *Zmanim*, vol. 13, no. 53, summer 1995, pp. 54–72 (in Hebrew). Partially cited in Yair Auron, *The Pain of Knowledge: Holocaust and Genocide Issues in Education*, Piscataway, 2005, p. 82.
4. Tom Segev, *The Seventh Million: The Israelis and the Holocaust*, New York, 2000; Peter Novick, *The Holocaust in American Life*, Boston, 1999.

Introduction, Words Laden with Pain

1. Raul Hilberg, *The Destruction of the European Jews*, 3rd edn, New Haven, CT, 2003.
2. Ibid., vol. 1, 'Preface to the First Edition' (1961), p. xv.
3. Jean-Michel Chaumont, *La Concurrence des victimes : Génocide, identité, reconnaissance*, Paris, 1997.
4. Esther Benbassa, *Suffering as Identity: The Jewish Paradigm*, London, 2009 (forthcoming at the time of writing – the reference in the original French edn is: *La Souffrance comme identité*, Paris, 2007, pp. 156–74).
5. United States Holocaust Memorial Museum, 'Frequently Asked Questions: About the Holocaust': www.ushmm.org/research/library/faq/details.php?topic=01#02
6. Zev Garber and Bruce Zuckerman, 'Why do we Call the Holocaust "The Holocaust"? An Inquiry into the Psychology of Labels', in Yehuda Bauer *et al.*, eds, *Remembering for the Future: Working Papers and Addenda*, vol. 2, *The Impact of the Holocaust on the Contemporary World*, Oxford, 1989, pp. 1882–3, repr. in Zev Garber, *Shoah: The Paradigmatic Genocide. Essays in Exegesis and Eisegesis*, Lanham, MD, 1994.

7. Ibid., p. 1886.

8. Arno Mayer, *Why did the Heavens Not Darken? The Final Solution in History,* New York, 1990, p. 16.

9. Michael Marrus, *The Holocaust in History,* London, 1988, p. 3.

10. Yad Vashem, 'The Holocaust: Definition and Preliminary Discussion': www1.yadvashem. org/Odot/prog/index_before_change_table.asp?gate=0-2

11. On this subject, see Neville Mandel, *The Arabs and Zionism before World War I,* Berkeley, CA, 1976, and Rashid Khalidi, *Palestinian Identity: The Construction of Modern National Consciousness,* New York, 1997.

12. Ibid.

13. See the population and immigration statistics in Walid Khalidi, ed., *From Haven to Conquest: Readings in Zionism and the Palestine Problem until 1948,* Washington, DC, 1987, pp. 841–3.

14. Mitchell Bard, 'British Restrictions on Jewish Immigration', Jewish Virtual Library: www.jewishvirtuallibrary.org/jsource/History/mandate.html

15. The standard, 2-vol. reference work on the reactions of the Palestinian Arabs to Zionism is still Yehoshua Porath, *The Emergence of the Palestinian-Arab National Movement, 1918–1929,* London, 1974, and *The Palestinian Arab National Movement, 1929–1939: From Riots to Rebellion,* London, 1977. For a vivid description of the circumstances surrounding the riots and the entire mandatory period, see Tom Segev, *One Palestine Complete: Jews and Arabs under the British Mandate,* New York, 2000.

16. Benny Morris, *Righteous Victims: A History of the Zionist–Arab Conflict, 1881–1998,* 2nd edn, New York, 2001, p. 107.

17. Bard, 'British Restrictions on Jewish Immigration'.

18. Central Bureau of Statistics, *Statistical Abstract of Israel 2007,* Jerusalem, 2007, table 4.2, p. 228.

19. Ze'ev Venia Hadari, *Second Exodus: The Full Story of Jewish Illegal Immigration to Palestine, 1945–1948,* London: Vallentine Mitchell, 1991, p. 3.

20. Israel Ministry of Foreign Affairs, 'Aliya and Absorption', 29 Oct. 2002 (www.mfa.gov. il/MFA/History/Modern+History/Centenary+of+Zionism/Aliya+and+Absorption. htm). See also Idith Zertal, *From Catastrophe to Power: Holocaust Survivors and the Emergence of Israel,* Berkeley, CA, 1998, p. 1.

21. Khalidi, *From Haven to Conquest,* pp. 842–3.

22. Central Bureau of Statistics, *Statistical Abstract 2007,* table 2.25, p. 158.

23. For an overview of pre-1939 Nazi policies towards the German Jews, see Richard Evans, *The Third Reich in Power 1933–1939,* New York, 2005, ch. 6: 'Toward the Racial Utopia'.

24. Lukasz Hirszowicz, *The Third Reich and the Arab East,* London, 1966, p. 32.

25. Francis Nicosia, 'Arab Nationalism and National Socialist Germany, 1933–1939: Ideological and Strategic Incompatibility', *International Journal of Middle East Studies,* vol. 12, no. 3 (Nov. 1980), pp. 358–9.

26. Francis Nicosia, *The Third Reich and the Palestine Question,* 2nd edn, New Brunswick, NJ, 2000, p. 212 (table).

27. On the Haavara agreement, ibid., ch. 3, 'The Development of the Haavara Transfer Agreement', pp. 29–49, as well as the same author's most recent book, which may be considered a standard reference work on the relations between Zionists and Nazis: Nicosia, *Zionism and Anti-Semitism in Nazi Germany,* New York, 2008; Edwin Black, *The Transfer Agreement: The Dramatic Story of the Pact between the Third Reich and Jewish Palestine,* 2nd edn, Washington, DC, 1999; 'Abd-ul-Rahmān 'Abdul-Ghani,

Almānia al-Nāziyya wa Filastīn 1933–1945, Beirut, 1995, pp. 48–186; and Tom Segev, *The Seventh Million: The Israelis and the Holocaust,* New York, 2000, ch. 1, 'The Streets are Paved with Money', pp. 15–34.

28. Segev, *Seventh Million,* p. 29.

29. United States Holocaust Memorial Museum, *Holocaust Encyclopedia,* 'German Jewish Refugees, 1933-1939': www.ushmm.org/wlc/article.php?lang=en&ModuleId=10005468

30. Central Bureau of Statistics, *Statistical Abstract of Israel 1985,* Jerusalem, 1985, table V/4, p. 154.

31. Segev, *One Palestine Complete,* p. 377.

32. Theodor Herzl, *The Jewish State: An Attempt at a Modern Solution of the Jewish Question,* London, 1972 (1st publ. in German in 1896), p. 8.

33. Shabtai Teveth, *Ben-Gurion: The Burning Ground, 1886–1948,* Boston, MA, 1987, p. 850. Michel Abitbol, *The Jews of North Africa during the Second World War,* Detroit, MI, 1989, p. 39.

34. Michel Abitbol, *The Jews of North Africa during the Second World War*, Detroit, MI, 1989, p. 39.

35. Teveth, *Ben-Gurion: The Burning Ground,* p. 848. For a thoroughgoing examination of the question of the attitude of the Yishuv's leaders during the Second World War, see Dina Porat, *The Blue and the Yellow Stars of David: The Zionist Leadership in Palestine and the Holocaust, 1939–1945,* Cambridge, MA, 1990. Stung by the 'post-Zionist' critique of Ben-Gurion on this subject – first and foremost, Tom Segev's – Shabtai Teveth later devoted a whole book to defending the founding father: *Ben-Gurion and the Holocaust,* New York, 1996. For a moderately apologetic discussion of Ben-Gurion's and Mapai's positions, see Hava Wagman Eshkoli, 'Three Attitudes toward the Holocaust within Mapai, 1933–1945', *Journal of Israeli History,* vol. 14, no. 1 (1993), pp. 73–94.

36. Cited in Segev, *Seventh Million,* p. 28.

37. Segev, *One Palestine, Complete,* p. 394.

38. Raul Hilberg, *Perpetrators, Victims, Bystanders: The Jewish Catastrophe 1933–1945,* New York, 1992, p. 227.

39. See Dina Porat, 'Al-domi: Palestinian Intellectuals and the Holocaust, 1943–1945', *Journal of Israeli History,* vol. 5, no. 1 (1984), pp. 97–124.

40. Thomas Kolsky, *Jews against Zionism: The American Council for Judaism, 1942–1948,* Philadelphia, 1990.

41. UNSCOP, 'Report to the General Assembly', *Official Records of the Second Session of the General Assembly,* suppl. 11, A/364, 3 Sept. 1947, United Nations, New York: http://domino.un.org/UNISPAL.NSF/9a798adbf322aff38525617b006d88d7/07175de9fa2de563852568d3006e10f3?OpenDocument

42. Adam Garfinkle, 'On the Origin, Meaning, Use and Abuse of a Phrase', *Middle Eastern Studies,* vol. 27, no. 4 (1991), pp. 539–50.

43. Segev, *One Palestine Complete,* p. 404.

44. Israel Zangwill, cited in Kevin MacDonald, 'Jewish Involvement in Shaping American Immigration Policy, 1881–1965: A Historical Review', *Population and Environment,* vol. 19, no. 4 (March 1998), pp. 311–12. On Zangwill, see Hani Faris, 'Israel Zangwill's Challenge to Zionism', *Journal of Palestine Studies,* vol. 4, no. 3 (Spring 1975), pp. 74–90.

45. See Beverley Hooper, 'Steinberg, Isaac Nachman (1888–1957)', *Australian Dictionary of Biography,* vol. 16, Melbourne, 2002, pp. 298–9: www.adb.online.anu.edu.au/biogs/A160362b.htm.

46. The full text of the 'Biltmore Program' is www.jewishvirtuallibrary.org/jsource/Zion-ism/BiltProg.html

47. Aaron Berman, *Nazism, the Jews, and American Zionism, 1933–1948,* Detroit, MI, 1990, p. 183.

48. Wyman, *The Abandonment of the Jews,* New York, 1983, p. 175.

49. Ibid., pp. 176–7. See also Carol Silverman, 'The American Jewish Community, the Roosevelt Administration, and the Holocaust', in Thomas Howard and William Ped-erson, eds, *Franklin D. Roosevelt and the Formation of the Modern World,* New York, 2003, pp. 188–207.

50. Cited in Segev, *Seventh Million,* p. 28.

51. Nicosia, *Zionism and Anti-Semitism,* p. 289.

52. Berman, *Nazism, the Jews, and American Zionism,* p. 181.

53. 'Evian Conference', *This Month in Holocaust History: July,* Yad Vashem, Jerusalem: www.yadvashem.org/about_holocaust/month_in_holocaust/july/july_lexicon/evian_con-ference.html

54. Edward Said, 'Bases for Coexistence', in *The End of the Peace Process: Oslo and After,* New York, 2001, p. 207. This article was originally published in Arabic translation in the daily *Al-Hayat,* 5 Nov. 1997; the original English version appeared a day later in *Al-Ahram Weekly.*

55. Ibid., pp. 207–8.

56. Joseph Massad, 'Palestinian and Jewish History: Recognition or Submission?', *Journal of Palestine Studies,* vol. 30, no. 1 (autumn 2000), p. 62.

57. See David Arnow's partisan argument, 'The Holocaust and the Birth of Israel: Reassess-ing the Causal Relationship', *Journal of Israeli History,* vol. 15, no. 3 (1994), pp. 257–81. See also the point made by Anita Shapira in her *Land and Power: The Zionist Resort to Force, 1881–1948,* New York, 1992, p. 342.

58. Yehuda Bauer, *Rethinking the Holocaust,* New Haven, CT, 2001, p. 258.

59. Ibid.

60. Segev, *Seventh Million,* p. 432.

61. Hannah Torok-Yablonka, 'The Recruitment of Holocaust Survivors during the War of Independence', *Journal of Israeli History,* vol. 13, no. 1 (1992), pp. 43–56.

62. Bauer, *Rethinking the Holocaust,* p. 259.

63. Said, 'Bases for Coexistence', p. 209.

64. Isaac Deutscher, 'Israel's Spiritual Climate' (originally publ. in *The Reporter,* April–May 1954), in *The Non-Jewish Jew and Other Essays,* London, 1968, p. 112.

65. Khalidi, 'Introduction', in idem, *From Haven to Conquest,* p. lxxii.

66. Bard, 'British Restrictions on Jewish Immigration'. Bevin was speaking before the annual congress of the Labour Party. As reported by Associated Press and quoted in the *New York Post,* 12 June 1946, he declared: 'The agitation in the U.S. for 100,000 Jews to be pushed into Palestine – and I do not want the Americans to misunderstand me – is because they do not want too many of them in New York.'

67. Segev, *One Palestine Complete,* p. 439n.

68. Segev, *Seventh Million,* p. 154.

69. Central Bureau of Statistics, *Statistical Abstract 2007,* table 4.2, p. 228.

70. Shlomo Ben-Ami, *Scars of War, Wounds of Peace: The Israeli–Arab Tragedy,* London, 2005, p. 28.

71. 'The Declaration of the Establishment of the State of Israel (May 14, 1948)', Jewish Virtual Library: www.jewishvirtuallibrary.org/jsource/History/Dec_of_Indep.html

72. For the current state of the debate on this question, see Benny Morris, *The Birth of the*

Palestinian Refugee Problem Revisited, Cambridge 2004 (originally pub. in 1988 as *The Birth of the Palestinian Refugee Problem, 1947–1949*) and Ilan Pappé, *The Ethnic Cleansing of Palestine,* Oxford, 2006.

73. Elias Sanbar, *Palestine 1948: L'Expulsion,* Washington, DC, 1984; Nur Masalha, *Expulsion of the Palestinians: The Concept of 'Transfer', in Zionist Political Thought, 1882–1948,* Washington, DC, 1992.

74. On the memory of the Nakba, see Ahmad Sa'di and Lila Abu-Lughod, eds, *Nakba: Palestine, 1948, and the Claims of Memory,* New York, 2007.

75. Mahmoud Darwish, 'Interview avec Hilit Yeshurun à Rabat Amon [Amman], 7 février 1996', *Hadarim,* no. 12 (spring 1996), pp. 172–98 (in Hebrew). Tr. into French in Mahmoud Darwish, *La Palestine comme métaphore: Entretiens,* Paris, 1997, p. 155.

76. Ruth Linn and Ilan Gur-Ze'ev, 'Holocaust as Metaphor: Arab and Israeli Use of the Same Symbol', *Metaphor and Symbolic Activity,* vol. 3, no. 11 (1996), p. 196. Note, however, that Mahmūd Fahmi Darwīsh published a book with the title *Kārithat Filastīn,* Baghdad, 1949, before the term *Nakba* had been established as the standard name for the Palestinian tragedy.

77. Linn and Gur-Ze'ev, 'Holocaust as Metaphor', p. 198.

78. Meir Litvak and Esther Webman, 'Perceptions of the Holocaust in Palestinian Public Discourse', *Israel Studies,* vol. 8, no. 3 (fall 2003), p. 130.

79. Ibid.

80. Meir Litvak and Esther Webman, *From Empathy to Denial: Arab Responses to the Holocaust,* London, 2009, p. 313.

81. Constantine Zurayk, *Maana al-Nakba,* Beirut, 1948, p. 5. An Eng. tr. of this book was publ. by Khayat's in Beirut in 1956 under the title *The Meaning of the Disaster.* The sentence quoted here has been directly translated from the Arabic. On Zurayk, see Aziz Al-Azmeh, *Qustantīn Zurayq: 'Arabiyyun lil-Qarn al-'Ishrīn,* Beirut, 2003.

82. Darwish, *La Palestine comme métaphore,* pp. 153–4 (emphasis added).

83. Pierre Bourdieu and Abdelmalek Sayad, *Le Déracinement : La Crise de l'agriculture traditionnelle en Algérie,* Paris, 1964.

84. Said, 'Bases for Coexistence', p. 208.

85. Morris, 'The Historiography of Deir Yassin', *Journal of Israeli History,* vol. 24, no. 1 (March 2005), p. 101. Srebrenica is the Bosnian city in which 8,000 people were slaughtered by the forces of the Serbian Republic of Bosnia in 1995.

86. On the circumstances under which the UN General Assembly resolution on the partition of Palestine was adopted, see Walid Khalidi, 'Revisiting the UNGA Partition Resolution', in Ilan Pappé, ed., *The Israel/Palestine Question: A Reader,* 2nd edn, London, 2007, pp. 97–114.

87. I. F. Stone, 'For a New Approach to the Israeli–Arab Conflict', *New York Review of Books,* 3 Aug. 1967, repr. in Gary Smith, ed., *Zionism: The Dream and the Reality. A Jewish Critique,* New York, 1974, p. 207.

88. Charles de Gaulle, press conference of 27 Nov. 1967. Lengthy excerpts from De Gaulle's address as well as a critical commentary on it may be found in Raymond Aron, *De Gaulle, Israel and the Jews,* New Brunswick, NJ, 2004. For much of the original French text of the address see www.swans.com/library/dossiers/gaulle67.html

89. *Les Temps Modernes,* no. 253bis (1967), special issue: 'Le Conflit israélo-arabe'.

90. Maxime Rodinson, 'Israël, fait colonial?', in *Le Conflit israélo-arabe,* pp. 17–88. Tr. into English in Rodinson, *Israel: A Colonial-Settler State?,* New York, 1973. In 1975, Bernard Avishai sought to challenge the validity of this term by drawing a subtle distinction between colonization and colonialism and pointing to the socialist orientation of the

Zionist movement ('Zionist Colonialism: Myth and Dilemma', repr. in Avishai, *A New Israel: Democracy in Crisis, 1973–1988,* New York, 1990, pp. 179–95). Another original discussion of the colonial label is Derek Penslar's attempt to draw a distinction between pre-1967 and post-1967 Israel, the latter alone being a colonial state in the author's view ('Zionism, Colonialism, Postcolonialism', in Anita Shapira and Derek Penslar, *Israeli Historical Revisionism: From Left to Right,* London, 2003, pp. 84–98). The same collection, edited by Shapira and Penslar, includes another critique of the 'Colonialist School' by Avi Bareli ('Forgetting Europe: Perspectives on the Debate about Zionism and Colonialism', pp. 99–120).

91. Morris, *Righteous Victims*, p. 676. Note however that Morris seems here to opt for Avishai's distinction by using the label 'colonizing' instead of 'colonial' or 'colonialist'. On the colonial nature of the Zionist enterprise, see Gabriel Piterberg, *The Returns of Zionism: Myths, Politics and Scholarship in Israel,* London, 2008, esp. ch. 2, 'The Zionist Colonization of Palestine in the Comparative Context of Settler Colonialism', pp. 51–92. See also Uri Ram, 'The Colonization Perspective in Israeli Sociology', in Pappé, *The Israel/Palestine Question*, pp. 53–77; and, in the same collection, Gershon Shafir, 'Zionism and Colonialism: A Comparative Approach', pp. 78–93.

92. Uri Ram, 'The Future of the Past in Israel: A Sociology of Knowledge Approach', in Benny Morris, ed., *Making Israel,* Ann Arbor, MI, 2007, p. 214. Two of the contributions to this work on the debate around the Israeli 'new historiography', by Yoav Gelber ('The History of Zionist Historiography: From Apologetics to Denial', pp. 47–80) and Moshe Lissak ('Critical and "Establishment" Sociology in Israel's Academic Community', pp. 178–201), represent further unconvincing attempts to deny the applicability of the 'colonialist paradigm' to Zionism and the state of Israel.

93. On the similarities between the southern African and Palestinian cases, see George Jabbour, *Settler Colonialism in Southern Africa and the Middle East,* Khartoum and Beirut, 1970.

94. International Rescue Committee, *Mortality in the Democratic Republic of Congo: An Ongoing Crisis,* New York, Jan. 2008 (www.theirc.org/special-report/congo-forgotten-crisis.html).

95. BBC, 'Poll: Global Views of USA Improve', 2 April 2008 (http://news.bbc.co.uk/1/shared/bsp/hi/pdfs/02_04_08_globalview.pdf). On this subject, see also BBC, 'Israel "Worried over World Image"', 13 Oct. 2004 (http://news.bbc.co.uk/1/hi/world/middle_east/3740682.stm)
and *Israel Today*, 'Survey: Israel Worst Brand Name in the World', 22 Nov. 2006 (http://www.israeltoday.co.il/default.aspx?tabid=178&nid=10395). The most recent poll available at the time of writing was conducted by the University of Maryland and publ. 1 July 2008: www.worldpublicopinion.org/pipa/articles/international_security_bt/503.php?lb=brglm&pnt=503&nid=&id=

96. 'Israeli Anger over EU "Threat" Poll', 3 Nov. 2003 (http://news.bbc.co.uk/1/hi/world/middle_east/3237277.stm)

I. THE TIME OF THE SHOAH

Arab Reactions to Nazism and Anti-Semitism, 1933–1947

Prelude

1. Raphael Patai, *The Arab Mind,* Long Island City, 2002 (1973).
2. Hillel Cohen, *Army of Shadows: Palestinian Collaboration with Zionism, 1917–1948,* Berkeley, CA, 2008.

3. Avi Shlaim, *Collusion across the Jordan: King Abdullah, the Zionist Movement and the Partition of Palestine,* Oxford, 1988.

4. Laura Zittrain Eisenberg, *My Enemy's Enemy: Lebanon in the Early Zionist Imagination, 1900–1948,* Detroit, MI, 1994.

5. On Egyptian 'liberal nationalism', see Nadav Safran, *Egypt in Search of Political Community: An Analysis of the Intellectual and Political Evolution of Egypt, 1804–1952,* Cambridge, MA, 1961.

Chapter 1: The Liberal Westernizers

1. Ian Buruma and Avishai Margalit, *Occidentalism: The West in the Eyes of its Enemies,* New York, 2004.

2. On the quarrel between the Slavophiles and Westernizers in Russia, see Andrzej Walicki, *The Slavophile Controversy: History of a Conservative Utopia in Nineteenth-Century Russian Thought,* Oxford, 1975 (Polish original, 1964), and Walicki, *A History of Russian Thought: From the Enlightenment to Marxism,* Stanford, CA, 1979 (Polish original, 1973).

3. See Walicki, *History of Russian Thought*, ch. 8: 'Belinsky and Different Variants of Westernism', pp. 135–51.

4. Safran, *Egypt in Search of Political Community*, p. 275, n. 1. Safran's book remains, notwithstanding the often justified criticisms and rectifications of it made by Israel Gershoni in particular (see the references below), an important contribution to the study of Egyptian liberalism in the first half of the twentieth century.

5. Joseph Achcar, 'La France et l'Angleterre dans le Proche-Orient: L'Évolution politique de la Syrie et du Liban, de la Palestine et de l'Irak', doctoral dissertation, University of Lyons, Lyons, 1934, pp. 89–91 (copies may be consulted at the Bibliothèque nationale de France and the Library of Congress).

6. Israel Gershoni, *Beyond Anti-Semitism: Egyptian Responses to German Nazism and Italian Fascism in the 1930s,* EUI Working Paper no. RSC 2001/32, San Domenico, 2001 – subtitle, p. 6. See also Gershoni, *Or ba-Zel: Mizraim we-ha-Fashism, 1922–1937* (in Hebrew) (Light in the Shade: Egypt and Fascism, 1922–1937), Tel Aviv, 1999. A German translation is forthcoming.

7. Gershoni, *Beyond Anti-Semitism*, p. 8.

8. Ibid., p. 11 (emphasis in the original).

9. Israel Gershoni, 'Egyptian Liberalism in an Age of "Crisis of Orientation": Al-Risāla's Reaction to Fascism and Nazism, 1933–39', *International Journal of Middle East Studies,* vol. 31, no. 4 (Nov. 1999), pp. 551–76.

10. On Al-Hakim in particular, in the same context, see Israel Gershoni, 'Confronting Nazism in Egypt: Tawfiq al-Hakim's Anti-Totalitarianism 1938–1945', *Tel Aviver Jahrbuch für deutsche Geschichte,* vol. 26 (1997), pp. 121–50.

11. On *Al-Risāla*, see also Israel Gershoni and James Jankowski, *Redefining the Egyptian Nation, 1930–1945,* Cambridge, 1995, pp. 63–4.

12. Gershoni, 'Egyptian Liberalism', p. 555.

13. Ibid., p. 564.

14. On the opinions on Palestine published in *Al-Risāla*, see Israel Gershoni and Jankowski, *Redefining the Egyptian Nation*, p. 174.

15. Gershoni, 'Egyptian Liberalism', p. 570.

16. Gershoni, '"Der verfolgte Jude": Al-Hilals Reaktionen auf den Antisemitismus in Europa und Hitlers Machtergreifung', in Gerhard Höpp, Peter Wien and René Wildangel, eds,

Blind für die Geschichte? Arabische Begegnungen mit dem Nationalsozialismus, Berlin, 2004, pp. 39–72.

17. Ibid., pp. 65–6.

18. Ami Ayalon, 'Egyptian Intellectuals versus Fascism and Nazism in the 1930s', in Uriel Dann, ed., *The Great Powers in the Middle East, 1919–1939,* New York, 1988, p. 402.

19. Philip Khoury, *Syria and the French Mandate: The Politics of Arab Nationalism 1920–1945,* London, 1987, pp. 549–52.

20. Ibid., p. 550.

21. Norman Stillman, *The Jews of Arab Lands in Modern Times,* Philadelphia, 1991, p. 100.

22. *Palestine Post,* 22 Feb. 1935, cited in René Wildangel, *Zwischen Achse und Mandatsmacht. Palästina und der Nationalsozialismus,* Berlin, 2007, p. 183.

23. Khoury, *Syria and the French Mandate,* p. 551.

24. 'Kalimat 'Abdul-Rahmān 'Azzām, bi-Ism Jam'iyyat al-Fikra al-'Arabiyya, fi Ijtimā' Nāblus fi Zikra Wa'd Balfour, 2/11/1935', in Bayān Nuwayhid al-Hūt, ed., *Wathā'iq al-Haraka al-Wataniyya al-Filastīniyya 1918–1939: Min Awrāq Akram al-Zu'aytir,* Beirut, 1979, p. 393. On the political education that 'Abdul-Rahmān 'Azzām received prior to his nomination as an Egyptian plenipotentiary minister in 1936, see Ralph Coury, *The Making of an Egyptian Arab Nationalist: The Early Years of Azzam Pasha, 1893–1936,* Reading, 1998.

25. Cited by Akram Zu'aytir in his diary: *Yawmiyyāt Akram Zu'aytir: Al-Haraka al-Wataniyya al-Filastīniyya 1935–1939,* Beirut, 1980, p. 477.

26. Ibid.

27. Edward Said, 'Review of Ahdaf Soueif's *In The Eye of the Sun*', *Times Literary Supplement,* 19 June 1992 (emphasis in the original). On Antonius and his intellectual and political role, the most detailed study is Susan Silsby Boyle, *Betrayal of Palestine: The Story of George Antonius,* Boulder, CO, 2001. The book includes a selected bibliography.

28. George Antonius, *The Arab Awakening: The Story of the Arab National Movement,* London, 1938, pp. 410–11.

29. Wildangel, *Zwischen Achse und Mandatsmacht.* See also idem, '"Der größte Feind der Menschheit": Der Nationalsozialismus in der arabischen öffentlichen Meinung in Palästina während des Zweiten Weltkrieges', in Höpp *et al., Blind für die Geschichte?,* pp. 115–54.

30. Wildangel, *Zwischen Achse und Mandatsmacht,* p. 181.

31. Rashid Khalidi, *The Iron Cage: The Story of the Palestinian Struggle for Statehood,* Boston, MA, 2006, p. 93. On *Filastīn,* see pp. 90–104.

32. Ibid., p. 94.

33. 'Abdul-Rahmān 'Abdul-Ghani, *Almāniya al-Nāziyya wa Filastīn 1933–1945,* Beirut, 1995, pp. 190–1. Among the works in Arabic on the relations between Nazi Germany and Palestine, 'Abdul-Ghani's is the most serious scholarly study. Based on an extensive examination of the primary sources, German and Arab, it provides a useful supplement to Hirszowicz's and Nicosia's well-known works on the same subject.

34. Wildangel, *Zwischen Achse und Mandatsmacht,* p. 147.

35. Cited in Nizām 'Abbāsi, *Al-'Ilāqāt al-Sahyūniyya al-Nāziyya wa Atharuha 'ala Filastīn wa Harakat al-Taharrur al-'Arabi 1933–1945,* Kuwait, 1984, pp. 75–6 (a facsimile may be found on p. 187).

36. Orayb Aref Najjar, '*Falastin* Editorial Writers, the Allies, World War II, and the Palestinian Question in the 21st century', *SIMILE: Studies in Media and Information Literacy Education,* vol. 3, no. 4 (Nov. 2003), p. 5.

37. Cited in ibid., p. 5.

38. Cited in Wildangel, *Zwischen Achse und Mandatmacht*, p. 267.

39. Tom Segev, *One Palestine, Complete: Jews and Arabs under the British Mandate,* New York, 2000, p. 437n.

40. Ibid., p. 462.

41. For the Arabic text, see *Al-Ahram*, 8 Oct. 1944. Eng. tr.: 'The Alexandria Protocol; October 7, 1944', *Department of State Bulletin*, vol. 16, no. 411 (18 May 1947), Washington, DC: Government Printing Office, 1947, also available in Khalil Muhammad Khalil, ed., *The Arab States and the Arab League: A Documentary Record*, vol. 2, Beirut, 1962, pp. 55–6, and in The Avalon Project at Yale Law School, http://avalon.law.yale.edu/20th_century/alex.asp

42. *Report of the Anglo-American Committee of Enquiry Regarding the Problems of European Jewry and Palestine,* Lausanne, 20 April 1946 (London, 1946), p. 30.

43. See Huri Azazian, *Al-Jāliyāt al-Armaniyya fi al-Bilād al-'Arabiyya,* Latakia, 1993, p. 83.

44. Abd al-Rahman Azzam ('Abdul-Rahmān 'Azzām), 'The Arab League and World Unity', in Sylvia Haim, ed., *Arab Nationalism: An Anthology,* Berkeley, CA, 1962, pp. 164–5. Similar arguments may be found in the articles published by the Lebanese Michel Chiha in 1945–7 and reproduced in a collection of Chiha's essays on Palestine tr. into English, *Palestine,* Beirut, 1969, repr. as *Palestine: Editorial Reflections of Michel Chiha 1944–55,* London, 2007.

45. UNSCOP, 'Report to the General Assembly', *Official Records of the Second Session of the General Assembly*, suppl. 11, New York, 3 Sept. 1947 (UNISPAL, http://domino.un.org/UNISPAL.NSF/99818751a6a4c9c6852560690077ef61/07175de9fa2de56385 2568d3006e10f3!OpenDocument).

46. Sub-Committee 2 of the ad hoc Committee of the UN General Assembly on the Palestinian Question, 'Draft Resolution on Jewish Refugees and Displaced Persons', *Yearbook of the United Nations 1947–48*, 1949.I.13, New York, 31 Dec. 1948 (UNISPAL, http://domino.un.org/UNISPAL.NSF/9a798adbf322aff38525617b006d88d7/5ce90 0d2de34aadf852562bd007002d2?OpenDocument). The text of the subcommittee's report and its draft resolutions may be found in Walid Khalidi, ed., *From Haven to Conquest,* Washington, DC, 1987, pp. 645–99.

47. Ibid., p. lxxii.

48. 'International Refugee Organization', *International Organization*, 2/1 (Feb. 1948), 130

Chapter 2: The Marxists

1. On the 'acrobatics' of Palestine's Communists, most of them Jews, on this question, see Musa Budeiri, *The Palestine Communist Party 1919–1948: Arab and Jew in the Struggle for Internationalism,* London, 1979, pp. 127–31.

2. Cited in Jane Degras, ed., *The Communist International 1919–1943: Documents,* vol. 3, *1929–1943*, London, 1965, p. 257.

3. Walter Laqueur, *Communism and Nationalism in the Middle East,* London, 1956, p. 93.

4. Israel Shahak, *Jewish History, Jewish Religion: The Weight of Three Thousand Years*, 2nd edn, London, 1997, pp. 71–2.

5. Francis Nicosia, *Zionism and Anti-Semitism in Nazi Germany,* New York, 2008, p. 95. It must be clear, however, as Nicosia shows, that beyond their common ethno-nationalist Central European roots, German Zionism and National Socialism had little in common.

Indeed, much of German Zionism was inclined toward the bi-nationalism of Martin Buber and Brit Shalom. The relationship between the Zionists and the Nazi regime after 1933 was essentially a pragmatic one. The Zionists had little choice but to appear to the Nazi regime as the best means to achieve the Nazi goal of removing Jews from Germany. They didn't like the Nazis or celebrate when the Nazis took power. By the same token, the Nazis, who loathed the Zionists as much as any other Jews because they were still Jews, used them nevertheless as a means to achieve the goals of their Jewish policy.

6. See, among other sources, the two chapters on Jabotinsky and his movement in Mitchell Cohen, *Zion and State: Nation, Class and the Shaping of Modern Israel,* Oxford, 1987, pp. 134–60; Yaacov Shavit, *Jabotinsky and the Revisionist Movement 1925–1948,* London, 1988, esp. pp. 350–72; and Colin Shindler, *The Triumph of Military Zionism: Nationalism and the Origins of the Israeli Right,* London, 2006. See also Lenni Brenner's vigorous indictment, *Zionism in the Age of the Dictators,* Westport, CT, 1983, as well as Nicosia's critique of this book, 'Victims as Perpetrators: German Zionism and Collaboration in Recent Historical Controversy', in Yehuda Bauer *et al.,* eds, *Remembering for the Future: Working Papers and Addenda,* vol. 2, *The Impact of the Holocaust on the Contemporary World,* Oxford, 1989, pp. 2134–46. On the Revisionists in particular, see Lenni Brenner, *The Iron Wall: Zionist Revisionism from Jabotinsky to Shamir,* London, 1984.

7. See Shabtai Teveth, *The Burning Ground, 1886–1948,* Boston, 1987, esp. ch. 26.

8. Ibid., ch. 29, p. 482.

9. On the convergence between Ben-Gurion and Jabotinsky-Begin, see Cohen, *Zion and State.*

10. Cited in Yūsuf Khattār al-Hilū, *Qissat al-Nasr al-Kabīr,* Beirut, 1985, p. 31.

11. This holds for Hilū's book, quoted in the previous note, and also for an earlier text, 'Abdallah Hannā's *Al-Haraka al-Munāhida lil-Fāshiyya fi Sūriya wa Lubnān 1933–1945,* Beirut, 1975. However, Hannā, in a few lines, attributes the eclipse of Communist anti-Fascist activity in 1939–41 to the repressive conditions created by the colonial authorities of Vichy France in Syria and Lebanon until their overthrow by British forces in June 1941; he does not so much as mention the German–Soviet Pact (pp. 85–6). On Communist anti-Fascist activities until 1939, see also Götz Nordbruch, *Nazism in Syria and Lebanon: The Ambivalence of the German Option, 1939–1945,* London, 2009, pp. 68–70.

12. Hannā Abu-Hannā, ed., *Mudhakkirāt Najāti Sidqi,* Beirut, 2001, pp. 165–7.

13. Ridwān al-Hilū, 'Fi al-Qadā' 'ala al-Fāshistiyya al-Nihāya al-Hatmiyya lil-Sahyūniyya', *Nidāl al-Sha'b,* March 1943, pp. 4–5.

14. Jacques Berque, *Egypt: Imperialism and Revolution,* London, 1972, p. 629 (emphasis in the original). On the Trotskyist tendency in Egypt in the period 1938–48, see Bashīr al-Sibā'i, *Marāya al-Intelligentsia,* Alexandria, 1995. The series of articles on the subject that Sibā'i reprints in his book is one of the best studies of Egyptian Trotskyism, but is inaccurate on certain points, notably the real relation of various participants, especially Henein and Kāmil, to Trotskyism, because the author did not have adequate documentation at his disposal. As Sibā'i himself acknowledges (p. 71), the history of this current has yet to be written. The most remarkable recent contribution on this same topic is the well-researched chapter on 'Georges Henein: Surrealism and Socialism' (written with Anne Alexander) in David Renton's book, *Dissident Marxism: Past Voices for Present Times,* London, 2004, pp. 82–103. For a Stalinist viewpoint on the history of the Trotskyist tendency, see Rif'at al- Sa'īd, *Tārīkh al-Munazzamāt al-Yasāriyya*

al-Misriyya 1940–1950, Cairo, 1976, pp. 153–65, 202–5. See Lotfallah Soliman's report on the 1943 discussions between the Egyptian Trotskyist group and the far-left Zionist organization Hashomer Hatzair in Soliman, *Pour une histoire profane de la Palestine,* Paris, 1989, pp. 92–3.

15. Saʿīd, *Al-Yasār al-Misri 1925–1940,* Beirut, 1972. See also, in the appendix, 'Mahdar Niqāsh maʿ Anwar Kāmil' (transcript of an interview with Anwar Kamil, Cairo: 14 Jan. 1969), pp. 252–7 (p. 252n.). In this interview, Kāmil himself stresses that his group, unlike the others, was made up of Egyptians. In the four years between the appearance of this book by Saʿīd and that of his book cited above, the author's tone underwent a radical change; the positive connotations gave way to Stalinist invective.

16. Anwar Kāmil, *Al-Sahyūniyya,* Cairo, 1944. On Kāmil and his pamphlet, see 'Abdul-Qādir Yāsīn, 'Al-Trotskiyyūn al-Misriyyūn wa Qadiyyat Filastīn', *Shuʾūn Filastīniyya,* no. 45 (May 1975), pp. 114–23.

17. I. Rennap, *Anti-Semitism and the Jewish Question,* with a preface by the British Communist MP William (Willie) Gallacher, London, 1942. On Rennap/Panner, see http://en.wikipedia.org/wiki/Israel_Panner

18. Group of Palestine Socialists, 'Zionism – An Outpost of Imperialism: Open Letter to Labour Party Conference', *Workers' International News,* vol. 5, no. 7 (Dec. 1944), pp. 4–11 (www.marxists.org/history/etol/newspape/win/vol05a/n007a/zionism.htm).

19. See Gershoni, *Beyond Anti-Semitism,* p. 18.

20. Kāmil, *Al-Sahyūniyya,* p. 5.

21. This information is provided by Anwar Kāmil who told Bashīr al-Sibāʿi this story in 1988. This was at a time when Sibāʿi, my source here, was preparing to release a 2nd edn of Kāmil's *Al-Sahyūniyya,* Cairo, 1989, with an introduction that he wrote himself.

22. Bernard Lazare, *Anti-Semitism: Its History and Causes,* repr. New York, 2005, pp. 239–40; http://www.fordham.edu/halsall/jewish/lazare-anti.html

23. Kāmil to 'Abdul-Qādir Yāsīn, in Yāsīn, 'Al-Trotskiyyūn al-Misriyyūn', p. 118.

24. Kāmil, *Al-Sahyūniyya,* pp. 59–60.

25. Yāsīn, 'Al-Trotskiyyūn al-Misriyyūn', p. 122.

26. Rifʿat al-Saʿīd, *Tārikh al-Munazzamāt al-Yasāriyya al-Misriyya 1940–1950,* Cairo, 1976, p. 159.

27. 'Extracts from an ECCI Statement on the Decision of the Poale Zion Not to Affiliate to the Third International', in Degras, ed., *The Communist International,* vol. 1, *1919–1922,* London, 1956, p. 366.

28. Laqueur, *Communism and Nationalism in the Middle East,* p. 91 (emphasis in the original).

29. Ibid., pp. 91–5.

30. Budeiri, *Palestine Communist Party 1919–1948,* p. 216.

31. Anita Shapira and Irit Keynan, 'The Survivors of the Holocaust', International School for Holocaust Studies, Yad Vashem, Jerusalem: www1.yadvashem.org/education/lessonplan/english/shapira/shapira.htm

32. See David Wyman, *The Abandonment of the Jews,* New York, 1984.

33. Group of Palestine Socialists, 'Zionism – An Outpost of Imperialism'. It is worth mentioning that the 'open letter' detected the beginning of a pro-Zionist shift in Moscow's position three years before the Soviet vote in favour of the partition of Palestine.

34. Peter Seidman, *Socialists and the Fight against Anti-Semitism: An Answer to the B'nai B'rith Anti-Defamation League,* New York, 1973, p. 30.

35. See Ilan Greilsammer, *Les Communistes israéliens,* Paris, 1978, p. 352.

36. Seidman, *Socialists and the Fight against Anti-Semitism*, pp. 23–30.
37. For an Egyptian example, see Joel Beinin, *Was the Red Flag Flying There? Marxist Politics and the Arab–Israeli Conflict in Egypt and Israel, 1948–1965*, London, 1990, p. 59. Beinin, however, is very much in error when he writes, in the same passage: 'This differentiation of Jews and Zionists characterized the Arab communists and divided them from the rest of the Arab national movement, which did not make this distinction.' The pages cited earlier suffice to show just how far off the mark the last assertion about 'the rest of the Arab national movement' is. For an Algerian example, see Michel Abitbol, *The Jews of North Africa during the Second World War*, Detroit, MI, 1989, p. 30.
38. Hanna Batatu, *The Old Social Classes and the Revolutionary Movements of Iraq: A Study of Iraq's Old Landed and Commercial Classes and of its Communists, Ba'athists, and Free Officers*, Princeton, NJ, 1978, p. 454.
39. Budeiri, *Palestine Communist Party*, p. 209. See also Zachary Lockman, *Comrades and Enemies: Arab and Jewish Workers in Palestine, 1906–1948*, Berkeley, CA, 1996, esp. pp. 307, 324–5.
40. Beinin, *Was the Red Flag Flying There?*, p. 57.
41. See Sa'id, *Al-Yasār al-Misri wa al-Qadiyya al-Filastīniyya*, Beirut, 1974.
42. Ibid., pp. 189–90.
43. On the perceptible shift in the attitude of the world Communist movement in 1947, see Greilsammer, *Les Communistes israéliens*, p. 127. On Moscow's stance at the UN in 1947, ibid., pp. 138–45, as well as Walid Khalidi, 'Introduction', in Khalidi, ed., *From Haven to Conquest*, pp. lxxii–lxxiv.
44. Batatu, *Old Social Classes*, p. 598.
45. Budeiri, *Palestine Communist Party*, p. 231; see also Greilsammer, *Les Communistes israéliens*, pp. 132–3. On the National Liberation League, see 'Umar Hilmi al-Ghūl's monograph, '*Usbat al-Taharrur al-Watani fi Filastīn: Nash'atuha wa Tatawwuruha wa Dawruha, 1943–1948*, Beirut, 1987.
46. See Gabriel Gorodetsky, 'The Soviet Union's Role in the Creation of the State of Israel', *Journal of Israeli History*, vol. 22, no. 1 (2003), pp. 4–20.
47. See the interview with Henri Curiel and the documents in Sa'id, *Al-Yasār al-Misri wa al-Qadiyya al-Filastīniyya*.
48. Budeiri, *Palestine Communist Party*, pp. 231–8.
49. 'Qarārāt al-Lujna al-Markaziyya li-'Usbat al-Taharrur al-Watani fi Filastīn', in Samīh Samāra, *Al-'Amal al-Shuyū'i fi Filastīn: Al-Tabaqa wa al-Sha'b fi Muwājahat al-Kūlūnyāliyya*, Beirut, 1979, pp. 354–5. Samīh Samāra's book reflects the critical treatment of the attitude of Arab Communists in 1947–8 that was encouraged by the Lebanese Communist Party beginning in the 1970s. Albeit published by the Lebanese CP's publishing house, Samāra's book included a preface by Emile Habibi, a member of the unconditionally pro-Soviet minority in 1947 who defended the 'orthodox' viewpoint. The Arab Communists who remained on the territory included within Israel in 1948, of whom Habibi is one of the best known, did not wait long to merge again with the Israeli Communist Party, to which most Jewish Communists belonged. The CP split again a few years later, in 1965, along essentially ethnic-political lines. On the Party's evolution after 1948, see Greilsammer, *Les Communistes israéliens*, and Sondra Miller Rubenstein, *The Communist Movement in Palestine and Israel, 1919–1984*, Boulder, CO, 1985. On the reactions of the Communists of Palestine to the 1947 partition, ibid., pp. 282–8, and Beinin, *Was the Red Flag Flying There?*, pp. 24–65, which also discusses Egyptian Communists' reactions.
50. Batatu, *Old Social Classes*, pp. 598–9.

51. On the Iraqi CP's position against the UN resolution on the partition of Palestine and the French CP's role in reversing it, see *Al-Hizb al-Shuyū'ī al-'Irāqī wa al-Mas'ala al-Filastīniya,* n.pl., 1971, pp. 43–52.

52. Batatu, *Old Social Classes,* pp. 598–9.

53. See Arnold Krammer, 'Arms for Independence: When the Soviet Bloc Supported Israel', *Wiener Library Bulletin,* vol. 22, no. 3, NS 12 (1968), pp. 19–23, repr. in Khalidi, ed., *From Haven to Conquest,* pp. 745–54.

Chapter 3: The Nationalists

1. Thomas Mayer, 'Egypt and the General Islamic Conference of Jerusalem in 1931', *Middle Eastern Studies,* 18/3 (1982), 318–19.

2. Stefan Wild, 'National Socialism in the Arab Near East between 1933 and 1939', *Die Welt des Islams,* vol. 25, no. 1/4 (1985), p. 130.

3. Shavit, *Jabotinsky and the Revisionist Movement,* p. 372.

4. Bernard Lewis, *Semites and Anti-Semites: An Inquiry into Conflict and Prejudice,* 1986, reissued with a new afterword, New York, 1999, p. 280, n. 9.

5. Wild, 'National Socialism in the Arab Near East', p. 131; Sami al-Jundi, *Al-Ba'th,* Beirut, 1969, p. 27 – cited in Wild from the extract tr. into English in Elie Kedourie, 'Arab Political Memoirs', *Encounter,* vol. 39, no. 5 (Nov. 1972), repr. in *Arab Political Memoirs and Other Studies,* London, 1974, p. 200.

6. Jalāl al-Sayyid, *Hizb al-Ba'th al-'Arabi,* Beirut, 1973.

7. Patrick Seale, *The Struggle for Syria: A Study of Post-War Arab Politics 1945–1958,* London, 1965, esp. ch. 14, 'The Ba'th and the Communists', pp. 148–63.

8. Nabil Kaylani, 'The Rise of the Syrian Ba'th, 1940–1958: Political Success, Party Failure', *International Journal of Middle East Studies,* vol. 3, no. 1 (Jan. 1972), pp. 3–23.

9. John Devlin, *The Baath Party: A History from its Origins to 1966,* Stanford, CA, 1976, pp. 7–22.

10. Batatu, *Old Social Classes,* esp. pp. 722–41.

11. Jundi, *Al-Ba'th,* p. 27, n. 1.

12. Kedourie, *Arab Political Memoirs,* p. 201.

13. Batatu, *Old Social Classes,* pp. 725–6; Seale, *Struggle for Syria,* pp. 149–50.

14. 'Abdallah Hannā, *Min al-Ittijāhāt al-Fikriyya fi Sūriyya wa Lubnān: Al-Nusf al-Awwal min al-Qarn al-'Ishrīn,* Damascus, 1987, pp. 109–13, 123. In 1973, Hannā published a book on the same subject that dealt only with the years 1920–45; in 1975, he followed up with another, quoted above, on the anti-fascist movement in Syria and Lebanon. The treatment of the topic in these two works is less extensive than that in his most recent book, cited here.

15. Ibid., pp. 112–13.

16. Seale, *Struggle for Syria,* p. 150; Kaylani, 'The Rise of the Syrian Ba'th', p. 4.

17. Hannā, *Min al-Ittijāhāt al-Fikriyya,* p. 138.

18. Jundi, *Al-Ba'th,* p. 31; Sayyid, *Hizb al-Ba'th al-'Arabi,* p. 15.

19. Jundi, *Al-Ba'th,* pp. 30–1.

20. Hazem Saghieh, *Qawmiyyū al-Mashriq al-'Arabi: Min Dreyfus ila Garaudy,* Beirut, 2000. On Arsūzi's thought see pp. 91–8.

21. Cited in ibid., p. 138, n. 19.

22. Jundi, *Al-Ba'th,* p. 27 – cited from the extract tr. into English in Elie Kedourie, *Arab Political Memoirs,* p. 200.

23. Zaki al-Arsūzi's main writings were brought together in his 'Complete Works' (*Al-Mu'allafāt al-Kāmila*), which are in fact rather incomplete; they were published

in 4 vols by the political command of the Syrian army in 1972–4. Generally nebulous and insipid, these writings cannot quite hide, even in the 1960s, their author's racial views.

24. Jundi, *Al-Ba'th*, p. 22.

25. Ibid., p. 23. In'ām al-Jundi, Sami's brother and a member of Aflaq-Bītār's competing group from the outset, has related how repulsive he found Arsūzi when he first met him (In'ām al-Jundi, 'Ba'd Ghiyāb Michel 'Aflaq: Da'wa li Tas'hīh al-Waqāi' wa Tadqīqiha', *Al-Yawm al-Sābi'*, 28 Aug. 1989, p. 20).

26. Sayyid, *Hizb al-Ba'th al-'Arabi*, p. 18.

27. Batatu, *Old Social Classes*, p. 724.

28. In'ām al-Jundi, 'Ba'd Ghiyāb Michel 'Aflaq'.

29. Sami al-Jundi, *Al-Ba'th*, p. 36.

30. Sayyid, *Hizb al-Ba'th al-'Arabi*, pp. 35–6.

31. Eric Rouleau, 'The Syrian Enigma: What is the Baath?', *New Left Review*, no. 1/45 (Sept.–Oct. 1967), pp. 53–65.

32. Ibid., p. 55.

33. Ibid., p. 56. On this subject, see Devlin, *Baath Party*, pp. 10–11.

34. Sami al-Jundi, *Al-Ba'th*, p. 29.

35. Rouleau, 'Syrian Enigma', p. 57.

36. See what Olivier Carré recounts about his May 1973 interview with Salāh Bītār in Beirut in *Le Nationalisme arabe*, Paris, 1996, p. 54. Despite its flimsiness, Rouleau's article provided the unique source for the claim by Bassam Tibi, in his University of Frankfurt doctoral dissertation, published in German in 1971 and in English translation a decade later, that Aflaq was 'full of enthusiasm for Rosenberg and Hitler' (Bassam Tibi, *Arab Nationalism: A Critical Enquiry*, 2nd edn, Basingstoke, 1990, p. 200). For a few years now, Bassam Tibi has been one of the authors who serve certain writers as a warrant for their Islamophobia.

37. Batatu, *Old Social Classes*, p. 731.

38. Michel 'Aflaq, 'Fi al-Qawmiyya al-'Arabiyya', in *Fī Sabīl al-Ba'ath*, 4th edn, Beirut, 1970, p. 123.

39. 'Aflaq, 'Bayna Ishtirākiyyatuna wa al-Shuyū'iyya wa al-Ishtirākiyya al-Wataniyya', in *Fi Sabīl al-Ba'ath*, 1st edn, Beirut, 1959, pp. 99–100. This article was not reprinted in the 1970 4th edn, in which anti-Communism is attenuated thanks to Aflaq's rapprochement with the Communists.

40. Nordbruch, *Nazism in Syria and Lebanon*, p. 120. Götz Nordbruch's book depicts the dominant political and intellectual currents in Syria and Lebanon at the time of Nazism. Although it is more nuanced than Stefan Wild's article, the image that emerges from it is one in which nationalist currents and Nazism's ideological influence on them are overrated at the expense of liberal or Marxist anti-Nazi currents. The 1944 pamphlet is a series of lectures given by Aflaq and Bītār in the early 1940s, and collected under the title: *Al-Qawmiyya al-'Arabiyya wa Mawqifuha min al-Shuyū'iyya*. The lectures are reprinted in Dhūqān Qarqūt, *Michel 'Aflaq: Al-Kitābāt al-Ūla*, Beirut, 1993, pp. 139–70.

41. Qarqūt, *Michel 'Aflaq*, p. 146.

42. Ibid., p. 170.

43. The text of the 'red book', *Kitāb al-Qawmiyya al-'Arabiyya* (an undated pamphlet probably published in 1935), is reprinted in full in Aziz Al-Azmeh, *Qustantīn Zurayq: 'Arabiyyun lil-Qarn al-'Ishrīn*, Beirut, 2003, pp. 120–35. Azmeh is exaggerating somewhat when he attributes to the influence of Nazism features common to several nineteenth-century European nationalisms (pp. 52–3). Whereas one key distinctive feature of Hitler's

brand of nationalism is its racism, the 'red book' explicitly excludes racism (p. 121), as well as anything that might divide an Arab nation defined in traditional fashion in terms of territory, language, culture, history and common aspirations (p. 120).

44. Lewis, *Semites and Anti-Semites*; the passage on the Baath inspired by Wild may be found on pp. 147–8.

45. Ralph Coury, 'The Demonisation of Pan-Arab Nationalism', *Race and Class*, vol. 46, no. 4 (2005), pp. 1–19.

46. A Dec. 2008 Google search for the words 'Sami Jundi Nazism' turned up nearly 700 pages on the internet; most of them reproduced the same vulgate, ascribing it, as a rule, to Lewis.

47. Basheer Nafi, *Arabism, Islamism and the Palestine Question, 1908–1941: A Political History*, Reading, 1998, p. 358.

48. Sayyid, *Hizb al-Ba'th al-'Arabi*, p. 205.

49. *Nidāl al-Ba'th*, vol. 1, *1943–1949*, Beirut, 1963, p. 175.

50. Sayyid, *Hizb al-Ba'th al-'Arabi*, pp. 45–50.

51. Nafi, *Arabism, Islamism and the Palestine Question*, p. 389, n. 125.

52. *Nidāl al-Ba'th*, p. 169.

53. Ibid., pp. 173–4.

54. Wildangel, *Zwischen Achse und Mandatsmacht*, pp. 40–1.

55. 'Aflaq, 'Lā Yantaziranna al-'Arab Zuhūr al-Mu'jiza', in *Fi Sabīl al-Ba'ath*, 4th edn, pp. 331–2.

56. *Al-Ba'th wa al-Qadiyya al-Filastīniyya: Bayānāt wa Mawāqif 1945–1965*, Beirut, 1975, pp. 7–56.

57. Ibid., pp. 44–9; also in *Nidāl al-Ba'th*, pp. 229–33. Bītār's signature appears only in the latter document.

58. Antūn Sa'āda (Antun Saadeh), *Nushū' al-Umam*. The whole of this text is available in Arabic on the SSNP website (www.ssnp.org/new/library/saadeh/nisho2_oumam/index.htm).

59. Seale, *Struggle for Syria*, ch. 8, 'Antun Sa'ada and his Party', p. 67.

60. Deutsches Generalkonsulat, 'Politischer Bericht. Inhalt: Aufdeckung einer umstürzlerischen Bewegung', Beirut, 22 Nov. 1935 (L327547-L327549) – facsimile reproduction in Jean Dāyih, *Sa'āda wa al-Nāziyya: Wathā'iq al-Khārijiyya al-Almāniyya*, n.pl. (probably Beirut), 1994, p. 52. The author of this apologetic work, himself a member of the SSNP, is bent on refuting the accusation of Nazism traditionally levelled against his party, but the document that he reproduces as his main exhibit tends rather to confirm the accusation.

61. Saghieh, *Qawmiyyū al-Mashriq al-'Arabi*, esp. pp. 195–249.

62. Ibid., p. 243.

63. Deutsches Generalkonsulat, 'Politischer Bericht', in Dāyih, *Sa'āda wa al-Nāziyya*, pp. 52–3.

64. Saadeh, cited ibid., p. 22. For a recent attempt to downplay the SSNP's fascist character by treating it as 'symbolic' and structural, see Christoph Schumann, 'Symbolische Aneignungen: Antūn Sa'ādas Radikalnationalismus in der Epoche des Faschismus', in Höpp *et al.*, eds, *Blind für die Geschichte?*, pp. 155–89. This less than convincing essay, which makes a selective utilization of the sources, is based on the judgements of a few former members of the party, who are not particularly inclined to damn their own past.

65. On 'clerical fascism', see Matthew Feldman and Marius Turda, eds, '"Clerical Fascism"

in Interwar Europe', special issue of *Totalitarian Movements and Political Religions*, vol. 8, no. 2 (2007).

66. See Zittrain Eisenberg, *My Enemy's Enemy*, pp. 126, 134.
67. Ibid., p. 83.
68. Ibid., pp. 136–8.
69. See Benny Morris, 'Israel and the Lebanese Phalange: The Birth of a Relationship, 1948–1951', *Journal of Israeli History*, vol. 5, no. 1 (1984), pp. 125–44.
70. See Alain Ménargues, *Les Secrets de la guerre du Liban: Du coup d'état de Béchir Gémayel aux massacres des camps palestiniens*, Paris, 2004.
71. See Jankowski, *Egypt's Young Rebels: 'Young Egypt,' 1933–1952*, Stanford, CA, 1975. (Like other authors, Jankowski transcribes the name of the organization as *Misr al-Fatāh* after its Egyptian colloquial pronunciation, instead of *Misr al-Fatāt*.) See also 'Ali Shalabi, *Misr al-Fatāt wa Dawruha fi al-Siyāsa al-Misriyya 1933–1941*, Cairo, 1982, the most detailed work on Ahmad Hussein's movement.
72. On the structure of 'Young Egypt', see Jankowski, *Egypt's Young Rebels*, pp. 14–17.
73. Ibid., pp. 39–41.
74. Ibid., p. 106.
75. Wolfgang Schwanitz, 'The German Middle Eastern Policy, 1871–1945', in Schwanitz, ed., *Germany and the Middle East, 1871–1945*, Princeton, NJ, 2004, p. 11. See also Lukasz Hirszowicz, *The Third Reich and the Arab East*, London, 1966, pp. 39–42.
76. Jankowski, *Egypt's Young Rebels*, pp. 20–1. Shalabi, *Misr al-Fatāt*, p. 437.
77. Ibid., p. 438.
78. Ibid., pp. 436–44.
79. Ibid., pp. 444–8.
80. Jankowski, *Egypt's Young Rebels*, p. 59.
81. Shalabi, *Misr al-Fatāt*, pp. 444–5.
82. See Ahmad Hussein's July 1938 open letter to Adolf Hitler, a long extract from which has been translated from the original Arabic text found in archives of the German Ministry of Foreign Affairs (Deutsches Auswartiges Amt, Akten betreffend Arabien, Pol. VII, 26, vol. 1, 293) by Stefan Wild, 'National Socialism in the Arab Near East', pp. 134–5.
83. Jankowski, *Egypt's Young Rebels*, pp. 112–13.
84. P. J. Vatikiotis, *Nasser and his Generation*, London, 1978, esp. ch. 3, 'The Young Egypt Society', pp. 67–84.
85. Rif'at al-Sa'īd, *Ahmad Husayn: Kalimāt wa Mawāqif*, Cairo, 1979.
86. Ibid., pp. 19–24.
87. Shalabi, *Misr al-Fatāt*, p. 446.
88. Ibid., pp. 453–4.
89. Jankowski, *Egypt's Young Rebels*, p. 39.
90. Khoury, *Syria and the French Mandate*, p. 447.
91. Resolution of 2 Dec. 1945, in Khalil, ed., *Arab States and Arab League*, p. 161.
92. Sa'īd, *Al-Yasār al-Misri wa al-Qadiyya al-Filastīniyya*, p. 43.
93. Jankowski, *Egypt's Young Rebels*, p. 91.
94. Soliman, *Pour une histoire profane de la Palestine*, p. 65.
95. Ibid., p. 66.
96. See Nasser's 1957 testimony before the Egyptian parliament, cited in Vatikiotis, *Nasser and his Generation*, p. 44, n. 30 (cited again on p. 60). See also David Wynne-Morgan, 'My Revolutionary Life: President Nasser's Own Story' (interviews with Nasser), *Sunday Times*, 17 June 1962, cited in Anouar Abdel-Malek, *Egypt: Military Society: The Army*

Regime, the Left, and Social Change under Nasser, New York, 1968, p. 418, n. 19, and Jankowski, *Egypt's Young Rebels,* p. 121.

97. Vatikiotis, *Nasser and his Generation,* p. 41.

98. Ibid., p. 60.

99. Ibid., p. 62.

100. Ibid., p. 82.

101. P. J. Vatikiotis, *The Egyptian Army in Politics: Pattern for New Nations?,* Bloomington, IN, 1961, p. 68.

102. Vatikiotis, *Nasser and his Generation,* p. 60.

103. Ibid., p. 78.

104. Anwar al-Sadāt, *Safaḥāt Majhūla,* Cairo, 1954, quoted here from the electronic edn (www.anwarsadat.org/book_info.asp?categorytemp=29&article_id=321&category_id=122). Eng. adaptation by Thomas Graham: Anwar El Sadat, *Revolt on the Nile,* London, 1957. Vatikiotis errs in describing the latter book as a translation of *Qissat al-Thawra Kāmilatan,* a work that Sadat published in 1956 (*The Egyptian Army in Politics,* p. 51). Vatikiotis repeats his mistake in *Nasser and his Generation,* p. 64, n. 10.

105. Anwar El Sadat, *In Search of Identity,* New York, 1977, p. 59.

106. Sadat, *Revolt on the Nile,* p. v.

107. Lewis, *Semites and Anti-Semites,* p. 159.

108. Ibid., pp. 158–9.

109. Sadat, *Revolt on the Nile,* pp. 34–5.

110. Soliman, *Pour une histoire profane de la Palestine,* pp. 67–8.

111. Sadāt, *Safaḥāt majhūla,* pp. 50–2.

112. Ibid., pp. 25–6.

113. Ibid., p. 26.

114. Wild, 'National Socialism in the Arab Near East', p. 136.

115. On the Iraqi Futuwwa, see, among other sources, Reeva Simon, *Iraq between the Two World Wars: The Creation and Implementation of a Nationalist Ideology,* New York, 1986, pp. 110–14, and Peter Wien, *Iraqi Arab Nationalism: Authoritarian, Totalitarian, and Pro-Fascist Inclinations, 1932–1941,* London: Routledge, 2006, pp. 88–112.

116. Foreign Office Document cited by Simon, *Iraq between the Two World Wars,* p. 113.

117. *Mudhakkirāt Akram al-Ḥūrāni,* vol. 1, Cairo, 2000, p. 156. On the 'ironshirts', see Khoury, *Syria and the French Mandate,* pp. 473–6. Ḥūrāni's gloss provides a welcome corrective to Nadav Safran, *Egypt in Search of Political Community,* p. 192, which comes perilously close to putting the Wafd's 'blueshirts' and Young Egypt's 'greenshirts' on the same level.

118. Wien, *Iraqi Arab Nationalism,* pp. 113–14.

119. See Hayyim Cohen, 'The Anti-Jewish *Farhūd* in Baghdad, 1941', *Middle Eastern Studies,* vol. 3, no. 1 (1966), p. 7.

120. Wien, *Iraqi Arab Nationalism,* pp. 109–12.

121. Simon, *Iraq between the Two World Wars,* pp. 154–60.

122. On the Al-Muthanna Club, see Wien, *Iraqi Arab Nationalism,* pp. 32–3, and Batatu, *Old Social Classes,* pp. 297–300.

123. Ja'far 'Abbās Hamīdi, *Min Wathā'iq al-Nawādi al-Qawmiyya fi al-'Irāq: Al-Muthanna bin Hāritha al-Shaibāni wa al-Ba'th al-'Arabi,* Baghdad, 1998.

124. Ibid., pp. 34–5.

125. Ibid., pp. 37–8.

126. Ibid., pp. 80–90.

127. Ibid., p. 90.

128. See Hirszowicz, *The Third Reich and the Arab East*, ch. 13, 'The Arab Legion and Mufti-Kilani Dispute', pp. 250–68. See also the report by Fawzi al-Qāwuqji, the most eminent of the Arab leaders, after the Mufti and Gaylāni, who found refuge in Berlin, in Khayriyyah Qāsimiyyah, ed., *Filastīn fī Mudhakkirāt al-Qāwuqji 1936–1948*, Beirut, 1975, pp. 96–114, and, further, Qāwuqji's long 7 Feb. 1942 letter to 'Ādil al-'Azmeh on the relations between the Mufti and Gaylāni in Qāsimiyyah, *Al-Ra'īl al-'Arabi al-Awwal: Hayāt wa Awrāq Nabīh wa 'Ādil al-'Azmeh*, London, 1991, pp. 429–32.
129. George Lenczowski, *The Middle East in World Affairs*, 4th edn, Ithaca, NY, 1980, p. 692.
130. Salāh-ud-Dīn al-Sabbāgh, *Fursān al-'Urūba: Mudhakkirāt al-'Aqīd al-Rukn Salāh-ud-Dīn al-Sabbāgh*, Rabat, 1994, p. 76.
131. Ibid., pp. 130–1.
132. Majid Khadduri, *Independent Iraq, 1932–1958: A Study in Iraqi Politics*, 2nd edn, London, 1960.
133. Ibid., pp. 214–17.
134. Ibid., p. 219.
135. Ibid., p. 229. See also Hirszowicz, *The Third Reich and the Arab East*, p. 106.
136. Sabbāgh, *Fursān al-'Urūba*, pp. 76–7.
137. Wild, 'National Socialism in the Arab Near East', p. 153.
138. Batatu, *Old Social Classes*, pp. 457–8.
139. Ibid., p. 459.
140. Ibid., p. 461.
141. The letter is here cited from Batatu's nearly complete translation, ibid., pp. 453–5.
142. Khoury, *Syria and the French Mandate*, p. 590.
143. Majid Khadduri, 'General Nuri's Flirtation with the Axis Powers', *Middle East Journal*, vol. 16, no. 3 (summer 1962), pp. 328–36.
144. Hirszowicz, *The Third Reich and the Arab East*, p. 308.
145. Qāsimiyyah, ed., *Filastīn fī Mudhakkirāt al-Qāwuqji 1936–1948*, p. 97 and n. 1.
146. Qāsimiyyah, *Al-Ra'īl al-'Arabi al-Awwal*, p. 424 (draft).
147. Ibid., pp. 438–9 (draft).
148. Ibid.
149. Ibid., pp. 441–2 (draft).
150. Ibid., p. 443 (draft).
151. Ibid.
152. Baruch Kimmerling and Joel Migdal, *The Palestinian People: A History*, Cambridge, MA, 2003, pp. 106–7.
153. Zu'aytir, *Yawmiyyāt Akram Zu'aytir*, p. 369.
154. Kedourie, 'The Break between Muslims and Jews in Iraq', in Mark Cohen and Abraham Udovitch, eds, *Jews among Arabs: Contacts and Boundaries*, Princeton, NJ, 1989, p. 30.
155. Ibid.
156. Zu'aytir, *Yawmiyyāt Akram Zu'aytir*, pp. 418–19.
157. Ibid., p. 597. Kedourie cites this passage in 'Break between Muslims and Jews', p. 29.
158. Zu'aytir, *Yawmiyyāt Akram Zu'aytir*, p. 597.
159. Wild, 'National Socialism in the Arab Near East', p. 137.
160. Sylvia Haim, 'Arabic Antisemitic Literature: Some Preliminary Notes', *Jewish Social Studies*, no. 17 (1955), p. 311.
161. Sylvia Haim, 'Islam and the Theory of Arab Nationalism', *Die Welt des Islams*, vol. 4, no. 2/3 (1955), pp. 133–4.

162. Wein, *Iraqi Arab Nationalism*, pp. 84–8.

163. Ibid., p. 115.

164. Ibid., pp. 44, 110.

165. Ibid., p. 51. Abraham Elkabir's typescript is held at the Babylonian Jewry Heritage Center in Or-Yehuda, Israel.

166. Kedourie, 'The Sack of Basra and the *Farhud* in Baghdad', in Kedourie, *Arab Political Memoirs*, p. 307.

167. Esther Meir-Glitzenstein, *Zionism in an Arab Country: Jews in Iraq in the 1940s*, London, 2004, pp. 18–19.

168. Cohen, 'Anti-Jewish *Farhūd* in Baghdad, 1941', p. 2.

169. Ibid., pp. 12–13.

170. Zvi Yehuda, 'Those Responsible for the *Farhud*: Lecture given by Dr. Zvi Yehuda on June 4, 06 at the Babylonian Heritage Center in Or-Yehuda during the Memorial Evening of the 129 Jewish Victims of the Farhud (The Pogrom of 1941 in Iraq)', www.sephardiccouncil.org/farhud06.pdf [accessed in 2008, link broken].

171. Wein, *Iraqi Arab Nationalism*, p. 138, n. 219.

172. Ibid., p. 108.

173. Esther Meir-Glitzenstein, 'The Farhud', *Holocaust Encyclopedia*, United States Holocaust Memorial Museum (my emphasis), www.ushmm.org/wlc/article.php?lang=en&ModuleId=10007277

174. The official figure was in fact '110 Jews and Muslims', to judge by the text of the report translated and published by Norman Stillman: 'The Report of the Iraqi Commission of Enquiry on the Farhūd (1941)', in Stillman, *The Jews of Arab Lands in Modern Times*, Philadelphia, 1991, p. 410.

175. Kedourie, 'Sack of Basra', p. 298.

176. Lewis, *Semites and Anti-Semites*, p. 158.

177. See Wien, *Iraqi Arab Nationalism*, p. 108.

178. Hayim Habousha, 'The Farhud' (New York: Midrash Ben Ish Hai), www.midrash.org/articles/farhud/

179. Nissim Rejwan, *The Jews of Iraq: 3000 Years of History and Culture*, London, 1985, pp. 223–4.

180. Robert Satloff, *Among the Righteous: Lost Stories from the Holocaust's Long Reach into Arab Land*, New York, 2006, p. 99.

181. Abitbol, *Jews of North Africa*, p. 139.

182. Stillman, *Jews of Arab Lands*, p. 113.

183. Ibid., p. 127.

184. Satloff, *Among the Righteous*, p. 191.

185. According to Meir-Glitzenstein, *Zionism in an Arab Country*, p. 5.

186. See Kedourie, 'Break between Muslims and Jews', pp. 45–59. On Nūri al-Saʿīd's anti-Semitic campaign, see also Shlomo Hillel, *Operation Babylon: Jewish Clandestine Activity in the Middle East 1946–51*, London, 1988, pp. 210–22. Finally, there is the interesting account by Naeim Giladi on all these events and, especially, the role of the British: 'The Jews of Iraq', *The Link*, vol. 31, no. 2 (April–May 1998), pp. 1–13 (www.ameu.org/uploads/vol31_issue2_1998.pdf).

Chapter 4: Reactionary and/or Fundamentalist Pan-Islamists

1. A good starting point for those seeking information on this period is Albert Hourani's classic work, reprinted several times since it first appeared in 1962, *Arabic Thought in the Liberal Age, 1798–1939*, Cambridge, 1983. On Hourani's book, see Donald Reid,

'Arabic Thought in the Liberal Age Twenty Years After', *International Journal of Middle East Studies*, vol. 14, no. 4 (Nov. 1982), pp. 541–57.

2. Elie Kedourie, *Afghani and 'Abduh: An Essay on Religious Unbelief and Political Activism in Modern Islam*, London, 1997.

3. On Afghani, the standard work is the voluminous biography by Nikki Keddie, *Sayyid Jamal ad-Din 'al-Afghani': A Political Biography*, Berkeley, CA, 1972.

4. On Pan-Islamism, see Jacob Landau, *The Politics of Pan-Islam: Ideology and Organization*, Oxford, 1994.

5. On the new Islamic 'orthodoxy', see the interesting reflections by Olivier Carré, *L'Islam laïque ou le retour à la Grande Tradition*, Paris, 1993.

6. On Rida and his turn toward fundamentalism, see Safran, *Egypt in Search of Political Community*, pp. 75–84, and Al-Sayyid Yūsuf, *Rashīd Rida wa al-'Awda ila Manhaj al-Salaf*, Cairo, 2000. For a summary of Rida's ideas and their intellectual context, see the classic work by Hamid Enayat, *Modern Islamic Political Thought: The Response of the Shī'ī and Sunnī Muslims to the Twentieth Century*, London, 2005.

7. Walicki, *Slavophile Controversy*, p. 454.

8. Muhammad Rashīd Ridā, 'Fātihat al-Mujallad al-Sābi' wa al-'Ishrūn', *Al-Manār*, vol. 27, no. 1 (13 April 1926), pp. 1–2.

9. On the concept of the 'Islamic state', see Enayat, *Modern Islamic Political Thought*, pp. 69–110.

10. See Richard Mitchell, *The Society of the Muslim Brothers*, New York, 1993, p. 186.

11. Ibid., p. 322 and nn. 73 and 74. On the relationship between the Brotherhood and Rashid Rida's legacy, see Safran, *Egypt in Search of Political Community*, pp. 231–2.

12. Ridā, 'Fātihat al-Mujallad al-Sābi'wa al-'Ishrūn', p. 2.

13. I have explained my view of the Saudi kingdom's role and its relations with the United States in *The Clash of Barbarisms: The Making of the New World Disorder*, 2nd edn, London and Boulder, CO, 2006.

14. Landau, *Politics of Pan-Islam*, p. 238.

15. See the succinct balance-sheet drawn up by Rida in his report to the last Islamic conference held in Jerusalem, in 1931, in Rídā, 'Al-Mu'tamar al-Islāmi al-'Ām fi Bayt al-Maqdis', *Al-Manār*, vol. 32, no. 2 (Feb. 1932), p. 116.

16. Ridā, 'Al-Za'īmān Shaukat 'Ali wa Muhammad 'Ali', *Al-Manār*, vol. 27, no. 7 (17 Oct. 1926), pp. 548–55.

17. On this subject see Abdelwahab Meddeb, *The Malady of Islam*, Cambridge, 2003.

18. Norman Stillman, 'Yahūd', in Peri Bearman *et al.*, eds, *Encyclopaedia of Islam*, Leiden, 2002– , vol. 11, p. 239.

19. Ibid.

20. Bernard Lewis, *The Jews of Islam*, Princeton, NJ, 1984, p. 85. For a comparison of the situation of the Jews in Christian Europe and the Muslim countries in the Middle Ages, see Mark Cohen, *Under Crescent and Cross: The Jews in the Middle Ages*, Princeton, NJ, 1996.

21. Lewis, *Jews of Islam*, pp. 170–1.

22. Ibid., p. 183.

23. Stillman, *Jews of Arab Lands*.

24. Lewis, *Semites and Anti-Semites*, p. 259.

25. Haim, 'Arabic Antisemitic Literature', p. 309.

26. See Neville Mandel, *The Arabs and Zionism before World War I* (Berkeley, CA, 1976, pp. 45–7.

27. Ibid., pp. 153–4.

28. Haim, 'Arabic Antisemitic Literature', p. 310, n. 12.

29. Mandel, *Arabs and Zionism*, pp. 193, 204.

30. Ibid., pp. 213–14.

31. Saghieh, *Qawmiyyū al-Mashriq al-'Arabi*, pp. 17–19.

32. Enayat, *Modern Islamic Political Thought*, p. 42.

33. Ridā, 'Fātihat al-Mujallad al-Sābi' wa al-'Ishrūn'.

34. See Ridā, 'Di'āyat al-Rafd wa al-Khurāfāt wa al-Tafrīq bayn al-Muslimīn', *Al-Manār*, vol. 29, no. 6 (14 Oct. 1928), pp. 424–32.

35. See Ridā, 'Al-Munāzara bayn Ahl al-Sunna wa al-Shī'a', *Al-Manār*, vol. 32, no. 2 (Feb. 1932), pp. 145–60.

36. Ridā, 'Fath al-Yahūd li Bāb al-Fitna fī al-Quds', *Al-Manār*, vol. 29, no. 6 (14 Oct. 1928), pp. 414–24.

37. On this question, see Mandel, *Arabs and Zionism*, p. 188.

38. Ridā, 'Thawrat Filastīn: Asbābuha wa Natā'ijuha', part 1, *Al-Manār*, vol. 30, no. 5 (1 Nov. 1929), pp. 391–2.

39. Ibid., p. 392.

40. Ibid.

41. See É. Conan, 'Les Secrets d'une manipulation antisémite', *L'Express* (16 Nov. 1999); www.phdn.org/antisem/protocoles/origines.html

42. Stillman, *Jews of Arab Lands*, pp. 104–5.

43. Stillman has published these documents in Eng. tr., ibid., pp. 351–2.

44. Daphne Tsimhoni, 'The Arab Christians and the Palestinian Arab National Movement during the Formative Stage', in Gabriel Ben-Dor, ed., *The Palestinians and the Middle East Conflict*, Ramat Gan, Israel, 1978, p. 79.

45. Lewis, *Semites and Anti-Semites*, p. 199.

46. Wild, 'Die arabische Rezeption der "Protokolle der Weisen von Zion"', in Rainer Brunner *et al.*, eds, *Islamstudien ohne Ende: Festschrift für Werner Ende zum 65. Geburtstag*, Würzburg, 2002, p. 519.

47. Gudrun Krämer takes up Wild's mistaken affirmation, but is careful to attribute it to him in its entirety, while rightly criticizing him for his arbitrary hypothesis about the circulation of the *Protocols*. See 'Anti-Semitism in the Muslim World: A Critical Review', *Die Welt des Islams*, vol. 46, no. 3 (2006), p. 257.

48. Ridā, 'Thawrat Filastīn: Asbābuha wa Natā'ijuha'. The resume and the citations that follow refer to part 1, already cited.

49. See the article by the Turkish Freemason Celil Layiktez, 'The History of Freemasonry in Turkey', 9 April 2001, www.freemasons-freemasonry.com/layiktez.html

50. Ridā, 'Thawrat Filastīn: Asbābuha wa Natā'ijuha', part 2, *Al-Manār*, vol. 30, no. 6 (1 Dec. 1929), pp. 450–68. The resume and citations that follow correspond to part 2.

51. Gustave Le Bon, *The World of Islamic Civilization*, New York, 1974. The French original was published in 1884 under the title *La Civilisation des Arabes*.

52. Ridā, 'Fatāwa al-Manār', *Al-Manār*, vol. 33, no. 4 (June 1933), pp. 273–5.

53. Ridā, 'Fatāwa al-Manār', *Al-Manār*, vol. 33, no. 5 (Sept. 1933), pp. 347–51.

54. *Al-Manār*, vol. 34, no. 1 (May 1934), pp. 73–5 and 76–8. Another report on the same subject had been published a few months previously in *Al-Manār*, vol. 33, no. 9 (28 Feb. 1934), pp. 692–6.

55. *Al-Manār*, vol. 34, no. 1 (May 1934), p. 78.

56. Ridā, 'Indhār wa Istitāba. Wayl lil-'Arab min Sharr qad Iqtarab', *Al-Manār*, vol. 34, no. 8 (5 March 1935), p. 606. The general message of this text is also endlessly repeated in

Rashid Rida's speech before the Muslim Young Men's Association, printed after it: 'Muhādarati fi Jam'iyyat al-Shubbān al-Muslimīn', pp. 607–11.

57. See e.g. Ridā, 'Al-Mu'tamar al-Islāmi al-'Ām', p. 131.

58. Ridā, 'Al-Shiqāq bayn al-'Arab al-Muslimīn', *Al-Manār*, vol. 34, no. 10 (3 May 1935), pp. 782–6.

59. On Shakib Arslan, see William Cleveland's remarkable political biography, *Islam Against the West: Shakib Arslan and the Campaign for Islamic Nationalism,* Austin, TX, and London, 1985; see also Martin Kramer's critique of this book in *Middle Eastern Studies*, vol. 23, no. 4 (1987), pp. 529–33. See further Ahmad al-Sharabāsi's 2-vol. work, focused on Arslan's literary output and including his letters to Rashid Ridā, *Amīr al-Bayān Shakīb Arslān,* Cairo, 1963, as well as Zāhir Al-Hasnāwi, *Shakīb Arslān: Al-Dawr al-Siyāsi al-Khafi,* Beirut, 2002.

60. Sharabāsi cites Arslan's Sunni wife, who affirms that her husband prayed, fasted and went on a pilgrimage to Mecca like all Muslims: *Amīr al-Bayān Shakīb Arslān,* vol. 1, p. 74.

61. Ibid., vol. 2, p. 832.

62. Cleveland, *Islam against the West*, pp. 128–30.

63. Ibid., p. 65.

64. Ibid., p. 74.

65. Khayriyyah Qāsimiyyah, ed., *Mudhakkirāt Fawzi al-Qāwuqji, 1914–1932*, vol. 1, Beirut, 1975, pp. 120–1.

66. Ibid., pp. 138–9.

67. On Arslan's relations with Italy, ibid., pp. 145–9, and Hasnāwi, *Shakīb Arslān,* pp. 159–75.

68. See Claudio Segré, 'Liberal and Fascist Italy in the Middle East, 1919–1939: The Elusive White Stallion', in Dann, ed., *Great Powers in Middle East,* p. 207.

69. An Eng. tr. of the letter has been published in Esco Foundation for Palestine, *Palestine: A Study of Jewish, Arab, and British Policies,* vol. 2, New Haven, CT, 1947, pp. 774–5.

70. Hasnāwi, *Shakīb Arslān,* p. 173.

71. Cleveland, *Islam against the West*, pp. 149–54.

72. Francis Nicosia, *The Third Reich and the Palestine Question,* 2nd edn, New Brunswick, NJ, 2000, pp. 88–9.

73. Wild cites passages from this article in 'National Socialism in the Arab Near East', pp. 141–2.

74. Cleveland, *Islam against the West*, p. 144.

75. Ibid., p. 201, n. 26.

76. Ibid., p. 144.

77. Nafi, *Arabism, Islamism and the Palestine Question*, p. 365.

78. Cleveland, *Islam against the West*, pp. 155–6.

79. Ibid., p. 143.

80. Wild, 'National Socialism in the Arab Near East', pp. 163–9.

81. Hirszowicz, *The Third Reich and the Arab East,* p. 130; Cleveland, *Islam against the West,* p. 156.

82. Ibid., p. 157.

83. Daniel Guérin, *Au service des colonisés 1930–1953,* Paris, 1954, p. 20.

84. On this subject in its relation to Islam, see my essay 'Orientalism in Reverse', *Radical Philosophy,* 151 (Sept./Oct. 2008), pp. 20–30.

85. Cleveland, *Islam against the West,* p. 138.

86. On Bourguiba's relations with Berlin and Rome, see Hirszowicz, *The Third Reich and the Arab East*, pp. 290–8.

87. Gerhard Höpp, ed., *Mufti-Papiere: Briefe, Memoranden, Redden und Aufrufe Amīn al-Husainīs aus dem Exil, 1940–1945*, Berlin, 2004, p. 219.

88. Philip Mattar, *The Mufti of Jerusalem: Al-Hajj Amīn al-Husaynī and the Palestinian National Movement*, rev. edn, New York, 1992, p. 107.

89. Yehoshua Porath, *The Palestinian Arab National Movement, 1929–1939: From Riots to Rebellion*, London, 1977, p. 214. On King Abdul-Aziz's role, see esp. pp. 204–25.

90. For the Arabic text of the telegram, see Nuwayhid al-Hūt, ed., *Wathā'iq al-Haraka al-Wataniyya*, doc. 267, p. 461.

91. Lenczowski, *Middle East in World Affairs*, pp. 578–9. On the Saudi stance during the Second World War, see also Esco Foundation for Palestine, *Palestine: A Study of Jewish, Arab, and British Policies*, pp. 961–70.

92. See Hirszowicz, *The Third Reich and the Arab East*, pp. 14–15, 47–61, 68–9; Uwe Pfullmann, 'German-Saudi Relations and their Actors on the Arabian Peninsula, 1924–1939', in Schwanitz, ed., *Germany and the Middle East*, pp. 144–6; and Michael Wolffsohn, 'The German–Saudi Arabian Arms Deal of 1936–1939 Reconsidered', in Dann, ed., *The Great Powers in the Middle East*, pp. 283–300.

93. Hirszowicz, *The Third Reich and the Arab East*, p. 580.

94. Ibid., p. 260n.

95. Memorandum of 20 June 1939, in *German Foreign Policy 1918–1945*, Series D (1937–1945), vol. 6, *The Last Months of Peace, March–August 1939*, London, 1956, p. 743. This 'line of thought' seems to have found increasing favour with the Nazi hierarchy. In his memoirs, Amin al-Husseini reports a remark that Heinrich Himmler, the head of the SS and the Gestapo, is supposed to have made to him during the Mufti's Berlin exile: 'Like all the rest of Europe, we had two opportunities to escape these massacres [the wars of religion, especially the Thirty Years' War – the Mufti erroneously writes 'The Hundred Years' War'], but we frittered both of them away. The first opportunity was provided by the Arabs' advance in the West (from Andalusia), and the second, by the Ottomans' advance in the East. It is unfortunate that the German people did more than any other to fend off these two advances, thus depriving Europe of the intellectual enlightenment and the flourishing culture of Islam.' ('Abdul-Karīm al-'Umar, ed., *Mudhakkirāt al-Hāj Amīn al-Husayni*, Damascus, 1999, p. 126.)

96. I have attempted to explain this in *The Clash of Barbarisms*, pp. 45–6.

97. On Roosevelt's meeting with Abdul-Aziz, see Thomas Lippman, 'The Day FDR Met Saudi Arabia's Ibn Saud', *The Link*, vol. 28, no. 2 (April–May 2005), pp. 2–12 (www.ameu.org/uploads/vol38_issue2_2005.pdf). Our main source on this subject is the report by Col. William Eddy, US plenipotentiary minister to the Saudi kingdom in 1944–1946, *F.D.R. Meets Ibn Saud* (1954), repr. Vista, 2005, www.ameu.org/uploads/FDR_IBNSAUD_2005.pdf

98. Ibid., p. 32.

99. Ibid., p. 33.

100. Montesquieu, *Mes Pensées*, Pensée 11, in idem, *Œuvres complètes,* Paris, 1964, p. 855. Eng. tr. in George Healy, 'Translator's Introduction' to Montesquieu, *The Persian Letters,* Indianapolis, IN, 1999, p. xix.

101. The best full-length biographies of Amin al-Husseini – those whose authors make a genuine attempt to be objective, although neither biography can be considered definitive – are Philip Mattar, *Mufti of Jerusalem*, and Zvi Elpeleg, *The Grand Mufti: Haj Amin al-Husaini, Founder of the Palestinian National Movement* (tr. from Hebrew),

London, 1993. These should be completed by the indispensable reference work on the Palestinian national movement under the British mandate, a book of more than 1000 pages: Bayān Nuwayhid al-Hūt, *Al-Qiyadāt wa al-Mu'assasāt al-Siyāsiyya fi Filastīn, 1917–1948,* Beirut, 1981. On the Mufti's relations with Nazism, see, besides the already cited works on German–Arab or German–Palestinian relations by Hirszowicz, Nicosia and 'Abdul-Ghani, 'Ali Muhāfaza, *Al-'Ilāqāt al-Almāniyya al-Filastīniyya, 1841–1945,* Beirut, 1981; Klaus Gensicke, *Der Mufti von Jerusalem, Amin el-Husseini, und die Nationalsozialisten,* Frankfurt, 1988; and Daniel Carpi, 'The Mufti of Jerusalem, Amin el-Husseini, and his Diplomatic Activity during World War II (October 1941–July 1943)', *Journal of Israeli History,* vol. 4, no. 1 (1983), pp. 101–31.

102. The standard work on the Islamic institutions of Palestine under British mandate is Uri Kupferschmidt, *The Supreme Muslim Council: Islam under the British Mandate for Palestine,* Leiden, 1987); on the status of the 'Grand Mufti', see esp. pp. 78–9.

103. Ibid., p. 20.

104. Ahmad al-Shuqayri, *Arba'ūn 'Āman fi al-Hayāt al-'Arabiyya wa al-Dawliyya,* Beirut, 1969, p. 142. Extracts from Shuqayri's memoirs have been translated and annotated by Kedourie, *Arab Political Memoirs,* pp. 188–92. On Mūsa Kāzim al-Husseini, see Hūt, *Al-Qiyadāt wa al-Mu'assasāt,* pp. 143–5.

105. On the Mufti's role as a force for moderation during the 1929 events, see Ilan Pappé, 'Haj Amin and the Buraq Revolt', *Jerusalem Quarterly File,* no. 18 (June 2003), pp. 6–16.

106. On the Jerusalem Conference, see Kupferschmidt, *Supreme Muslim Council,* pp. 187–220; Hūt, *Al-Qiyadāt wa al-Mu'assasāt,* pp. 243–9; and Thomas Mayer, 'Egypt and the General Islamic Conference of Jerusalem in 1931', *Middle Eastern Studies,* vol. 18, no. 3 (1982), pp. 311–22.

107. Ridā, 'Al-Mu'tamar al-Islāmi al-'Ām fi Bayt al-Maqdis'.

108. Hūt, *Al-Qiyadāt,* p. 249.

109. Ibid., p. 270; on Hizb al-Istiqlāl, see esp. pp. 263–78.

110. Ibid., p. 275.

111. Kupferschmidt, *Supreme Muslim Council,* pp. 48–52.

112. Kimmerling and Migdal, *Palestinian People,* p. 108.

113. Hūt, *Al-Qiyadāt,* pp. 702–3.

114. Ibid., pp. 664–5.

115. On 'Izz-ul-Dīn al-Qassām and the Qassāmists, see Muhsin Sālih, *Al-Tayyar al-Islāmi fi Filastīn wa Atharuhu fi Harakat al-Jihād 1917–1948,* Kuwait, 1988, and Abdullah Schleifer, 'The Life and Thought of 'Izz-id-Din al-Qassām', *Islamic Quarterly,* vol. 23, no. 2 (1980), pp. 61–81.

116. Ibid., p. 63.

117. In the abridged (and bowdlerized) version of Schleifer's article published under the title 'Izz al-Din al-Qassām: Preacher and *Mujahid*', in Edmund Burke, III, *Struggle and Survival in the Modern Middle East,* London, 1993, pp. 164–78, the coffin episode has been dropped. All that remains is the mention of Qassām's 'good humour' (p. 167).

118. Schleifer, 'Life and Thought of 'Izz-id-Din al-Qassām', p. 64.

119. Ibid., p. 73.

120. Sālih, *Al-Tayyar al-Islāmi fi Filastīn,* p. 304.

121. Porath, *Palestinian Arab National Movement,* p. 141.

122. See Farhad Khosrokhavar, *Inside Jihadism: Understanding Jihadi Movements Worldwide,* Boulder, CO, 2009.

123. Sālih, *Al-Tayyar al-Islāmi fi Filastīn,* p. 366.

124. Hūt, *Al-Qiyadāt,* p. 405.

125. Zu'aytir, *Yawmiyyāt Akram Zu'aytir*, p. 54.

126. Porath, *Palestinian Arab National Movement*, p. 162.

127. Ibid., pp. 262–3.

128. Hūt, *Al-Qiyadāt*, p. 405.

129. Kimmerling and Migdal, *Palestinian People*, p. 124.

130. Zu'aytir, *Yawmiyyāt Akram Zu'aytir*, p. 69.

131. The report of the Anglo-American Committee of Inquiry on Palestine in 1946 describes these factions as follows: 'On the one side stand two small but important parties: the Conservative Aliyah Hadashah (New Settlers), drawn chiefly from colonists of German and western European extraction, and Hashomer Hatzair, a socialist party which, while demanding the right of unrestricted immigration and land settlement, challenges the concept of the Jewish State and particularly emphasises the need for cooperation with the Arabs. Hashomer Hatzair, though it did not appear before us, published shortly before we left Jerusalem a striking pamphlet in support of bi-nationalism. Very close to Hashomer Hatzair, but without its socialist ideology, stands Dr. Magnes and his small Ihud group, whose importance is far greater than its numbers. Taken altogether, these Palestinian critics of the Biltmore Programme [the international Zionist conference that met in New York's Biltmore Hotel in May 1942, officially adopted, for the first time, the goal of a Jewish state ("Jewish Commonwealth") in Palestine] certainly do not exceed at the moment one-quarter of the Jewish population in Palestine. But they represent a constructive minority.' *Report of the Anglo-American Committee of Enquiry Regarding the Problems of European Jewry and Palestine*, Lausanne, 20 April 1946, London, 1946, pp. 26–7.

132. Adolf Hitler, *Mein Kampf*, vol. 2, ch. 14; Eng. tr. by James Murphy, London, 1939, www.greatwar.nl/books/meinkampf/meinkampf.pdf

133. Nicosia, *The Third Reich and the Palestine Question*, pp. 85–6. See also Gensicke, *Der Mufti von Jerusalem*, pp. 45–6.

134. Cited in 'Abdul-Ghani, *Almāniya al-Nāziyya wa Filastīn*, p. 202.

135. Cited in 'Abbāsi, *Al-'Ilāqāt al-Sahyūniyya al-Nāziyya*, p. 76.

136. Porath, *Palestinian Arab National Movement*, p. 194.

137. Ibid., p. 213.

138. Zu'aytir, *Yawmiyyāt Akram Zu'aytir*, p. 205.

139. Shuqayri, *Arba'ūn 'Āman*, p. 159.

140. Porath, *Palestinian Arab National Movement*, pp. 228–30.

141. Hirszowicz, *The Third Reich and the Arab East*, pp. 29–33. The anti-Semitic ideology of the Nazis promoted the contradictory notions that the Jews, being racially inferior, were incapable of building a viable state, on the one hand, and on the other, that any independent Jewish state in Palestine or elsewhere would be unacceptable because it would provide the 'world Jewry' with a power base from which to conduct their international conspiracy.

142. Ibid., p. 34.

143. 'The propaganda in the villages and towns to buy arms and to prepare for the resumption of violence was carried out by the *Qādis* and *Imāms*, and other dependents of the President of the SMC [Supreme Muslim Council], Istiqlalist leaders and rebel commanders, especially the Qassāmites. The latter enlisted volunteers and trained the villagers in the use of arms.' Porath, *Palestinian Arab National Movement*, pp. 233–4.

144. Louis Denisty, *Le Grand Mufti et le nationalisme palestinien: Haj Amin al-Hussayni, la France et la Grande-Bretagne face à la révolte arabe de 1936–1939*, Paris, 2006, p. 42.

145. Porath, *Palestinian Arab National Movement*, pp. 236–7.

146. Hūt, *Al-Qiyadāt*, p. 382.
147. Ibid., p. 397.
148. Cited ibid.
149. Zu'aytir, *Yawmiyyāt Akram Zu'aytir*, p. 596.
150. Porath, *Palestinian Arab National Movement*, pp. 290–1.
151. Ibid., pp. 291–2.
152. Mattar, *Mufti of Jerusalem*, p. 116.
153. Ibid., pp. 123–4.
154. Muhsin Sālih's *Al-Tayyār al-Islāmi fi Filastīn wa Atharuhu fi Harakat al-Jihād 1917-1948*, Maktabat al-Falāh, 1988.
155. See Kimmerling and Migdal, *Palestinian People*, p. 124.
156. 'Fetwà di Amin el-Husseini per la guerra santa del maggio', *Oriente Moderno*, 21 (Jan.–Dec. 1941), p. 552.
157. Khadduri, *Independent Iraq*, p. 224.
158. Hirszowicz, *The Third Reich and the Arab East*, pp. 252–3.
159. Ibid., p. 254.
160. Antonio J. Muñoz, *Lions of the Desert: Arab Volunteers in the German Army 1941–1945*, 2nd edn, New York, n.d., p. 28. Elsewhere, Munōz signs essays with the acronym USMC next to his name, indicating that he belonged or still belongs to the Marine Corps.
161. This was far too few, the Spanish author of the far-right Carlos Caballero Jurado complains, pointing to the contrast with the hundreds of thousands of soldiers from the Maghreb mobilized, he says, by Franco for his war against the Republicans: *La espada del Islam: Voluntarios árabes en la Wehrmacht*, 2nd edn, Granada, 1999, p. 209. The figure is a matter of debate among Spanish historians. According to Gustau Nerín, *La guerra que vino de África*, Barcelona, 2005, pp. 171–2, the most trustworthy estimates range from 62,000 to 87,000. Caballero consoles himself by supposing that, circumstances allowing, there would have been many more 'Arab volunteers' ready to fight against Communism. This is the same writer who makes the utterly preposterous claim that the 1941 German offensive against the USSR 'was enthusiastically hailed throughout the Arab world' (Jurada, *La espada del Islam*, p. 129).
162. Belkacem Recham, 'Les Militaires nord-africains pendant la Seconde Guerre mondiale', conference paper 2007: http://colloque-algerie.ens-lsh.fr/communication.php3?id_article=262. See also www.ldh-toulon.net/spip.php?article525
163. See Gerhard Höpp, 'In the Shadow of the Moon: Arab Inmates in Nazi Concentration Camps', in Schwanitz, ed., *Germany and the Middle East*, pp. 216–40, as well as the last product of Höpp's research, 'Der verdrängte Diskurs: Arabische Opfer des Nationalsozialismus', in Höpp *et al.*, eds, *Blind für die Geschichte?*, pp. 215–68. Höpp's work on the Arab victims of Nazism has been translated and published in Arabic under the title *Al-'Arab fi al-Mahraqa al-Nāziyya: Dahāya Mansiyyūn?*, Damascus, 2006. Let us note, in this connection, those other victims of Nazism, all too often forgotten: the Blacks. Hannah Arendt, as everyone knows, emphasizes that totalitarianism has its roots in the colonial experience. This line of descent is a very direct one in the case of Nazi Germany. See Firpo Carr, *Germany's Black Holocaust, 1890–1945*, Kearney, 2003. On forgotten victims from throughout the Third World, see also Rheinisches JournalistInnenbüro, '*Unsere Opfer zählen nicht': Die Dritte Welt im Zweiten Weltkrieg*, Hamburg, 2005.
164. Höpp, 'Der verdrängte Diskurs', p. 246.
165. On these people as well, see Höpp, 'Salud wa Salam: Araber im Spanischen Bürgerkrieg', *Inamo*, no. 33 (spring 2003), pp. 53–5.
166. Höpp, 'In the Shadow of the Moon', p. 216.

167. Höpp, *Mufti-Papiere*, p. 233.

168. Ibid., p. 235.

169. Stephen Schwartz, 'The Jews, the Serbs, and the Truth', *FrontPageMagazine.com*, 21 March 2005 (www.frontpagemag.com/Articles/Read.aspx?GUID=B7E86308-CEC1-4CCA-8D1A-655FF9563F2F). On the Handschar Division, see also Marko Attila Hoare, *The History of Bosnia: From the Middle Ages to the Present Day*, London, 2007, in particular ch. 5, 'The Bosnian Revolution, 1941–5', pp. 249–308.

170. 'Umar, ed., *Mudhakkirāt al-Hāj Amīn al-Husayni*, pp. 129–40. 'Abdul-Karīm al-'Umar, who had worked with Husseini, was in 1999 still styling himself as the 'Secretary of the Executive Bureau' of the Higher Arab Committee of Palestine, which, after the Mufti's death, was reorganized under his son's lead on a recommendation from Saudi King Faisal.

171. Ibid., pp. 140–1.

172. Ibid., p. 240.

173. Schwartz, 'Jews, Serbs, and Truth'.

174. 'Umar, *Mudhakkirāt al-Hāj Amīn al-Husayni*, p. 142. On the training centre in Dresden, see Titus Lenk, 'Die SS-Mullah-Schule und die Arbeitsgemeinschaft Turkestan in Dresden', 25 Nov. 2006, http://zukunft-braucht-erinnerung.de/zweiter-weltkrieg/ueberfall-auf-die-sowjetunion/611.html

175. 'Umar, *Mudhakkirāt al-Hāj Amīn al-Husayni*, p. 101.

176. Ibid., p. 118.

177. Höpp, *Mufti-Papiere*, pp. 107–12, 134–41 (original texts and translations).

178. 'Umar, *Mudhakkirāt al-Hāj Amīn al-Husayni*, pp. 119–20.

179. Ibid., p. 128.

180. Ibid., pp. 196–7.

181. Ibid., p. 197.

182. Ibid., p. 170.

183. Raul Hilberg, *The Destruction of the European Jews*, 3rd edn, vol. 3, New Haven, 2003, pp. 1301–21.

184. See www.ushmm.org/wlc/article.php?lang=en&ModuleId=10005161, for 'Jewish Population of Europe in 1933'.

185. 'Umar, *Mudhakkirāt al-Hāj Amīn al-Husayni*, pp. 126–7.

186. Ibid., pp. 127, 162.

187. Ibid., pp. 192–4.

188. Höpp, *Mufti-Papiere*, pp. 179–81.

189. Ibid., p. 182.

190. 'Umar, *Mudhakkirāt al-Hāj Amīn al-Husayni*, p. 195.

191. Ibid., p. 194.

192. Edgar Ansel Mowrer, 'Official Documents Convict Mufti of Complicity in 6,000,000 Murders', *New York Post*, 13 June 1946.

193. Maurice Pearlman, *Mufti of Jerusalem. The Story of Haj Amin El Husseini*, London, 1947, p. 74.

194. Höpp, *Mufti-Papiere*, p. 192.

195. 'Umar, *Mudhakkirāt al-Hāj Amīn al-Husayni*, p. 164.

196. Ibid., p. 165.

197. Anthony De Luca fails to note the inconsistency of the Mufti's explanations when he points out, rightly, that al-Husseini went far beyond mere opportunistic collaboration: see his '"Der Grossmufti" in Berlin: The Politics of Collaboration', *International Journal of Middle East Studies*, vol. 10, no. 1 (Feb. 1979), pp. 125–38.

198. Höpp, *Mufti-Papiere*, pp. 93–7.

199. See Conrad Black, *Franklin Delano Roosevelt: Champion of Freedom,* New York, 2003, p. 4.

200. Höpp, *Mufti-Papiere*, pp. 96–7.

201. Ibid., pp. 147–8.

202. Hirszowicz, *Third Reich*, pp. 263 and 315.

203. See, on this subject, the monumental work by Milan Hauner, *India in Axis Strategy: Germany, Japan, and Indian Nationalists in the Second World War,* Stuttgart, 1981. Hauner's book is an essential reference work for anyone working on the history of German–Arab relations under Nazism.

204. Höpp, *Mufti-Papiere*, pp. 192–3, 196–7.

205. Samāhat al-Sayyid Muhammad Amīn al-Husayni, *Haqā'iq 'an Qadiyyat Filastīn*, 2nd edn, Cairo, 1956, p. 28.

206. 'Umar, *Mudhakkirāt al-Hāj Amīn al-Husayni*, esp. pp. 155–70. Zvi Elpeleg's brief summary of Amin al-Husseini's anti-Semitic remarks (*Grand Mufti*, p. 71) – which cites the Hebrew tr. of the Mufti's memoirs rather than the Arabic original – gives a very faint idea of them.

207. 'Umar, *Mudhakkirāt al-Hāj Amīn al-Husayni*, p. 217.

208. Ibid., p. 161.

209. Qāsimiyyah, *Filastīn fi Mudhakkirāt al-Qāwuqji*, p. 129.

210. Hūt, *Al-Qiyadāt*, p. 479.

211. Ibid., pp. 460–2.

212. Ibid., p. 465.

213. The Mufti reproduces his letter to the Arab ministers in his memoirs: 'Umar, *Mudhakkirāt al-Hāj Amīn al-Husayni*, pp. 312–15.

214. Ad Hoc Committee on Palestine, Press Release, United Nations, New York, 18 Oct. 1947, http://domino.un.org/unispal.nsf/fd807e46661e3689852570d00069e918/ff89 4bc0a67066ad85256935006dc65f/$FILE/gapal21.pdf

215. Abu Iyad, with Eric Rouleau, *My Home, my Land: A Narrative of the Palestinian Struggle,* New York, 1981, p. 137.

216. Ibid., p. 214.

217. Arno Mayer, *Plowshares into Swords: From Zionism to Israel,* London, 2008, p. 217.

218. Interview of 1955 conducted by Jean Lacouture, cited in idem, *Nasser, a Biography,* New York, 1973, pp. 279–80.

219. Simha Flapan, *The Birth of Israel: Myths and Realities,* New York, 1987, p. 58.

220. See Shlaim, *Collusion across the Jordan,* and Zvi Elpeleg, 'Why was "Independent Palestine" Never Created in 1948?', *Jerusalem Quarterly,* 50 (Spring 1989), 3–22.

221. United Nations General Assembly, 'Continuation of the discussion on the progress report of the United Nations Mediator on Palestine', Paris, 22 Nov. 1948, p. 704 (http://domino.un.org/pdfs/AC1SR207.pdf).

222. Husayni, *Haqā'iq 'an Qadiyyat Filastīn*, p. 117.

223. 'Umar, *Mudhakkirāt al-Hāj Amīn al-Husayni*, pp. 222–3.

224. Elpeleg, *Grand Mufti*, p. 165.

225. Ibid.

226. The standard work on the Muslim Brotherhood's relationship to Palestine down to the Nakba is Abd Al-Fattah M. El-Awaisi, *The Muslim Brothers and the Palestine Question 1928–1947,* London, 1998. See also Sālih, *Al-Tayyar al-Islāmi fi Filastīn*, pp. 433–51, and Gershoni, 'The Muslim Brothers and the Arab Revolt in Palestine, 1936–39', *Middle Eastern Studies,* vol. 22, no. 3 (1986), pp. 367–97. All three writers underscore the

convergence of views and the close collaboration between the Muslim Brothers and the Mufti.

227. Awaisi, *Muslim Brothers and Palestine Question*, p. 153.

228. Ibid., p. 154.

229. Ibid., pp. 6–8.

230. Ibid., p. 18.

231. Ibid., p. 8.

232. Hassan al-Banna, *Majmūʿat Rasāʾil al-Imām al-Shahīd Hassan al-Banna,* n.pl., n.d., p. 263.

233. Awaisi, *Muslim Brothers and Palestine Question*, p. 189.

234. ʿAbduh Dasūqi, 'Al-Faqīd al-Mujāhid al-Hāj Muhammad Amīn al-Husayni Mufti Filastīn', www.ikhwanonline.com/Article.asp?ArtID=21830&SecID=0.

235. Hilberg, *Destruction of European Jews*, pp. 1152–3.

236. Hannah Arendt, *Eichmann in Jerusalem: A Report on the Banality of Evil,* New York, 1994, p. 10. See also Idith Zertal, *Israel's Holocaust and the Politics of Nationhood,* Cambridge, 2005, pp. 100–2.

237. Arendt, *Eichmann in Jerusalem*, p. 13.

238. Tom Segev, *The Seventh Million: The Israelis and the Holocaust,* New York, 2000, p. 425.

239. Israel Gutman, ed. in chief, *Encyclopedia of the Holocaust*, 4 vols, New York, 1990.

240. Peter Novick, *The Holocaust in American Life,* Boston, MA, 1999, p. 158.

241. Ibid., p. 157.

242. Meir Litvak and Esther Webman, *From Empathy to Denial: Arab Responses to the Holocaust,* London, 2009, pp. 297–8.

243. Ibid., p. 298.

244. See the site of the Palestinian American Research Center (PARC), http://parc-us-pal.org/

245. Litvak and Webman, *From Empathy to Denial*, p. 300.

246. Abu Iyad, *My Home, my Land*, p. 33.

247. Ibid., pp. 33–4 (emphasis in the original).

248. Litvak and Webman, *From Empathy to Denial*, p. 300 (my emphasis).

249. Ibid., p. 303.

250. Al-Jabha al-Shaʿbiyya al-Dīmuqrātiyya li-Tahrīr Filastīn, *Malāmih Tatawwur al-Nidāl al-Filastīni,* n.pl., n.d. [*c.* 1969], pp. 22–3.

251. Zertal, *Israel's Holocaust*, pp. 174–6.

252. David Dalin and John Rothmann, *Icon of Evil: Hitler's Mufti and the Rise of Radical Islam,* New York, 2008.

253. Ibid., pp. 141–2.

254. Ibid., pp. 6, 47.

255. Ibid., p. 35.

256. Ibid., p. 38.

257. Ibid., p. 40.

258. Ibid., p. 42.

259. Segev, 'Courting Hitler', *New York Times*, 28 Sept. 2008.

260. Matthias Küntzel, *Jihad and Jew-Hatred: Islamism, Nazism and the Roots of 9/11,* New York, 2007.

261. Ibid., p. xxiv.

262. Jeffrey Goldberg, 'Seeds of Hate', *New York Times*, 6 Jan. 2008.

263. Chuck Morse, *The Nazi Connection to Islamic Terrorism: Adolf Hitler and Haj Amin al-Husseini*, Lincoln, NE, 2003.

264. Ibid., p. xi.

265. Klaus-Michael Mallmann and Martin Cüppers, *Halbmond und Hakenkreuz: Das Dritte Reich, die Araber und Palästina*, Darmstadt, 2006.

266. Wildangel, *Zwischen Achse und Mandatsmacht*, p. 344.

267. Mallman and Cüppers, *Halbmond und Hakenkreuz*, p. 250.

268. 'Rashīd 'Alī al-Gaylānī', *Encyclopaedia Britannica*, www.britannica.com/EBchecked/topic/491697/Rashid-Ali-al-Gaylani

269. Mallmann and Cüppers, *Halbmond und Hakenkreuz*, pp. 26, 34.

270. Ibid., p. 160.

271. Ibid., p. 258.

272. Francis Nicosia, Review of Mallmann and Cüppers, *Halbmond und Hakenkreuz*, *Holocaust and Genocide Studies*, vol. 22, no. 1 (spring 2008), p. 127.

273. Ibid.

II. THE TIME OF THE NAKBA

Arab Attitudes to the Jews and the Holocaust from 1948 to the Present

Prelude

1. Meir Litvak and Esther Webman, *From Empathy to Denial: Arab Responses to the Holocaust*, London, 2009, p. 19.

2. Yehoshafat Harkabi, *Arab Attitudes to Israel*, London, 1972.

3. Ibid., p. xx.

4. Ibid., p. xxi.

5. Ibid., pp. 466–72.

6. Yehoshafat Harkabi, *Israel's Fateful Decisions*, London, 1988). The original Hebrew version was published in 1986 and went through three edns before the English tr. appeared. It is dedicated to 'the victims of their leaders – Jews and Arabs'.

7. Harkabi, *Arab Attitudes to Israel*, pp. 473–6.

8. Ibid., pp. 384–449.

9. Nissim Rejwan, *Arab Aims and Israeli Attitudes: A Critique of Yehoshafat Harkabi's Prognosis of the Arab–Israeli Conflict*, Jerusalem, 2000. This short book is based on essays published several years earlier. See the essay that David Green has written on Rejwan: 'The Outsider', *Nextbook*, 26 Jan. 2007, www.tabletmag.com/arts-and-culture/books/901/the-outsider/

10. Rejwan, *Arab Aims and Israeli Attitudes*, p. 4.

11. Ibid., p. 48.

12. Harkabi, *Arab Attitudes to Israel*, 2nd edn, Jerusalem, 1976, pp. 529–39.

13. Harkabi, *Israel's Fateful Decisions*, p. 31.

14. Manfred Gerstenfeld, 'The Development of Arab Anti-Semitism: Interview with Meir Litvak', Feb. 2003, www.jcpa.org/JCPA/Templates/ShowPage.asp?DRIT=3&DBID=1&LNGID=1&TMID=111&FID=624&PID=0&IID=741&TTL=The_Development_of_Arab_Anti-Semitism.

15. Litvak and Webman, *From Empathy to Denial*, p. 2.

16. Ibid.

17. Ibid., p. 4.

18. Ibid., p. 13.

19. See 'About Us': www.memri.org/

20. Ibid.

21. Benny Morris, *1948: A History of the First Arab-Israeli War,* New Haven, CT, 2008.

22. Benny Morris, *The Birth of the Palestinian Refugee Problem, 1947–1949,* Cambridge, 1987.

23. Simha Flapan, *The Birth of Israel: Myths and Realities,* New York, 1987.

24. Benny Morris, 'The New Historiography: Israel Confronts its Past', *Tikkun* (Nov.–Dec. 1988), pp. 19–23, 99–102; repr. in Morris, ed., *Making Israel,* Ann Arbor, MI, 2007, pp. 11–28. On the debate around the Israeli 'new historiography', see also, in the same collection, Avi Shlaim, 'The Debate about 1948', pp. 124–46.

25. On post-Zionism, see esp. Uri Ram, 'The Future of the Past in Israel: A Sociology of Knowledge Approach', ibid., pp. 202–30, and, on the crisis of post-Zionism, the series of three articles published by Dalia Shehori in *Haaretz* on 21 and 28 April and 5 May 2004. See also Ilan Pappé, 'The Post-Zionist Discourse in Israel: 1990–2001', *Holy Land Studies,* vol. 1, no. 1 (Sept. 2002), pp. 9–35.

26. Morris, 'New Historiography', p. 15.

27. The Palestinian work on 1948 that is the most nearly contemporaneous with the Israeli 'new historiography', and, at the same time, the most thorough, is Elias Sanbar, *Palestine 1948: L'Expulsion,* Washington, DC, 1984.

28. Flapan, *Birth of Israel,* p. 9.

29. Nur Masalha, 'A Critique of Benny Morris', *Journal of Palestine Studies,* vol. 21, no. 1 (fall 1991), pp. 90–7. In the same issue of the *Journal of Palestine Studies,* Masalha's critique is preceded by another radical critique, Norman Finkelstein, 'Myths, Old and New', pp. 66–89, and followed by Benny Morris's response to his two critics, 'Response to Finkelstein and Masalha', pp. 98–114. See also Masalha's later *Expulsion of the Palestinians: The Concept of 'Transfer' in Zionist Political Thought, 1882–1948,* Washington, DC, 1992, and Finkelstein's '"Born of War, Not by Design": Benny Morris's "Happy Median" Myth', ch. 3 of his *Image and Reality of the Israel-Palestine Conflict,* London, 1995, pp. 51–87.

30. Segev, *One Palestine Complete,* New York, 2000, p. 407.

31. Benny Morris, *The Birth of the Palestinian Refugee Problem Revisited,* Cambridge, 2004, pp. 5–6. The revised edn includes a new chapter: 'The Idea of "Transfer" in Zionist Thinking before 1948', pp. 39–64. For a good critical analysis of this work and Morris's subsequent trajectory, see Joel Beinin, 'No More Tears: Benny Morris and the Road Back from Liberal Zionism', *Middle East Report* (MERIP), no. 230 (spring 2004), pp. 38–45.

32. Morris, 'Revisiting the Palestinian Exodus of 1948', in Eugene Rogan and Avi Shlaim, eds, *The War for Palestine: Rewriting the History of 1948,* Cambridge, 2001, p. 56.

33. Ram, 'Future of the Past in Israel.'

34. Ram, cited in Shehori, 'Post-Zionism didn't Die, it's Badly Injured', *Haaretz,* 28 April 2004. See also Uri Ram, 'Historiosophical Foundations of the Historical Strife in Israel', in Anita Shapira and Derek Penslar, *Israeli Historical Revisionism: From Left to Right,* London, 2003, pp. 43–61. In any case, this neo-Zionism is not very 'neo', in that it has roots in Revisionism and bears the direct influence of what Bernard Avishai called, in 1985, 'A New Zionism for Greater Israel' in *The Tragedy of Zionism: Revolution and Democracy in the Land of Israel,* New York, 1985, pp. 235–71.

35. Ari Shavit, 'Survival of the Fittest', interview with Benny Morris, *Haaretz,* 9 Jan. 2004.

36. Ibid.

37. Ibid.

38. Morris, *1948*, pp. 398–9.
39. Gilbert Achcar, 'Zionism and Peace: From the Allon Plan to the Washington Accords' (1994), in idem, *Eastern Cauldron: Islam, Afghanistan, Palestine and Iraq in a Marxist Mirror,* New York, 2004, pp. 209–10.
40. Shavit, 'Survival of the Fittest'.
41. Ibid.
42. Ibid.
43. Carl Schmitt, *Theorie des Partisanen*, Berlin, 1963, p. 95.
44. Morris, *1948*, pp. 405–6. On the myth of the 'purity of arms', see Finkelstein, *Image and Reality*, pp. 110–20.
45. Morris, *1948*, p. 392.
46. Ibid., p. 393.
47. Ibid.
48. Ibid., p. 394.
49. Shlaim, 'No Sentiments in War', *Guardian*, 31 May 2008.
50. Rejwan, *Arab Aims and Israeli Attitudes*, p. 19.

Chapter 5: The Nasser Years (1948–1967)

1. Orayb Aref Najjar, '*Falastin* Editorial Writers, the Allies, World War II, and the Palestinian Question in the 21st Century', *SIMILE: Studies in Media and Information Literacy Education*, vol. 3, no. 4 (Nov. 2003), p. 11.
2. Morris, *1948*, p. 402.
3. Madawi Al-Rasheed, 'Saudi Arabia and the 1948 Palestine War: Beyond Official History'. This original unabridged text of a contribution to Rogan and Shlaim, eds, *The War for Palestine: Rewriting the History of 1948*, 2nd edn, Cambridge, 2007, pp. 228–47, has been published on the website of Madawi Al-Rasheed, a native of Saudi Arabia and a professor at the University of London. www.madawialrasheed.org/index.php/site/more/133/
4. On this subject, see, for example, P. J. Vatikiotis, *The Egyptian Army in Politics: Pattern for New Nations?*, Bloomington, IN, 1961, pp. 44–68; Jean Lacouture, *Nasser: A Biography,* New York, 1973), pp. 68–73; Ahmad Hamrūsh, *Qissat Thawrat 23 Yuliu,* vol. 1, *Misr wa al-'Askariyyūn,* Beirut, 1974, pp. 143–6, as well as the reports by those who made the Revolution, ibid., vol. 4, *Shuhūd Thawrat 23 Yūliū,* Beirut, 1977. On his own account, Hamrūsh himself was, until 1939, while still in secondary school, a member of Young Egypt; he became a Communist in 1945 (ibid., pp. 36–7).
5. James Jankowski, *Nasser's Egypt, Arab Nationalism, and the United Arab Republic,* Boulder, CO, 2002, p. 15.
6. Gamal Abdel-Nasser, *Falsafat al-Thawra wa al Mīthāq,* Beirut, 1970, p. 21. Tr. into English as Gamal Abdul Nasser, *Egypt's Liberation: The Philosophy of the Revolution,* Washington, DC, 1955, p. 24. On Nasser's relationship to Cohen, see Lacouture, *Nasser: A Biography*, pp. 261–7.
7. Bernard Lewis, 'Pan-Arabism', in *From Babel to Dragomans*, New York, 2004, p. 176.
8. Cited in Lacouture, *Nasser: A Biography*, p. 265.
9. Laura James, *Nasser at War: Arab Images of the Enemy,* Basingstoke, 2006, pp. 7–8.
10. http://nasser.bibalex.org/main.aspx
11. http://nasser.bibalex.org/Speeches/browser.aspx?SID=92
12. Jean Lacouture, *Nasser,* Paris, 1971, p. 236. Part of this sentence, cited in the original French version of Lacouture's book, is missing in the English tr., which reads: 'At your

age, we too were demanding arms to throw us out!' (Lacouture, *Nasser: A Biography*, p. 271).

13. Abdul Nasser, *Egypt's Liberation*, p. 98. In the original Arabic version of this book, Nasser writes 'colonialism' (*istiʿmar*), not 'imperialism'. Abdel-Nasser, *Falsafat al-Thawra*, p. 97.

14. James, *Nasser at War*, p. 95.

15. http://nasser.bibalex.org/Speeches/browser.aspx?SID=348

16. http://nasser.bibalex.org/Speeches/browser.aspx?SID=3

17. http://nasser.bibalex.org/Speeches/browser.aspx?SID=7

18. Harkabi, *Arab Attitudes to Israel*, p. 2.

19. Constitution of the African National Congress, adopted at the ANC National Conference, June 1991, www.anc.org.za/ancdocs/history/const/constanc.html

20. Michel Aflaq, 'Sirāʿ al-ʿArab maʿ al-Istiʿmār wa al-Sahyūniyya', answers to questions posed by the newspaper *Al-Jamhūr* (also published in the newspaper *Al-Baʿth*, no. 63), in *Nidāl al-Baʿth*, vol. 3, *1954–1958*, Beirut, 1964, p. 283.

21. For a detailed examination of the history of Shuqayri's remarks and the hostile reactions of the Arab governments, including Egypt's, see Moshe Shemesh, 'Did Shuqayri Call for "Throwing the Jews into the Sea"?', *Israel Studies*, vol. 8, no. 2 (summer 2003), pp. 70–81.

22. A comprehensive inventory of Ahmed Shuqayri's positions may be found in the commemorative work about him by Khayriyyah Qasimiyyah, *Ahmad al-Shuqayri, Zaʿiman Filastīnīyyan wa Rāʾidan ʿArabiyyan*, Kuwait, 1987.

23. On Nasser's policy towards Israel, see Lacouture, *Nasser: A Biography*, pp. 261–343, and Robert Stephens, *Nasser: A Political Biography*, London, 1971, pp. 435–559.

24. http://nasser.bibalex.org/Speeches/browser.aspx?SID=1274

25. http://nasser.bibalex.org/Speeches/browser.aspx?SID=1289

26. Elie Podeh, 'Demonizing the Other: Israeli Perceptions of Nasser and Nasserism', in Podeh and Onn Winckler, eds, *Rethinking Nasserism: Revolution and Historical Memory in Modern Egypt*, Gainesville, FL, 2004, pp. 72–99. See also Segev, *Seventh Million*, pp. 297, 390–1.

27. See Segev, *1967: Israel, the War, and the Year that Transformed the Middle East*, New York, 2007, p. 284.

28. Segev, *Seventh Million*, pp. 390–1.

29. Harkabi, *Arab Attitudes to Israel*, p. 198.

30. Rejwan, *Israel's Years of Bogus Grandeur: From the Six Day War to the First Intifada*, Austin, TX, 2006, p. 70. This volume of Rejwan's memoirs consists mainly of letters written between 1967 and 1988.

31. Ibid., pp. 133–4.

32. Keith Wheelock, *Nasser's New Egypt: A Critical Analysis*, London, 1960, p. 48.

33. Beinin, *The Dispersion of Egyptian Jewry: Culture, Politics, and the Formation of a Modern Diaspora*, Berkeley, CA, 1998, p. 19. On Israel's political exploitation of the affair, ibid, ch. 4, pp. 90–117.

34. Ibid., p. 87. On the situation of the Egyptian Jews after 1948 and under Nasser, as well as the Zionist campaign revolving around the comparison of Nasserism to Nazism, see also Michael Laskier, 'From War to War: The Jews of Egypt from 1948 to 1970', *Studies in Zionism (Journal of Israeli History)*, vol. 7, no. 1 (1986), pp. 111–47.

35. Maurice Roumani, *The Case of the Jews from Arab Countries: A Neglected Issue*, Tel Aviv, 1983, p. 2.

36. Ibid.

37. Michel Abitbol, *Juifs et Arabes au XXème siècle,* Paris, 2006, p. 139. Mention should also be made of Nathan Weinstock's very tendentious book on this subject, *Une si longue présence: Comment le monde arabe a perdu ses Juifs, 1947–1967,* Paris, 2008. Its basic line of argument should be compared with what Weinstock, a former radical anti-Zionist become an Islamophobic neo-Zionist, wrote on the same subject forty years earlier: *Le Sionisme contre Israël,* Paris, 1969, pp. 299–300.

38. For concise descriptions of the events in Iraq, see Rejwan, *The Jews of Iraq: 3000 Years of History and Culture,* London, 1985, pp. 243–8, and Philip Mendes's fine summary, 'The Forgotten Refugees: The Causes of the Post-1948 Jewish Exodus from Arab Countries', *Australian Journal of Jewish Studies,* vol. 16 (2002), pp. 120–34, www.palestineremembered.com/Articles/General/Story2127.html

39. Yehouda Shenhav, 'The Jews of Iraq, Zionist Ideology, and the Property of the Palestinian Refugees of 1948', *International Journal of Middle East Studies,* 31/4 (Nov. 1999), p. 605.

40. 'Interview Given by his Excellency President Gamal Abdel-Nasser to Mr R. K. Karanjia, Editor of *Blitz Newsmagazine* of India, 28 September 1958', in Abdel-Nasser, *Speeches and Press Interviews 1958,* Cairo, n.d., p. 402. The Arabic version is at http://nasser.bibalex.org/Speeches/browser.aspx?SID=681

41. Harkabi, *Arab Attitudes to Israel,* p. 231.

42. Ibid., pp. 229–37.

43. Ibid., p. 233.

44. Ibid., p. 237.

45. Litvak and Webman, *From Empathy to Denial,* p. 7.

46. http://nasser.bibalex.org/Speeches/browser.aspx?SID=576

47. http://nasser.bibalex.org/Speeches/browser.aspx?SID=1272

48. Litvak and Webman, *From Empathy to Denial,* p. 280.

49. On the question of German reparations and the controversy they sparked in Israel itself, part 4 of Segev's excellent *Seventh Million* (pp. 189–252) is indispensable.

50. Litvak and Webman, *From Empathy to Denial,* pp. 59–91.

51. Ibid., p. 78.

52. On the Eichmann trial and the attendant controversies, see, again, Segev, *Seventh Million,* pp. 323–66.

53. Ibid., pp. 327–8.

54. Idith Zertal, *Israel's Holocaust and the Politics of Nationhood,* Cambridge, 2005, p. 100. On the exploitation of the Eichmann trial in Israel, see pp. 91–163 of Zertal's excellent book.

55. See Tamara Feinstein, ed., 'The CIA and Nazi War Criminals', *National Security Archive Electronic Briefing Book,* no. 146 (www.gwu.edu/~nsarchiv/NSAEBB/NSAEBB146/index.htm). The same website contains all the documents, introduced, edited, and censured by the CIA's official historian: Kevin Ruffner, ed., *Forging an Intelligence Partnership: CIA and the Origins of the BND, 1945–49,* Langley, 1999. See also Richard Breitman, Norman Goda, Timothy Naftali and Robert Wolfe, *U.S. Intelligence and the Nazis,* Washington, DC, 2004; repr. Cambridge, 2005. On the Eichmann affair, see Naftali, 'The CIA and Eichmann Associates', ibid. (2005 edn), pp. 337–74.

56. Kevin Ruffner, 'A Persistent Emotional Issue: CIA's Support to the Nazi War Criminal Investigations', CIA, 2007, www.cia.gov/library/center-for-the-study-of-intelligence/kent-csi/docs/v40i5a12p.htm

57. Hannah Arendt, *Eichmann in Jerusalem: A Report on the Banality of Evil,* New York, 1994, p. 17 (emphasis in the original).

58. Ibid., pp. 18–19.

59. Litvak and Webman, *From Empathy to Denial*, pp. 93–129.

60. Ibid., p. 98.

61. Bernard Lewis, *Semites and Anti-Semites: An Inquiry into Conflict and Prejudice*, 2nd edn, New York, 1999, p. 162.

62. Hannah Arendt simply described what she had managed to read about Arab reactions to the Eichmann trial in Israeli and American newspapers (*Eichmann in Jerusalem*, p. 13); she had no way of knowing more, unlike Harkabi and Wistrich.

63. Litvak and Webman, *From Empathy to Denial*, pp. 123–4.

64. Ibid., p. 124.

65. Ibid., p. 117.

66. Ibid., p. 128.

67. http://nasser.bibalex.org/Speeches/browser.aspx?SID=1109

68. http://nasser.bibalex.org/Speeches/browser.aspx?SID=1111

69. http://nasser.bibalex.org/Speeches/browser.aspx?SID=1115

70. Abdel-Nasser, 'Letter to Prof. Erhard, Chancellor of the German Federal Republic', *Al-Ahram*, 16 May 1965, cited in Harkabi, *Arab Attitudes to Israel*, p. 178.

71. http://nasser.bibalex.org/Speeches/browser.aspx?SID=1135

72. http://nasser.bibalex.org/Speeches/browser.aspx?SID=1247

73. http://nasser.bibalex.org/Speeches/browser.aspx?SID=1279

74. Harkabi, *Arab Attitudes to Israel*, pp. 176–7.

75. Litvak and Webman, *From Empathy to Denial*, pp. 215–42.

76. Ibid., p. 215.

77. Ibid.

78. Segev, *Seventh Million*, p. 24n.

79. *I. F. Stone's Weekly*, vol. 12, no. 19 (1 June 1964), pp. 1–2.

80. Harkabi, *Arab Attitudes to Israel*, pp. 277–8.

81. Lewis, *Semites and Anti-Semites*, p. 162.

82. Litvak and Webman, *From Empathy to Denial*, p. 161.

83. Gerhard Frey, '"Krieg mit Israel unvermeidbar": NZ-Interview mit Staatspräsident Nasser', *Deutsche National-Zeitung und Soldaten-Zeitung*, vol. 14, no. 18 (1 May 1964), p. 3.

84. Roger Garaudy, *Les Mythes fondateurs de la politique israélienne, La Vieille Taupe*, no. 2 (Winter 1995). Eng. tr., *The Mythical Foundations of Israeli Policy,* London, 1997.

85. Mohamed Hassanein Heikal, 'Muqaddimat al-Tab'a al-'Arabiyya', in Roger Garaudy, *Al-Asātīr al-Mu'assisa lil-Siyāsa al-Isra'īliyya*, Cairo, 1998, pp. 7–8. This Eng. tr. of the preface is a slightly modified version of the one published by the journal of American Holocaust deniers, *Journal of Historical Review*, vol. 19, no. 6 (Nov.–Dec. 2000), p. 30, www.ihr.org/jhr/v19/v19n6p30_Heikal.html

Chapter 6: The PLO Years (1967–1988)

1. On the Iraqi Baath's anti-Semitism in the post-1967 period, see Samir Al-Khalil (pseudonym of Kanan Makiya), *Republic of Fear: The Politics of Modern Iraq*, London, 1989, pp. 47–58.

2. Ibrāhīm Maqādima, *Ma'ālim fī al-Tarīq ila Tahrīr Filastīn*, Gaza, 1994, p. 254, cited by Khaled Hroub in *Hamās: Al-Fikr wa al-Mumārasa al-Siyāsiyya*, Beirut, 1996, p. 29. The citation is abridged in the Eng. version of Hroub's book, *Hamas: Political Thought and Practice,* Washington, DC, 2000, p. 29.

3. PLO Charter, adopted in 1964. Arabic text in Qāsimiyyah, *Ahmad al-Shuqayri*, p. 572 (Eng. tr. at www.un.int/palestine/PLO/PNA2.html).

4. Palestinian National Charter, amended in 1968, www.palestineinarabic.com/Docs/other_doc/Palestinian_National_Charter_1968_A.pdf (Eng. tr. at www.un.int/palestine/PLO/PNAcharter.html).

5. See the Palestinian sources cited by Yehoshafat Harkabi in *The Palestinian Covenant and its Meaning*, London, 1979, pp. 43–7.

6. On the early relations between the Muslim Brothers and Fatah's founders, see Hroub, *Hamās*, pp. 23–9, and *Hamas*, pp. 25–9.

7. Address to the Second International Conference in Support of the Arab Peoples, Cairo, 28 Jan. 1969 – cited in Mohammad Rasheed, *Toward a Democratic State in Palestine*, Beirut, 1970, pp. 11–13.

8. Al-Jabha al-Shaʿbiyya li-Tahrīr Filastīn, Report of the Congress of February 1969, part I, pp. 39–40 – cited in Sadik Jalal Al-Azm (Sādiq Jalāl al-ʿAzm), *Dirāsāt Yasāriyya hawl al-Qadiyya al-Filastīniyya*, Beirut, 1970, pp. 56–7 (n. 36), 58. Eng. tr. in Leila Kadi, ed., *Basic Political Documents of the Armed Palestinians Resistance Movement*, Beirut, 1969, pp. 224–5.

9. ʿAl-Muqāwama. Kayf Tufakkir? Kayf Taʿmal? Kayf Tuwājih al-Hādir? Kayf Tara al-Mustaqbal? Hiwār bayn "Fatah" wa ʿAl-Talīʿa', *Al-Talīʿa*, vol. 5, no. 6 (June 1969), pp. 51–87. Eng. tr. in Kadi, ed., *Basic Political Documents*, pp. 39–100. Abu Iyad says that he put forward the idea of a democratic Palestine 'where Muslims, Christians, and Jews would live together in complete equality' as early as 10 Oct. 1968, in a press conference (Abu Iyad, with Eric Rouleau, *My Home, my Land: A Narrative of the Palestinian Struggle*, New York, 1981, p. 65).

10. Rasheed, *Toward a Democratic State*, pp. 14–15.

11. Ibid., p. 16.

12. Ibid., pp. 25–6.

13. Elias Sanbar, 'Post-scriptum', to Michel Warschawski, *Israël-Palestine: Le Défi binational*, Paris, 2001, p. 138. Eng. tr. of the quotation in Gilbert Achcar, *The Israeli Dilemma: A Debate between Two Left-Wing Jews. Letters between Marcel Liebman and Ralph Miliband*, London, 2006, pp. 73–4.

14. Ibid., p. 139.

15. Al-Jabha al-Shaʿbiyya al-Dīmuqrātiyya li-Tahrīr Filastīn, *Harakat al-Muqāwama al-Filastīniyya fi Wāqiʿiha al-Rāhin: Dirāsa Naqdiyya*, Beirut, 1969, p. 166. Eng. tr. in Kadi, ed., *Basic Political Documents*, pp. 173–4 (tr. modified in light of the Arabic original).

16. Rasheed, *Toward a Democratic State*, pp. 40–1.

17. Harkabi, *Palestinian Covenant*, p. 53.

18. On the evolution of the debate on a Palestinian state, see the excellent study by Alain Gresh, *The PLO: The Struggle Within. Toward an Independent Palestinian State*, London, 1985.

19. Resolution of the Eighth PNC, held in Cairo in Feb.–March 1971, cited in Harkabi, *Palestinian Covenant*, p. 51. The original Arabic text is http://bait-al-maqdis.ahlam-ontada.com/montada-f13/topic-t377.htm

20. Harkabi, *Palestinian Covenant*, pp. 55–7.

21. Peter Novick, *The Holocaust in American Life*, Boston, MA, 1999, p. 148. The indispensable work on this question is, of course, Tom Segev, *1967*.

22. Lotfallah Soliman, 'Un transfert de culpabilité', in 'Le Conflit israélo-arabe', *Les Temps Modernes*, special issue, no. 253bis (1967), pp. 270–1 (emphasis in the original).

23. David Shipler, *Arabs and Jews: Wounded Spirits in a Promised Land,* New York, 1987, p. 343.

24. Ibid.

25. Mahmoud Darwish, *Yawmiyyāt al-Huzn al-ʿĀdi,* Beirut, 1973, p. 56. Darwish's exasperation led him to make this flagrant overstatement, which does not reflect his basic thinking.

26. Litvak and Webman, *From Empathy to Denial,* p. 191.

27. Saul Friedländer, *Réflexions sur l'avenir d'Israël,* Paris, 1969, pp. 155–6.

28. Ibid., p. 156.

29. Excerpted from *Siah Lohamin* (in Hebrew, Interviews with combatants), Tel Aviv, 1968, p. 160, cited in French by Friedländer, *Réflexions sur l'avenir d'Israël,* p. 185.

30. Pierre Vidal-Naquet, 'Pour un ami disparu : Hommage à Marcel Liebman', *Revue d'études Palestinian,* no. 30 (winter 1989), repr. in Vidal-Naquet, *Les Juifs, la mémoire et le présent,* Paris, 1995, p. 496.

31. Marcel Liebman, 'Israël à 25 ans', *Mai,* no. 29 (May–June 1973), p. 43, cited in Vidal-Naquet, *Les Juifs, la mémoire et le présent,* p. 495. Cited in Eng. tr. in Achcar, *The Israeli Dilemma,* p. 5.

32. United Nations, General Assembly Resolution 3379 (30), 'Elimination of all forms of Racial Discrimination', 10 Nov. 1975 (UNISPAL, http://domino.un.org/UNISPAL. NSF/9a798adbf322aff38525617b006d88d7/761c1063530766a7052566a2005b74d1?O penDocument).

33. See James Adams, *The Unnatural Alliance,* London, 1984. On the development of the Israeli nuclear arms programme and Israel's collaboration with the apartheid regime in this connection, see Seymour Hersh, *The Samson Option: Israel, America and the Bomb,* New York, 1991. On the relations between Israel and South Africa and the parallels between the kinds of apartheid practised in the two countries, see Chris McGreal's two long articles in the *Guardian,* 'Worlds Apart' and 'Brothers in Arms – Israel's Secret Pact with Pretoria', 6 and 7 Feb. 2006, (www.guardian.co.uk/world/2006/feb/06/southafrica.israel; www.guardian.co.uk/world/2006/feb/07/southafrica.israel).

34. Segev, *Seventh Million,* p. 375n.

35. Ibid., p. 399.

36. Ibid. One of the first denunciations of Israel's exploitation of the Holocaust to be made in the country itself dates from 1980. This was an essay by the Israeli writer Boaz Evron, an Eng. tr. of which was published the following year in *Journal of Palestine Studies* under the title 'The Holocaust: Learning the Wrong Lessons', vol. 10, no. 3 (spring 1981), pp. 16–26.

37. Segev, *Seventh Million,* p. 399.

38. *Yedioth Ahronoth,* 21 June 1982, cited by Segev, *Seventh Million,* p. 401.

39. According to Yoav Gelber, 'The History of Zionist Historiography', in Morris, *Making Israel,* p. 71. Gelber notes that German immigrant newspapers in Palestine, which he describes as being 'disappointed', used expressions such as *Yishuvnazism* and *Nazionismus* in 1942.

40. Shlomo Shmelzman, letter published in *Haaretz,* 11 Aug. 1982, cited in Noam Chomsky, *Fateful Triangle: The United States, Israel and the Palestinians,* Cambridge, 1999, p. 257.

41. Shipler, *Arabs and Jews,* p. 349.

42. Cited in Shlaim, *The Iron Wall: Israel and the Arab World,* New York, 2000, p. 411.

43. Cited by Michael Marrus in 'Is there a New Antisemitism?', in Michael Curtis, ed., *Antisemitism in the Contemporary World,* Boulder, CO, 1986, p. 177.

44. Segev, *Seventh Million*, p. 399.
45. Alan Hart, *Arafat: Terrorist or Peacemaker?*, 3rd edn, London, 1987, p. 439. For a concise, reflective critique of other declarations by Yasser Arafat, see Vidal-Naquet, 'Arafat et les Juifs', in *Les Juifs, la mémoire et le présent*, pp. 503–5.
46. Shipler, *Arabs and Jews*, p. 336.
47. Shlaim, *Iron Wall*, p. 454.

Chapter 7. The Years of the Islamic Resistances (1988 to the Present)

1. Michel Warschawski, *On the Border,* Cambridge, MA, 2005, p. 181.
2. Ibid., pp. 185–6. See also Harkabi, *Israel's Fateful Decisions*, ch. 4, pp. 141–99, 'Nationalist Religious Judaism'.
3. Flapan, *Birth of Israel*, p. 239.
4. Foundation for Middle East Peace, 'Sources of Population for West Bank and Gaza Strip Settlements, 1993 to 2004', www.fmep.org/settlement_info/settlement-info-and-tables/stats-data/sources-of-population-for-west-bank-and-gaza-strip-settlements-1993-to-2004
5. Efrat Weiss, 'Settlers' Birth Rate Three Times Higher than Other Israelis', *YNet*, 21 Feb. 2007, www.ynetnews.com/articles/0,7340,L-3367908,00.html
6. Avihai Nudel, 'Prof. Moshe Zimmerman: The Children of the Settlers in Hebron are Exactly like the Hitler Youth', *Yerushalayim*, 28 April 1995, published in the file on the 'Zimmerman affair' prepared by Israel Shahak, www.kokhavivpublications.com/2002/forum/israel_fund_demo/shahak_zimmerman.html
7. Arnon Groiss, *Jews, Israel and Peace in the Palestinian Authority Textbooks: The New Textbooks for Grades 5 and 10,* New York and Jerusalem, 2005, p. 4: www.impact-se.org/docs/reports/PA/PA2005.pdf
8. Amal Saad-Ghorayeb, *Hizbu'llah: Politics and Religion,* London, 2002, p. 169.
9. Ibid., p. 173.
10. Ibid., pp. 181–2.
11. Ze'ev Schiff and Ehud Ya'ari, *Intifada: The Palestinian Uprising. Israel's Third Front*, New York, 1991, pp. 224–5. On the tardy change in the Israeli attitude, which came in summer 1988, see pp. 237–9.
12. The Charter is, of course, available on the internet. The original Arab text may be consulted at www.islamonline.net/Arabic/doc/2004/03/article11.SHTML (Eng. tr. at www.palestinecenter.org/cpap/documents/charter.html).
13. Hroub, *Hamas*, p. 51.
14. Hroub, *Hamās*, p. 55.
15. Khālid Abul-'Amrayn, *Hamās: Harakat al-Muqāwama al-Islāmiyya fī Filastīn,* Cairo, 2000, p. 323 (this book was completed in summer 1997, as the author's preface indicates).
16. Muhammad Barhūma, 'Fahm al-Haraka lil-Ākhar al-Sahyūni wa al-Gharbi', in Jawād al-Hamad and Iyād al-Barghūti, eds, *Dirāsa fī al-Fikr al-Siyāsi li-Harakat al-Muqāwama al-Islāmiyya (Hamās), 1987–1996,* Amman, 1997, pp. 143–4.
17. Helga Baumgarten, *Hamas: Der politische Islam in Palästina,* Munich, 2006, pp. 65–6.
18. Cited in Orly Halpern, 'Hamas Working on New Charter', *Jerusalem Post*, 16 Feb. 2006.
19. Azzam Tamimi, *Hamas: Unwritten Chapters,* London, 2007, pp. 148–9.
20. Ibid., p. 150.
21. Ibid., p. 155.

22. Halpern, 'Hamas Working on New Charter'.

23. Jeroen Gunning, *Hamas in Politics: Democracy, Religion, Violence,* London, 2007, p. 202.

24. Ibid., pp. 1–3.

25. The original Arabic text is available on the website of the list 'Block for Change and Reform', Hamas's group in the legislature (www.islah.ps/new/index.php?scid=8).

26. 'Nabdha 'an Harakat Hamās', 15 Sept. 2006: www.palestine-info.info/ar/default. aspx?xyz= U6Qq7k%2bcOd87MDI46m9rUxJEpMO%2bi1s7YjyNYgnCrGxy9Lp hpYtjbpN10jo4ZpAEj22uHhDqul1JcP2sHDtgZlJCR3C2afNaApr%2bmcrhAOq3 FNcmJIzvxLcU9gqBHHcqmhfrDvamPtU%3d#4

27. Muhammad Hussein Fadlallah to the Danish Prime Minister (in Arabic), 19 Feb. 2008 (http://arabic.bayynat.org.lb/nachatat/bayan_19022008.htm).

28. Aluma Solnick, 'Based on Koranic Verses, Interpretations, and Traditions, Muslim Clerics State: The Jews are the Descendants of Apes, Pigs, And Other Animals', *MEMRI Special Report,* no. 11, 1 Nov. 2002, http://memri.org/bin/articles.cgi?Page=archives &Area=sr&ID=SR01102

29. John Mearsheimer and Stephen Walt, 'The Israel Lobby', *London Review of Books,* vol. 28, no. 6 (23 March 2006), pp. 3–12; *The Israel Lobby and U.S. Foreign Policy,* New York, 2007.

30. Hassan Nasrallah, 'Nida' Samāhat al-Amīn al-'Ām al-Sayyid Hasan Nasr-Allāh ila al-Umma,' 29 July 2006: www.moqawama.org/essaydetails.php?eid=7815&cid=319. On the relationship between the summer 2006 war and the policy of the USA in the region, see Gilbert Achcar with Michel Warschawski, *The 33-Day War: Israel's War on Hezbollah in Lebanon and its Consequences,* Boulder, CO, and London, 2007.

31. Hassan Nasrallah, 'Al-Sayyid Nasr-Allāh fi Dhikra Arba'īn al-Imām al-Husayn: Fashal Harb Tammuz huwa Fashal lil-Mashrū' al-Amīrkī fi al-Mintaqa', 9 March 2007: www. moqawama.org/essaydetails.php?eid=2146&cid=138

32. Harkabi, *Arab Attitudes to Israel*, pp. 298–9.

33. Cited in Novick, *Holocaust in American Life*, p. 249.

34. Anne Kornblut and Charles Sennott, 'Bush Seeks Nato Solidarity', *Boston Globe,* 21 Nov. 2002.

35. Philippe Boggio, 'Infantilisation de la politique, déréalisation de la violence', interview with Claude Lanzmann, *Marianne,* 31 May 1999, http://m.marianne2.fr/index.php?a ction=article&numero=152975#1

36. Zertal, *Israel's Holocaust*, p. 4.

37. Avraham Burg, *The Holocaust is Over: We Must Rise from its Ashes,* New York, 2008, pp. 208–9.

38. Pierre Vidal-Naquet, 'Theses on Revisionism,' in *Assassins of Memory: Essays on the Denial of the Holocaust*, New York, 1992, p. 96, www.anti-rev.org/textes/ VidalNaquet85a/.

39. Pierre Vidal-Naquet died in 2006.

40. For a full treatment of Holocaust deniers that takes the trouble to refute their theses soberly and in detail without, be it noted, seizing the opportunity to defend Israel and vilify the Arabs (something that merits emphasis, as it is on the way to becoming a rarity in the literature on Holocaust denial), see Michael Shermer and Alex Grobman, *Denying History: Who Says the Holocaust Never Happened and Why do They Say it?,* Berkeley, CA, 2000. This book does not, however, discuss Garaudy, who, to be sure, has not added anything new to the arguments of the Holocaust deniers.

322 THE ARABS AND THE HOLOCAUST

41. A rather complete overview of the Garaudy affair may be found in Litvak and Webman, *From Empathy to Denial*, pp. 340–50.

42. Sālih Zahr-ul-Dīn, *Al-Khalfiyya al-Tārikhiyya li Muhākamat Roger Garaudy,* Beirut, 1998.

43. Ibid., pp. 195–256.

44. 'Abdul-Wahāb al-Masīrī (Abdelwahab Elmessiri), *Al-Sahyūniyya wa al-Nāziyya wa Nihāyat al-Tārīkh,* Cairo, 1997. In 2007, Abdelwahab Elmessiri was elected co-ordinator of the Egyptian protest organization Kefaya, which had been created three years earlier out of the movement of solidarity with the second Palestinian Intifada and against the US invasion of Iraq. He died in July 2008.

45. 'Abdul-Wahāb Al-Masīrī, *Mawsū'at al-Yahūd wa al-Yahūdiyya wa al-Sahyūniyya*, 8 vols, Cairo, 1999. This encyclopedia has since been published on internet (www.elmessiri. com/encyclopedia). The work contains flagrant errors: thus it defines the term 'Shoah' as the Hebrew tr. of the Greek term 'Holocaust', and the Arab term '*mahraqa*' as a tr. of 'Shoah' (www.elmessiri.com/encyclopedia/JEWISH/ENCYCLOPID/MG2/GZ4/BA4/MD03.HTM)

46. Masīrī, *Al-Sihyūniyya*, p. 98, and *Mawsū'at al-Yahūd*: www.elmessiri.com/encyclopedia/JEWISH/ENCYCLOPID/MG2/GZ4/BA5/MD04/M0203.HTM

47. www.elmessiri.com/encyclopedia/JEWISH/ENCYCLOPID/MG2/GZ4/BA2/MD16/M0163.HTM

48. Edward Said, 'A Desolation, and they Called it Peace', *Al-Ahram Weekly Online*, no. 383, 25 June 1998 (http://weekly.ahram.org.eg/1998/383/op2.htm). Repr. in Edward Said, *The End of the Peace Process: Oslo and After,* New York, 2001, under the title 'Breaking the Deadlock: A Third Way', pp. 285–6.

49. Litvak and Webman, *From Empathy to Denial*, p. 333.

50. Saghieh, *Difā'an 'an al-Salām,* Beirut, 1997, pp. 63–4. There exists a doctoral dissertation in Arab studies on this pamphlet and its author: Matthijs Kronemeijer, 'An Arab Voice of Compromise: Hazem Saghieh's "In Defense of Peace" (1997)', University of Utrecht, 2005. It is at http://igitur-archive.library.uu.nl/student-theses/2006-0324-082630/An%20Arab%20Voice%20of%20Compromise.doc

51. On the difficulty of this undertaking, see Aviv Lavie, 'Partners in Pain: Arabs Study the Holocaust', *Haaretz*, 5 Feb. 2003, www.counterpunch.org/lavie02122003.html

52. 'Arafat Touched by "Sad Story" of Anne Frank as he Tours Site', *Reuters News Service*, 31 March 1998 (http://archive.deseretnews.com/archive/621570/Arafat-touched-by-sad-story-of-Anne-Frank-as-he-tours-site.html).

53. Elise Friedmann, 'Israel Dismisses Arafat's Visit to the Anne Frank House', *Jewish Telegraphic Agency*, 3 April 1998 (www.jewishsf.com/content/2-0-/module/displaystory/story_id/8403/edition_id/159/format/html/displaystory.html).

54. 'Nidā' al-Sha'b al-Filastīni fi al-Dhikra al-Khamsīn lil-Nakba' (excerpts), *Majallat al-Dirāsāt al-Filastīniyya*, vol. 9, no. 35 (summer 1998), pp. 219–21 (www.palestine-studies.org/files/word/mdf/8232.doc). Approximate English translations of the Call may be found on the internet. The one that best reflects the Arab original, although it is not entirely faithful to it, is available at www.jmcc.org/media/report/98/May/4c.htm

55. Jamāl Mansūr, *Al-Risāla*, 13 April 2000, cited in 'Palestinians Debate Including the Holocaust in the Curriculum', *Special Dispatch*, no. 187, 22 Feb. 2001, MEMRI, www.memri.org/bin/articles.cgi?Page=archives&Area=sd&ID=SP18701

56. See Mouna Naim, 'L'Appel de quatorze intellectuels arabes contre une conférence négationniste', *Le Monde*, 16 March 2001.

57. The text of Said's message may be found, together with several other texts on the 2001 Holocaust denial conference and its repercussions, on the American organizers' website: www.ihr.org/conference/beirutconf/

58. Mark Weber, 'An Anti-Holocaust Intifada Grows among the Arabs', www.ihr.org/jhr/v20/v20n3p-3_Weber.html.

59. www.freearabvoice.org/

60. See 'Iranian Leaders: Statements and Positions', MEMRI, 5 Jan. 2006, http://memri.org/bin/articles.cgi?Page=archives&Area=sr&ID=SR3906#_ednref15. Mahmoud Ahmadinejad repeated his revisionist comments in a speech delivered on 6 Oct. 2007; extracts, recorded and translated by MEMRI, http://memri.org/bin/articles.cgi?Page=archives&Area=sd&ID=SP174807

61. Hassan Nasrallah, excerpts from speeches, recorded and translated by MEMRI, http://memri.org/bin/articles.cgi?Page=archives&Area=sd&ID=SP108806

62. Mahmoud Ahmadinejad, 8 Dec. 2005, MEMRI TV, clip 956, transcript at www.memritv.org/clip_transcript/en/956.htm

63. Segev, *Seventh Million*, p. 120n. It goes without saying that such a state would not have been, as Ben-Gurion envisaged it, a substitute for the one that the Zionist movement intended to create in Palestine, but rather a supplement to it.

64. I have stated my viewpoint on the (in)appropriateness and political utility of Ahmadinejad's declaration in Noam Chomsky and Gilbert Achcar, *Perilous Power: The Middle East and U.S. Foreign Policy*, ed. Stephen Shalom, Boulder, CO, 2007, pp. 139–40.

65. Ghassān Sharbil, 'Al-Amīn al-'Ām li Hizb Allāh Yatahaddath ila al-Hayāt', *Al-Hayat*, 19 Jan. 2006.

66. Khaled Hroub, 'Irān, wa Hamās, wa al-Ikhwān al-Muslimūn ... wa Inkār al-Mahraqa', *Al-Hayat*, 12 Jan. 2006. Hroub has published a number of essays against Holocaust denial, such as the recent 'Qirā'atān fī "al-Holocaust": Al-Tawzīf al-Isra'īli wa al-Inkārāt al-'Arabiyya', *Al-Hayat*, 10 Feb. 2008 (Eng. tr. at www.kibush.co.il/show_file.asp?num=25377).

67. Pierre Abi-Sa'b, 'Kafāna Sukhfan!', *Al-Akhbar*, 9 Dec. 2006.

68. Azmi Bishara, 'Wujūh Inkār al-Mahraqa al-Nāziyya', *Al-Hayat*, 14 Dec. 2006; 'Ways of Denial', *Al-Ahram Weekly*, no. 825, 21 Dec. 2006, http://weekly.ahram.org.eg/2006/825/op2.htm

69. 'Israeli Minister Warns of Palestinian "Holocaust"', *Guardian*, 29 Feb. 2008, www.guardian.co.uk/world/2008/feb/29/israelandthepalestinians1

70. 'Israel Warns Gaza of "Shoah"', *Reuters*, 29 Feb. 2008, www.reuters.com/article/worldNews/idUSL2868601720080229?pageNumber=2&virtualBrandChannel=0

71. A very solemn intervention in this debate, by someone above all suspicion of Holocaust denial, circulated widely during the attack that Israel launched on Gaza in Dec. 2008, although it had been written eighteen months earlier. This was Richard Falk's essay 'Slouching toward a Palestinian Holocaust', *TFF*, 29 June 2007, www.transnational.org/Area_MiddleEast/2007/Falk_PalestineGenocide.html

72. Yael Branovsky, 'Shoah Survivors Hoard Food in Face of Financial Crisis', www.ynetnews.com/articles/0,7340,L-3662375,00.html

73. Norman Finkelstein, *The Holocaust Industry: Reflection on the Exploitation of Jewish Suffering*, London, 2000, p. 5.

74. See Nur Masalha, *The Politics of Denial: Israel and the Palestinian Refugee Problem*, London, 2003.

75. See the Institute's website, which uses the Arab equivalent of the word 'Shoah', *al-Kāritha* (catastrophe), to designate the event: www.alkaritha.org/. On the Nazareth Museum,

see Charles Radin, 'Muslim Opens Holocaust Museum in Israel', *Boston Globe*, 6 May 2005, and Donald Macintyre, 'The Holocaust through Arab Eyes', *Independent*, 17 May 2005.

76. Didier Pollefeyt, 'Between a Dangerous Memory and a Memory in Danger: The Israeli–Palestinian Struggle from a Christian Post-Holocaust Perspective', in Leonard Grob and John Roth, eds, *Anguished Hope: Holocaust Scholars Confront the Palestinian–Israeli Conflict*, Grand Rapids, MI, 2008, p. 146.

77. Fadi Eyadat and the Associated Press, 'Poll: Over 25% of Israeli Arabs Say Holocaust Never Happened', *Haaretz*, 18 March 2007.

78. E. Shohama, N. Shiloaha and R. Kalisman, 'Arab Teachers and Holocaust Education', *Teaching and Teacher Education*, 19 (2003), pp. 609–25.

79. Fadi Eyadat, 'Poll: 40% of Israeli Arabs Believe Holocaust Never Happened', *Haaretz*, 17 May 2009.

80. Joseph Samaha, 'Istighlāl al-Mahraqa,' *Al-Hayat*, 28 March 2001.

Conclusion: Stigmas and Stigmatization

1. René Descartes, *Discourse on the Method of Rightly Conducting One's Reason and of Seeking Truth in the Sciences*, http://www.gutenberg.org/files/59/59-h/59-h.htm

2. See Isaac Deutscher, *The Non-Jewish Jew and Other Essays,* London, 1968.

3. See Martin Buber, 'Zionism and "Zionism"', an extract from *A Land of Two Peoples* (1948), in Adam Shatz, ed., *Prophets Outcast: A Century of Dissident Jewish Writing about Zionism and Israel,* New York, 2004, pp. 56–9. It is to statist Zionism in contrast with his own Zionism that Buber reserved the quote marks. However, in historical perspective, they should rather be distinguishing his brand.

4. Mark Cohen, *Under Crescent and Cross: The Jews in the Middle Ages,* Princeton, NJ, 1996, pp. 3–14. Cohen points to the role that Jews from Arab countries played in forging the 'counter-myth' which he describes as, in some sense, the product of a rivalry with the Ashkenazim and their status as victims of the Holocaust (pp. 12–13). But this is far from being the rule. For a contribution by an Arab Jew at variance with Zionist views, see Abraham Serfaty, 'Le Judaïsme marocain et le sionisme', *Souffles*, 15 (3rd quarter 1969), pp. 24–37, www.lehman.cuny.edu/deanhum/langlit/french/souffles/s15/5.html

5. Bernard Lewis, *Semites and Anti-Semites: An Inquiry into Conflict and Prejudice*, 2nd edn, New York, 1999, p. 20. The same idea about the Israeli–Arab conflict is repeated in the last chapter of the book: 'This conflict may be clouded by prejudice; it may be influenced in its expression by prejudice. It is not caused by prejudice' (p. 242).

6. Ibid., pp. 22–3.

7. Ibid., p. 241.

8. Ibid., pp. 241–2.

9. Michael Marrus, 'Is there a New Antisemitism?', in Michael Curtis, ed., *Antisemitism in the Contemporary World,* Boulder, CO, 1986, p. 180.

10. Ibid., p. 174.

11. Brian Klug, 'The Myth of the New Anti-Semitism', *The Nation*, 2 Feb. 2004, www.thenation.com/doc/20040202/klug. See also his 'The State of Zionism', *The Nation*, 18 June 2007, www.thenation.com/doc/20070618/klug

12. See, among other publications by Wistrich, the propaganda brochure *Muslim Anti-Semitism: A Clear and Present Danger*, published by the American Jewish Committee, New York, 2002.

13. Yehuda Bauer, 'Antisemitism and Anti-Zionism: New and Old', in Wistrich, ed., *Anti-Zionism and Antisemitism in the Contemporary World,* New York, 1990, p. 207.

14. The English text of the 'Working Definition of Antisemitism' is at http://fra.europa. eu/fraWebsite/material/pub/AS/AS-WorkingDefinition-draft.pdf. This text has been translated into thirty-two languages by the European Forum on Antisemitism, an organization with ties to the American Jewish Committee, that was founded in 2008 at a meeting in Berlin attended by leading Jewish personalities from fifteen European countries, Israel and the USA. The translations are available at www.european-forum-on-antisemitism.org/working-definition-of-antisemitism

15. Frank Stern, *The Whitewashing of the Yellow Badge: Antisemitism and Philosemitism in Postwar Germany,* Oxford, 1992, p. 337.

16. Cited in Stern, *Whitewashing of Yellow Badge,* p. 402.

17. Ibid., p. 382.

18. Eleonore Sterling, 'Judenfreunde – Judenfeinde', *Die Zeit,* 50 (10 Dec. 1965); www. zeit.de/1965/50/Judenfreunde-Judenfeinde. See also Frank Stern, 'Der geschönte Judenfleck', in Jüdisches Museum der Stadt Wien, ed., *Die Macht der Bilder,* Vienna, 1995, pp. 398–402.

19. Cited in Stern, *Whitewashing of the Yellow Badge,* p. 383.

20. Ibid., pp. 396–403.

21. Ibid., p. 432.

22. Ibid., p. 430.

23. Ibid., p. 434.

24. 'Rede von Bundeskanzlerin Angela Merkel vor der Knesset in Jerusalem', 18 March 2008, available, with Eng. tr., at www.bundesregierung.de/Content/DE/Rede/2008/03/2008-03-18-rede-merkel-vor-der-knesset.html

25. P. Belkin, *Germany's Relations with Israel,* Washington, DC, 2007, pp. 5–6.

26. 'Germany's Transformation', *Jerusalem Post,* editorial, 24 Aug. 2006, www.jpost.com/ servlet/Satellite?cid=1154525933256&pagename=JPost%2FJPArticle%2FShowFull

27. Lewis, *Semites and Anti-Semites,* p. 253.

28. For a commendable effort not to separate the question of anti-Semitism from that of Islamophobia in Europe, see John Bunzl and Alexandra Senfft, eds, *Zwischen Antisemitismus und Islamophobie: Vorurteile und Projektionen in Europa und Nahost,* Hamburg, 2008.

29. Pierre-André Taguieff, to cite only one example, maligns Maxime Rodinson and Ilan Halévi the length of one whole chapter of his book *Les Protocoles des Sages de Sion: Un faux et ses usages dans le siècle,* Paris, 1992, pp. 315–39.

30. On this subject, see Roni Stauber, '*Realpolitik* and the Burden of the Past: Israeli Diplomacy and the "Other Germany"', *Israel Studies,* vol. 8, no. 3 (Fall 2003), pp. 100–22.

31. *Harry S. Truman 1947 Diary,* 21 July 1947, Truman Library, Independence, MO, www. trumanlibrary.org/diary/page21.htm

32. See Norman Stillman, 'Antisemitism in the Contemporary Arab World', in Curtis, *Antisemitism,* p. 72.

33. On the evolution of the Muslim Brothers' attitude to Nasser between 1956 and 1967, see Emmanuel Sivan, 'Radical Islam and the Arab-Israeli Conflict', ibid., pp. 62–4.

34. Ibid., pp. 65–6. For a thorough presentation of Qutb's views on the Jews, see Olivier Carré, *Mystique et politique: Lecture révolutionnaire du Coran par Sayyid Qutb, Frère musulman radical,* Paris, 1984, ch. 3, 'Juifs et chrétiens dans la société islamique idéale du *Zilâl*', pp. 103–22.

35. Anwar al-Sadat, 'Khitāb al-Ra'īs Anwar al-Sadāt fi al-Ihtifāl bi Zikra al-Mawlid al-Nabawi

al-Sharīf', *Al-Ahram*, 26 April 1972, www.anwarsadat.org/articletemplate_lang.
asp?templet_id=49&category=&categorytemp=29&category_id=367&parent=29

36. Mahmoud Abbas, *Al-Wajh al-Ākhar: Al-ʿAlāqa al-Sirriyya bayn al-Nāziyya wa al-Sahyūniyya,* Amman, 1984.

37. Robert Faurisson, *Haqīqat Ghuraf al-Ghāz al-Nāziyya*, with a preface by Mahmoud Abbas, Amman, 1983.

38. Nathan Glazer, 'Anti-Zionism: A Global Phenomenon', in Curtis, *Antisemitism*, p. 163, emphasis in the original.

39. Ibid., p. 160.

40. Ibid., p. 159.

41. Bernard Lewis, 'The Anti-Zionist Resolution', *Foreign Affairs* (Oct. 1976), 54–64, repr. in Lewis, *From Babel to Dragomans,* New York, 2004, p. 275.

42. Glazer, 'Anti-Zionism', p. 160 (emphasis in the original).

43. Ibid., p. 162.

44. Ibid., p. 163.

45. David Grossman, 'Speech at the Rabin Memorial', *Haaretz*, 5 Nov. 2006, www.haaretz.com/hasen/spages/784034.html

46. On conditions in the West Bank and Gaza, see Eyal Weizman's excellent work, *Hollow Land: Israel's Architecture of Occupation*, London, 2007. Interesting essays on the racist structures of the Israeli state, as well as the oppression experiences by the Palestinians, may also be found in Ronit Lentin, ed., *Thinking Palestine*, London, 2008.

47. Daniel Bar-Tal and Yona Teichman, *Stereotypes and Prejudice in Conflict: Representations of Arabs in Israeli Jewish Society,* Cambridge, 2005, pp. 154–6. See also an essay by Ismael Abu-Saad, a professor at the Ben-Gurion University in the Negev, 'The Portrayal of Arabs in Textbooks in the Jewish School System in Israel', *Arab Studies Quarterly*, vol. 29, no. 1 (Winter 2007), pp. 21–38.

48. See 'Prevailing View among Israeli Jews: Israel, Too, Bears Responsibility in Overall Israeli–Arab/Palestinian Conflict', which presents the study and states a few results; this text is at www.tc.columbia.edu/news/article.htm?id=6811

49. Akiva Eldar, 'Is an Israeli Jewish Sense of Victimization Perpetuating the Conflict with Palestinians?', *Haaretz*, 30 Jan. 2009, www.haaretz.com/hasen/spages/1060061.html

50. Sami Smooha, *Index of Arab–Jewish Relations 2004,* Haifa, 2005, p. 113; http://soc.haifa.ac.il/~s.smooha/download/IndexArabJewishRelations2004.pdf

51. Ibid., pp. 31, 114–16.

52. Avraham Burg, *The Holocaust is Over: We Must Rise from its Ashes,* New York, 2008, pp. 236–7.

53. Ibid, p. 192.

54. See n. 3 above.

55. Theodor Herzl, *The Jewish State: An Attempt at a Modern Solution of the Jewish Question,* London, 1972, p. 30.

56. Maxime Rodinson, *Israel: A Colonial-Settler State?,* New York, 1973, p. 77.

57. 'Israel Protests UN Chief Ban Ki-Moon's Use of Term "Nakba"', *Haaretz*, 16 May 2008 www.haaretz.com/hasen/spages/984009.html

58. 'FM Livni's address at the closing plenary session of the Israel Presidential Conference', www.mfa.gov.il/MFA/About+the+Ministry/Foreign+Minister+Livni/Speeches+interviews/FM%20Livni%20address%20to%20Israel%20Presidential%20Conference%2015-May-2008

59. Israel Shahak, *Jewish History, Jewish Religion,* 2nd edn, London, 1997, p. 103.

60. Burg, *Holocaust is Over*, p. 152.

61. Ibid., p. 171.
62. Edward Said, 'Bases for Coexistence' (1997) in *The End of the Peace Process: Oslo and After,* New York, 2001, p. 206.
63. Ibid., p. 209.
64. Burg, *Holocaust is Over*, pp. 83–4.
65. Joseph Samaha, *Salām 'Ābir: Nahwa Hal 'Arabi lil-Mas'ala al-Yahūdiyya,* Beirut, 1993, p. 112.
66. Meir Litvak and Esther Webman, *From Empathy to Denial: Arab Responses to the Holocaust,* London, 2009, p. 363.
67. Ibid., p. 372.
68. Ibid., p. 373.
69. Roi Mandel, 'Naalin Holds Holocaust Exhibit', *Ynet*, 27 Jan. 2009, www.ynetnews. com/articles/0,7340,L-3662822,00.html
70. A commendable effort to promote such mutual recognition has yielded a book of dialogue and a confrontation of different narratives on the Israeli–Palestinian conflict: Robert Rotberg, ed., *Israeli and Palestinian Narratives of Conflict: History's Double Helix*, Bloomington, IN, 2006.
71 Samaha, *Salām 'Ābir*, p. 109.
72 See Ella Shohat, 'Sephardim in Israel: Zionism from the Standpoint of its Jewish Victims', Social Text, no. 19/20 (autumn 1988), pp. 1–35, repr. in Shatz, ed., *Prophets Outcast*, pp. 278–322.

Bibliography

For reasons of space, this list of the publications cited in this book does not include articles of daily newspapers, nor documents that are available exclusively on the internet. Each work is cited only once. If a work has more than one author, it is cited under the name of the author mentioned first on the title page. Individual contributions to collections or collective works are not listed separately: only the collection is.[*]

Abbas, Mahmoud, *Al-Wajh al-Ākhar: Al-'Alāqa al-Sirriyya bayn al-Nāziyya wa al-Sahyūniyya*, Amman: Dār Ibn Rushd, 1984.

'Abbāsi, Nizām, *Al-'Ilāqāt al-Sahyūniyya al-Nāziyya wa Atharuha 'ala Filastīn wa Harakat al-Taharrur al-'Arabi 1933-1945*, Kuwait: Kādhima, 1984.

Abdel-Malek, Anouar, *Egypt: Military Society: The Army Regime, the Left, and Social Change under Nasser*, New York: Random House, 1968.

'Abdul-Ghani, 'Abd-ul-Rahmān, *Almāniya al-Nāziyya wa Filastīn 1933–1945*, Beirut: Mu'assasat al-Dirāsat al-Filastīniyya, 1995.

'Abdul-Nāsir, Gamāl [Abdel-Nasser, Gamal], *Falsafat al-Thawra wa al Mīthāq*, Beirut: Dār al-Ma'rifa wa Dār al-Qalam, 1970.

——*Speeches and Press Interviews 1958*, Cairo: Information Department UAR, Le Caire, n.d.

——*The Philosophy of the Revolution*, Washington, DC: Public Affairs (Eng. tr. of *Falsafat al-Thawra*), 1955.

——See also Frey, 1964.

Abitbol, Michel, *Juifs et Arabes au XXème siècle*, Paris: Perrin, 2006.

——*The Jews of North Africa during the Second World War*, Detroit: Wayne State University Press, 1989.

Abu-Hannā, Hannā, ed., *Mudhakkirāt Najāti Sidqi*, Beirut: Mu'assasat al-Dirāsāt al-Filastīniyya, 2001.

Abu Iyad [Salāh Khalaf, aka Abu-Iyyād], with Rouleau, Eric, *My Home, My Land: A Narrative of the Palestinian Struggle*, New York: Times Books, 1981.

——(1969), 'Al-Muqāwama. Kayf Tufakkir? Kayf Ta'mal? Kayf Tuwājih al-Hādir? Kayf Tara al-Mustaqbal? Hiwār bayn "Fatah" wa "Al-Talī'a"' (Abu Iyad interviewed by Lutfi al-Khūli), *Al-Talī'a*, vol. 5, no. 6 (June 1969), pp. 51–87 (Eng. tr. in Kadi, 1969: 39–100).

Abul-'Amrayn, Khālid, *Hamās: Harakat al-Muqāwama al-Islāmiyya fi Filastīn*, Cairo: Markaz al-Hadāra al-'Arabiyya, 2000.

---

[*]   I am grateful to Jo Kelcey for her help in assembling this bibliography.

Abu-Saad, Ismael, 'The Portrayal of Arabs in Textbooks in the Jewish School System in Israel' *Arab Studies Quarterly*, vol. 29, no. 1 (Winter 2007), pp. 21–38.

Achcar, Gilbert, 'Orientalism in Reverse', *Radical Philosophy*, 151 (Sept./Oct. 2008), pp. 20–30.

——with Warschawski, Michel, *The 33-Day War: Israel's War on Hezbollah in Lebanon and its Consequences*, London: Saqi; Boulder, CO: Paradigm, 2007.

——*The Israeli Dilemma: A Debate between Two Left-Wing Jews: Letters between Marcel Liebman and Ralph Miliband*, London: Merlin, 2006.

——*The Clash of Barbarisms: The Making of the New World Disorder*, 2nd edn, London: Saqi; Boulder, CO: Paradigm, 2006.

——*Eastern Cauldron: Islam, Afghanistan, Palestine and Iraq in a Marxist Mirror*, New York: Monthly Review Press, 2004.

Achcar, Joseph, *La France et l'Angleterre dans le Proche-Orient: L'Evolution politique de la Syrie et du Liban, de la Palestine et de l'Irak*, Lyons: Thèse, Imprimerie M. Martin, 1934.

Adams, James, *The Unnatural Alliance*, London: Quartet, 1984.

Aflaq, Michel, *Fi Sabīl al-Ba'ath*, 4th rev. edn, Beirut: Dār al-Talī'a, 1970.

——*Fi Sabīl al-Ba'ath*, 1st edn, Beirut: Dār al-Talī'a, 1959.

Antonius, George, *The Arab Awakening: The Story of the Arab National Movement*, London: Hamish Hamilton, 1938.

Arendt, Hannah, *Eichmann in Jerusalem: A Report on the Banality of Evil*, New York: Penguin, 1994.

Arnow, David, 'The Holocaust and the Birth of Israel: Reassessing the Causal Relationship', *Journal of Israeli History*, vol. 15, no. 3 (1994), pp. 257–81.

Aron, Raymond, *De Gaulle, Israel and the Jews*, New Brunswick, NJ: Transaction, 2004.

Auron, Yair, *The Pain of Knowledge: Holocaust and Genocide Issues in Education*, Piscataway, NJ: Transaction, 2005.

Avishai, Bernard, *A New Israel: Democracy in Crisis, 1973–1988*, New York: Ticknor & Fields, 1990.

——*The Tragedy of Zionism: Revolution and Democracy in the Land of Israel*, New York: Farrar Straus Giroux, 1985.

El-Awaisi, Abd Al-Fattah M., *The Muslim Brothers and the Palestine Question 1928–1947*, London: Tauris Academic Studies, 1998.

Azazian, Huri, *Al-Jāliyāt al-Armaniyya fi al-Bilād al-'Arabiyya*, Latakia: Dār al-Hiwār, 1993.

al-'Azm, Sādiq Jalāl [Al-Azm, Sadik Jalal], *Dirāsāt Yasāriyya hawl al-Qadiyya al-Filastīniyya*, Beirut: Dār al-Talī'a, 1970.

al-Azmeh, 'Aziz, *Qustantīn Zurayq: 'Arabiyyun lil-Qarn al-'Ishrīn*, Beirut: Mu'assasat al-Dirāsāt al-Filastīniyya, 2003.

al-Banna, Hassan, *Majmū'at Rasā'il al-Imām al-Shahīd Hassan al-Banna*, n.pl.: Dār al-Hadāra al-Islamıyya, n.d.

Bar-Tal, Daniel, and Teichman, Yona, *Stereotypes and Prejudice in Conflict: Representations of Arabs in Israeli Jewish Society*, Cambridge: Cambridge University Press, 2005

Batatu, Hanna, *The Old Social Classes and the Revolutionary Movements of Iraq: A Study of Iraq's Old landed and Commercial Classes and of its Communists, Ba'athists, and Free Officers*, Princeton, NJ: Princeton University Press, 1978

Bauer, Yehuda, *Rethinking the Holocaust*, New Haven, CT: Yale University Press, 2001.

——*et al.*, eds, *Remembering for the Future: Working Papers and Addenda, vol. 2, The Impact of the Holocaust on the Contemporary World*, Oxford: Pergamon, 1989.

Baumgarten, Helga, *Hamas: Der politische Islam in Palästina*, Munich: Diederichs, 2006.

Bearman, Peri, *et al.*, eds, *The Encyclopaedia of Islam*, 2nd edn, Leiden: Brill (Online), 2002–.

Beinin, Joel, 'No More Tears: Benny Morris and the Road Back from Liberal Zionism', *Middle East Report* (MERIP), no. 230 (Spring 2004), pp. 38–45.

——*The Dispersion of Egyptian Jewry: Culture, Politics, and the Formation of a Modern Diaspora*, Berkeley, CA: University of California Press, 1998.

——*Was the Red Flag Flying There? Marxist Politics and the Arab-Israeli Conflict in Egypt and Israel, 1948–1965*, London: I. B. Tauris, 1990.

Belkin, Paul, *Germany's Relations with Israel: Background and Implications for German Middle East Policy*, Washington, DC: Congressional Research Service, 2007.

Ben-Ami, Shlomo, *Scars of War, Wounds of Peace: The Israeli-Arab Tragedy*, London: Weidenfeld & Nicolson, 2005.

Benbassa, Esther, *Suffering as Identity: The Jewish Paradigm*, London: Verso, 2009.

Ben-Dor, Gabriel, ed., *The Palestinians and the Middle East Conflict*, Ramat Gan: Turtledove, 1978.

Berman, Aaron, *Nazism, the Jews, and American Zionism, 1933–1948*, Detroit: Wayne State University Press, 1990.

Berque, Jacques, *Egypt: Imperialism and Revolution*, London: Faber & Faber, 1972.

Black, Conrad, *Franklin Delano Roosevelt: Champion of Freedom*, New York: Public Affairs, 2003.

Black, Edwin, *The Transfer Agreement: The Dramatic Story of the Pact between the Third Reich and Jewish Palestine*, 2nd edn, Washington, DC: Dialog Press, 1999.

Bourdieu, Pierre, and Sayad, Abdelmalek, *Le Déracinement : La Crise de l'agriculture traditionnelle en Algérie*, Paris: Minuit, 1964.

Boyle, Susan Silsby, *Betrayal of Palestine: The Story of George Antonius*, Boulder, CO: Westview, 2001.

Breitman, Richard *et al.*, *U.S. Intelligence and the Nazis*, Cambridge: Cambridge University Press, 2005.

Brenner, Lenni, *The Iron Wall: Zionist Revisionism from Jabotinsky to Shamir*, London: Zed, 1984.

——*Zionism in the Age of the Dictators*, Westport, CT: Lawrence Hill & Co., 1983.

Brunner, Rainer *et al.*, eds, *Islamstudien ohne Ende: Festschrift für Werner Ende zum 65. Geburtstag*, Würzburg: Ergon Verlag, 2002.

Budeiri, Musa, *The Palestine Communist Party 1919–1948: Arab and Jew in the Struggle for Internationalism*, London: Ithaca, 1979.

Bunzl, John, and Senfft, Alexandra, eds, *Zwischen Antisemitismus und Islamophobie: Vorurteile und Projektionen in Europa und Nahost*, Hamburg: VSA, 2008.

Burg, Avraham, *The Holocaust is Over: We Must Rise from its Ashes*, New York: Palgrave Macmillan, 2008.

Burke, III, Edmund, ed., *Struggle and Survival in the Modern Middle East*, London: I. B. Tauris, 1993.

Buruma, Ian, and Margalit, Avishai, *Occidentalism: The West in the Eyes of its Enemies*, New York: Penguin, 2004.

Carpi, Daniel, 'The Mufti of Jerusalem, Amin el-Husseini, and his Diplomatic Activity during World War II (Oct. 1941–July 1943)', *Journal of Israeli History*, vol. 4, no. 1 (1983), pp. 101–31.

Carr, Firpo, *Germany's Black Holocaust, 1890–1945*, Kearney, NE: Morris, 2003.

Carré, Olivier, *Le Nationalisme arabe*, Paris: Payot, 1996.

——*L'Islam laïque ou le retour à la Grande Tradition*, Paris: Armand Colin, 1993.

——*Mystique et politique : Lecture révolutionnaire du Coran par Sayyid Qutb, Frère musulman radical*, Paris: Presses de la FNSP and Cerf, 1984.

Cattaruzza, Marina *et al.*, eds., *Storia della Shoah. La crisi dell'Europa, lo sterminio degli ebrei e la memoria del XX secolo*, 2 vols, Turin: UTET, 2005–6.

Chaumont, Jean-Michel, *La Concurrence des victimes : Génocide, identité, reconnaissance*, Paris: La Découverte, 1997.

Chiha, Michel, *Palestine*, Beirut: Trident, 1969; repr. *Palestine: Editorial Reflections of Michel Chiha 1944–55*, London: Stacey International, 2007.

Chomsky, Noam, *Fateful Triangle: The United States, Israel and the Palestinians*, Cambridge, MA: South End Press, 1999.

——and Achcar, Gilbert, *Perilous Power: The Middle East and U.S. Foreign Policy*, ed. Stephen Shalom, Boulder, CO: Paradigm, 2007.

Cleveland, William, *Islam Against the West: Shakib Arslan and the Campaign for Islamic Nationalism*, Austin, TX: University of Texas Press, and London: Saqi, 1985.

Cohen, Hayyim, 'The Anti-Jewish *Farhūd* in Baghdad, 1941', *Middle Eastern Studies*, vol. 3, no. 1 (1966), pp. 2–17.

Cohen, Hillel, *Army of Shadows: Palestinian Collaboration with Zionism, 1917–1948*, Berkeley, CA: University of California Press, 2008.

Cohen, Mark, *Under Crescent and Cross: The Jews in the Middle Ages*, Princeton, NJ: Princeton University Press, 1996.

——and Udovitch, Abraham, eds, *Jews among Arabs: Contacts and Boundaries*, Princeton, NJ: Darwin, 1989.

Cohen, Mitchell, *Zion and State: Nation, Class and the Shaping of Modern Israel*, Oxford: Basil Blackwell, 1987.

Conan, Éric, 'Les Secrets d'une manipulation antisémite', *L'Express*, 16 Nov. 1999.

Coury, Ralph, 'The Demonisation of Pan-Arab Nationalism', *Race and Class*, vol. 46, no. 4 (2005), pp. 1–19.

——*The Making of an Egyptian Arab Nationalist: The Early Years of Azzam Pasha, 1893–1936*, Reading: Ithaca, 1998.

Curtis, Michael, ed., *Antisemitism in the Contemporary World*, Boulder, CO: Westview, 1986.

Dalin, David, and Rothmann, John, *Icon of Evil: Hitler's Mufti and the Rise of Radical Islam*, New York: Random House, 2008.

Dann, Uriel, ed., *The Great Powers in the Middle East, 1919–1939*, New York: Holmes & Meier, 1988.

Darwish, Mahmoud, *La Palestine comme métaphore: Entretiens*, Paris: Actes Sud, 1997.

——*Yawmiyyāt al-Huzn al-'Ādi*, Beirut: Markaz al-Abhāth—Munazzamat al-Tahrīr al-Filastīnıyya, and Al-Mu'assasa al-'Arabiyya lil-Dirāsāt wa al-Nashr, 1973.

Dāyih, Jean, *Saāda wa al-Nāziyya: Wathā'iq al-Khārijiyya al-Almāniyya*, n.pl.: Fajr al-Nahda, 1994.

Degras, Jane, ed., ed., *The Communist International 1919–1943: Documents*, vol. 3, *1929–1943*, London: Oxford University Press, 1965.

—— *The Communist International*, vol. 1, *1919–1922*, London: Oxford University Press, 1956.

De Luca, Anthony, '"Der Grossmufti" in Berlin: The Politics of Collaboration', *International Journal of Middle East Studies*, vol. 10, no. 1 (Feb. 1979), pp. 125–38.

Denisty, Louis, *Le Grand Mufti et le nationalisme palestinien: Haj Amin al-Hussayni, La France et la Grande-Bretagne face à la révolte arabe de 1936–1939*, Paris, L'Harmattan, 2006.

Deutscher, Isaac, *The Non-Jewish Jew and Other Essays*, London: Oxford University Press, 1968.

Devlin, John, *The Baath Party: A History from its Origins to 1966*, Stanford, CA: Hoover Institution Press, 1976.

Eddy, William, *F.D.R. Meets Ibn Saud* (1954), Vista, CA: Selwa Press, 2005.

Eisenberg, Laura Zittrain, *My Enemy's Enemy: Lebanon in the Early Zionist Imagination, 1900–1948*, Detroit: Wayne State University Press, 1994.

Elpeleg, Zvi, *The Grand Mufti: Haj Amin al-Hussaini, Founder of the Palestinian National Movement*, London: Frank Cass, 1993.

——'Why was "Independent Palestine" Never Created in 1948?', *Jerusalem Quarterly*, no. 50 (Spring 1989), pp. 3–22.

Enayat, Hamid, *Modern Islamic Political Thought: The Response of the Shī'ī and Sunnī Muslims to the Twentieth Century*, London: I. B. Tauris, 2005.

Esco Foundation for Palestine, *Palestine: A Study of Jewish, Arab, and British Policies*, vol. 2, New Haven, CT: Yale University Press, 1947.

Eshkoli, Hava Wagman, 'Three Attitudes toward the Holocaust within Mapai, 1933–1945', *Journal of Israeli History*, vol. 14, no. 1 (1993), pp. 73–94.

Evans, Richard, *The Third Reich in Power 1933–1939*, New York: Penguin, 2005.

Evron, Boaz, 'The Holocaust: Learning the Wrong Lessons', *Journal of Palestine Studies*, vol. 10, no. 3 (Spring 1981), pp. 16–26.

Faris, Hani, 'Israel Zangwill's Challenge to Zionism', *Journal of Palestine Studies*, vol. 4, no. 3 (Spring 1975), pp. 74–90.

Faurisson, Robert, *Haqīqat Ghuraf al-Ghāz al-Nāziyya* (with a preface by Mahmoud Abbas), Amman: Dār al-Karmil, 1983.

Feldman, Matthew, and Turda, Marius, eds, '"Clerical Fascism" in Interwar Europe', special issue of *Totalitarian Movements and Political Religions*, vol. 8, no. 2 (2007).

Finkelstein, Norman, *The Holocaust Industry: Reflection on the Exploitation of Jewish Suffering*, London: Verso, 2000.

——*Image and Reality of the Israel–Palestine Conflict*, London: Verso, 1995.

——'Myths, Old and New', *Journal of Palestine Studies*, vol. 21, no. 1 (Fall 1991), pp. 66–89.

Flapan, Simha, *The Birth of Israel: Myths and Realities*, New York: Pantheon, 1987.

Frey, Gerhard, '"Krieg mit Israel unvermeidbar": NZ-Interview mit Staatspräsident Nasser', *Deutsche National-Zeitung und Soldaten-Zeitung*, vol. 14, no. 18 (1 May 1964), pp. 1, 3–4.

Friedländer, Saul, *Réflexions sur l'avenir d'Israël*, Paris: Seuil, 1969.

Garaudy, Roger, *Al-Asātīr al-Mu'assisa lil-Siyāsa al-Isra'īliyya* (with a preface by Mohamed Hasanein Heikal, 'Muqaddimat al-Tab'a al-'Arabiyya', pp. 5–11), Cairo: Dār al-Shurūq, 1998.

——*The Mythical Foundations of Israeli Policy*, London: Studies Forum International, 1997.

Garber, Zev, *Shoah: The Paradigmatic Genocide: Essays in Exegesis and Eisegesis*, Lanham, MD: University Press of America, 1994.

Garfinkle, Adam, 'On the Origin, Meaning, Use and Abuse of a Phrase', *Middle Eastern Studies*, vol. 27, no. 4 (1991), pp. 539–50.

Gensicke, Klaus, *Der Mufti von Jerusalem, Amin el-Husseini, und die Nationalsozialisten*, Frankfurt: Peter Lang, 1988.

Gershoni, Israel, *Beyond Anti-Semitism: Egyptian Responses to German Nazism and Italian Fascism in the 1930s*, San Domenico: EUI Working Paper no. RSC 2001/32.

——'Egyptian Liberalism in an Age of "Crisis of Orientation": Al-Risālā's Reaction to Fascism and Nazism, 1933–39', *International Journal of Middle East Studies*, vol. 31, no. 4 (Nov. 1999), pp. 551–76.

——'Confronting Nazism in Egypt: Tawfiq al-Hakim's Anti-Totalitarianism 1938–1945', *Tel Aviver Jahrbuch für deutsche Geschichte*, vol. 26 (1997), pp. 121–50.

——and Jankowski, James, *Redefining the Egyptian Nation, 1930–1945*, Cambridge: Cambridge University Press, 1995.

——'The Muslim Brothers and the Arab Revolt in Palestine, 1936–39', *Middle Eastern Studies*, vol. 22, no. 3 (1986), pp. 367–97.

al-Ghūl, 'Umar Hilmi, *'Usbat al-Taharrur al-Watani fi Filastīn: Nash'atuha wa Tatawwuruha wa Dawruha, 1943–1948*, Beirut: Mukhtārāt, 1987.

Giladi, Naeim, 'The Jews of Iraq', *The Link*, vol. 31, no. 2 (April–May 1998).

Gorodetsky, Gabriel, 'The Soviet Union's Role in the Creation of the State of Israel', *Journal of Israeli History*, vol. 22, no. 1 (2003), pp. 4–20.

Greilsammer, Ilan, *Les Communistes israéliens*, Paris: FNSP, 1978.

Gresh, Alain, *The PLO: The Struggle Within: Toward an Independent Palestinian State*, London: Zed, 1985.

Grob, Leonard, and Roth, John, eds, *Anguished Hope: Holocaust Scholars Confront the Palestinian-Israeli Conflict*, Grand Rapids, MI: Eerdmans, 2008.

Guérin, Daniel, *Au service des colonisés 1930–1953*, Paris: Minuit, 1954.

Gunning, Jeroen, *Hamas in Politics: Democracy, Religion, Violence*, London: Hurst, 2007.

Gutman, Israel, ed. in chief, *Encyclopedia of the Holocaust*, 4 vols, New York: Macmillan, 1990.

Hadari, Ze'ev Venia, *Second Exodus: The Full Story of Jewish Illegal Immigration to Palestine, 1945–1948*, London: Vallentine Mitchell, 1991.

Haim, Sylvia, ed., *Arab Nationalism: An Anthology*, Berkeley, CA: University of California Press, 1962.

——'Arabic Antisemitic Literature: Some Preliminary Notes', *Jewish Social Studies*, no. 17 (1955), pp. 307–12.

——'Islam and the Theory of Arab Nationalism', *Die Welt des Islams*, vol. 4, nos. 2/3 (1955), pp. 124–49.

al-Hamad, Jawād, and al-Barghūti, Iyād, eds, *Dirāsa fi al-Fikr al-Siyāsi li Harakat al-Muqāwama al-Islāmiyya (Hamās), 1987–1996*, Amman: Dār al-Bashīr, 1997.

Hamīdi, Ja'far 'Abbās, *Min Wathā'iq al-Nawādi al-Qawmiyya fi al-'Irāq: Al-Muthanna bin Hāritha al-Shaibāni wa al-Ba'th al-'Arabi*, Baghdad: Bayt al-Hikma, 1998.

Hamrūsh, Ahmad, *Qissat Thawrat 23 Yuliu*, vol. 4, *Shuhūd Thawrat 23 Yūliū*, Beirut: Al-Mu'assasa al 'Arabiyya lil-Dirāsāt wa al-Nashr, 1977.

——*Qissat Thawrat 23 Yuliu*, vol. 1, *Misr wa al-'Askariyyun*, Beirut: Al-Mu'assasa al-'Arabiyya lil-Dirasat wa al-Nashr, 1974.

Hannā, 'Abdallah, *Min al-Ittijāhāt al-Fikriyya fi Sūriyya wa Lubnān: Al-Nusf al-Awwal min al-Qarn al-'Ishrīn*, Damascus: Al-Ahāli, 1987.

——*Al-Haraka al-Munāhida lil-Fāshiyya fi Sūriya wa Lubnān 1933–1945*, Beirut: Dār al-Fārābi, 1975.

Harkabi, Yehoshafat, *Israel's Fateful Decisions*, London: I. B. Tauris, 1988.

——*The Palestinian Covenant and its Meaning*, London: Vallentine, Mitchell & Co., 1979.

——*Arab Attitudes to Israel*, London: Vallentine, Mitchell & Co., 1972; 2nd edn, Jerusalem: Keter, 1976.

Hart, Alan, *Arafat: Terrorist or Peacemaker?*, 3rd edn, London: Sidgwick & Jackson, 1987.

al-Hasnāwi, Zāhir, *Shakīb Arslān: Al-Dawr al-Siyāsi al-Khafi*, Beirut: Riad El-Rayess, 2002.

Hauner, Milan, *India in Axis Strategy: Germany, Japan, and Indian Nationalists in the Second World War*, Stuttgart: Klett-Cota, 1981.

Heikal, Mohamed Hasanein, 'Foreword to the Arabic Edition of Garaudy's The Founding Myths of Modern Israel', *Journal of Historical Review*, vol. 19, no. 6 (Nov.–Dec. 2000), p. 30.

Hersh, Seymour, *The Samson Option: Israel, America and the Bomb*, New York: Random House, 1991.

Herzl, Theodor, *The Jewish State: An Attempt at a Modern Solution of the Jewish Question*, London: H. Pordes, 1972.

Hilberg, Raul, *The Destruction of the European Jews*, 3rd edn, New Haven, CT: Yale University Press, 2003.

——*Perpetrators, Victims, Bystanders: The Jewish Catastrophe 1933–1945*, New York: HarperCollins. 1992.

Hillel, Shlomo, *Operation Babylon: Jewish Clandestine Activity in the Middle East 1946–51*, London: Collins, 1988.

al-Hilū, Ridwān, 'Fi al-Qadā' 'ala al-Fāshistiyya al-Nihāya al-Hatmiyya lil-Sahyūniyya', *Nidāl al-Sha'b* (March 1943), pp. 4–5.

al-Hilū, Yūsuf Khattār, *Qissat al-Nasr al-Kabīr*, Beirut: Dār al-Fārābi, 1985.

Hirszowicz, Lukasz, *The Third Reich and the Arab East*, London: Routledge & Kegan Paul, 1966.

Hitler, Adolf, *Mein Kampf*, Eng. tr. James Murphy, London: Hurst & Blackett, 1939.

Hizb al-Ba'th al-'Arabi al-Ishtirāki, *Al-Ba'th wa al-Qadiyya al-Filastīniyya. Bayānāt wa Mawāqif 1945–1965*, Beirut: Al-Mu'assasa al-'Arabiyya lil-Dirāsāt wa al-Nashr, 1975.

——*Nidāl al-Ba'th*, vol. 1, *1943–1949*, vol. 3, *1954–1958*, Beirut: Dār al-Talī'a, 1963, 1964.

al-Hizb al-Shuyū'i al-'Irāqi – al-Qiyāda al-Markaziya, *Al-Hizb al-Shuyū'i al-'Irāqi wa al-Mas'ala al-Filastīniya*, n.pl.: Min Manshūrāt al-Hizb al-Shuyū'i al-'Irāqi (al-Qiyāda al-Markaziya), 1971.

Hoare, Marko Attila, *The History of Bosnia: From the Middle Ages to the Present Day*, London: Saqi, 2007.

Höpp, Gerhard, *Al-'Arab fi al-Mahraqa al-Nāziyya: Dahāya Mansiyyūn?*, Damascus: Dār al-Amwāj, 2006.

——ed., *Mufti-Papiere: Briefe, Memoranden, Redden und Aufrufe Amīn al-Husainis aus dem Exil, 1940–1945*, Berlin: Klaus Schwarz, 2004.

——'Salud wa Salam. Araber im Spanischen Bürgerkrieg', *Inamo*, no. 33 (Spring 2003), pp. 53–5.

Höpp, Gerhard, Wien, Peter, and Wildangel, René, eds, *Blind für die Geschichte? Arabische Begegnungen mit dem Nationalsozialismus*, Berlin: Klaus Schwarz, 2004.

Hourani, Albert, *Arabic Thought in the Liberal Age, 1798–1939*, Cambridge: Cambridge University Press, 1983.

Howard, Thomas, and Pederson, William, eds, *Franklin D. Roosevelt and the Formation of the Modern World*, New York: M. E. Sharpe, 2003.

Hroub, Khaled, *Hamas: Political Thought and Practice*, Washington, DC: Institute for Palestine Studies, 2000.

——*Hamās: Al-Fikr wa al-Mumārasa al-Siyāsiyya*, Beirut: Mu'assasat al-Dirāsāt al-Filastīniyya, 1996.

al-Hūrāni, Akram, *Mudhakkirāt Akram al-Hūrāni*, vol. 1, Cairo: Maktabat al-Madbūli, 2000.

al-Husayni, Muhammad Amīn [Al-Husseini, Muhammad Amin], *Haqā'iq 'an Qadiyyat Filastīn*, 2nd edn, Cairo: Maktab al-Hay'a al-'Arabiyya al-'Ulya li Filastīn, 1956.

——'Fetwà di Amin el-Husseini per la guerra santa del maggio', *Oriente Moderno*, 21 (Jan.–Dec. 1941), pp. 552–3.

——See also 'Umar, ed., 1999; Höpp, ed., 2004.

al-Hūt, Bayān Nuwayhid, *Al-Qiyadāt wa al-Mu'assasāt al-Siyāsiyya fi Filastīn, 1917–1948*, Beirut: Mu'assasat al-Dirāsāt al-Filastīniyya, 1981.

——ed., *Wathā'iq al-Haraka al-Wataniyya al-Filastīniyya 1918–1939: Min Awrāq Akram al-Zu'aytir*, Beirut: Mu'assasat al-Dirāsāt al-Filastīniyya, 1979.

International Organization Foundation, 'International Refugee Organization', *International Organization*, vol. 2, no. 1 (Feb. 1948), pp. 130–2.

Jabbour, George, *Settler Colonialism in Southern Africa and the Middle East*, Khartoum: University of Khartoum, and Beirut: PLO Research Center, 1970.

al-Jabha, al-Sha'biyya al-Dīmuqrātiyya li-Tahrīr Filastīn, *Malāmih Tatawwur al-Nidāl al-Filastīni*, n.pl., n.d. [c. 1969].

——*Harakat al-Muqāwama al-Filastīniyya fi Wāqi'iha al-Rāhin: Dirāsa Naqdiyya*, Beirut: Dār al-Talī'a, 1969.

James, Laura, *Nasser at War: Arab Images of the Enemy*, Basingstoke: Palgrave Macmillan, 2006.

Jankowski, James, *Nasser's Egypt, Arab Nationalism, and the United Arab Republic*, Boulder, CO: Lynne Rienner, 2002.

——*Egypt's Young Rebels: 'Young Egypt,' 1933–1952*, Stanford, CA: Hoover Institution Press, 1975.

Jüdisches Museum der Stadt Wien, ed., *Die Macht der Bilder. Antisemitische Vorurteile und Mythen*, Vienna: Picus, 1995.

al-Jundi, In'am, 'Ba'ad Ghiyāb Michel 'Aflaq: Da'wa li Tas'hīh al-Waqāi' wa Tadqīqiha', *Al-Yawm al-Sābi'*, 28 Aug. 1989, p. 20.

al-Jundi, Sami [Sāmi], *Al-Ba'th*, Beirut: Dār al-Nahār, 1969.

Jurado, Carlos Caballero, *La espada del Islam: Voluntarios árabes en la Wehrmacht*, 2nd edn, Granada: García Híspan, 1999.

Kadi, Leila, ed., *Basic Political Documents of the Armed Palestinians Resistance Movement*, Beirut: PLO Research Center, 1969.

Kāmil, Anwar, *Al-Sahyūniyya*, Cairo: Dār al-Matbū'āt al-Shaabiyya, 1944; ed. Bashīr Al-Sibā'i, Cairo: Maktabat Madbūli, 1989.

Kaylani, Nabil, 'The Rise of the Syrian Ba'th, 1940–1958: Political Success, Party Failure', *International Journal of Middle East Studies*, vol. 3, no. 1 (Jan. 1972), pp. 3–23.

Keddie, Nikki, *Sayyid Jamal ad-Din 'al-Afghani: A Political Biography*, Berkeley, CA: University of California Press, 1972.

Kedourie, Elie, *Afghani and 'Abduh: An Essay on Religious Unbelief and Political Activism in Modern Islam*, London: Frank Cass, 1997.

——*Arab Political Memoirs and Other Studies*, London: Frank Cass, 1974.

Khadduri, Majid, 'General Nuri's Flirtation with the Axis Powers', *Middle East Journal*, vol. 16, no. 3 (Summer 1962), pp. 328–36.

——*Independent Iraq, 1932–1958: A Study in Iraqi Politics*, 2nd edn, London: Oxford University Press, 1960.

Khalidi, Rashid, *The Iron Cage: The Story of the Palestinian Struggle for Statehood*, Boston, MA: Beacon Press, 2006.

——*Palestinian Identity: The Construction of Modern National Consciousness*, New York: Columbia University Press, 1997.

Khalidi, Walid, ed., *From Haven to Conquest: Readings in Zionism and the Palestine Problem until 1948*, Washington, DC: Institute for Palestine Studies, 1987.

Khalil, Khalil Muhammad, ed., *The Arab States and the Arab League: A Documentary Record*, vol. 2, Beirut: Khayats, 1962.

al-Khalil, Samir [pseudonym of Kanan Makiya, Kan'ān Makkiyya], *Republic of Fear: The Politics of Modern Iraq*, London: Hutchinson Radius, 1989.

Khosrokhavar, Farhad, *Inside Jihadism: Understanding Jihadi Movements Worldwide*, Boulder, CO: Paradigm, 2009.

Khoury, Philip, *Syria and the French Mandate: The Politics of Arab Nationalism 1920–1945*, London: I. B. Tauris, 1987.

Kimmerling Baruch, and Migdal, Joel, *The Palestinian People: A History*, Cambridge, MA: Harvard University Press, 2003.

Kolsky, Thomas, *Jews against Zionism: The American Council for Judaism, 1942–1948*, Philadelphia: Temple University Press, 1990.

Krämer, Gudrun, 'Anti-Semitism in the Muslim World: A Critical Review', *Die Welt des Islams*, vol. 46, no. 3 (2006), pp. 243–76.

Kramer, Martin, 'Review of Cleveland, *Islam Against the West: Shakib Arslan and the Campaign for Islamic Nationalism*', *Middle Eastern Studies*, vol. 23, no. 4 (1987), pp. 529–33.

Küntzel, Matthias, *Jihad and Jew-Hatred: Islamism, Nazism and the Roots of 9/11*, New York: Telos, 2007.

Kupferschmidt, Uri, *The Supreme Muslim Council: Islam under the British Mandate for Palestine*, Leiden: Brill, 1987.

Lacouture, Jean, *Nasser: A Biography*, New York: Alfred A. Knopf, 1973.

——*Nasser*, Paris: Seuil, 1971.

Lammers, Donald, 'Fascism, Communism, and the Foreign Office, 1937–39', *Journal of Contemporary History*, vol. 6, no. 3 (1971), pp. 66–86.

Landau, Jacob, *The Politics of Pan-Islam: Ideology and Organization*, Oxford: Clarendon Press, 1994.

Laqueur, Walter, *Communism and Nationalism in the Middle East*, London: Routledge & Kegan Paul, 1956.

Laskier, Michael, 'From War to War: The Jews of Egypt from 1948 to 1970', *Studies in Zionism (Journal of Israeli History)*, vol. 7, no. 1 (1986), pp. 111–47.

Lazare, Bernard, *Antisemitism: Its History and Causes*, New York: Cosimo, 2005.

Le Bon, Gustave, *The World of Islamic Civilization*, New York: Tudor, 1974.

Lenczowski, George, *The Middle East in World Affairs*, 4th edn, Ithaca, NY: Cornell University Press, 1980.

Lentin, Ronit, ed., *Thinking Palestine*, London: Zed, 2008.

Lewis, Bernard, *From Babel to Dragomans: Interpreting the Middle East*, New York: Oxford University Press, 2004.

——*Semites and Anti-Semites: An Inquiry into Conflict and Prejudice*, reissued with a new afterword, New York: W. W. Norton & Co., 1999.

——*The Jews of Islam*, Princeton, NJ: Princeton University Press, 1984.

Linn, Ruth, and Gur-Ze'ev, Ilan, 'Holocaust as Metaphor: Arab and Israeli Use of the Same Symbol', *Metaphor and Symbolic Activity*, vol. 3, no. 11 (1996), pp. 195–206.

Lippman, Thomas, 'The Day FDR met Saudi Arabia's Ibn Saud', *The Link*, vol. 28, no. 2 (April–May 2005), pp. 2–12.

Litvak, Meir, and Webman, Esther, *From Empathy to Denial: Arab Responses to the Holocaust*, London: Hurst & Co., 2009.

——'Perceptions of the Holocaust in Palestinian Public Discourse', *Israel Studies*, vol. 8, no. 3 (Fall 2003), pp. 123–40.

Lockman, Zachary, *Comrades and Enemies: Arab and Jewish Workers in Palestine, 1906–1948*, Berkeley, CA: University of California Press, 1996.

MacDonald, Kevin, 'Jewish Involvement in Shaping American Immigration Policy, 1881–1965: A Historical Review', *Population and Environment*, vol. 19, no. 4 (March 1998), pp. 311–12.

Mallmann, Klaus-Michael, and Cüppers, Martin, *Halbmond und Hakenkreuz: Das Dritte Reich, die Araber und Palästina*, Darmstadt: WBG, 2006.

Mandel, Neville, *The Arabs and Zionism before World War I*, Berkeley, CA: University of California Press, 1976.

Maqādima, Ibrāhīm, *Ma'ālim fi al-Tarīq ila Tahrīr Filastīn*, Gaza: Alīm, 1994.

Marrus, Michael, *The Holocaust in History*, London: Weidenfeld & Nicolson, 1988.

Masalha, Nur, *The Politics of Denial: Israel and the Palestinian Refugee Problem,* London: Pluto, 2003.

——*Expulsion of the Palestinians: The Concept of 'Transfer' in Zionist Political Thought, 1882–1948*, Washington, DC: Institute for Palestine Studies, 1992.

——'A Critique of Benny Morris', *Journal of Palestine Studies*, vol. 21, no. 1 (Fall 1991), pp. 90–7.

al-Masîri, Abdul-Wahâb [Elmessiri, Abdelwahab], *Mawsū'at al-Yahūd wa al-Yahūdiyya wa al-Sahyūniyya*, 8 vols, Cairo: Dār al-Shurūq, 1999.

——*Al-Sahyūniyya wa al-Nāziyya wa Nihāyat al-Tārikh*, Cairo: Dār al-Shurūq, 1997.

Massad, Joseph, 'Palestinian and Jewish History: Recognition or Submission?', *Journal of Palestine Studies*, vol. 30, no. 1 (Autumn 2000), pp. 52–67.

Mattar, Philip, *The Mufti of Jerusalem: Al-Hajj Amin al-Husayni and the Palestinian National Movement*, rev. edn, New York: Columbia University Press, 1992.

Mayer, Arno, *Plowshares into Swords: From Zionism to Israel*, London: Verso, 2008.

——*Why did the Heavens not Darken? The Final Solution in History*, New York: Pantheon Books, 1990.

Mayer, Thomas, 'Egypt and the General Islamic Conference of Jerusalem in 1931', *Middle Eastern Studies*, vol. 18, no. 3 (1982), pp. 311–22.

Mearsheimer, John, and Walt, Stephen, *The Israel Lobby and U.S. Foreign Policy*, New York: Farrar, Strauss & Giroux, 2007.

——'The Israel Lobby', *London Review of Books*, vol. 28, no. 6, 23 March 2006, pp. 3–12.

Meddeb, Abdelwahab, *The Malady of Islam*, Cambridge, MA: Basic Books, 2003.

Meir-Glitzenstein, Esther, *Zionism in an Arab Country: Jews in Iraq in the 1940s*, London: Routledge, 2004.

Ménargues, Alain, *Les Secrets de la guerre du Liban: Du coup d'état de Béchir Gémayel aux massacres des camps palestiniens*, Paris: Albin Michel, 2004.

Mendes, Philip, 'The Forgotten Refugees: The Causes of the Post-1948 Jewish Exodus from Arab Countries', *Australian Journal of Jewish Studies*, vol. 16 (2002), pp. 120–34.

Mitchell, Richard, *The Society of the Muslim Brothers*, New York: Oxford University Press, 1993.

Montesquieu, *The Persian Letters* (with an introd. by the translator, George Healy, pp. vii–xix), Indianapolis: Hackett, 1999.

——*Œuvres complètes*, Paris: Seuil, 1964.

Morris, Benny, *1948: A History of the First Arab-Israeli War*, New Haven, CT: Yale University Press, 2008.

——ed., *Making Israel*, Ann Arbor, MI: University of Michigan Press, 2007.

——'The Historiography of Deir Yassin', *Journal of Israeli History*, vol. 24, no. 1 (March 2005), pp. 79–107.

——*The Birth of the Palestinian Refugee Problem Revisited*, Cambridge: Cambridge University Press, 2004.

——*Righteous Victims: A History of the Zionist–Arab Conflict, 1881–1998*, 2nd edn, New York: Vintage, 2001.

——'Response to Finkelstein and Masalha', *Journal of Palestine Studies*, vol. 21, no. 1 (Fall 1991), pp. 98–114.

——*The Birth of the Palestinian Refugee Problem, 1947-1949*, Cambridge: Cambridge University Press, 1987.

——'Israel and the Lebanese Phalange: The Birth of a Relationship, 1948–1951', *Journal of Israeli History*, vol. 5, no. 1 (1984), pp. 125–44.

Morse, Chuck, *The Nazi Connection to Islamic Terrorism: Adolf Hitler and Haj Amin al-Husseini*, Lincoln, NE: iUniverse, 2003.

Muhāfaza, 'Ali, *Al-'Ilāqāt al-Almāniyya al-Filastīniyya, 1841–1945*, Beirut: Al-Mu'assasa al-'Arabiyya lil-Dirāsāt wa al-Nashr, 1981.

Muñoz, Antonio J., *Lions of the Desert: Arab Volunteers in the German Army 1941–1945*, 2nd edn, New York: Axis Europa, n.d.

Nafi, Basheer, *Arabism, Islamism and the Palestine Question, 1908–1941: A Political History*, Reading: Ithaca, 1998.

Najjar, Orayb Aref, 'Falastin Editorial Writers, the Allies, World War II, and the Palestinian Question in the 21st Century', *SIMILE: Studies in Media and Information Literacy Education*, vol. 3, no. 4 (Nov. 2003), pp. 1–15.

Nerin, Gustau, *La guerra que vino de África*, Barcelona: Critica, 2005.

Nicosia, Francis, *Zionism and Anti-Semitism in Nazi Germany*, New York: Cambridge University Press, 2008

——'Review of Mallmann and Cüppers, *Halbmond und Hakenkreuz*', *Holocaust and Genocide Studies*, vol. 22, no. 1 (Spring 2008), pp. 125–8.

——*The Third Reich and the Palestine Question*, 2nd edn, New Brunswick, NJ: Transaction, 2000.

——'Arab Nationalism and National Socialist Germany, 1933–1939: Ideological and Strategic Incompatibility', *International Journal of Middle East Studies*, vol. 12, no. 3 (Nov. 1980), pp. 351–72.

Nordbruch, Götz, *Nazism in Syria and Lebanon: The Ambivalence of the German Option, 1939–1945*, London: Routledge, 2009.

Novick, Peter, *The Holocaust in American Life*, Boston, MA: Houghton Mifflin, 1999.

Pappé, Ilan, ed., *The Israel/Palestine Question: A Reader*, 2nd edn, London: Routledge, 2007.

——*The Ethnic Cleansing of Palestine*, Oxford: Oneworld, 2006.

——'Haj Amin and the Buraq Revolt', *Jerusalem Quarterly File*, no. 18 (June 2003), pp. 6–16.

——'The Post-Zionist Discourse in Israel: 1990–2001', *Holy Land Studies*, vol. 1, no. 1 (Sept. 2002), pp. 9–35.

Patai, Raphael, *The Arab Mind*, Long Island City, NY: The Hatherleigh Press, 2002.

Pearlman, Maurice, *Mufti of Jerusalem: The Story of Haj Amin El Husseini*, London: Victor Gollancz, 1947.

Piterberg, Gabriel, *The Returns of Zionism: Myths, Politics and Scholarship in Israel*, London: Verso, 2008.

Podeh, Elie, and Winckler, Onn, eds, *Rethinking Nasserism: Revolution and Historical Memory in Modern Egypt*, Gainesville, FL: University Press of Florida, 2004.

Porat, Dina, *The Blue and the Yellow Stars of David: The Zionist Leadership in Palestine and the Holocaust, 1939–1945*, Cambridge, MA: Harvard University Press, 1990.

——'Al-domi: Palestinian Intellectuals and the Holocaust, 1943–1945', *Journal of Israeli History*, vol. 5, no. 1 (1984), pp. 97–124.

Porath, Yehoshua, *The Palestinian Arab National Movement, 1929–1939: From Riots to Rebellion*, London: Cass, 1977.

——*The Emergence of the Palestinian-Arab National Movement, 1918–1929*, London: Cass, 1974.

Qarqūt, Dhūqān, *Michel 'Aflaq: Al-Kitābāt al-Ūla*, Beirut: Al-Mu'assasa al-'Arabiyya lil-Dirāsāt wa al-Nashr, 1993.

Qāsimiyyah, Khayriyyah, *Al-Ra'īl al-'Arabi al-Awwal: Hayāt wa Awrāq Nabīh wa 'Ādil al-'Azmeh*, London: Riad El-Rayyes, 1991.

——*Ahmad al-Shuqayri, Za'iman Filastīnīyyan wa Ra'idan 'Arabiyyan*, Kuwait: Lujnat Takhlīd Dhikra al-Mujāhid Ahmad al-Shuqayri, 1987.

——ed., *Filastīn fi Mudhakkirāt al-Qāwuqji 1936–1948*, Beirut: Dār al-Quds, 1975.

——*Mudhakkirāt Fawzi al-Qāwuqji, 1914–1932*, Beirut: Dār al-Quds, 1975.

al-Qāwuqji, Fawzi, see Qāsimiyyah, ed., 1975.

Rasheed, Mohammad, *Toward a Democratic State in Palestine*, Beirut: PLO Research Center, 1970.

Reid, Donald, 'Arabic Thought in the Liberal Age Twenty Years After', *International Journal of Middle East Studies*, vol. 14, no. 4 (Nov. 1982), pp. 541–57.

Rejwan, Nissim, *Israel's Years of Bogus Grandeur: From the Six Day War to the First Intifada*, Austin, TX: University of Texas Press, 2006.

——*Arab Aims and Israeli Attitudes: A Critique of Yehoshafat Harkabi's Prognosis of the Arab–Israeli Conflict*, Jerusalem: Hebrew University of Jerusalem, 2000.

——*The Jews of Iraq: 3000 Years of History and Culture*, London: Weidenfeld & Nicolson, 1985.

Rennap, Israel, *Anti-Semitism and the Jewish Question*, with a preface by William Gallacher, London: Lawrence & Wishart, 1942.

Renton, David, *Dissident Marxism: Past Voices for Present Times*, London: Zed, 2004.

Rheinisches Journalist Innenbüro, *'Unsere Opfer zählen nicht': Die Dritte Welt im Zweiten Weltkrieg*, Hamburg: Assoziation A, 2005.

Ridā, Muhammad Rashīd, 'Al-Shiqāq bayn al-'Arab al-Muslimīn', *Al-Manār*, vol. 34, no. 10 (3 May 1935), pp. 782–6.

——'Indhār wa Istitāba. Wayl lil-'Arab min Sharr qad Iqtarab', *Al-Manār*, vol. 34, no. 8 (5 March 1935), pp. 601–6.

——'Muhādarati fi Jam'iyyat al-Shubbān al-Muslimīn', *Al-Manār*, vol. 34, no. 8 (5 March 1935), pp. 607–11.

——"Fatāwa al-Manār," *Al-Manār*, vol. 33, no. 4 (June 1933), pp. 273–5; no. 5 (Sept. 1933), pp. 347–51.

——'Al-Munāzara bayn Ahl al-Sunna wa al-Shī'a', *Al-Manār*, vol. 32, no. 2 (Feb. 1932), pp. 145–60.

——'Al-Mu'tamar al-Islāmi al-'Ām fi Bayt al-Maqdis', *Al-Manār*, vol. 32, no. 2 (Feb. 1932), pp. 113–32.

——'Thawrat Filastīn: Asbābuha wa Natā'ijuha', part 1, *Al-Manār*, vol. 30, no. 5 (1 Nov. 1929), pp. 385–93; part 2, *Al-Manār*, vol. 30, no. 6 (1 Dec. 1929), pp. 450–68.

——'Di'āyat al-Rafd wa al-Khurāfāt wa al-Tafrīq bayn al-Muslimīn', *Al-Manār*, vol. 29, no. 6 (14 Oct. 1928), pp. 424–32.

——'Fath al-Yahūd li Bāb al-Fitna fi al-Quds', *Al-Manār*, vol. 29, no. 6 (14 Oct. 1928), pp. 414–24.

——'Al-Za'īmān Shaukat 'Ali wa Muhammad 'Ali', *Al-Manār*, vol. 27, no. 7 (17 Oct. 1926), pp. 548–55.

——'Fātihat al-Mujallad al-Sābi' wa al-'Ishrūn', *Al-Manār*, vol. 27, no. 1 (13 April 1926), pp. 1–18.

Rodinson, Maxime, *Israel: A Colonial-Settler State?*, New York: Monad Press, 1973.

Rogan, Eugene, and Shlaim, Avi, eds, *The War for Palestine: Rewriting the History of 1948*, 2nd edn, Cambridge: Cambridge University Press, 2007.

——*The War for Palestine: Rewriting the History of 1948*, Cambridge: Cambridge University Press, 2001.

Rotberg, Robert, ed., *Israeli and Palestinian Narratives of Conflict: History's Double Helix*, Bloomington, IN: Indiana University Press, 2006.

Rouleau, Eric, 'The Syrian Enigma: What is the Baath?', *New Left Review*, no. I/45 (Sept.–Oct. 1967), pp. 53–65.

Roumani, Maurice, *The Case of the Jews from Arab Countries: A Neglected Issue*, Tel Aviv: World Organization of Jews from Arab Countries, 1983.

Rubenstein, Sondra Miller, *The Communist Movement in Palestine and Israel, 1919–1984*, Boulder, CO: Westview, 1984.

Ruffner, Kevin, ed., *Forging an Intelligence Partnership: CIA and the Origins of the BND, 1945–49*, Langley, VA: CIA History Staff, 1999,

Saad-Ghorayeb, Amal, *Hizbu'llah: Politics and Religion*, London: Pluto, 2002.

al-Sabbāgh, Salāh-ud-Dīn, *Fursān al-'Urūba: Mudhakkirāt al-'Aqīd al-Rukn Salāh-ud-Dīn al-Sabbāgh*, Rabat: Tanit, 1994.

al-Sadāt, Anwar [El-Sadat, Anwar], *In Search of Identity: An Autobiography*, New York: Harper & Row, 1977.

——*Revolt on the Nile*, tr. and ed. Thomas Graham, London: Allan Wingate, 1957.

——*Safahāt Majhūla*, Cairo: Dār al-Tahrīr, 1954.

Sa'di, Ahmad, and Abu-Lughod, Lila, eds, *Nakba: Palestine, 1948, and the Claims of Memory*, New York: Columbia University Press, 2007.

Safran, Nadav, *Egypt in Search of Political Community: An Analysis of the Intellectual and Political Evolution of Egypt, 1804–1952*, Cambridge, MA: Harvard University Press, 1961.

Saghieh, Hazem, *Qawmiyyū al-Mashriq al-'Arabi: Min Dreyfus ila Garaudy*, Beirut: Riad El-Rayyes, 2000.

——*Difā'an 'an al-Salām*, Beirut: Dār al-Nahar, 1997.

Said, Edward (2001), *The End of the Peace Process: Oslo and After*, New York: Vintage, 2001.

al-Saʿīd, Rifʿat (1979), *Ahmad Hussein: Kalimāt wa Mawāqif*, Cairo: Al-ʿArabi, 1979.

——*Tārīkh al-Munazzamāt al-Yasāriyya al-Misriyya 1940–1950*, Cairo: Dār al-Thaqāfa al-Jadīda, 1976.

——*Al-Yasār al-Misri wa al-Qadiyya al-Filastīniyya*, Beirut: Dār al-Fārābi, 1974.

——*Al-Yasār al-Misri 1925–1940*, Beirut: Dār al-Talīʿa, 1972.

Sālih, Muhsin, *Al-Tayyār al-Islāmi fi Filastīn wa Atharuhu fi Harakat al-Jihād 1917–1948*, Kuwait: Maktabat al-Falāh, 1988.

Samaha, Joseph, *Salām ʿĀbir: Nahwa Hal ʿArabi lil-Mas ʾala al-Yahūdiyya*, Beirut: Dār al-Nahār, 1993.

Samāra, Samīh, *Al-ʿAmal al-Shuyūʿi fi Filastīn: Al-Tabaqa wa al-Shaʿb fi Muwājahat al-Kūlūnyāliyya*, Beirut: Dār al-Farābi, 1979.

Sanbar, Elias, *Palestine 1948 : L'expulsion*, Washington, DC: Livres de la Revue d'études palestiniennes, Institute for Palestine Studies, 1984.

Sartre, Jean-Paul, ed., 'Le Conflit israélo-arabe', special issue, *Les Temps modernes*, no. 253bis (1967).

Satloff, Robert, *Among the Righteous: Lost Stories from the Holocaust's Long Reach into Arab Land*, New York: Public Affairs, 2006.

al-Sayyid, Jalāl (1973), *Hizb al-Baʿth al-ʿArabi*, Beirut: Dār al-Nahār, 1973.

Schiff, Ze'ev, and Ya'ari, Ehud, *Intifada: The Palestinian Uprising. Israel's Third Front*, New York: Touchstone, 1991.

Schleifer, Abdullah, 'The Life and Thought of ʿIzz-id-Din al-Qassam', *Islamic Quarterly*, vol. 23, no. 2 (1980), pp. 61–81.

Schmitt, Carl, *Theorie des Partisanen: Zwischenbemerkung zum Begriff des Politischen*, Berlin: Duncker & Humblot, 1963.

Schwanitz, Wolfgang, ed., *Germany and the Middle East, 1871–1945*, Princeton, NJ: Markus Wiener, 2004.

Seale, Patrick, *The Struggle for Syria: A Study of Post-War Arab Politics 1945–1958*, London: Oxford University Press, 1965.

Segev, Tom, *1967: Israel, the War, and the Year that Transformed the Middle East*, New York: Metropolitan, 2007.

——*One Palestine, Complete: Jews and Arabs under the British Mandate*, New York: Metropolitan, 2000.

——*The Seventh Million: The Israelis and the Holocaust*, New York: Owl Books, 2000.

Seidman, Peter, *Socialists and the Fight Against Anti-Semitism: An Answer to the B'nai B'rith Anti-Defamation League*, New York: Pathfinder, 1973.

Shahak, Israel, *Jewish History, Jewish Religion: The Weight of Three Thousand Years*, 2nd edn, London: Pluto, 1997.

Shalabi ʿAli, *Misr al-Fatāt wa Dawruha fi al-Siyāsa al-Misriyya 1933–1941*, Cairo: Dār al-Kitāb al-Jāmiʿi, 1982.

Shapira, Anita, *Land and Power: The Zionist Resort to Force, 1881–1948*, New York: Oxford University Press, 1992.

——and Penslar, Derek, *Israeli Historical Revisionism: From Left to Right*, London: Frank Cass, 2003.

al-Sharabāsi, Ahmad, *Amīr al-Bayān Shakīb Arslān*, Cairo: Dal al-Kitāb al-ʿArabi, 1963.

Shatz, Adam, ed., *Prophets Outcast: A Century of Dissident Jewish Writing about Zionism and Israel*, New York: Nation Books, 2004.

Shavit, Yaacov, *Jabotinsky and the Revisionist Movement 1925–1948*, London: Frank Cass, 1988.

Shemesh, Moshe, 'Did Shuqayri Call for "Throwing the Jews into the Sea"?', *Israel Studies*, vol. 8, no. 2 (Summer 2003), pp. 70–81.

Shenhav, Yehouda, 'The Jews of Iraq, Zionist Ideology, and the Property of the Palestinian Refugees of 1948: An Anomaly of National Accounting', *International Journal of Middle East Studies*, vol. 31, no. 4 (Nov. 1999), pp. 605–30.

Shermer, Michael, and Grobman, Alex, *Denying History: Who Says the Holocaust Never Happened and Why Do They Say It?*, Berkeley, CA: University of California Press, 2000.

Shindler, Colin, *The Triumph of Military Zionism: Nationalism and the Origins of the Israeli Right*, London: I. B. Tauris, 2006.

Shipler, David, *Arabs and Jews: Wounded Spirits in a Promised Land*, New York: Penguin, 1987.

Shlaim, Avi, *The Iron Wall: Israel and the Arab World*, New York: W. W. Norton & Co., 2000.

——*Collusion across the Jordan: King Abdullah, the Zionist Movement and the Partition of Palestine*, Oxford: Clarendon Press, 1988.

Shohama, Edna, Shiloaha, Neomi, and Kalisman, Raya, 'Arab Teachers and Holocaust Education: Arab Teachers Study Holocaust Education in Israel', *Teaching and Teacher Education*, no. 19 (2003), pp. 609–25.

Shohat, Ella, 'Sephardim in Israel: Zionism from the Standpoint of its Jewish Victims', *Social Text*, no. 19/20 (Autumn 1988), pp. 1–35.

al-Shuqayri, Ahmad, *Arba'ūn 'Āman fi al-Hayāt al-'Arabiyya wa al-Dawliyya*, Beirut: Dār al-Nahār, 1969.

——See also Qāsimiyyah, 1987.

al-Sibā'i, Bashīr, *Marāya al-Intelligentsia*, Alexandria: Dār al-Nīl, 1995.

Simon, Reeva, *Iraq between the Two World Wars: The Creation and Implementation of a Nationalist Ideology*, New York: Columbia University Press, 1986.

Smith, Gary, ed., *Zionism: The Dream and the Reality. A Jewish Critique*, New York: Barnes & Noble, 1974.

Soliman, Lotfallah, *Pour une histoire profane de la Palestine*, Paris: La Découverte, 1989.

Stauber, Roni, '*Realpolitik* and the Burden of the Past: Israeli Diplomacy and the "Other Germany"', *Israel Studies*, vol. 8, no. 3 (2003), pp. 100–22.

Stephens, Robert, *Nasser: A Political Biography*, London: Allen Lane Penguin, 1971.

Sterling, Eleonore, 'Judenfreunde—Judenfeinde: Fragwürdiger Philosemitismus in der Bundesrepublik', *Die Zeit*, no. 50 (10 Dec. 1965).

Stern, Frank, *The Whitewashing of the Yellow Badge: Antisemitism and Philosemitism in Postwar Germany*, Oxford: Pergamon, 1992.

Stillman, Norman, *The Jews of Arab Lands in Modern Times*, Philadelphia: Jewish Publication Society, 1991.

Taguieff, Pierre-André, *Les Protocoles des Sages de Sion: Un faux et ses usages dans le siècle*, Paris: Berg international, 1992.

Tamimi, Azzam, *Hamas: Unwritten Chapters*, London: C. Hurst & Co., 2007.

Teveth, Shabtai, *Ben-Gurion and the Holocaust*, New York: Harcourt Brace & Co., 1996.

——*Ben-Gurion: The Burning Ground, 1886–1948*, Boston, MA: Houghton Mifflin, 1987.

Tibi, Bassam, *Arab Nationalism: A Critical Enquiry*, 2nd edn, Basingstoke: Macmillan, 1990.

Torok-Yablonka, Hannah, 'The Recruitment of Holocaust Survivors during the War of Independence', *Journal of Israeli History*, vol. 13, no. 1 (1992), pp. 43–56.

al-'Umar, 'Abdul-Karīm, ed., *Mudhakkirāt al-Hāj Amīn al-Husayni*, Damascus: Al-Ahāli, 1999.

Vatikiotis, P. J., *Nasser and his Generation*, London: Croom Helm, 1978.

——*The Egyptian Army in Politics: Pattern for New Nations?*, Bloomington, IN: Indiana University Press, 1961.

Vidal-Naquet, Pierre, *Les Juifs, la mémoire et le présent*, Paris: Points, 1995.

——*Assassins of Memory: Essays on the Denial of the Holocaust*, New York: Columbia University Press, 1992.

Walicki, Andrzej, *A History of Russian Thought: From the Enlightenment to Marxism*, Stanford, CA: Stanford University Press, 1979.

——*The Slavophile Controversy: History of a Conservative Utopia in Nineteenth-Century Russian Thought*, Oxford: Clarendon Press, 1975.

Warschawski, Michel, *On the Border*, Cambridge, MA: South End Press, 2005.

——*Israël-Palestine: Le Défi binational*, with a 'Post-scriptum' by Elias Sanbar (pp. 125–44), Paris: Textuel, 2001.

Weinstock, Nathan, *Une si longue présence: Comment le monde arabe a perdu ses Juifs, 1947–1967*, Paris: Plon, 2008.

——*Le Sionisme contre Israël*, Paris: Maspero, 1969.

Weizman, Eyal, *Hollow Land: Israel's Architecture of Occupation*, London: Verso, 2007.

Wheelock, Keith, *Nasser's New Egypt: A Critical Analysis*, London: Atlantic, 1960.

Wien, Peter, *Iraqi Arab Nationalism: Authoritarian, Totalitarian, and Pro-Fascist Inclinations, 1932–1941*, London: Routledge, 2006.

Wild, Stefan, 'National Socialism in the Arab Near East between 1933 and 1939', *Die Welt des Islams*, vol. 25, no. 1/4 (1985), pp. 126–73.

Wildangel, René, *Zwischen Achse und Mandatsmacht: Palästina und der Nationalsozialismus*, Berlin: Klaus Schwarz, 2007.

Wistrich, Robert, *Muslim Anti-Semitism: A Clear and Present Danger*, New York: American Jewish Committee, 2002.

——ed., *Anti-Zionism and Antisemitism in the Contemporary World*, New York: New York University Press, 1990.

Wyman, David, *The Abandonment of the Jews: America and the Holocaust 1941–1945*, New York: Pantheon Books, 1984.

Yāsīn, 'Abdul-Qādir, 'Al-Trotskiyyūn al-Misriyyūn wa Qadiyyat Filastīn', *Shu'ūn Filastīniyya*, no. 45 (May 1975), pp. 114–23.

Yūsuf, Al-Sayyid, *Rashīd Rida wa al-'Awda ila Manhaj al-Salaf*, Cairo: Mirīt, 2000.

Zahr-ul-Dīn, Sālih, *Al-Khalfiyya al-Tārikhiyya li Muhākamat Roger Garaudy*, Beirut: Al-Markaz al-'Arabi li al-Abhāth wa al-Tawthīq, 1998.

Zertal, Idith, *Israel's Holocaust and the Politics of Nationhood*, Cambridge: Cambridge University Press, 2005.

——*From Catastrophe to Power: Holocaust Survivors and the Emergence of Israel*, Berkeley, CA: University of California Press, 1998.

Zu'aytir, Akram, *Yawmiyyāt Akram Zu'aytir: Al-Haraka al-Wataniyya al-Filastīniyya 1935–1939*, Beirut: Mu'assasat al-Dirāsat al-Filastīniyya, 1980.

——See also Hūt, ed., 1979.

Zurayq, Qustantīn [Zurayk, Constantine], *The Meaning of the Disaster*, Beirut: Khayats, 1956.

——*Maana al-Nakba,* Beirut: Dār al-'Ilm lil-Malāyīn, 1948.
—— See also Azmeh, 2003.

Official documents

Central Bureau of Statistics, *Statistical Abstract of Israel 2007,* Jerusalem: Central Bureau of Statistics, 2007.

'Nidā' al-Sha'b al-Filastīni fi al-Zikra al-Khamsīn lil-Nakba' (excerpts), *Majallat al-Dirāsāt al-Filastīniyya,* vol. 9, no. 35 (Summer 1998), pp. 219–21.

UK Government, *German Foreign Policy 1918-1945,* Series D (1937-1945), vol. VI, *The Last Months of Peace, March-August 1939,* London: Her Majesty's Stationery Office, 1956.

——*Report of the Anglo-American Committee of Enquiry Regarding the Problems of European Jewry and Palestine,* Lausanne, 20 April 1946, London: His Majesty's Stationery Office, 1946.

US Government, 'The Alexandria Protocol; October 7, 1944,' *Department of State Bulletin,* vol. 16, no. 411 (18 May 1947), Washington, DC: Government Printing Office.

Index